Moineddin Jablonski a

"The strength of the Chishtis
of their message of love and service to all. This enabled their teaching to resonate in modern times with western hearts. *Illuminating the Shadow* brings to life through his correspondence and other writing the spiritual quest of Moineddin Carl Jablonski (1942-2001), a contemporary American Chisti master. Pir Moineddin, following in the footsteps of Hazrat Inayat Khan and Murshid Sufi Ahmed Murad Chisti, adapted traditional eastern Sufi teachings to serve the needs of western seekers—a socio-religious phenomenon of the last hundred years.

"Neil Douglas-Klotz's skillful presentation of his teacher's life and writings is a powerful memorial to the sincerity and uncompromising honesty of Pir Moineddin who, despite sickness and outer adversity, left the legacy of the Sufi Ruhaniat, which has brought light and delight to many questing hearts. A book of subtle messages which will challenge and inspire any serious seeker, regardless of ethnic or religious background."

—**Muneera Haeri**, author of *The Chishtis: A Living Light* and co-author with Shaykh Fadhlalla Haeri of *Sufi Links*

"This book illuminates, in his own words, the life of a gentle and gifted soul. Over the three decades I knew Moineddin Jablonski we enjoyed many intimacies, including countless hours of music-making, the study of Sufism under his guidance, and open, spacious darshans. I thought I knew him well. But in reading Illuminating the Shadow I received a newly clear, coherent picture of the whole man in all his glories and tortures, and I've come to love him as never before. Thanks to this savvy presentation of his writings, Moineddin's vision can now light the way for many more seekers of the realized life."

—**W. A. Mathieu**, author of *The Listening Book*

"*Illuminating The Shadow* is a rich compendium of anecdote and teaching of the eclectic and universalist shaman, Moineddin Carl Jablonski, direct heir to Samuel Lewis, Sufi and Zen master. Articulately collated and edited by Neil Douglas-Klotz, *Illuminating The Shadow* is an important read for anyone interested in the Light and Shadow of our human story, and the journey of the soul. Douglas-Klotz adds to the current mystical wisdom stream with this poignant exposition of the life, love and laughter of this Sufi leader and humble practitioner."

—**Mariam Baker**, author of *Woman as Divine: Tales of the Goddess*

"Read this book for its editorial comments and ... then dip into this transparent mystery of my friend, Moineddin Jablonski, in this tribute/ debt paid/ responsibility unavoided/ head bowed effort/ by the editor, Neil Douglas-Klotz."
—**Mansur Johnson**, author of *Shamcher*, and *Murshid*, and the compiler and editor of *Big Tales*

"Moineddin Jablonski came to a true realization of heart and manifested a capacity for great love. This helped him, in a natural and unassuming way, to guide and hold together the community of Murshid Samuel Lewis' mureeds, which included various teachers who had been empowered by Murshid Sam or Pir Vilayat. Moineddin realized the need for all of us to acknowledge the psychological realm where we are often at the mercy of our ego-demands.

"He took on the difficult task of getting everyone to see that they would be held accountable for their actions. His numerous letters and writings clearly reveal his depth of thought. And while his manner was saintly and refined, at the same time he stood eternally strong in his relationship with his teacher and united with the great blood stream of Oneness, in which we live and move and have our being. He worked for harmony between all the lineages that trace themselves to Pir-o-Murshid Hazrat Inayat Khan. All this and more made him a highly effective Pir, as this excellent book bears witness."
—**Wali Ali Meyer**, co-author of *Physicians of the Heart*

"Neil Douglas Klotz has carefully assembled an essential contribution to the Sufi lineage's story. *Illuminating the Shadow* is rich with letters, poems, quotes, and stories. Yet I found fascinating Pir Moineddin's own description of his physical illness, with inner and outer guidance, over the last 20 years of his life."
—**Tamam Kahn**, author of *Untold: A History of the Wives of the Prophet Muhammad*

"This book transmits! It reveals the life and work of a Sufi dedicated to the pursuit of truth wherever it may lead. In the presence of his remarkable Murshid SAM, whose teacher was the great Sufi Hazrat Inayat Khan, we readers are invited to join in the caravan. Neil Douglas-Klotz has found the exact passages in Moineddin's writing that connect us to the divine source that

infused all aspects of his life. Ultimately, we can see him as a full human being who was doing the work."
—**Carol Sill**, author of *Human Ecology: Notes on the Sacred Element Work* and manager of the Shamcher Bryn Beorse archives

"The meeting with Pir Moineddin was a great event in my young years, in response to the fact that I was so much longing to experience harmony between the organizations which answered the call of the Bringer of the Message of Spiritual Liberty. In full confidence and knowing no one, I went to Hawaii for the first time and I was deeply impressed when meeting Pir Moineddin. Following exchanges of thoughts regarding the future, I was so deeply grateful to receive his agreement to my proposal for the creation of a Federation of the Sufi Message where there would be no President nor a one-man Leader. The Federation would be governed by a committee, with a secretary to handle the correspondence. Now yearly Federation Retreats are organised either in the USA or in Europe, offering the Sufi brothers and sisters a new home where all can meet as one loving family, regardless of the differences of the organisations' characteristics."
—**Pir Hidayat Inayat Khan**, Sufi Movement International, son of Pir-o-Murshid Hazrat Inayat Khan and author of *Reflections on Spiritual Liberty*

"While our teacher, Murshid Samuel Lewis was alive, he made it very clear that Moineddin Jablonski would be his successor. We all understood why: Moineddin's inner life, his graceful manner of expression, and the depth of his insight. Now thanks to this wonderful publication, you the reader have a chance to meet Moineddin through his written expressions. Deep gratitude to Moineddin for his service and eloquence in the written word, and the same gratitude to the editors who have made it possible for so many more of us to have a relationship with the spirit of Moineddin."

—**Pir Shabda Kahn**, Sufi Ruhaniat International, co-author of *Physicians of the Heart*

Illuminating the Shadow
The Life, Love and Laughter of a 20th century Sufi
Moineddin Jablonski

Other titles by Moineddin Jablonski

A Gift of Life: Aphorisms and Poems

Illuminating the Shadow

The Life, Love and Laughter
of a 20th century Sufi

Moineddin Jablonski

EDITED BY
NEIL DOUGLAS-KLOTZ

RUHANIAT
PRESS

Illuminating the Shadow:
The Life, Love and Laughter of a 20th century Sufi.

Published by Ruhaniat Press.
Copyright 2016 Sufi Ruhaniat International.

The writings of Moineddin Jablonski are copyright 2001 Sufi Ruhaniat International.
Introduction and notes copyright 2016 Neil Douglas-Klotz.
The excerpt of "Piktor's Metamorphosis" in Appendix II is reprinted with permission from *C.G. Jung and Hermann Hesse: A Record of Two Friendships* by Miquel Serrano.
All rights reserved. Copyright 1977 Daimon Verlag,
Am Klosterplatz, Hauptstrasse 85, CH-8840 Einsiedelm, Switzerland. www. daimon.ch.
The photos on pages 21, 24 and 237 are copyright Mansur Johnson 2016, reprinted with permission, all rights reserved: www.mansurjohnson.com. Cover photo: Ayesha Graham.

This edition All rights reserved. Except for brief quotations in critical articles or reviews, no part of this book may be reproduced or transmitted in any form or by any means electronic or mechanical, including photocopying, recording, or by any information storage and retrieval system, without permission in writing from Sufi Ruhaniat International, 410 Precita Avenue, San Francisco, CA 94110 USA. www.ruhaniat.org.

ISBN-13: 978-1530006335
ISBN-10: 1530006333
Printed in the United States of America.
Cover and interior design by Hauke Jelaluddin Sturm, www.designconsort.de.

The only royalty from this book goes to Moineddin Jablonski's children. Please purchase only authorized print and ebook versions. Your support of the author's right and that of his surviving children is greatly appreciated.

Content

Preface	9
Editor's Introduction	10

I. Prologue: Meeting the Teacher– Murshid Samuel L. Lewis — 17

Editor's note	17
Murshid S.A.M.: Trickster, Madzub or Master (1991)	19
The Early Days of the Dances (1975)	26
How the Dances Began (Email 1999)	31
Daily Life with Murshid (1978)	32
Three Zen Anecdotes (1987)	36
One-Quarter Leprechaun (1987)	37
Visiting Hours (1987)	38
The Stoic Yogi (1991)	39
Two Anecdotes About Murshid S.A.M. (1997)	40
The Flavor of Murshid S.A.M.'s Transmission (interview 1992)	41
Cult of Personality (poem 1978)	47
The Non-Pointing Finger and the Moon (poem 1977)	48
The Passing of a Rishi (poem 1977)	49
On the 26th Urs of Murshid Samuel L. Lewis (email 1997)	50

II. Continuing a Sufi Transmission — 53

Editor's Note	53
The Walk of Pluto (1972-4)	55
Reflections on "The Walk of Christ" (1975)	57
Meeting Suleiman Dede of the Mevlevis (1976)	59
Lama Maqbara Camp (Letter 1976)	61
Remembering Our Origins (1976)	62
Letter to the Lama Foundation (1977)	64
Pir-o-Murshid Samuel L. Lewis (1983)	66
Shards of a Broken Vessel (1977)	68
Open Letter to All Mureeds (1977)	69
Silsila Sufian (1977)	73
Initiation (1977)	74
Individuating as a Sufi Tariqa (letters 1978–79)	75

Update and Sufi Counseling (letter 1978)	84
Blackbirds and Signposts (letter 1978)	86
About Dissolving (letters 1978)	87
Receiving the Pilgrims (letter 1979)	90
It's Happening.... (letter 1979)	93
A Sufi Life, Part I: Carrying On (1979)	95
An Exchange: Pir Barkat Ali and Pir Moineddin (letters 1979)	106

III. Healing Heart and Mind 113

Editor's note	113
Life More Abundant: The Power of Thought and Feeling (1979)	115
On the Breath: Practices for Healing Mind, Heart and Soul (1979)	133
The Bird Creates Its Nest: Heart and Concentration (1979)	136
Love, Relationship and Bayat (letter 1979)	152
A Sufi Life, Part II: Effacement and Facing Death (1979)	155
A Spark Borrowed From the Blaze: Will, Wish and Desire (1979)	169
The Ultimate Season (poem 1979)	191
About Effacement and Nirvana (letter 1979)	192
Last Poem (1979)	195
Releasing Negative Impressions (letter 1980)	196
The Kidneys of Our Hearts (letter 1980)	198
A Large Golden Key (letter 1980)	199

IV. Depths of the Self and Soul 201

Editor's note:	201
Ferment of the Earth's Evolution: "We Are All Becoming Bridges" (1992)	204
Snapshots from Maui (letter 1981)	211
Thinking About Getting a Milk Goat (letter 1982)	212
Renewing, Rebuilding (letters 1983)	213
"The Message is in the Sphere" (letter 1983)	214
Beginning Life Counseling (letter 1984)	215
Abandon Tension... (letter 1984)	216
Messages from the Inner Community (letter 1984)	217
Metamorphosis (letter 1984)	219
Celebrate the Search (letter 1984)	220

No Escaping Anymo' (letter 1985)	221
Honesty (letter 1987)	222
Beseeching the Breath (poem 1988)	223
Look to the Source (brochure 1989)	224
Grief (essay 1989)	226
The Big "D" (poem 1990)	228
Winged Kidney (letter 1990)	229
Writing Through the Pain (letter 1991)	231
Shiva (poem 1991)	232
Breaking the Spell (poem 1991)	233
Crucifixion (letter 1991)	234
Illuminating the Shadow (essay 1996)	235
Uniting the one to the One (essay 2000)	241

V. An Evolving Sufi Path — 259

Editor's note:	259
Mureeds Rights (letter 1984)	262
Sufi Practice, Psychology and Gender Issues (letter 1984)	264
Jamiat Agenda I (letter 1985)	266
Funding the Work (letter 1985)	268
Moths (letter 1985)	269
Continuing the Conversation (letter 1985)	270
An Open Letter to Moineddin (letter 1986)	271
Bottom of the Milk of Life (letter 1986)	272
Reconciliation, Guts and Guidance (letter 1986)	273
The Making of a Sufi Teacher (letters 1986)	274
Winged Apple? (letter 1987)	278
One Ceaseless Ko-an (letter 1987)	279
Ethical Standards for Teachers (letter 1987)	280
The Path of the Ruhaniat (letter 1987)	282
Jamiat Agenda II (letter 1987)	283
New Directions in Universal Worship (letter 1988)	285
The Link of Initiation (letter 1988)	287
Ancestry, Death and Dying (letter 1990)	289
A Spiritual Switzerland? (letter 1990)	291
Ancestry, Part II (letter 1991)	293
Relations with Lama Foundation (letter 1992)	294
Another Step in the Dance (email 1995)	296
A Southwest Sufi Community (email 1995)	298
An Inclusive Spiritual Path? (email 1997)	301

The Voice of the Turtle (email 1998)	303
Bismillah and Buddhism (email 1997)	304
For the Murshids Circle... (emails 1997)	305
Support for the Dances of Universal Peace Network (letter 1997)	309
Time to Descend (email 1997)	311
If You're Going Through Hell... (email 1998)	312
The Invocation (email 1998)	313
Sacred Vowels (email 1999)	314
Happy Birthday, Murshid (email 1999)	315
Thanksgiving (email 1999)	316
A Federation of the Sufi Message (emails 1996–2000)	317
Preparations for Dying (2000)	333
Last Urs (2001)	335
Instructions for the Pir (1998)	336

VI. Epilogue 339

Flying Clouds (poem 1977)	340
Acid Trip, 1966 (poem 1991)	341
Bull in a China Shop (poem 1994)	342
Wings (poem 2000)	343
The Wind (poem 2000)	344
Acknowledgements	346
Appendix I: Eulogy—Pir Moineddin Carl Jablonski, 1942–2001	347
Appendix II: Piktor's Metamorphosis by Hermann Hesse	351
Glossary	355
Index	367
The Sufi Ruhaniat International	385
The Sufi Soulwork Foundation	386

Preface

On the evening before he became ill, Moineddin and I were on the phone planning our families' semi-annual trip to Priest Lake in North Idaho and then on (in an old blue Toyota Land Cruiser, which he loved to drive) to Northwest Sufi Camp. Suddenly, the next morning, he was in ICU for his final illness. He had endured so much illness, yet I mention his planning a summer trip to remind us all he wasn't planning to die right then. He had things to do, places to go and children to watch get to their next stages in life. He was quite full of life until the illness that marked the end of his life.

When I first read this book, it touched me deeply, reminding me of the strength, endurance, power, intelligence, humor, and creativity of Moineddin. He was open to new ideas, willing to take a stand in defense of new as well as old ideas of merit (even when those ideas weren't particularly popular), willing to write and speak with great openness and tenderness of his own healing in the physical as well as psychological realms, and willing to illuminate the path toward a strong and sensitive and possible future for all.

Moineddin brought psychological awareness through SoulWork to complement the strong legacy of spiritual teachings from the Sufi teachers Pir-o-Murshid Inayat Khan, Murshid Samuel Lewis and others. Politically, he reminded us of the very real ills of "isms" (racism, sexism, fundamentalisms) and of the need to work toward solutions for the very real environmental issues we face.

Moineddin shepherded the Sufi Ruhaniat for thirty years, guiding its transformation from a San Francisco-based center to an international organization with a global focus, a land-based community in New Mexico, and Sufi teachings as well as Dances of Universal Peace in cities and communities on very nearly every continent!

Moineddin's last charge to the youth, and a reminder to us all:

> *Unite the above and below,*
> *cherish freedom over power,*
> *renew the world!*

Quan Yin (Lynne Williams, M.D.)
March 2016

Editor's Introduction

Toward the beginning of the 20th century, a new phenomenon began to appear in the reported history of religion and spirituality: "Western" students of "Eastern" teachers. On one level, it was and is the age-old story of seekers travelling from one world to another and returning with wisdom's treasure. No doubt, this has occurred since people began to travel far away from home; however, given the way modern history developed, we learned more about it after European colonialism began to cut its harsh swath of influence through the rest of the ancient world. In the 20th century, these one-off occurrences of seeking (and sometimes finding) began to snowball into an avalanche of what scholars now call "new religious movements." Not coincidentally, this occured just as Europe and the rest of the West found its own ancient world of community and village life drastically interrupted by the reality of world wars that dominated the 20th century.

During the recent era, whole generations were sacrificed to the new political gods of commercial-industrial-militarism. The security of ordered family and community life began to disintegrate. Science and religion were also at war. And with increasing urgency, humanity found itself with bills to pay for its past treatment of the environment as a limitless larder and resource stockpile. All of this led to the rise of what is now called modern psychology and psychotherapy; however, as one of its proponents remarked candidly in a book of the same title, "We've had a hundred years of psychotherapy, and the world's getting worse." Psychology usually lacked the tools to touch the real heart of meaning and purpose, a contact with the numinous that was beyond the sense of fixing an individual "self." Other solutions needed to be found, and many began to look for them in the spiritualities of the ancient world, given that spiritual experience had often been suffocated with religious formalism in much of the modern one.

The scholar of religion Andrew Rawlinson (1997) collated the stories of a large number of Western students of Eastern teachers, and called the Sufi Murshid and Zen master Samuel L. Lewis (1896-1971) one of the first exponents of "experiential comparative religion." Murshid S.A.M. (Sufi Ahmed Murad), best known for his creation of the Dances of Universal Peace, lived virtually his entire life in semi-obscurity. A mureed (Sufi student) of Hazrat Inayat Khan, his teacher had charged him with being a leader in what was called the "brotherhood" work in the Sufi Movement (the latest iteration of a number of organizations founded by the Indian

Sufi, who came to the West in 1910). For Samuel Lewis this meant that, among other things, he would help bring the world of the mystic and esotericist into dialogue with contemporary culture and science. Lewis approached the task with enthusiasm and courage, as detailed in this editor's earlier collection *Sufi Vision and Initiation* (1985).

Yet we would know little if anything about Samuel Lewis's life and work if it were not for the community of young people, mostly hippies in the San Francisco, California area, whom he galvanized in the late 1960s to continue his work, both the Dances of Universal Peace and the Sufi lineage and organization currently called the Sufi Ruhaniat International. Carl "Moineddin" Jablonski (1942-2001), the person whom Samuel Lewis designated his spiritual successor and whom he entrusted with the responsibility for continuing his spiritual transmission, is the subject of this book.

Like *Sufi Vision*, my goal here was to allow the subject's own words, woven together, to reveal a very human life, with all of the changing perspectives that both looking back and looking forward provide one. We might call biography the historian's pseudo-scientific yet subjective approach to a life, "facts" woven together with a particular attitude and style. Likewise, hagiography is the religionist's glossing over of fact to produce an idealized picture of a useful icon. The present book aims at something between autobiography and found "actuality"—combining Moineddin's refined writing and commentary with interviews, letters, emails and unpublished poetry. (A selection of poems that he wished kept together as one volume was published in 2007 as *The Gift of Life*, available from the Sufi Ruhaniat.) These beads are threaded together to reveal the necklace of service and devotion that formed the last thirty years of his life, from age twenty-nine to his passing at fifty-nine.

Imagine, if you will, being entrusted (burdened?) at age 29 with the spiritual lineage of an intensely magnetic figure like Murshid Samuel Lewis. One has only to view the film *Sunseed* (or the out-takes of Samuel Lewis entitled *Dance to Glory*) to appreciate how difficult it must have been for his young students to carry on after his passing in 1971. Yet almost to a person, those who did carry on report that it was like Samuel Lewis was still with them. Nothing, they say, changed. According to Samuel Lewis himself, the connection between murshid and mureed is in no way dependent on one or both being in the body. In classical Sufism, this inner connection is called by various names: *fana-fi-Sheikh* or *fana-fi-Pir*. The continuance of a living transmission in the Sufi lineages or tariqas depends on it. Without it, some of the various orders and tariqas have simply become family patronage systems, dependent on a strong *paterfamilias* to take care of everyone, or societies of historical anachronism with a (neo)religious tinge.

Murshid Samuel Lewis spent his entire life on the Sufi and Zen paths, changing and being changed by the spiritual practices of his teachers. Toward the end of his life he also sought psychotherapy with a friend of his, Dr. Blanche Baker, who had been a student of the Carl Rogers school of "unconditional positive regard." We know a few of the difficulties that Samuel Lewis encountered in his life from his own writings. We will know much more when the extensive research of Murshid Wali Ali Meyer and his team culminates in a thorough biography that is currently underway. Yet virtually all of Samuel Lewis' turbulent life of change and transformation took place out of the public eye. What we see in *Dance to Glory* is the wise, energetic teacher, seasoned by life's ups and downs, seemingly master of both the inner and outer life.

To continue what Murshid Samuel Lewis began at the end of his life left Moineddin Jablonski with a very difficult task. At age 29, he had his own further inner growth and transformation ahead of him. Even having attained the state of spiritual realization that Murshid S.A.M. recognized in him, he would still need to "work out his salvation with diligence," in the parting words of the Buddha. This grist of life's mill affects every conscious person, no matter how it manifests. With age, it leads to either wisdom or rigid dependence on habit, depending on how one handles the "neglected" aspects of life. The basic questions that the Buddha confronted—old age, illness, poverty, death—are multiplied by modern ones in our mixed, multi-cultural societies, such as violence, betrayal, relationship, divorce, gender relations, social justice and community. And as the spiritual director of the esoteric lineage that Murshid S.A.M. represented, as well as the organizational head of the Sufi Islamia Ruhaniat Society, all of this "working out" necessarily happened in public. Add to this the ever-present challenge of a genetic predisposition to kidney failure. In this light, the transformation—both personal and organizational—that Moineddin accomplished is nothing short of a wonder.

Illuminating the Shadow consists of five sections, a five-act drama that sheds some light on what it can mean to remain true to one's *dharma* or *din,* the purpose of one's life, which can be experienced as both a joy and a duty. In Moineddin's case, this challenge occurred under the most trying personal circumstances, while at the same time he guided others, individually and collectively.

Moineddin's letters and emails remain the richest untapped repository of his wisdom. *Inshallah* (the One willing), this book will help inspire the efforts and funds necessary for a full-scale collation and scanning of this correspondence, much like what occurred for Murshid Samuel L. Lewis and which can be found at the website www.murshidsam.org. This book would not have been possible without the help of Moineddin's students and friends, many of whom contributed letters and emails to fill in some of the gaps in the story. (See the Acknowledgments section at the end of the book.)

Section One, *Meeting the Teacher,* is the "overture"—a selection of Moineddin's writings, interviews, stories, letters, emails and poems about his relationship with Murshid Samuel Lewis. This relationship with the teacher of his heart defined his adult life, but did not limit him from creating his own identity and destiny. In this section, we see Moineddin evaluating and re-evaluating the five years he spent with Murshid S.A.M. as well as using those experiences to illuminate and transform his path.

Section Two, *Continuing a Sufi Transmission,* sets the scene and introduces the characters. We see Moineddin carry on after Murshid Samuel Lewis' passing, attempting to maintain *fana-fi-Pir*—an open inner channel to his teacher—as well as to provide the type of guidance and direction that S.A.M. did. When not in a state of *fana,* he tried to maintain the practice of *tasawwuri Murshid,* acting as if in the presence of the teacher.

Later in life, he described this task as "one ceaseless ko-an." At the same time that he had his own inner growth to accomplish, many of his fellow students expected him to act as the same magnetic, always-on figure that Murshid S.A.M. had been in the three to five years that they had been with him. While many undoubtedly (even if subconsciously) wanted such a "hero" figure, many also wanted and needed to make their own mistakes and discover their own dharma. In the name of this, they also wanted more democracy, more "doing their own thing." So Moineddin experienced a balancing act between too much "togetherness" and too much "looseness," the community strands woven too closely or too loosely.

On another level, Murshid S.A.M. had clearly acted as what Sufis call a *malik,* a master who can sometimes be kind, sometimes harsh, always acting in the *now.* Murshid Samuel Lewis writes in his paper *Malikiyyat:* "Those on the path of the Malik are not necessarily called upon to be outwardly polite in conventional ways.... This is confusing to others. The inner light operates according to the needs of the moment and not according to any philosophical principle." This immediacy and presence, connected to love and guidance, caught the hearts of Murshid's students.

Yet when Moineddin acted in similar contradictory and unconventional ways, his fellow students sometimes found this difficult to accept.

In Section Three, *Healing Heart and Mind*, crisis looms. The pieces here come from the crucial period in 1979 during which Moineddin was facing imminent death due to kidney failure. They show him bringing all of his spiritual training to bear on mental-emotional healing, both for himself and for his community. The section mixes a formal commentary on Hazrat Inayat Khan's writing on "mental purification"—a project that Murshid S.A.M. began but didn't finish—with an interview and other writings from the time. They reveal a very clear channel, but also a very tortured human being—as one of the Sufi metaphors has it, "a tavern in a ruin." Moineddin throws himself into (as he supposes) completing his work and leaving the transmission in good order for his then-successor, his wife Fatima.

In Section Four, *Depths of the Self and Soul,* we fast forward a few years and find Moineddin somehow resurrected, living in Hawaii. The story of how and why this occurred gradually unfolds. Following a successful kidney transplant, he began to integrate his life as a more complete human being. It was not enough to simply act as a clear channel for Murshid Samuel Lewis' transmission, the substance of the channel itself needed to change. He found that he was not only the light in the lamp, but the lamp itself. The selections here focus on his inner process during the last twenty years of his life. During the same time, he continued to serve as the spiritual director of the Ruhaniat community, with only the occasional visits to the mainland that the organization could afford.

Section Five, *An Evolving Sufi Path,* is a parallel view of the same period, but showing Moineddin guiding a modern, and postmodern, Sufi lineage with increasing insight and wisdom won from the process of his own life. Here we see him gradually transforming the way that the ancient Sufi lineages functioned in order to meet the needs of the world today: toward increasing social, gender and ecological justice. At the same time, the inner guidance that he was able to provide individual mureeds becomes stronger and stronger. In classical Sufi terms, *fana*—effacement in the teacher—merges with *baqa*—full realization of one's humanity as part of the "hidden treasure" through which Allah is discovering new experiences every moment.

In this sense, both the reality of the ancient Sufi transmission as well the truth of life here-and-now come together in his life.

Looking back some 15 years after Moineddin's passing, what he created—in personal and collective terms—seems even more important. Everywhere in its "homeland," the mystical path of the Sufi is under threat from Islamism of one sort or another. Sufi shrines, libraries and dargahs (the gravesites of the saints) are attacked and destroyed. Living teachers go undercover or flee. As with Tibetan Buddhism, we may have already reached the point where authentic Sufism is kept alive in the West, from whence it may at some point be able to return to its origin. Inshallah.

Moineddin was my personal guide in Sufism, so any picture presented here can never be objective. I trust that his own voice will ring clearly through any false notes in my own. Moineddin wanted to be called Moineddin, not "Murshid." He famously wrote, "I am not Murshid, we are Murshid. I don't have all of the answers. We may have all the answers." What I found most moving in stringing together the prayer beads of his life from these papers, physical and electronic, was his adamantine self-honesty. Even when he was honestly wrong, he was as honest as he could be. But most often, at least in relation to me as a mureed, he was right and guided me away from many potentially fatal potholes in life toward those that were still very bumpy but would not break an axle.

I thought I knew him very well, but with the help of his other friends and students, who provided letters and emails for this project, I find I probably only understood him a little. His own life's motto can be summed up in the words of the Prophet Muhammad that he paraphrases in a letter to a fellow mureed of Murshid Samuel Lewis: "O Allah, I have never known you as you really are."

Some consolation then, that we are in good company if we view the purpose of life, the Sufi *din,* as a horizon that constantly recedes as we move towards it.

"We are indeed entering a new era of humanity, a time of massive inner and outer change and growth. Earth herself is giving birth to what she must become. Upheaval—personal, societal, and geologic—are the labor and birth pangs which will create greater consciousness of spiritual reality for all. As each one of us is moved into Soul-consciousness, and we are being so moved, we will select our own modes of spiritual realization. What we now know as 'Sufism' will become vastly expanded and transformed. It will be like the reported meeting of Inayat Khan and Nyogen Senzaki. They entered samadhi together, 'and Sufism and Zen became like yesterday's dream.'" –Moineddin Jablonski

Neil Douglas-Klotz
April 2016

I. Prologue: Meeting the Teacher– Murshid Samuel L. Lewis

Editor's note

In the Sufi world, one determines the genuineness of mystics by asking them to speak about their teacher rather than about themselves.

Moineddin spoke and wrote frequently about meeting and living with his teacher, Murshid Samuel L. Lewis (Sufi Ahmed Murad Chisti, S.A.M.). Throughout his life, he re-evaluated this crucial five years from 1966 to 1971. As Samuel Lewis's successor, it seems that he was continually making sense of both his personal history and what mystical experience—and the Sufi path in general—could mean today.

This section begins with an article from 1991 that serves as an introduction to Moineddin's voice, as well as his way of mixing personal reflection together with spiritual inspiration. The other pieces here juxtapose early and later writings about the first Dances of Universal Peace and about the essence of his teacher's transmission and lineage. The anecdotes and poems reflect as much Moineddin's sense of humor as Murshid S.A.M.'s. The final selection, written about four years before Moineddin's passing, finds him musing about the paradoxical and bittersweet nature of a Sufi "urs"—the teacher's passing seen as his or her "wedding day" with the divine Beloved.

Murshid S.A.M.: Trickster, Madzub or Master (1991)

All Sufis everywhere affirm that God is The Only Being. The Trickster reveals this reality through shape-shifting, or phenomena. The Madzub conveys it through atmosphere, or essence. The Master demonstrates a balance of essence and phenomena, thereby appearing divine and human at the same time.

Understand, friends, that all these beings are God-realized. The Trickster's tricks are played by God, the Madzub's mystic trance is God's alone, the Master's balance shows God awake on all planes. Indeed, the Master may use many means to bring us to balanced realization, but the Trickster and Madzub will transmit a certain drunkenness according to their predispositions. Tricksters and Madzubs are not primarily plugged into the human world; the Master is ever human.

In 1956, Murshid S.A.M. wrote to a young Pir Vilayat Khan: "Perhaps the most wonderful thing in life would be if you would let me play to you the role Shams Tabriz played to Mevlana Rumi." As you will recall, Shams Tabriz was the spiritual firestorm who burned all of Jelaluddin Rumi's bridges to the finite world behind him, and brought him to a place of overwhelming mystical intimacy. Murshid S.A.M.'s invitation to Pir Vilayat was no ordinary valentine, but an offer to share the cup of God-realization—"a challenge and a chalice," as New Age teacher Frida Waterhouse expressed it.

Naturally, the "challenge" aspect might make Pir Vilayat ask the question, Who does this Samuel Lewis think he is? By what right does he presume such authority? So forward, in fact, was Murshid S.A.M.'s general behavior toward people, that the "chalice" aspect was often lost to view.

Lost to view, that is, until the hippie generation came along. Suddenly, Murshid S.A.M. found himself becoming the Pied Piper of the flower children. He was rejected by the Establishment, but accepted with open arms and hearts by the hippies. He played his music and charmed the young people away from the obsolete values of their elders, into the "inaccessible" mountain of spiritual reality.

Many of his first mureeds combined the spiritual practices he gave them with LSD, psilocybin and other psychedelics—not exactly with his blessing, but not without it either. So powerful were the highs generated by this precocious alchemy, that ordinary consciousness was transformed into visionary experience. One man reported that he became God-conscious while intoning the *zikr* on a kazoo, while a woman told how Inayat Khan came to her and played the cello until all her pain disappeared.

Clearly, the Norman Rockwell version of reality no longer made sense to minds and hearts that were launched willy-nilly into the fourth dimension. The brightly-colored clothing, long hair, open hugging and new slang showed a picture that would no longer be crammed into the limitations of society's traditional frame.

Around this time—we are speaking of the mid-1960's—a handful of hippies began to visit India and other cultures regarded as exotic. The hippies noticed that certain people in these cultures were intoxicated like themselves—not from alcohol as in the West, but from botanical psychedelics used sacramentally to stimulate the awareness of divine states of consciousness. Other flower children joined the ceremonies of the Native American Church, which uses the peyote cactus as its communion food. All these journeys, inner and outer, brought new hope to a generation seeking confirmation for its radical and mystical views.

Everything soon developed into a grand love affair. The hippie phenomenon attracted large numbers of Eastern teachers to the West, and the love generation in turn sought teachers who could tell them what their experiences meant, and point a way toward enlightenment.

Most of these teachers were firmly against the use of psychedelics on the spiritual path. Others, Murshid S.A.M. among them, were not so adamant, preferring to use spiritual dance and song to wean their students away from chemical and botanical dependency. But a few initiated their apprentices even more profoundly into the mysteries of "power plants"—shamans whose role as guide and healer to their native community serves from matriarchal times as the model for spiritual schools today.

Now that we have sketched a background, let us see whether Murshid S.A.M. comes to light primarily as Trickster, Madzub or Master. Was Murshid S.A.M. a Trickster, a shape-shifter? I once saw him manifest as a leprechaun. He was giving a talk to a small group of mureeds, when suddenly in place of the man a leprechaun appeared. The lecture continued, but I was privy for the time being to a secret realm of Murshid S.A.M.'s psyche. When I asked him about it afterward, he replied, "That's right, I'm one-quarter leprechaun!" I didn't think to ask what the other three quarters were....

There is a tremendous spirit of play in the Trickster, often with mischievous intent. In this connection, we can trace the influence of the Jinn plane, and understand why the Quran warns against association with Jinn spirits. They will not be fettered by orthodox assumptions about reality, and are linked to the fire element, which is quick to show its temper, quick to destroy comfortable human constructs. Yet as playful and full of tricks as Murshid S.A.M. was on earth, it is clear that the Trickster was a ploy in his overall purpose, not dominant or central.

Even Hazrat Inayat Khan shifted his shape occasionally. Look at the many portraits taken in states of attunement to the different messengers of God. The very contours of his face changed from picture to picture, to accommodate the potent rays emanating from the inner planes. This is shape-shifting of the highest order, for it demonstrates how The Only Being can display itself through the spectrum of human ideals. It suggests that all shape-shifting has its origin in the strength of one's attunement to extraordinary reality levels.

Murshid S.A.M. often identified with the prankish Krishna, another Trickster personality—especially in interactions with women. Recall how Krishna steals the saris of the milkmaids when they go to the river to bathe. He glimpses them from his hiding place in a nearby tree. But it is all a ruse. The whole purpose is to get their attention, through whatever handy means, so that the divine message can be directly imparted. Notice how Krishna's play calls to mind the Christian scripture: "Naked you come into the world, and naked you go."

Radha, of all the milkmaids, proves to be most receptive to the spiritual presence, and becomes Krishna's beloved. She embodies the

Attunement to Krishna Photo: Mansur Johnson

human soul ready to be touched by the hand of divine love and follow the light of the divine glance ever deeper into mystery.

Bacchus was another teaching mask worn by Murshid S.A.M. He taught the Bacchus dance to his women disciples. Like Krishna, Bacchus is associated with the divine intoxication. He too is charged with bringing the spiritual message in the form of intoxicating love to women. His mission is premeditated, however, compared to Krishna's unbroken and spontaneous connection to the divine flow. In this regard, Bacchus is masquerading his ecstasy in service to a conscious spiritual objective. The Krishna archetype retains a direct identity with the innocence of youthful desire and love, while Bacchus is a grown man serving these impulses as an instrument.

But in the Bhagavad Gita, Krishna is pictured as the consummate Master, instructing Arjuna to fight the battle of life without attachment to sentimentality. The feminine and masculine principles, *jemal* and *jelal* in Sufi terms, are demonstrated in Krishna's dealings with the gopis and Arjuna respectively. With the milkmaids Krishna traffics in love and delight; with Arjuna he exhorts the use of the sword until the prince wins his birthright of spiritual sovereignty. Both stories have Krishna as their protagonist. How can this be so? It is so because Krishna is Master of both paths, the feminine and the masculine, called *bhakti* and *jnana* in Hindu terminology.

These stories are not about some lucky fellow who wakes up and finds himself surrounded by beautiful young women, or about a soldier boy who cuts down his enemies until he controls the world—though if we looked closely we would find parts of ourselves that want it to be that way.

What the stories mean is that we have feelings on the feminine side of emotional sensitivity, love and nurturance, and feelings on the masculine side of earnest will to achieve meaningful goals. We are to honor both sides, feminine and masculine, as the two halves of the psyche which, when united in sacred inner marriage, form the wholeness of wise love.

Coming now to the Madzub, let us be clear that we are talking about a soul plunged irretrievably in that dimension of spiritual essence called "the night of power." The Sufi legend of Leila and Majnun shows the condition of the Madzub: an utter wreck of a personality until he finds his beloved Leila. The name Majnun means "mad" or "crazy," the name Leila means "dark night." Until the soul of Majnun enters the "dark night" of spiritual eternity, he behaves as one possessed.

There is a beautiful story told in Attar's "The Conference of the Birds." Majnun is crying, sifting the dust of the road over and over through his fingers. A friend asks him what he is doing. "I am looking for Leila," he says. "But Majnun," the friend replies, "how do you expect to find Leila in the dust of the road? Surely she is not there." Majnun looks into his friend's eyes and says, "I look for her everywhere in the hope of finding her somewhere."

Murshid S.A.M. occasionally spoke of the Madzubs he met during his travels in the East. One man, called the "Madzub of Lahore," was highly regarded by Sufis near and far. Murshid S.A.M.'s Goddaughter from Pakistan, Saadia Khawar Khan, told me, "Madzub-sahib is in constant realization of 'grand night.'"

Another Madzub loved to play softball with the young boys of the district. He would play "roaming outfielder" and catch seemingly impossible fly balls hit by the boys. And there was one who stationed himself by a blind curve on a mountain road. Every time a vehicle would approach the curve, the Madzub would run and wave wildly to warn drivers coming from the opposite direction.

Hazrat Inayat Khan once asked a Madzub, "Are you a thief?" to test the truth of his *madzubiat*. The Madzub replied, "Yes"— though he never pinched a penny in his life. Inayat's question could as easily have been, "Are you a woman? a goldfinch? a terrorist?" The God-realized see themselves reflected in each and all.

Sri Ramakrishna used to visit the quarter of the prostitutes in his city, and would enter *samadhi* as he gazed at them: living embodiments of the Divine Mother Whom he worshipped. The prostitutes in turn would become transfigured for the duration of the saint's rapture.

Was Murshid S.A.M. a Madzub? He did experience phases of his life when the pull of the divine attraction was extreme, but he always kept the ideal of the Master before him and succeeded more often than not by merging with his ideal. Some may disagree, citing examples of his having shaving cream in his ears when going to market, or sometimes forgetting to zip up his fly. All these things and more are true, but rather than show a personality overwhelmed by the world of essence, they reveal a character committed, body and soul, to the improvement of human beings on the earth-plane. His priorities were feeding people and world peace, and sometimes this meant that his hair would go uncombed, his dentures unbrushed. This is no different from the behavior of Handel when he wrote *The Messiah*.

Poetically contrasting the state of the Madzub and the stage of the Master, Hazrat Inayat Khan writes in Nirtan:

"I am the wine of the Holy Sacrament; my very being is intoxication; those who drink of my cup and yet keep sober will certainly be illuminated;

but those who do not assimilate it will be beside themselves and exposed to the ridicule of the world."

Murshid S.A.M. said simply, "The Madzubs I met became sober in my presence."

Looking, then, into Murshid S.A.M.'s role as Master, it is important to recognize his function as an *Abdal* in the Spiritual Hierarchy. Murshid described the *Abdal* as "one who is prepared to surrender his or her ego-state and preferred lifestyle in order to manifest the Will of God—not once, but from moment to moment." This may explain why many, even his close disciples, became frustrated at his seeming inconsistency. The woman he called "Mother Divine," lifelong friend Vocha Fiske, told us, "Outwardly your Murshid is like a great whirlwind, but inside he is pure peace."

He once took us aside and made us swear an oath not to repeat what he was about to say until after he died. We swore not to say anything. Then he said, "During World War II, I was taken out of my body every night for weeks on end. I was part of a team headed by Abdul Qadir Jilani. The only rule was that you couldn't look to the right or left to see who your companions were. That wasn't important. You paid attention to your leader. We would travel over the battlefields, eventually arriving at the gas chambers where the Jews and other 'undesirables' were being executed. Our job was to enter the souls of the victims and assist their transition to the next world. This is the work of the Spiritual Hierarchy, and it is no fun."

And yet, Murshid S.A.M. had more actual fun than anybody I've ever met. He confided on his 73rd birthday, "My alter-ego Puck is not such a polite guy. You know what Puck's motto is, don't you?

Attunement to Muhammad.   Photo: Mansur Johnson

Puck's motto is: strugglin', smugglin' and snugglin'!" He later explained, "When things get too serious, I bring in comedy. And when things get too comic, I bring in the serious side. Did I tell you I can also be the world's biggest fool if left to my own devices? But if you put a mureed in need in front of me, I suddenly turn into a wise man. What do you think of that?"

Who is Murshid S.A.M. really? Why not ask him yourself? The next time you sit down to a cup of tea, pour a cup for him too. If someone comes along and asks who the extra cup is for, tell him or her it's for a friend—maybe *that very person*....

The Early Days of the Dances (1975)

(Editor's note: This short article first appeared as the introduction to a booklet accompanying the Sufi Dance and Song Album, *published in 1975.)*

It is the late sixties and within the castle-like walls of Scott Hall (a big round tower of the Presbyterian Seminary which overlooks San Anselmo in Marin County) a voice rings out loud and clear:

"Everyone form a circle!"

Not everyone has arrived yet, but a few of the youthful ex-hippies begin to link hands. Others present for the first time are still standing around.

"I said everyone form a circle!"

After the second ringing command, the circle is rapidly formed. The leader of the meeting is Murshid Samuel L. Lewis, a spiritual teacher in the Sufi tradition, who is introducing his audience of young seekers to the Dances of Universal Peace. In a few moments, Murshid formally opens the meeting, asking everyone to recite the Sufi Invocation:

"Toward the One, the Perfection of Love, Harmony and Beauty, the Only Being, United with all the Illuminated Souls who form the Embodiment of the Master, the Spirit of Guidance."

There is a short silence.

"Now let's repeat the Bismillah.... Bismillah, er-Rahman, er-Rahim. We begin in the Name of Allah, Most Merciful and Compassionate."

The Dancing begins. Throughout the evening the Names of God penetrate and fill the space, building an atmosphere of joy. The Dance arena becomes peaceful, bringing everyone out of the "realism" of surface life and into the reality of heart, through chanting God's Names.

The Dances of Universal Peace, a compendium of group-dances set to sacred phrases from the various world religions, came to and through Murshid during the last seven years of his life. These Dances have continued to come in inspiration through his followers since his passing on January 15, 1971.

Starting in the spring of 1969, Murshid began getting less and less sleep at night due to the increasing activity of his visionary consciousness. As Murshid put it: "Allah (God) keeps me up at night so I can receive these visions of new Dances." Often it would take two or three days before a Dance which Murshid had witnessed in vision would filter down to the mental realm, to be later translated into written instruction.

The first few Dances that came were simple follow-the-leader type Dances using either "Allah, Allah" or "Om Sri Ram Jai Ram Jai Jai Ram" as the kindling phrase, the Divine Name of God which stands at the center of the Dances. In Murshid's own words he gives the secret:
"No dance is a Spiritual Dance because it is called that; it does not mean a certain form or technique, nor a ritual. What must remain is the sacred phrase; this, the sacred phrase, and not the form, is the foundation of development along this line."

Gradually other movements were added, mostly drawn from different folk-dances Murshid knew, for he had been a diligent folk-dance aficionado earlier in his life. Murshid said he was actually very timid as a youth and that he joined a folk-dance club to overcome his shyness. He used folk-dance movements from all over the world, borrowing from places he had visited during his trips abroad in 1956 and again in 1962.

As was Murshid's manner, he wrote incessantly to his old friends to let them know the astounding new developments in his life, friends who like Murshid were in their sixties and seventies. Many of his old friends congratulated him, some merely wrote his remarks off as the antics of an already eccentric man, while the young people began to experience more and more the well of *baraka* (Arabic for the magnetic love-blessings which impregnate a mystic's atmosphere) that had long remained untapped through a lifelong pattern of rejection by his peers.

At the same time, Murshid cultivated a steady correspondence with humor columnist Art Hoppe of the San Francisco Chronicle and wrote repeatedly with tongue-in-cheek: "Art, I have failed miserably as a Pied Piper. Only the young show up!"

Finally, Murshid's old folk-dance club invited him to bring his group of young ex-hippies (Murshid's term) to perform for the club's special anniversary celebration. This was the first public performance of what became the Dances of Universal Peace. Later, public performances of the Dances were to occur in Precita Park opposite the Mentorgarten, Murshid's San Francisco home, and in cathedrals and temples in California and elsewhere since his passing. In fact, the Dances are now an international phenomenon.

By the time Murshid visited Los Angeles in June of 1969 with two of his disciples, several new Dances had become regular features at the weekly meetings. He wasted no time demonstrating (or 'angel-strating' as he would pun) these new Dances with just three people, himself and his two students, for his Los Angeles friends—right in their living rooms! Murshid wasn't the type to let such behavior fall short of its intended purpose, even if it proved momentarily embarrassing to his hosts. If they were still Murshid's friends this late in life, they were probably used to it. His young followers took everything mostly in stride, although a few doses of social embarrassment at the hands of Murshid were always in store!

The legendary Ruth St. Denis, whom Murshid referred to as his 'fairy godmother,' played the role of confirming angel in his efforts to gain support for the Dances. It was after Murshid visited the tomb of Sheikh Selim Chishti, a Sufi Saint, at Fathepur Sikri in India that he began his Dance work in earnest. Murshid had entered a state of mystical absorption wherein the theme "Dance of Universal Peace" was disclosed. At the tombsite he performed his first attempt of the Dance of Universal Peace in which a human being, incorporating the religious expressions of humanity through millennia, dances in devotion to God and God dances with loving compassion through him or her.

When Murshid returned to this country he visited "Miss Ruth" and said:

"Srimati (Mother Divine), I have the answer to all the world's problems."

"What is it?" she asked.

"I'm going to teach little children how to Walk," he replied.

"You've got it, you've got it, you've got it!" exclaimed Miss Ruth.

Murshid felt that basic rhythms should be introduced to children early in life, and that training in Walk could be part of every child's upbringing, without any somber overtones. With this happily-applied training in Walk, it would be a matter of but another step and the Dance could unfold with full consciousness.

He would remark to Miss Ruth: "You taught me how to draw these Dances right out of the cosmos, right from the space." Miss Ruth had inspired Murshid not only to continue his efforts to spread Spiritual Dancing, but also to attune to the dance-ful moods and modes in the atmosphere within and around us, and to bring the inspirations into manifest portrayal.

Back in January of 1967, shortly after the first few ex(ing)-hippies discovered Murshid living in a two-room apartment on Clementina Street, an alleyway south of Market Street, Murshid suffered what he termed "an attack of food-poisoning." Later, another friend told us that Murshid had actually had a heart attack, but he didn't want his young disciples to know it was that serious.

At the time of his attack there were about ten disciples who attended his talks regularly. When he took sick we prepared to visit him at the Chinese Hospital (the same hospital where he was later to die) on Jackson

Street. When we got there Murshid was ashen-faced and could hardly talk. Murshid's lifelong friend Joe Miller was there with his wife Guin. Joe tried to pep Murshid up with a few well-chosen words. Dr. Ajari Warwick, a Zen teacher, was there from time to time, and Murshid later said it may have been Dr. Warwick's healing puja ceremony—performed on the spot—that helped spur him back to physical health.

It was that hospital stay that Murshid would speak of later:

"There I was flat on my back in the hospital and Allah decides that is when He is going to manifest, when I have no choice but to accept!"

Then Murshid went on to describe the vision vouchsafed to him: "I saw a mountain at the top of which there was a little trickle of water, and, after the water had gone down the slope a little bit, it became a sizeable stream. Then the stream became a rushing river, which in turn became a mighty river with several tributaries. As the river neared the plain the flowing water was so strong it could not be stopped, and would continue to flow until it merged into the ocean."

"Do you know what that means?" Murshid would ask. Then he would answer: "It means that I have completed my first stage as a spiritual teacher—that's the little trickle at the top. Next will be the period of expanding to thirty disciples. And after that to sixty and after that to a hundred disciples. Then, after the vision, God says to me, 'I make you spiritual leader of the hippies.'"

Through the trial of near-death Murshid emerged stronger than before, and declared that the promise of spiritual unfoldment for him together with his disciples was a confirmation of the commission he had received five years earlier from his Pir-O-Murshid (Sufi teacher) in Pakistan: "You will cause fifty thousand Americans to chant 'Allah'." We little realized how joyous a way Murshid would provide for us and the world when he gave out the Dances.

It has been four years since Murshid's passing, years which have witnessed an increase in the repertoire of the Dances, the quality now developing beyond the rough-hewn manner we were capable of in the beginning, and the scope of the Dances now opening to a world perspective. Murshid saw this development shortly before he left the world and expressed his vision to the Women's Dance Class, a group of women disciples who met for the purpose of refining the Dances, inaugurating more graceful movements to coordinate the similarly refined singing of God's Names:

"The next step will be to establish Jewish and Christian Dances. We already have Mantric Dances, Dervish Dances and Mystery Dances.

After that we will have Dances for all religions. And then we will begin to work on having Angelic Dances, Dances which will take you very high."

These Dances have come, are coming, and with them an ability to deepen the Dance experience with both new and old Dances. It would not be proper to say that the Angelic Dances are too different from other types of sacred Dances. Angelic Dances simply express the exaltation in all of us which comes when our human limitations are overcome through an act of blessing another, or through losing oneself in the love (which asks for no return) of another. So really every Dance can be an Angelic Dance, yet there are certain sacred phrases, certain movements of grace, which promote the utterly translucent Angelic moods hidden within us.

But there may be even deeper experiences open to the Spiritual Dancer. Murshid has written in his poem "Suras of the New Age": "When the Dervish whirls, the Angels tremble." This shows that the Angels can become entrapped by a devotion which sees God as if through a window-glass, while the Dervish, or Sufi has, like Shiva or Krishna, become identical with God through dancing *the dance* that illuminates and integrates all planes of our being, all aspects of our personality from the seen to the Unseen.

> "THE WATCHER IS THE PRAYERFUL DEVOTEE,
> BUT THE DANCER BECOMES DIVINE."
> (from Murshid's poem "Siva, Siva")

To dance the Divine Dance we can follow the footsteps of the Masters, Saints and Prophets of humanity. We can dance the Dance of the Divine Messengers, giving to all the blessing of God which we see naturally in a loving mother, a kind father, an innocent child, a helpful friend and in an inspiring teacher. We can dance to improve ourselves; we can dance to overcome ourselves. We can even dance to find ourselves.

All these purposes of Spiritual Dancing are answered when we begin to feel the Divine Presence more and more as we dance.

This is being offered in the hope that multitudes of people will be able to take up the Dances of Universal Peace in a real way, by remaining centered and confident in the endeavor toward fuller awakening.

How the Dances Began (Email 1999)

5 April 1999

Thanks for the news about the Silver City Dance meeting. It got me to thinking about the genesis of the Dances. As you know, they started out small and without any fanfare.

Murshid S.A.M. had a handful of disciples in 1967, to whom he began to give the *darshan* [blessing through the glance] of Krishna, Buddha, Jesus, and Muhammad on a semi-regular basis, say every month or so. He wouldn't give everybody all the *darshans*, he'd just ask each mureed who their favorite messenger of God was, and then he'd give them the *darshan* of that messenger. To the more advanced disciples, or to those who had more inner capacity, he would eventually give all the *darshans*—although Muhammad he reserved only for a few.

The next stage was the *tasawwuri* Walks of Moses, Jesus, and Muhammad—and for some of the women, the Walks of Mary and Fatima.

This seemed to be the groundwork for the Dances which would come later. He also gave us the Walks using the centers (chakras), but I can't recall if they came before, or after, the initial Dances that consisted of the Allah and Ramnam Snake Dances, plus the Three Wazifas Dance (Subhan Allah, Alhamdulillah, Allah Ho Akbar).

After those first Dances, which he demonstrated to his friends and colleagues using as few as two or three of us in someone's living room, the Dances began coming to him in vision more regularly. He would often complain that he didn't get any sleep because God kept showing him new Dances all night long. During this process, the Dances also became more complex in terms of movements. The Wazifa Walks, which he referred to as "super-psychiatry," also came through at this time (circa spring 1968).

The first more complex Dances included the Dervish Dance Cycle, the Introductory Bismillah Dance with Spins, and the Er-Rahman, Er-Rahim Dance for partners. Later came the Kalama Dance, the Nembutsu Dance, the Om Nama Shivaya Dance for partners, the Hare Krishna, Hare Rama Dance, and all the rest.

That's how I remember things unfolding, although now that more than thirty years have passed I could be mistaken in some of the details. I mainly want to show that everything happens through stages and patterns of development.

Love, Moineddin

Daily Life with Murshid (1978)

(Written between September 15, 1978 and October 20, 1978 as the beginning of an autobiography.)

The experiences vouchsafed to heart and soul from the inner planes are a sign and a proof that God-Allah is Ever Living, Eternal. But certain Mahayana Buddhists have declared, "*Samsara* and *nirvana* are one." This would indicate that the daily life, and the examples shown by the living teacher on earth, have a value which augments the truth of the inner world and at the same time exemplifies the words of the Psalmist: "The earth is the Lord's, and the fullness thereof."

Thus, the incidents, adventures, even anecdotes connected with the actual life of the living teacher can be a teaching equal to any experience "arrayed in other-worldly splendor." For if the teacher is realized, the *baraka* from the inner planes will permeate his every action, his every word, his every thought and feeling. He will strive every moment of his life to fulfill the words of the prayer Nabi [of Hazrat Inayat Khan]: "Thou, my master, makest earth a paradise."

Much of the daily life of Murshid Sufi Ahmed Murad Chisti has been recorded in the book *In the Garden* published by Lama Foundation [recently republished by Sufi Ruhaniat International], as well as in the voluminous diaries he kept. Much more promises to be compiled in a biography being written by Masheikh Wali Ali Meyer, Murshid's chief secretary. But I should like to add the following four examples from Murshid's daily life, examples which only hint at the range of "inconsistent" behaviors of a real teacher.

***

Shortly after Fatima and I met Murshid, we invited him to spend a weekend in our cottage in Bolinas, a small seacoast village north of San Francisco. As was his habit, Murshid rose early and went out to pull weeds in the garden. He came in just as Fatima was setting breakfast on the table.

We enjoyed ourselves greatly, for the food and the conversation were equally wonderful. Then the mood suddenly changed. Murshid began to speak very seriously and softly, yet with tremendously increased strength and power.

And he said, "You must swear not to mention what I am going to tell you until after I have died." Naturally, Fatima and I agreed to the confidence.

Then Murshid gave each of us a penetrating yet unified glance and said very slowly and deliberately, "I have eaten locusts."

It is not necessary to disclose the impression this remark had upon us.

***

A few weeks after Murshid moved from his small Clementina Street apartment to the Mentorgarten on Precita Avenue in San Francisco, he asked Fatima and me to come for our first formal spiritual lesson at three o'clock the following Sunday afternoon. We were very happy to receive this invitation, and said we would be there.

But as the days passed we somehow allowed the priority of the lesson to slip from our minds, and by the time Sunday arrived my friend Mansur and I had instead made arrangements to climb Mount Tamalpais with Ajari Warwick, a local Buddhist teacher. And Fatima had opted to stay home the whole day and meet us at the Mentorgarten around six o'clock, as it was our custom to eat Sunday supper with Murshid.

Now, to climb Mount Tamalpais takes several hours; even the descent takes a lot of time. Not only did Mansur and I take our time with the climb and descent, we even took our time driving from Marin County to San Francisco, where we stopped at a Mexican restaurant and had a leisurely meal, after which we drove to Murshid's home.

Mansur and I, and Fatima and Jemila, who drove in together from Bolinas, arrived simultaneously around suppertime. Even then I didn't have a clue as to the seriousness of our first error in upsetting Murshid's schedule and robbing him of his invaluable time.

And again I experienced the whole atmosphere suddenly change, only this time it was a change much like the ominous moment of stillness that precedes a tornado. Then, in front of everyone, Murshid singled me out and scolded me with such force and fire that it took six full months to rid myself of the impression of that reprimand—although Murshid dropped the subject in a split second.

For the first time in my life I was struck by the direct wrath of a Master, a Master who until that moment had shown nothing but tenderness and loving-kindness. After the scolding, all Murshid said was, "I don't like to be this way." And he said it with all feeling and compassion.

Then he went back into the kitchen and resumed cooking supper for those of us who were there. After supper he prepared himself spiritually for the Dharma Night meeting that was to follow.

***

Murshid used to divide his time between staying at the Mentorgarten in San Francisco and the Garden of Inayat, the Novato Sufi khankah in Marin County. The lion's share of clerical work was done in San Francisco, while the creation and maintenance of the gardens, both vegetable and floral, was a chief concentration at his Novato home.

During one particularly rainy winter, before the new sidewalk was poured, there was a section of sunken walkway by a corner of the Garden of Inayat that used to fill whenever it rained. At such times it became impossible to walk around the house without getting soaked to the ankles. But as we young disciples tended to "overlook" such earth-plane problems, we never gave the deep puddle much consideration. So, after giving us several weeks of rainy weather to test our intentions, Murshid took it upon himself one wet morning to solve the problem.

He donned his slicker and rubbers, went to the tool shed and got an adze-hoe, and returned to the puddle area. His concentration was vigorous and intense as he began to hoe a channel from the puddle leading toward the street some distance away. He continued for several minutes in this fashion, his "faithful" disciples (including the writer) looking on from the window inside the warm house.

But before Murshid had channeled ten feet, the hoe suddenly caved in a large chunk of earth, and the puddle of water began to drain quickly and efficiently. He had struck a gopher hole, a main tunnel it would seem from the amount of water that disappeared into it. Not only was Murshid's intuition operating fully (consciously or unconsciously, who can say?), but the gophers which had been ravaging our gardens for months also disappeared!

***

I spent six months in various hospitals with a severe kidney disease through the summer and fall of 1970. I was released from Moffitt Hospital in San Francisco the day after Thanksgiving. My physical condition at that time was extremely weak, so to build up my strength I used to walk around the block every afternoon. This was during the five year period we lived at the Garden of Inayat.

One particularly Indian summery afternoon on my walk around the block I noticed that Murshid and Rufus, Hassan and Jayanara's dog, had taken a gambol up the hill behind the Garden of Inayat (since levelled by gigantic bulldozers to make room for the freeway there now).

As if my sight had opened wider, I clearly saw not an old Murshid in his seventies but the figure of a young boy romping with his pet dog. This perception made me feel inspired to increase my own efforts toward strength and health, for up to that moment I had been feeling quite like an old man. Then I completed my circuit of the block and went indoors to rest.

When Murshid returned half an hour later I could not contain my enthusiasm. I immediately remarked, "Murshid, Murshid, when I saw you and Rufus a few minutes ago on the hill you reminded me of an eight-year-old boy!"

"Shh! Not so loud, you'll tell everyone my secret!" Then he gave me a big grin of assurance that I had, so to speak, seen truly.

Several years later I related this story to the Reverend Joe Miller (who is likewise in his seventies and often is immersed in the young boy stage of realization). Joe's rejoinder went something like this: "Yes, I remember times when S.A.M. would look like a newborn infant, and other times he could be older than God."

Three Zen Anecdotes (1987)

In the summer of 1967, while walking with Murshid S.A.M. in Golden Gate Park, I had asked him a string of questions about Zen. He nodded and answered much like a parent responds to the chatter of a young child. Finally, after he had taken enough of my pestering, he drew his breath and stated, "A Zen master has to be able to play with the Buddha like it was a football."

* * *

During a Gatha class at the Garden of Inayat, Murshid S.A.M. once shared the following: "There is a saying, 'Bodhisattvas live among mountains.' This can have two meanings. One is that bodhisattvas live in actual mountainous regions. The second is that bodhisattvas consort with those who are like mountains in stature."

* * *

After explaining that certain actors in the Japanese Noh Drama are able to express sounds of eternity by concentrating deep in the throat center, Murshid S.A.M. added, "There are three types of statement a Zen master can make. One, true for the moment. Two, true for an entire cycle of time. And three, true for eternity.

"None of these is more nor less true than any other."

One-Quarter Leprechaun (1987)

When I first met Murshid S.A.M. he lived on Clementina Street, an alleyway between Folsom and Howard in downtown San Francisco. He had a two-room apartment with plastic curtains that rustled noisily whenever the breeze gusted through the window. The bathroom was outside and down the hall, shared with a man who had a parrot and whose TV was always too loud. Despite the odd surroundings, Murshid made his students feel like they had entered a temple of warmth and light. He burned fragrant incense, placing sticks on the mantle next to the white plaster Quan Yin, and on the toilet tank in the bathroom.

The five or six students that attended the weekly meetings sat on folding metal chairs facing Murshid who sat on the edge of his single bed and talked to us "of cabbages and kings"—adding short meditations and other practices throughout the lecture.

One particular night I kept noticing a tendency for Murshid to appear smaller than he was, and he was only five feet two inches in human guise. He struck me as being a leprechaun, one of the "little people" spoken of in the myths and fairy tales of cultures worldwide. I decided to ask him about it after the meeting.

"Murshid, when you were talking tonight, I kept seeing you as a leprechaun. Are you part leprechaun?" I was totally serious.

Murshid's answer was so fast that I almost didn't catch the words, flying more from the mischievous gleam in his eyes than from his lips.

"One-quarter!" he winked, happy to share a glimpse of his treasure from the repository of faerie.

Visiting Hours (1987)

During the 19-day period Murshid S.A.M. was hospitalized before his death, he was visited by three disciples of Yogi Bhajan, the Sikh teacher. As they entered the room, Murshid stirred from his semi-comatose state.
"Who's there?" he asked. "Is it my disciples?"
The visitors hemmed and hawed, embarrassed by the question. Finally one of the Sikhs replied.
"Murshid, isn't everyone your disciple?"
"Everyone my disciple," Murshid murmured. "Everyone my disciple, everyone my disciple...."
The visit was over, and the Sikhs tip-toed out.

***

When Murshid S.A.M. was in the large ward at San Francisco General Hospital following his fall down the Mentorgarten stairs, a handful of mureeds went to see how he was doing. While there, Murshid's long-time friend Joe Miller walked in and, displaying an assurance lacking in the mureeds, went directly to the bedside.
"Hey, S.A.M. , it's your old pal Joe," he whispered.
"Huh, what!" Murshid reacted, opening his eyes indeterminately.
"It's your old pal Joe," he repeated. All of a sudden Murshid reached out and grabbed Joe's arm, yelling, "Take it!" Joe looked perplexed.
"TAKE IT!" Murshid yelled again, raising his voice and tightening his grip on the arm. Joe acted more dumbfounded.
"*TAKE IT!!!*" roared Murshid with finality, shaking Joe's arm clear to the socket.
"*I'M TAKING IT, I'M TAKING IT!!!*" Joe shouted back with equal vigor.
The ultimatum had been answered. Murshid lay back and was silent.

The Stoic Yogi (1991)

Bolinas, California, 1967. On a chilly October night, Fatima (my wife at the time) and I rode a couple of miles down the road in a friend's pickup truck to visit Mansur and Jemila's where Murshid S.A.M. was staying for the day. The plan was to spend two or three hours, and then drive Murshid back with us to spend the night at our house.

It was common for Murshid to "house-hop" between Mansur and Jemila's, Hassan and Jayanara's up on the mesa, and our house because he didn't want people to think he was playing favorites. He made a point of staying equal amounts of time at each home, and the whole arrangement flowed quite naturally. We knew he loved each of us with his whole heart.

When we arrived, Jemila was cleaning up after her two-year-old son Nathan's supper. Murshid and Mansur were playing honeymoon bridge on a small table in the living room. A fire was going in the fireplace, and the TV was on. Everyone said hello to everyone else, and the evening took shape.

Nathan watched TV for a while and then went to bed. Murshid and Mansur continued to play cards. And the rest of us lit a joint of marijuana and passed it around, Murshid abstaining as usual. We settled in and watched the movie "The Horse's Mouth" with Alec Guinness on the small black and white TV.

Around eleven o'clock we began to say our good-byes to each other, and Murshid came outside into the chilly air with Fatima and me and our friend to be driven back to our place to spend the night. Because there were four of us now, and the cab of the truck would only hold three persons, I opted to sit in the back for the drive home—clad inappropriately in a T-shirt.

As the wind began to whip around me, I realized that I had but two choices before me: either I could curl up and suffer; or I could brace myself and face the chill head-on. As I chose the latter, I distinctly heard the words, "Sit like a stoic yogi!" So I did, and as the truck drove on, I experienced a wonderful and bracing feeling that opened up my pores and deepened my breathing.

By the time we arrived home, I was totally invigorated. I couldn't contain the pride I felt in having accomplished a degree of heretofore unknown physical and mental mastery, and I rushed up to Murshid and said, "Murshid, I sat like a stoic yogi!"

"Yes," Murshid fired back, "and you smoked a yogic stogie!"

Two Anecdotes About Murshid S.A.M. (1997)

(Editor's note: At one point, an editor of one of the Ruhaniat newsletters began to gather written anecdotes from mureeds of Murshid Samuel L. Lewis. Moineddin sent in these two.)

Sometime in 1970 I was taking Murshid's dictation in the Garden of Inayat office. The mailman came and delivered a junk-mail ad about a new best-seller called *Your Erogenous Zones*. Murshid opened the envelope and skimmed over the ad, then he turned to me and said, "I can't explain it, but my whole body is like one big erogenous zone."

* * *

Murshid S.A.M. would frequently tell the young people who attended his meetings, "I could play very unfair with you, but I won't. All I would have to do would be to ask you one simple question -- and it's not what you think. The question would be, 'Are you lonely?' Now, see how unfair that would be?

"But I want you all to know that at a certain point in your spiritual evolution you come to a place where you're never lonely again. What do you think of that?

Photo: Fatima Lassar

The Flavor of Murshid S.A.M.'s Transmission (interview 1992)

(Editor's note: The following interview was conducted via email in 1992 between Moineddin and Vasheest Davenport, the editor of the Sound, *a newsletter of the San Francisco Bay area Sufi communities. This is part one; part two of the interview appears later in this book as "Ferment of the Earth's Evolution" in part IV.)*

The Sound: *You have been the spiritual director of SIRS for over twenty years now. Based upon that experience, what essential qualities distinguish this order, and what directions do you see SIRS taking in the future?*

Moineddin: I think the essential qualities of the Sufi Islamia Ruhaniat Society (SIRS) can be found living in the hearts of the Mureeds as: sincere seeking; devoted practice; deep inner experience; universal vision. We are developing in our own lives the God-realization not only of Murshid S.A.M. and Hazrat Inayat Khan, but of all the Illuminated Souls, male and female, of all times and places and cultures and schools.

Does that sound extravagant? It isn't really. The Sufi Invocation is our basic and primary teaching. We encourage a strong, vital and open approach to personal and spiritual wholeness. We are not afraid to be ourselves. We are daring in our quest to reach beyond ourselves. Presently we are learning the difficult lessons of love in the schoolhouse of Earth, but truly we are citizens of the starry Cosmos ... What can I say?

Our Sufi initiation and practice unite us as sisters and brothers on the spiritual path. We're a family. We love. We fight. We're eclectic. We're open. We're innovative. We're a lot of things the more orthodox Sufi schools say we shouldn't be. God bless them, but we are who we are. As to the future, we will continue to eat, dance and pray with the peoples of the world—and with each other—as the simplest and best means to unify hearts and create peace. We will also utilize the tremendous love our community has developed to organize compassionate and focused responses to the suffering of homeless people, people with AIDS, and other victims of personal and collective catastrophe. In short, we will become more committed and active in addressing the growing helplessness and hopelessness felt by so many in our society. I see the Cheragas and Cherags [ministers of the Universal Worship begun by Hazrat Inayat Khan] taking the lead here, but we will all be involved in one way or another.

The Sound: *What flavor did Murshid S.A.M. contribute to Sufism, and how is SIRS carrying that flavor forward?*

Moineddin: I originally went to Murshid because I was looking for a Zen master. A friend of mine said, "There's a seventy year old man named S.A.M. you've got to meet. He says he's a Zen master, and I believe him." This was in 1967. When I met him I believed he was a Zen master too! I attended his meetings twice a week for almost a month before he ever mentioned the word "Sufi." I had no idea what he was talking about so I asked, "What is Sufi?"

He explained, "I have the knowledge of more than one path, actually several. I've been waiting to see which path I should use with the young people beginning to come to me. They seem to be interested in love, real love, so I think the Sufi approach would be best. The Sufis I have met are very big on love, generally bigger than the Zen people—who are very fine in their way—but the love-realization of the Sufis has touched me deepest."

That was my introduction to Murshid's "flavor." There was nothing theoretical about S.A.M. If you were interested in "flavor," he would take you to a Chinese restaurant. Or an Indian restaurant, or an Afghan restaurant, or an Indonesian restaurant, or a Greek restaurant, or an Armenian restaurant. He said, "I believe in the United Nations of the stomach."

He delighted in poking fun at long-faced (and usually long-winded) religionists. "Give us Allah in Heaven, and Baskin-Robbins on Earth," he quipped. "We celebrate the feasts of all religions, and the fasts of none!"

Murshid also loved to cook for his disciples. He knew he had the *baraka* that comes with spiritual mastery, and he put it in everything he cooked. It didn't matter if the brown rice was burned or the salad had dirt in it. It didn't matter if he regularly tracked mud from the garden onto the kitchen floor. Or peed on the toilet seat. We loved him and he loved us. We cared for him and he cared for us. We were his family.

Murshid's friends became our friends. I speak here of Joe and Guin Miller, Frida Waterhouse, Shamcher Beorse, Vocha Fiske, Ted Reich, Eugene Wagner, Ajari Warwick, Murshida Vera, Shemseddin Ahmed, Paul Reps. After Murshid died, the list grew to include Zalman Schachter-Shalomi, Lamala, Pandit Pran Nath, Hayat Stadlinger, Pir Kaleemi, Karunamayee and others. I want to include Pir Vilayat here too. His loving guidance, even when we could not accept it, has been instrumental in making us who and what we are today. Vilayat and I are now friends.

We have been truly blessed to have so many friends, all of whom have shared their love and enlightened perspectives with us over the years. Many of us owe our very sanity to the humor and guidance of these friends during our times of personal failure and group conflict. Like Murshid, they picked us up, dusted us off, and lovingly placed us back in the front lines of life.

But the "flavor" I liked most about Murshid was his ability to integrate—with lightning immediacy and total love—the spiritual and the commonplace in his own personality. Murshid really was like Baskin-Robbins [the American ice cream business]. He had thirty-two flavors and more! If you sometimes got a scoop of licorice and didn't like it, well, that was tough. His often challenging exterior went hand in hand with his Awakened Heart.

Murshid's contribution to Sufism was himself. We carry his work forward, individually and as a group, by being who we are.

The Sound: *Do you sense the presence of the* silsila *as an active source of guidance in your work?*

Moineddin: Since some of the readers may not be familiar with the term *silsila*, let's begin with Murshid S.A.M.'s definition. He writes, "The Hierarchical Chain, known as the *Silsila Sufian*, is a linkage of realized personalities whose teachings reflect the age in which they have lived and functioned. There are many such Chains, each associated with a particular Sufi order."

In other words, a *silsila* is a formal lineage of spiritual successors to the Prophet Muhammad. Sufis invoke their *silsilas* to honor the hard-won illumination of their direct spiritual ancestors, and to open themselves to the transforming *baraka* that flows as an inner current of God-realization through the Chain.

It was actually Pir Vilayat who introduced us to the *silsila* of the Chishti Order. Murshid S.A.M. never mentioned it, as far as I recall. My first experience with invoking the full Chishti silsila was when Pir Vilayat assigned it as a retreat practice in 1971. I found it to be very effective in strengthening my attunement to the deep golden light of the Chishti transmission. I continued to use it on and off for the next ten years, chiefly as an introduction to my concentration upon mureeds. That practice stopped in 1981 when I entered, willy-nilly, a new cycle in my life.

I now work simply with the Sufi Invocation of Hazrat Inayat Khan.

The Sound: *Over the past decade or so there has been much questioning, even controversy, regarding what constitutes the nature of the spiritual teacher. How would you define the terms Sheikh, Khalif, Murshid and Pir, as used in SIRS?*

Moineddin: Joe Miller, who was an honorary Murshid in SIRS, put it this way: "Sometimes there's not much difference between a Sheikh and a jerk!" It sounds like a joke. But it is also a challenge to each one of us to keep working on the *koan* of personal integrity.

Every initiator in the Sufi Islamia Ruhaniat Society is supposed to have some kind of experience in God-realization. But what is God-realization if it doesn't reach right down into our lower chakras and show us, after the ecstasy of union has gone, ever-new layers of painful unfinished business waiting to be compassionately embraced and worked with? Controversial to some, this is the psychological aspect of Sufi practice, called *Mujahida*, and it will not be ignored. Unless we practice *Mujahida* ourselves, we cannot truly work with the negative emotional patterns of mureeds.

We see the spiritual aspect of Sufi practice in the film *Sunseed* when Amertat Cohn (off camera) asks Murshid:

"What do you want to do before you die?"

Murshid: "Before I die? (laughter) It's awkward when one has contact with immortality direct.... I want to see two or three of my disciples reach a stage of spiritual realization. Then I can die in peace."

Amertat: "What would it be that would show you that some of your disciples had attained—"

Murshid: "I would see the light shining out through them. Actually shining. Not verbal, but manifestable. 'Let thy light so shine before men (and women and children) that they would know thy good works, and glorify the Father (Mother) which is in Heaven.'"

Initiations of Sheikh(a), Khalif(a) and Murshid(a) in the Ruhaniat are given inwardly on the basis of spiritual realization, and outwardly on the basis of individual temperament and capacity. Pir Vilayat has suggested that a Sheikh(a) will tend to have an independent personality, be flexible, and have a wide latitude of expression. A Khalif(a) will work hard to tame the personality, and will generally represent the Pir(a). A Murshid(a), whose heart must be as sensitive as a glass bell, may normally undergo one or more "crucifixions" in the course of his or her development in the cause of God. The Pir(a) is the successor, prepared or not, to the preceding Pir(a).

We, the senior initiators in SIRS, have tended to follow these guidelines, and especially our own intuition, when initiating advanced mureeds to the teaching grades.

Yet while all these designations are born of real experiences in the inner world, we live in a time when titles are going the way of the dinosaur. We wear them modestly, or not at all. In Hazrat Inayat Khan's *The Birth of the New Era*, he says, "Titles will have little importance; signs of honor will become conspicuous."

I would like to finish this question by saying that we are indeed entering a new era of humanity, a time of massive inner and outer change and growth. Earth herself is giving birth to what she must become. Upheaval—personal, societal, and geologic—are the labor and birth pangs which will create greater consciousness of spiritual reality for all.

As each one of us is moved into Soul-consciousness, and we are being so moved, we will select our own modes of spiritual realization. What we now know as "Sufism" will become vastly expanded and transformed. It will be like the reported meeting of Inayat Khan and Nyogen Senzaki. They entered *samadhi* together, "and Sufism and Zen became like yesterday's dream."

The Sound: *The Quran uses the term* dhikr *perhaps several hundred times, and to the Sufi, it is the central practice—in fact, all practice can be seen as* dhikr. *What does this term, which translates as "remembrance," imply to you?*

Moineddin: There are many varied interpretations and unique applications of the sacred phrase known variously as *dhikr, zikr, zikar,* etc. For instance, Inayat Khan calls *La Ellah Ha, El Allah Hoo* "the first Zikar" (his spellings). By "the first Zikar" he means the entire phrase, plus the seed phrases *El Allah Hoo; Allah Hoo;* and *Hoo.* These four phrases are given to mureeds one at a time over months and sometimes years, until only the sound *Hoo,* the Essence, remains.

The purpose of "the first Zikar" is to bring mureeds by stages to the realization of Allah as pure and formless Spiritual Essence, which the Hindus call *Sat-Chit-Ananda.* This is the movement that Pir Vilayat calls "the dismantling of consciousness into the Absolute." Until one has lost oneself in the absolute Being of Allah, one is not truly prepared to go on to "the second Zikar," "the third Zikar" and so on, which involve incarnating the Divine Qualities. The first Zikar ends with spiritual realization. The Zikars that follow begin with it. In this way, Muhammad's practice of self-realization has become the ideal for Sufis everywhere.

The Dewdrop slips into the Shining Sea; the Shining Sea slips into the Dewdrop. Muhammad becomes Allah; Allah becomes Muhammad. "Make God a Reality, and God will make you the Truth" (Hazrat Inayat Khan). It is in this complete sense that Sufis know "zikr" as their core practice.

Murshid S.A.M. cautions, "All spiritual practice has a developmental side, and a phenomenal side. Sufis emphasize development at all times."

Did I mention that zikr is the cry of the Lover to the Beloved?

Cult of Personality (poem 1978)

(Editor's note: Written October 16, 1978, this poem appeared in Bismillah: A Journal of the Heart, *vol. 3, issue 4 in 1978.)*

Nyogen Senzaki was the Buddha
of this age.
Papa Ramdas was the Avatar
of this age.
Hazrat Inayat Khan was the Pir
of this age.
Sufi Ahmed Murad Chisti was the Dervish
of this age.

Is this insight, or opinion?

Seekers of Truth, abandon such concepts!
Salvation's call is heard clearly:
Deeper than thought, beyond mind.

The Non-Pointing Finger and the Moon (poem 1977)

Murshid led his "kids" up Bernal Hill,
led us and walked with us.
The green slopes grew
bright during the climb;
we noticed things best
in the presence
of an All-disclosing heart.

Birds wakened our eyes
by fluttering, or pecking for grubs;
our ears flew toward the children
who called out, "Hippies!"
But never did this man
point his finger at the moon.

He climbed hills with us—
and the moon split,
the grass cried, "Yes!"

The Passing of a Rishi (poem 1977)

His body, like a conch-shell
washed up on some distant beach,
empty of all save music in the
chambers that once held vital breath—
this being smiles a rarer smile now.

He shared wholesomeness of Heart,
Breath and Glance
with the handful of dust
that attended him. Now
that dust has begun to circulate
anew: through bodies, hearts
and minds once thought to be
past repair.

The music of the conch sounds
anew:
Anahata, Om!
Sahasrara, Om!
Om, Siddhi, Om!

On the 26th Urs of Murshid Samuel L. Lewis (email 1997)

15 January 1997

Dear Friends,

I thought I'd share some personal thoughts and feelings on this 26th *urs* day of Murshid Samuel Lewis, Sufi Ahmed Murad Chisti.
In the four years I knew Murshid (1967 - 1971) he never used the word *urs*. The only time he mentioned the anniversary of Murshid Inayat Khan's death was when he took a handful of us to visit the Sufi rock in Fairfax. After we had each taken a turn sitting on the rock's 'friendship seat' and were walking back to the car, he said, "Today is the anniversary of the day Inayat Khan died."
He said this with the feeling you would expect of one who loved his teacher. It was a simple statement from a man who missed his teacher's human manifestation. And he let it go at that. There was no mention of a "divine betrothal in the heavens" or any other special sentiment.
Murshid liked birthdays much more than death days.
Inayat Khan taught that the Sufi and the Bodhisattva were the same. The Bodhisattva is one who foregoes entering *nirvana* for the sake of saving humanity. So there is a real question if Sufis, upon their physical death, enter into "ultimate union with the Beloved" as many mureeds commonly imagine.
A Bodhisattva, in my opinion, is united with the Beloved even while on Earth. The departure from the physical plane is simply the removal of an outer cloak worn to protect one from the elements.
Murshid S.A.M. said, "I'm too busy to go into *samadhi* anymore." I don't fancy he is any less busy working in the inner planes, probably quite the opposite.
And yet the day Murshid died in Chinese Hospital on Jackson Street, it was special. On the grossest level, Saul (upon instructions from Joe Miller) literally threatened to kick me in the butt with his heavy engineer's boot if I didn't snap out of my state of shock. This proved to be a great blessing, as it moved me immediately into the practice of *fikr* [*zikr* on the breath] from which I was able to coordinate the movement of people in and out of the room where Murshid lay in state.

On a more subtle level, the living radiance emanating from Murshid's "lifeless body" (ha ha!) created an atmosphere of silence and peace that deeply affected all who entered the room.

On this day, I remember the thing about Murshid that impressed me most. He combined the ordinary and the extraordinary in a way that could make you laugh and cry at the same time.

Love and blessings,
Moineddin

II. Continuing a Sufi Transmission

Editor's Note

During the first ten years after Murshid S.A.M.'s passing (1971-1981), Moineddin's letters and interviews reveal him "keeping the faith"— teaching mureeds and harmonizing the various individual teachers who had been brother and sister mureeds of Samuel Lewis. He also met visiting Sufi teachers from other lineages and corresponded with Murshid S.A.M.'s Sufi contacts and guides (such as W.D. Begg and Sufi Barkat Ali), explaining to them how the transmission that Samuel Lewis represented was continuing.

Relations with Sufis in the East were not his largest challenge, however. In the last few years before his passing, Murshid Samuel Lewis had decided to work together with one of the sons of Hazrat Inayat Khan, Vilayat, who had formed the Sufi Order in the West. Murshid S.A.M. and Pir Vilayat's "togetherness" was, however, always a bit fraught. This created yet another difficult balancing act for Moineddin. As some of the selections below describe, this delicate balance was disrupted when Pir Vilayat issued several ultimatums that Moineddin and most of the senior disciples of Murshid S.A.M. could not accept. No doubt this "individuation" of the two streams was inevitable, yet the way in which it occurred was painful for many on both sides.

During the latter part of this time, Moineddin was on dialysis, his kidneys failing again, with no hope for a transplant in sight. He began to plan for his passing, as the letter to Murshid Wali Ali indicates. As part of this, he sent a delegation of mureeds to Turkey, Pakistan and India in 1979 to introduce his wife Fatima, his designated successor at the time, to the Sufi colleagues and teachers of Murshid Samuel Lewis who were still alive and to receive their blessing. During nearly two months on the road, the group met with Sheikhs Suleiman Dede of the Mevelvi order and Muzaffer Effendi of the Halveti-Jerrahi order in Turkey, Sufi Barkat Ali and Shemseddin Ahmed in Pakistan, and Mother Krishnabai, the Dalai Lama and W.D. Begg in India. Moineddin reflects on this trip, as well as the state of the budding Sufi community in the first part of his interview from 1979-1980.

The Walk of Pluto (1972-4)

(Editor's note: Murshid Samuel Lewis created walking meditations based on attunements to the planets as a form of "astrological yoga." He felt that, if his students were going to use astrology, they should work with their direct experience of the energies involved in a scientific, yet devotional way. Moineddin writes: "Murshid Samuel Lewis left his body before writing the final paper in this series on Pluto.... Before the Pluto practice is attempted, one should be thoroughly steeped in most, if not all, of the other planetary attunements. The breath associated with Pluto will come of itself when the instructions are fulfilled." The poem at the beginning of his paper on Pluto is from a "libretto" Moineddin wrote for a planetary pageant in which Sufi mureeds would embody each planet through movement.)

Holy Being, What is thy secret?
"Pluto has become All.
Our spheres embody the curved space
which is as a mother's womb for our divine repose,
while the father's essence shines in our every atom.
The saints of earth enact the mystery
of our blessed state."

Pluto represents the integration (meaning "blending, with growth") of all the other planets. From the standpoint of an individual ego-outlook, Pluto is almost meaningless. Pluto is the being of the group, and group-unity is Pluto's function. But this does not mean group-unity as a mob or even as an army. Sufism teaches "unity, not uniformity," and it is this unity at all levels that shows Pluto in operation.

The Pluto concentration is good for communes and communities, and for leaders of communes or communities who are called upon to represent the ideals and goals of the group to the world at large. This is the practical side. The spiritual side may result in cases of actual awakening much in the same sense as Walt Whitman's realization, "in all men I see myself." It must be remembered that these lessons are given as yoga practices, and not as empty techniques. All the verbal instruction must be combined with devotion if these practices are to bear fruit.

Pluto has been called "the walk of the saint." Like a saint, Pluto does not represent a limited ego-self, but regards the group as its own being. The Kabbalists have a term for this: *Adam Kadmon*, the Grand or Original Human Being. This *Adam Kadmon* is really the whole humanity, with each individual acting like a cell in the overall organism, working on earth to promote all phases and aspects of sisterhood/brotherhood, while at the same time experiencing on the higher planes the consciousness of "Alpha and Omega."

Murshid Samuel L. Lewis remarked, "When you are doing Pluto your head must be in heaven, and your feet must be on earth." The attunements associated with the planet Pluto are to feel the "halo" center located about twelve inches above the crown center, and to feel equally the feet securely on the ground. The entire body is experienced as God's temple, and if more strength is needed, the backbone can be felt to be like a brass rod. The ever-expanding sense of one's aura is felt to be the means whereby one unites with others to further the divine cause.

When a group wishes to attune to the Plutonic norms, the common halo center may be felt somewhere above the group at the central focus. Many Dances of Universal Peace bring this attunement about easily and without particular effort. However, for those who wish to deepen their experience, a certain exertion is necessary at the beginning and perhaps throughout.

Pluto represents transcendence and immanence together. It is living in harmony. It is "united with all," above and beyond the Jupiterian outlook. It has a real spiritualizing effect upon the being, as contrasted with etheric and quietistic effects of some practices that lead to somnolence. The Walk and Spin of Pluto can lead to human perfection, so long as the vision of the whole is maintained. All virtues are there. "It is the Walk of the New Age" in the words of Murshid Samuel L. Lewis.

Reflections on "The Walk of Christ" (1975)

(Editor's note: Moineddin wrote the following on February 11, 1975. We might contrast it with the "Walk of Pluto" above in that, when harmony was not possible, Moineddin felt most attuned to crucifixion during this time of his life. It was published by Ruhaniat mureeds as a short letterpress broadside in 1979, as a commemoration of what was expected to be his imminent departure.)

THE WALK OF CHRIST
by Hazrat Inayat Khan

A crown of thorns on His head
And a bed of thorns beneath His feet
And thorns pricking wherever he resteth
The palm of His helping hand
Still with unshaking faith
And unbroken hope
With closed eyes yet with open heart
His head in heaven
And His feet on earth
He walketh gently with all His trust
In Him who hath sent Him.

REFLECTIONS ON THE WALK OF CHRIST

These words of Hazrat Inayat Khan present living signs of the crucifixion of Christ, a crucifixion which took place not only on the Last Day, but every moment of his life. Every thought, every feeling, every word, every deed was born through the fiery gamut of the Stations of the Cross. Every step of the way was trodden in the knowledge that the way led to Golgotha, the "place of the skull."

Far more, these words present living signs of the resurrection of Christ, a renascence that can take place every moment of our life. For the stations of resurrection dwell within each of life's crosses, like the rose-blooms dwell amid the thorns. The earthly crowning of the thorns, and the heavenly coronation are like the play of shadow and sunlight, commingling of the world of effort with the greater world of Grace.

"I am the Vine and ye are the branches," did Jesus declare. Neither shadows nor thorns did he call his kindred, but rays of his heart-sun, branches of his breath-vine. The illuminated souls of Christ's disciples are the fruits by which he is truly known.

Body and mind are crucified that the heart may live, yet even the heart must pour forth its own blood in praise of the living soul, the blood of spirit. Attachment to the idols of this world nails our vision to the skull and crossbones; yet, the Master's glance resurrects new life within the shattered figures of humanity. Verily, the sight of God is constant through the open heart.

Unshaken faith? Unbroken hope? What man or woman can say these things? These are divine words uttered by the God within. With our heads raised to heaven, and our feet firmly on the earth, we shall learn to walk the heavens and to perceive the inner condition of earth. Complainers are crushed beneath the weight of life's crosses. But with all trust placed in the Father who hath known us even before we became known, we shall walk gently from cross and thorn to crown and bloom, from divine limitation to divine perfection.

Meeting Suleiman Dede of the Mevlevis (1976)

(In the following report, entitled "Message from Marin" Moineddin describes the May 5, 1976 meeting between the Ruhaniat community and Sheikh Suleiman Dede at Hurkalya, the Sufi khankah in Marin County, California. It was published in the June-July 1976 issue of Bismillah.)

Fiona had called from Berkeley several weeks ago and asked if we were interested in hosting the venerable Suleiman Dede, head Sheikh of the Mevlevi Order of Sufis. By all means, I replied, we would love to meet him. Reshad Feild (an old friend and sort of gadfly) would be present as the Sheikh's chief travelling companion, so we would also have an opportunity to renew that acquaintanceship.

As the weeks passed and the day of Suleiman Dede's visit drew near, all of my normal concentrations seemed to pale and everything became like a background to the forthcoming event: the meeting between the Mevlevis and the Chishtis. (Have you read in Volume II, page 60, where Hazrat Inayat Khan writes: "A branch of this Order (the Mevlevis) came to India in ancient times, and was known as the Chistia school of Sufis"?)

Some of you may recall a similar meeting a few years ago in San Francisco where a number of Bay Area Sufis attended the formal *sema* [*the ceremony of turning*] of the Mevlevis at Masonic Auditorium. Afterwards, Allaudin [*Mathieu*] led us in singing many of our Sufi songs for our Mevlevi brethren. The hearts that were kindled at that meeting built a bridge in the unseen that allowed Sheikh Suleiman to visit us here May 5.

None of the 100 or so mureeds and friends knew quite what to expect. At five minutes before eight o'clock, David Bellach, a mureed of Sheikh Suleiman, telephoned and said they would be a few minutes late. So we decided to begin on time with the prayer Saum [of Hazrat Inayat Khan], followed by the opening Bismillah Dance. We had to use both front rooms to accommodate the oversize crowd. As soon as we finished the Dance, we were told that the Sheikh was on his way down the steps.

Rushing out to greet him, I was struck by an oddity. Many of the local Sufis wore robes to the meeting. Sheikh Suleiman wore a very respectable looking dark suit and tie. Yet, he seemed eminently spiritual, much more at ease in fact than us robe-wearers! As he entered through the kitchen door (we closed off the main entrance because a swarm of bees had nested nearby) we sang the *As-Salaam Aleikhum* greeting song.

Suleiman Dede responded by placing his hand over his heart and saying a few of the Ninety-Nine Names of Allah. He then led us into the chapel and we all sat down and sang songs for about an hour, interspersed by short addresses from Reshad. It proceeded to get very high, flash bulbs were popping off all over the place, and Shabda led us on into ecstasy through more singing. Then Suleiman asked specially that the women sing a song by themselves.

Several of the women from the Sufi Choir got up and sang "What Wondrous Love" with the *Ishk Allah Mahebud Lillah* counterpoint. After a few cycles of the song, Suleiman stood up—rather a moment in itself as he is very old in years and small of frame—and motioned people to move aside. He wanted a place to Turn. And as he proceeded to Turn, ever so slowly with steps simply of feeling and not at all the formal step-over turning motion associated with his tradition, the room became filled with increasing reverence. The faces of so many present began to bloom like flowers in the light of the Sheikh's devotion to Allah.

When the women finished their song and Suleiman sat down again, we started to sing the Kalama Dance melody and gradually introduced the counterpoint. After a few minutes, Suleiman Dede began to weave his own *zikr* into the fabric of the harmony. Pretty soon we all found ourselves following the Sheikh leading *zikr*: *La ilaha, el Allah*—then more abbreviated versions until we finished with the *Huu*. The evening had come to a close. We rose and followed the follower of Mevlana to the door.

And what an evening! After Suleiman left with his small entourage, we returned to the chapel long enough to say the prayer Salat—feeling the influx of *baraka* that had been generated.

And as I conclude this account, my normal concentrations once again begin to assume a place in the background, and one feels the onset of the Lama Maqbara Camp, where we shall attempt to build a pilgrim's shelter near Murshid's gravesite. Ya Fattah!

Lama Maqbara Camp (Letter 1976)

(From a letter to a mureed.)

Everything feels so right. We just had our formal dedication of the site here this morning. We began by meditating in silence at the grave itself, then proceeded a few yards away to the Dance ground for purification breaths and a Dance, and finally traipsed a little further down to the Pilgrim's Hut site.

When we were at the grave in silent meditation I closed my eyes and saw the faces of many present, especially Asha [*Greer, another mureed of Murshid S.A.M. and one of the founders of the Lama Foundation*].

So for the preamble to the dedication I said:

"I both saw Murshid and I didn't see him. I didn't see him as such, but I saw many faces of those here present. And I realized that this is how we are to see him—in each other. Without this realization all the visions in the world will remain empty."

Remembering Our Origins (1976)

(Originally published in Bismillah *magazine, December 1976.)*

The title "Remembering Our Origins" is open to many levels of interpretation. For instance, in the Book of Job (1:21) we read, "Naked came I out of my mother's womb, and naked shall I return thither." This refers Kabbalistically to the soul's innate purity which has been born from God's immaculacy and which, once the identifications with body, mind and personality have been divested, becomes like the dew-drop that, in the words of Sir Edwin Arnold, "slips into the shining sea."

This is our origin of origins, and it is the prayer of all the saints that we never forget the beginning-less land of our soul's birth. When we hear that "Abraham came from the Land of Ur (World of Light)" we divine the same meaning. And in the Upanishads we read again and again that God is "Source and Goal."

But there are other kinds of origins, origins which are perhaps not so pristine. In fact, it may not be proper to call them *origins* at all, because they represent stages in life that have appeared subsequent to our prior nakedness and innocence. Nevertheless, let us refer to these later stages as *origins*, since they do provide, each in its own way, the starting points in our need for the spiritual path.

Too often we tend to regard our pasts as unworthy, and this leads to guilt-complexes. On the one hand we come to terms with our state of relative unworthiness, or coarseness, or limitation, and this propels us to seek a higher way. On the other hand, it is easy to go overboard in hating the past, or worse, condemning the image of ourselves in the past. It would be much better to find a bit of humor in the situation, for the light of humor can clear away many dark clouds. Or, as our friend Joe Miller puts it, "Without a sense of humor, there is no end to the abyss of idiocy into which we can sink!"

Let me relate a story in which Murshid effectively punctured one of my bubbles. It was in June of 1969 when Zeinob and I drove Murshid to Los Angeles to visit some of his old friends, as well as to meet a new friend, Premanand Trikkanad, the grandson of Papa Ramdas. After spending a lot of time driving around the Los Angeles freeways, staying here and there, Murshid decided to visit Fred and Corinne Reinhold, a couple he had introduced during his beachcombing days at the dunes of Oceano. As we entered the living room to shake hands with the Reinholds, Murshid remarked perfectly casually, "This is my disciple,

Carl (he used given names often with old friends). Yes, I picked him right up out of the gutter."

Murshid frequently put his disciples on the spot like that. You could never tell how or when it was going to happen.

And many was the time I witnessed Murshid telling one young lady disciple or another, "If you keep on bemoaning your past, I'm going to fix you. I'll take you to meet a girl who really has a hard past, and make you listen to her story! Now, what do you think of that?"

So, dear friends, let us remember how fortunate we are to have discovered the path to the living God. For the Spirit of Guidance—even if it manifests humorously or without social grace—has chosen us for its testing-ground. It is all to get us to see the put-on of our "lesser nakedness" for what it is, and to help us attain the "greater nakedness" spoken of by Job.

At Lama Foundation, 1976

Letter to the Lama Foundation (1977)

Sufi Islamia Ruhaniat Society
(The San Francisco Area Branch of the Sufi Order)

June 15, 1977
Dear Trustees and Members of the Lama Foundation:

We wish to write to you as Trustees in our own right of an Order dedicated to ideals and goals similar to those you have espoused. The inspiring example that Lama Foundation has been to spiritual seekers throughout the world is of considerable magnitude. From its very beginnings, Lama Foundation has been established upon the rock of Work and Prayer, and has been dedicated to the openness—with direction—that any real venture into a New Age of humanity would require.

As we understand it, the problem facing Lama Foundation in its function as an open spiritual community is the present by-law arrangement which permits any one permanent member to absolutely veto the plans and visions of all the other permanent members. Personalities aside, perhaps it is possible that such a course may have served its purpose and should now be rendered obsolete by your vote.

Any amendment of your choosing—even so simple a revision as to allow one dissension and still permit resolutions to pass when the majority outlook is obvious—would insure the continuation and growth of Lama Foundation as an open spiritual community.

The other issue which we feel needs your attention concerns the Maqbara, or gravesite, of Murshid Samuel Lewis. Although technically this tomb is situated on National Forest land, it behooves the Lama Trustees and Members to protect in a definite and legally secure fashion the right of all spiritual seekers of whatever orientation to make pilgrimage thereto—"until time shall be no more."

As you are no doubt aware, the Maqbara has not been a site of pilgrimage limited to any one particular spiritual outlook. Murshid Lewis' gravesite has received the blessings of such Buddhist luminaries as Grand Master Kyung Bo Seo of Korea, and of Joshu Sasaki Roshi of Southern California, to name two—though there are certainly more known and unknown.

In a letter dated February 11, 1970, Murshid Samuel Lewis wrote the following words to Lama Foundation: "'What I give to you, you must share with others (Hazrat Inayat Khan).' Other than a spiritual recognition, I cannot and do not ask for anything." Murshid Lewis did share of his life and being at Lama Foundation on three occasions during his lifetime, and now continues to share of his life and being there for eternity.

We ask your deep consideration upon these matters.

With love and blessings,

Moineddin Jablonski, Fatima Jablonski,
Wali Ali Meyer, Halim Welch, Hassan Herz, Amina Erickson

(Editor's note: After many years, the Lama Foundation did modify its policy of consensus-only for making major decisions. In the late 1980s, land was traded with the US Forest Service so that the gravesite of Murshid Samuel Lewis is now on Lama property.)

Pir-o-Murshid Samuel L. Lewis (1983)

(Editor's note: Moineddin circulated the following article, dated March 3, 1983, to the senior leaders of the Ruhaniat. It recounts briefly the history of the Sufi Ruhaniat's individuation as a separate Sufi order or tariqa.*)*

In the first months of 1967, when the handful of young people (many of whom were soon to become his disciples) met Samuel Lewis at his small apartment on Clementina Street in San Francisco, he was called "Sam" by one and all, except for one Chinese-Irish youth who, out of respect, addressed him as "Mister Lewis." The young men from the Christian Holy Order of Mans, who occasionally attended Samuel Lewis' meetings, called him "Doctor Sam." He was also called "Sufi Ahmed Murad Chisti" by his Sufi colleagues, and "S.A.M." by those who appreciated the acrostic designation of the initials of his spiritual name; but the young people did not know this at the time.

During July of that year, after returning to the doorstep of his new home (the Mentorgarten, on Precita Avenue) following a Walks class conducted along the various sidewalks of the Bernal Heights district, "Sam" turned to his fledgling disciples and said, "I am to be called Murshid now. It means spiritual teacher in Persian. I was told to do this. It is not my doing." He then walked up the stairs, and the new disciples called him Murshid ever after, with nary a slip back to "Sam" except once or twice in the first couple of weeks after the change.

Now, Samuel Lewis never referred to himself as Pir-o-Murshid. In fact, he often stated that until he had had at least two illuminated disciples he would never let himself be called Murshid. Only after he had two such pupils (and he had them, but this was before his meeting with the young people), and following his public reception as a Murshid by Pir-o-Murshid Sufi Barkat Ali in Salarwala, West Pakistan in 1963, would he let himself be theoretically accounted a Murshid. Even so, he waited until the summer of 1967 to be so known. All of this was behavior based upon listening to the voice of the Spirit of Guidance.

At a class for disciples held at his alternate home, the Garden of Inayat in Marin County, in late summer of 1969, he mentioned a book he had recently bought titled *The Tidjaniyya.* "I have just read an account of Ahmed Tidjani's spiritual experiences. He founded a Sufi Order in North Africa. Well, I have had all of the experiences he has written about, plus a lot more. And I would never dream of starting my own Order."

Nevertheless, in the summer of 1970, due to a temporary impasse with Pir Vilayat Khan, then and now head of the Sufi Order in the West founded by his father, Pir-o-Murshid Hazrat Inayat Khan, Murshid and his chief secretary, Wali Ali Meyer, now a Masheikh, drew up a constitution, complete with by-laws and esoteric rules, for the formation of the Sufi Islamia Ruhaniat Society.

But the impasse was soon resolved, and in the years following Murshid's death in January 1971, the Sufi Islamia Ruhaniat Society functioned, as it did during his lifetime, as an autonomously constituted center operating within the general framework of the Sufi Order. However, in the summer of 1977 it became apparent that Pir Vilayat's directives to the Sufi Order were becoming increasingly difficult to abide for the Ruhaniat Society— as it had several special transmissions and commissions to foster and protect, and these areas of work were in danger of being overlooked or phased out.

Thus, in November of 1977, the Sufi Islamia Ruhaniat Society became, along with its constitutionally independent status, a functionally autonomous spiritual order with its own school, grades, classwork and areas of interest, all based upon the foundations laid down by Pir-o-Murshid Inayat Khan. Of course, the Ruhaniat Order had always been reckoned a spiritual order in its own right, with its unique lines of transmission. But now this new order needed to begin to channel and manifest its love and blessings on its own merits and initiative, and with the aid of God.

So, while Samuel Lewis avoided being called Pir-o-Murshid during his lifetime, he is now entitled as such "by default," as he might say. His being continues to rouse the divine fire of realized love, intelligence and strength in the inmost hearts of his disciples and followers. In addition, he is fulfilling all the requirements of the prayer of Murshid Inayat Khan, called Pir, which begins: "Inspirer of my mind, consoler of my heart, healer of my spirit...."

The man who tried to harmonize with all Sufi Orders, never calling himself Pir-o-Murshid, often did refer to his work as an *Abdal*, a helper in the spiritual hierarchy of illuminated souls, which is several grades higher than that of Pir. He said, "An *Abdal* has to manifest continually whatever lesson must be learned in the immediate moment, and thus seems to be possessed of a constantly changing personality."

Many of the lessons we must learn are hard lessons, and many we make hard. Some others may be easier to master, and our own ease makes them so. But all of our lessons, and we are here only to learn them, are given out from the Book of Love authored by the Hand of God.

Shards of a Broken Vessel (1977)

(Editor's note: The following aphorisms were published in the October 1977 issue of The Message, *the magazine of the Sufi Order in the West, shortly before the formal separation of the Ruhaniat from it. Taken together, we might consider them Moineddin's articulation of what he felt to be his spiritual work during his first ten years as director of the Ruhaniat.)*

God will test those who desire His nearness, with the fires of distance.
The 99 Names are the food and drink of the lovers of Allah.
The real crucifixion is separation from the Beloved.
Lover of truth is he who truly loves.
What appears to be sadness, may be the extremest joy.
Respect is more difficult to learn than love.
If Murshid does not like to think about my shortcomings,
    then I will not dwell on them.
The breath is enough,
    the heart is enough,
    the eye is enough,
    the atmosphere is enough.
The spiritual seeker must break free
    of the gravity-pull of mass culture.
Stability attracts.
To expect a movie star to play Jesus Christ,
    is like asking a five-year-old to play a romantic lead;
    it is not part of the experience of either to do so.
A fish slaps upon the dry ground; my heart yearns for His Ocean.
A grain of irritation is lodged in the heart of man;
    if he will give thanks, a pearl will form.
Description is a window; example is an open door.

Open Letter to All Mureeds (1977)

(The following three pieces appeared in a special "organizational" issue of the Ruhaniat's Bismillah *magazine, issued in December 1977 (Vol. 3 No. 1) following the November 6 meeting in which the Ruhaniat separated from the Sufi Order in the West of Pir Vilayat.)*

Beloved Mureeds of the Ruhaniat,
Greetings to you all in the Name of Allah!

I had intended to write something entitled "Where We Have Been, Where We are Going." But in looking over Wali Ali's masterful and comprehensive article elsewhere in this issue, I see that he has covered the subject *where we have been* most clearly. And *where we are going* is, as ever, totally in the hands of Allah. So I shall simply speak with you in a familiar and personal vein.

Today, as is my habit every Friday morning, I am working in Murshid Samuel L. Lewis's office at the Garden of Inayat in Novato. As many of you know, we were privileged to live here for three years with Murshid before Allah called him away from earthly functions. During those years with Murshid, I acted frequently as his secretary, taking dictation in this same office as my secretary, Fatima [Roberts], is now taking from me. It is like a "spiritual constitutional" to be able to work in this fine and refining atmosphere. One's whole vision tends to clear; and we wish to thank Hassan and Jayanara for allowing us to spend this time in their home.

If any one theme could be said to exemplify the life and being of our Murshid, one would have to point to his emphasis on and manifestation of *integration*. This integration (meaning blending and balance—with growth) is the most signal challenge before us all, as individuals and as a group. I heard Murshid remark several times that the most fulfilled and fulfilling moments of his entire life were the two or three occasions when he was able, through grace and transmission of dharma, to function simultaneously at all levels of consciousness. Nor should we regard such experiences as beyond the reach of most mureeds. As the Chinese say, "the journey of a thousand miles begins with the first step." And as Hazrat Inayat Khan says, balance is the state of individual progress *and* consideration for others.

Before speaking practically to the question of integrative functioning, permit me to say a few more words about Murshid Sufi Ahmed Murad

"If we are right, follow us in the Name of Allah. But if we go astray, show us the straight way in Allah's name."

These are the words of Abu Bakr Siddiq, the first khalif of Muhammad, in his opening speech to the people of Medina after the death of their Prophet.

Faithfully with all love and blessings,

Murshid Moineddin

Silsila Sufian (1977)

TOWARD THE ONE, THE PERFECTION OF LOVE, HARMONY, AND BEAUTY, THE ONLY BEING, UNITED WITH ALL THE ILLUMINATED SOULS WHO FORM THE EMBODIMENT OF THE MASTER, THE SPIRIT OF GUIDANCE.

According to Hazrat Inayat Khan's "The Unity of Religious Ideals," the Spiritual Hierarchy is as real or more real than creation itself. The hierarchical chain, known as the *silsila sufian*, is a linkage of realized personalities whose teachings reflect the age in which they have lived and functioned. There are many such chains, each associated with a particular Sufi order.

In keeping with the last words of Prophet Muhammad, "I am Wisdom, and Ali is the Door," most Sufi orders have regarded Hazrat Ali as the esoteric successor to the Prophet, and therefore he is placed at the head of most *silsilas*. However, according to certain writings of Murshid Samuel Lewis, there are at least two Sufi orders that place Hazrat Abu Bakr, Muhammad's first khalif, at the head of their *silsilas*. The point here is that it is quite possible that more than one disciple may inherit the esoteric transmission from the teacher; and that groups of mureeds and devotees will be drawn to the blessed names and forms that appeal most to them. It is thus that different chains are wrought.

Having been associated these past several years with the Sufi Order in the West conducted by Pir Vilayat Khan, we of the Ruhaniat have naturally used the *silsila* he has published. But as the guidance of Pir Vilayat has been called into question as a result of issues raised by his "Declaration," we feel that the line of transmission to the Ruhaniat from Hazrat Inayat Khan and others of the holy chain is more directly through the being and teachings of Murshid Sufi Ahmed Murad Chisti.

The invocation of the *silsila sufian* is definitely an esoteric practice (usually given during a spiritual retreat), and if mureeds wish to practice the invocation of the *silsila*, they should obtain permission from their initiator. A simpler and perfectly valid alternative would be to invoke the messengers named in the prayer Salat [of Hazrat Inayat Khan], followed by mention of Hazrat Inayat Khan, Murshid Sufi Ahmed Murad Chisti and any other illuminated soul whom one feels is a continuing inspiration and protection in his or her spiritual life. Any mureed may do this simpler version if inwardly moved to do so—without specific permission from the teacher.

Finally, one should place the name of one's initiator at the end of the chain, followed by one's own name as a faithful son or daughter of the initiator.

Initiation (1977)

Representatives of the Sufi Islamia Ruhaniat Society who are authorized to perform a ceremony of sacred initiation will henceforth initiate mureeds *"into the path of Sufism."*

This is in keeping with guidance received from Murshid Samuel Lewis that "a member of one Sufi order is automatically a member of all Sufi orders." On an exoteric level such a statement may invite problems of protocol, but on an esoteric level the meaning is quite clear: the Sufi orders, all of them if they are real, have Allah, the Merciful and Compassionate, as their source, sustenance and goal.

For this reason we feel that the sacred pledge, or *bayat*, is to the "path of Sufism," as this provides full scope for the experience of brother/sisterhood, whereas to limit one's pledge to the narrow outlooks found in some orders is alien to the breadth of spirit natural to this day and age.

There must also be the sacred feeling between initiator and mureed. For without this feeling there is little chance to cultivate the spiritual soil in which the seed of *fana-fi-sheikh* is to be sown. We of the Ruhaniat wish to strike a path with our feet firmly set upon the sacred ground of Sufism, and such a process involves *fana-fi-sheikh* as a foundation practice.

Initiations are given as a sacred trust in the name of Allah, who is All-Mercy and All-Compassion; in the name of Hazrat Inayat Khan who brought the Message of Sufism to the Western world; in the name of Murshid Sufi Ahmed Murad Chisti who so recently has restored a dormant Sufism in the West to its proper and vital level; and in the name of any other illuminated soul(s), known or unknown to the world, whom the initiator may be inspired to call upon as a patron and protector over the *bayat*.

Individuating as a Sufi Tariqa (letters 1978)

January 7, 1978

Dear Taj Inayat,
Beloved One of Allah, as-salaam aleikhum!

We were very happy to receive your recent letter. Indeed it has been too long since we have communicated with each other.

The Berkeley group is hosting Murshid S.A.M.'s urs this year, and I have asked Murshida Vera to organize Hazrat Inayat's urs on February 5. She has secured the same church hall where we do our Dance meetings for the occasion. I was more than slightly disappointed to learn that the offer by the Marin Women's Class to do the Beautiful Hu Dance at Hazrat Inayat Khan's urs (a class, incidentally, formed of mureeds from both the Sufi Order and the Ruhaniat) was turned down, apparently not by Murshida, but by Vakil and perhaps Sikander also.

The new format of the *Message* [the Sufi Order magazine] is very attractive. It seems to be easier to read somehow. While I have not as yet had a chance to peruse the whole issue which arrived in yesterday's mail, I did get to read the entirety of Pir's article "The Next Step." I was surprised to have been misquoted by Pir, and feel that a correction should be included in the next issue.

Pir quotes me as saying: "...the day will come when the Sufi Order will be free of ego leadership..." My actual statement, delivered by Fatima in my absence, was: "The day of ego leadership is coming to a close; it will be replaced by an age of real spiritual democracy in which the group will function as a single being. This group will function according to the ideal of 'unity not uniformity,' and will practice above all else to see God in each other."

To me, the gist of my remark is pretty close to the theme of Pir's "New Year's Greeting" in which he says that we are now awakening to the divinity of humanity rather than of limited individuals. Nor in going over the tapes from the November 6 meeting of Pir with the Bay area mureeds could I discover where Wali Ali says, "...at least SIRS has a real teacher." To me, Pir Vilayat is a real teacher and has been a real teacher for as long as I have known him. Every confirmation he has given has been real, even more than what one normally considers as real, in his spiritual transmissions.

I am sorry that Pir feels a betrayal of sorts in my statement, yet its meaning was certainly intended to be more general than personal. Nor has there been a lessening of good faith between the two groups. Naturally, there will always be eruptions of annoyance and the jumping to conclusions on the part of some, and these are sadly the thought-forms which receive the most attention in our culture. But the finer and better realities continue unabated too.

My only real complaint is that I am not being kept apprised by Sikander of vital news coming out of the Sufi Order and the Abode. I seem to be the last one to hear things. This is not a good situation in which to maintain awareness and friendship across group boundaries.

Also, I am not sure if Pir has reversed his decision to permit mureeds of either organization to retain an initiator belonging to another group. Could you clarify this question for me?

On other matters, the Pod [the meditation hut at the Sufi khankah in San Anselmo] is now painted the same color as Hurkalya (bark), but needs one more coat before the project is finished. But the rains keep coming with such regularity that it is impossible to set a date to finish it at this time.

Keep well, dear friends....

With love and blessings,
Moineddin, Fatima and All

***

February 10, 1978

(Letter to W.D. Begg, a Sufi correspondent of Murshid Samuel Lewis in Ajmir, India and author of two books on the early Chishti Sufi saints including Moineddin Chishti, Nizamuddin Auliya and others.)

As-salaam aleikhum!

One has read your letter of January 23 to Masheikh Wali Ali Meyer, one's closest spiritual brother. Many is the time when I sat in this office and took Murshid Sufi Ahmed Murad Chisti's letters in dictation to you. This was, of course, several years ago during his lifetime on earth. May the renewal of our correspondence after so long a lapse be propitious for the work of the followers of Khwaja Gharib Nawaz [Moineddin Chishti], *inshallah*.

One writes this letter with faith and trust in the Living Allah that you and your colleagues will hear the cry of one's heart. Five years ago at a large gathering of Sufi mureeds Pir Vilayat Inayat Khan told the story of how, when he was ten years old, his blessed father Hazrat Inayat Khan confirmed him as his spiritual successor. After telling the story, Pir Vilayat called me to come in front of the group. He then took off his sandals and handed them to me; next he removed the *tasbih* he was wearing and placed it over my head in blessing. He then took both my hands and led me in a circular dance motion and chanted *"El Allah Hu!"* several times. This event is recorded on film, and indicates that at that point in time Pir Vilayat regarded this person as one who should succeed him spiritually, or at least stand as protector of the divine Message until the year 2000 A.D. when his son Seraphiel Inayat Khan would come of age.

But times and people are subject to all kinds of changes. Two years ago one sensed that Pir Vilayat's real successor, in so many ways, was his own wife Taj Inayat Khan. I had a meeting with Pir Vilayat at that time and suggested seriously to him to consider drawing up new legal papers that would insure the succession—or at least the regency for Seraphiel—go to Taj Inayat. Pir Vilayat agreed with me.

Now, the above story may or may not be connected with Murshid Sufi Ahmed Murad Chisti's appointment of this person as *his* khalif and spiritual successor, confirmation of which was given by him many times verbally in the presence of witnesses, once on his death-bed in a dictated statement which we have on file, and even once on some film footage (with sound) which we also have in our archives. Needless to say, Murshid Sufi Ahmed Murad Chisti has been one's guiding light on the path of Sufism from the very first, and one considers his appointment and confirmation as paramount to any other initiations one may have received along the way.

Having lived with Murshid Sufi Ahmed Murad Chisti in his khankah, the Garden of Inayat, for three years until his death on January 15, 1971, one can affirm that he endeavored every moment of his life to fulfill the responsibilities placed on his shoulders by his first Sufi teacher, Hazrat Inayat Khan. If you are at all familiar with the teachings presented by Hazrat Inayat Khan and Murshid Sufi Ahmed Murad Chisti (and indeed of Pir Vilayat Inayat Khan) to Western peoples, you will see that Sufism is considered to be the very heart of all faiths, and not just the mysticism of Islam. This point is stressed over and over and over again, and I include with this letter some pertinent materials for your perusal. It must be remembered that the United States and the European Community of nations are not fundamentally Islamic in their religious outlooks, despite the fact that Sufism teaches that all the world's *Avatars, Pagyambars, Nabis* and *Rassouls* are united in essence. "We make no distinctions or differences among them...."[Holy Qur'an].

Murshid's last words to me (shortly after his passing) from *Malakut*, before his ascension into *Djabrut*, stand as living testimonial to all the above points: "If Islam wishes to be the supreme religion, it will have to prove it by its better deeds, and not by claims or words. Otherwise, Islam must take its place alongside the other religions of the world in the spirit of absolute brotherhood."

The matter of schism also needs some explanation. We have tried in the *Bismillah* magazine to present as clear a picture of the realities, as we see them, which have led to the dividing of the Sufi Islamia Ruhaniat Society from the Sufi Order of Pir Vilayat Khan. It is no doubt difficult for you and your colleagues to appreciate our position. The issue is not in reality based upon the use or non-use of intoxicants or drugs. The fundamental issue is really based upon Pir Vilayat's denial of the mureeds of Murshid Sufi Ahmed Murad Chisti full scope within the Sufi Order to carry out the teachings with which he entrusted us. As this denial left us no choice—except the choice of either dying out or becoming a class of subordinates—we chose to stand upon the spiritual principles taught to us, through the grace of Allah, by our beloved Murshid. We deeply feel that his *baraka* and living spirit are with us in our endeavors.

As much as we are disappointed by the schism, we feel that our hand was forced to make such a move. Praise be to Allah that the members of each group continue to maintain beautiful and enduring friendships as one would expect of real Sufis!

We shall continue to adhere to the profound and comprehensive teachings bestowed upon the Western world by Pir-o-Murshid Hazrat Inayat Khan, *inshallah*. We shall strive to fulfill the lessons given both as teachings and living example by our Murshid Sufi Ahmed Murad Chisti. And we shall trust, *inshallah*, that this letter will speak to the ears of your hearts....

Bismillah, Er Rahman Er Rahim...
Praise be to Allah,
The Cherisher and Sustainer of the Worlds:
Most Gracious, Most Merciful,
Master of the Day of Judgment.

*Thee do we worship,
and Thine aid we seek.
Show us the straight way,
The way of those on whom
Thou has bestowed Thy grace,
Those whose portion is not wrath
and who go not astray.
Amin.*

Faithfully, with all love and blessings,
Murshid Moineddin Jablonski

***

February 13, 1978

(Editor's note: Letter to a mureed, who suggested deleting the word "Islamia" from the name of the organization.)

Beloved One of Allah,
Wa aleikhum as-salaam!
Your letter of February 12 to hand. Thank you for sharing such depth of feeling with Wali Ali and me.

My understanding is that Murshid received the name "Sufi Islamia Ruhaniat Society" from Pir Dewwal Sherif of the University of Islamabad in Allahabad, Pakistan. Now, there may be a suggestion, through verbal association, that this name means we are Islamic (speaking here of the orthodox religion called Islam).

But Murshid definitely told me that our purpose is to restore these terms to their original meaning, and not get caught up in the rigmarole of "the Five Pillars that became five-thousand." (That was one of Murshid's comments regarding an "Islam" based more on folkways and local cultural trips than upon anything Muhammad gave.)

Here are Murshid's directives concerning the terms in the name of our Society:

1) *Sufi:* Divine Wisdom and Love as experience.
2) *Islamia:* All those processes which lead one in, with and toward the realization known as *nafs alima*, the "peace which passeth all understanding."

3) *Ruhaniat:* The entire range of spiritual manifestation, from *missal* (the sphere just beyond earth or matter as such) all the way to *Lahut*, the absolute divinity.

4) *Society:* Living, working, praying, singing and dancing together.

Now, I understand from Zeinob [*another original mureed of Murshid Samuel Lewis*] that her husband, Mojtaba, knows another attribution for the term *ruhaniat*. He says a *ruhaniat* is a type of holy person or dervish (as I recall Zeinob's words). Mojtaba plans to write a more complete explanation of this, and other terms, so that we can communicate the information to everyone through the *Bismillah*.

Love to you, and to Shamcher and Evelyn. Thanks again for sharing your ideas.

Faithfully, with love and blessing,
Moineddin

***

February 17, 1978

Mishala al 'Ayan
Majaanian Trust/Lux Qmina Order
Karama Tower, Moonridge Sanctuary
Anderson, CA

Dear Mishala al 'Ayan,
Beloved One of Allah, as-salaam aleikhum!

Your "Appeal for Reconciliation" is perhaps the clearest and strongest prayer for unity that one has seen. One senses a sincerity that goes beyond the usual opinions and reactions associated with such divisions as have recently occurred in the Sufi Work in the West.

However, one must emphasize that the issue of psychedelics and drugs, far from being Pir Vilayat's sole concern, was a subterfuge to cover even deeper and more controversial issues. One does not wish to malign the being of Pir Vilayat Khan; we are all very human beings and subject to shortcomings and blind spots. One will also not engage in any bickering or back-biting, for Pir Vilayat has indeed proved in the years since my own Murshid's passing to be a rare jewel amongst the general run of gurus, avatars and self-styled saviors. One shall always be grateful for the guidance and association that formed the core of one's endeavors with Pir Vilayat in the Sufi work.

The real reason (and this is perhaps nothing but an opinion) for the break in policy between the Sufi Order and the Sufi Islamia Ruhaniat Society is that the God-given transmissions from our first Sufi teacher, Murshid Samuel L. Lewis (Sufi Ahmed Murad Chisti) were gradually and inevitably being squeezed out of the picture of the overall Sufi Work. Naturally, Pir Vilayat, as his blessed father's spiritual successor, would wish for greater and broader recognition of the teachings given by Pir-o-Murshid Hazrat Inayat Khan. And the Ruhaniat Society too has held and continues to hold an identical viewpoint with regard to the dissemination of Hazrat Inayat's "music."

But the odd element introduced in recent months through Pir Vilayat has been a definite movement to de-emphasize the Spiritual Dancing, the commentaries upon the works of Hazrat Inayat Khan, and the being of Murshid Samuel L. Lewis. All these blessed gifts given to spiritual seekers—and his living example and being above all—deserve better treatment than that accorded by Pir Vilayat Khan. (We send under separate cover our organizational issue of *Bismillah: a Journal of the Heart*, so that you might peruse Murshid's account of his "Six Interviews with Hazrat Inayat Khan" [Reprinted in the book *Sufi Vision and Initiation*]. It should become clear that Pir-o-Murshid Inayat's loving and serious disposition toward his mureed, Samuel Lewis, is shown beyond any doubt.)

Now, there are those who feel that this schism is similar to a divorce; but one's own feeling is that this division is part of a natural process of development—much like the inevitable going in separate (though not separationist) directions of two strong brothers. There is no harm or shame in brothers, each according to the light of his ideal, seeking to travel by the path which will prove to be in line with one's deepest impulse.

One has written frankly to Pir Vilayat concerning many of the above matters, but one has also tempered such frankness with the heartfelt wish that "our two streams might someday, God-willing, reunite to form a mighty river." (The confluence of the Ganges and Jumna rivers at Allahabad springs to mind.)

Your proposal of compromise is certainly wise. Yet, without some definite promise from Pir Vilayat to permit a greater scope for the spiritual transmissions of a tried and true Sufi Master, and here one is speaking of Murshid Samuel Lewis, our hands are virtually tied. As mentioned before, this is the nut to be cracked, and this is the issue which more than anything else led to our decision to strike the path most in accord with our ideal.

I, for one, would be interested and even overjoyed to agree to such a compromise solution. While divisions may effect a certain development, one must admit that confusions and separations are just not much fun.

With all love and blessings to you and with special thanks for your Appeal for Reconciliation,

Murshid Moineddin Jablonski

cc: Pir Vilayat Inayat Khan
Masheikh Wali Ali Meyer

***

June 9, 1978

(letter to Hidayat Inayat Khan, the younger son of Hazrat Inayat Khan.)

Blessed Hidayat,
Beloved One of Allah, peace and blessings be with you!

Your recent letter, and the copy of your speech given in New York City, are deeply appreciated. Your letter discloses all the wealth of an inspired heart, while your speech reveals the musician's ability to sustain a theme over an extended time with undiminished clarity. I have taken the liberty of giving both your letter and speech to our *Bismillah* editor for publication. I trust this meets with your approval.

As you can see by the new return address at the top of this letter, my family has moved from Hurkalya (where you visited with us) to Petaluma, which is located further north. We have yet to formally name our new khankah, but all impressions point toward "Noor Mahal," *inshallah*. This name came spontaneously to my wife Fatima during a recent family meeting; it takes into account your sainted sister's influence, as well as the divine light that is all-important in any spiritual undertaking. *Noor Mahal* means "the light of the court"—which certainly coincided with the size and style of the structure, with the courtly feeling of the grounds.

Your prayers for our spiritual success would be most gratefully requested. And our prayers and good wishes are with you in your endeavor to further harmonize East and West through your compositions, which so beautifully reflect your blessed father's music.

Before I close, let me express to you the feeling I have when I listen to the opus from the "Message Symphony." One feels a beginning from somewhere high up in the mountains as from a clear spring of water. Then it forms a rivulet which in its journey through hill and dale meets in confluence with other similar streams, and becomes a river. This river, like the Message itself, "makes its way by itself" and reveals all of the bitter and sweet encounters that the human soul experiences through life. Ultimately, this river becomes a mighty force drawing all other streams into its current of blessing, and finally joins with ocean of vast illumination and absolute spiritual liberty. (But my words of description are nothing compared to the reality of the music.)

With all love and blessings,
Moineddin Jablonski

Update and Sufi Counseling (letter 1978)

(Editor's note: From a letter to a mureed.)

January 13, 1978
Wa-aleikhum as-salaam!

After two or three weeks of not knowing whether I would live or die (the mind entertains such notions at times!), I prayed to Allah to help me "turn the corner" and I would do the rest. So, by the time New Year's came around the problem was discovered and corrected. It turned out to be a very simple matter: I was simply leaving my dialysis sessions five to seven pounds heavier than I should have. Now that I have re-discovered what is called my "dry weight" I am feeling fit and chipper. Of course, it helped greatly to have received two transfusions in the interim.

Also, the training for home dialysis continues to improve with each session. Fatima is stronger in the field of dialysis theory than I, but I am now able to fulfill most of the practical applications by following the written instructions prepared for us as trainees. We should, *inshallah*, be dialyzing at home by approximately February 1.

Your report of *Ishk Allah Mahebood Lillah* becoming real experience fills your Murshid's heart with exaltation. When tears of joy rain down, the flowers of earth, like the first crocuses which pierce through the crust of snow, grow high.

Indeed, habituation to alcoholic beverages can be more deadening to one's inner spirit than one realizes. It is a matter of experience of many mureeds that when alcohol is cut out from their intake, spiritual unfoldment may begin immediately, even dramatically.

Wali Ali's suggestion that you and Victoria offer some sort of course in counseling through the Sufi School next fall sounds interesting. This is an area which must be approached with a great deal of care. For what is counseling? The standard psychological approach has been simply to mold the human personality to "fit" into certain societal modes, modes which at best may be questioned in terms of any real spiritual value.

Apparently the whole Gestalt movement in psychology has been a refutation of this trend. The Gestalt approach may even herald in its own way the unity principle which must come into play if the entire spectrum of human personality is to be considered of worth.

But I confess to a nagging doubt whenever I have considered the possibilities of opening up the field of counseling to practitioners who have not as yet awakened spiritually. Good intentions are not enough. College degrees are not enough. It takes more than that. It takes the ability to carry burdens and pains within the universe of one's heart—not sentimentality—but strength and willingness and knowledge of how to fulfill the Biblical injunction: "In Allah's presence there is no darkness at all."

Even partial awakening on the part of a counselor may prove to be worse than no awakening at all. Because one with partial awakening may become so excited about the little flash they have received that they make a mountain out of a molehill, as it were. It is most important to consider these matters to their fullest extent before assuming the right and qualification to proceed where even the Messengers of God have permitted life to provide the needed lessons for people, rather than to assume that they could do it of and by themselves.

"Faith (Iman) and self-confidence are one." (Hazrat Inayat Khan)

With all love and blessings,
Moineddin

Blackbirds and Signposts (letter 1978)

(Editor's note: A letter to Masheikh Wali Ali Meyer)
August 17, 1978

Dear Masheikh,
As-salaam aleikhum!
The weather is very beautiful today. There is a blackbird in one of our fig trees at the moment. He seems to have discovered too that the figs are ripe enough to eat. So far we have had a plentitude of loquats, domestic plums and pears, and the persimmons and walnuts aren't all that far behind. Anyhow, nature is a boon to the one who cultivates its inner and outer aspects.

You have seen some of my correspondence regarding impressions of one's "concluding chapters in life." Even two years ago I would have been scared of this prospect—mostly because at that time I felt that Murshid's trust in me as khalif was nowhere near to being fulfilled. But I feel differently today. Today I feel that I have entered into an irreversible process that must culminate, as indeed all lives must someday culminate, in so-called "death."

Every indication inwardly and outwardly points out the signposts and milestones on this road. So I am taking pains to put my house in good order. My will is clear, the succession is clear, and the incidental instructions will become clear when the time comes, *inshallah*. I believe this is what Murshid wants; for Murshid himself departed in advance of his own presentiments. For instance, I feel that he really wanted to train his chief disciples further as teachers before leaving the earth. But Allah knows best.

I have a proposal for you: I would be interested, and hope you are too, in arranging for you to come to Noor Mahal and give *darshan* to the Marin and Sonoma mureeds, and I would go to Mentorgarten at the same time and give *darshan* to the S.F. mureeds. An exchange of our particular energies would, I feel, be beneficial all around. What do you think? (Saturdays in the a.m. are best for me.)

With all love and blessings,
Moineddin

(Editor's note: This exchange of darshan sessions did subsequently occur in 1978.)

About Dissolving (letters 1978)

(Editor's note: The following correspondence was with Shamcher Beorse, an original mureed of Hazrat Inayat Khan and an economist, solar engineer and wise mentor to many in the Ruhaniat Sufi community. He passed away at the age of 84 two years later. For an archive of his extensive writing and work, see http://www.shamcher.org/ and https://shamcher.wordpress.com)

2 December 1978

Dear Moineddin,

You know about the faces one goes through. After enthusiastically accepting sublime mental and heart teachings, there comes a time when all that dissolves into an at-first amorphous nothing, then gradually to be perceived in an entirely different form or rather in no form whatever, and one even conceives how one's original teacher had gone through all that and taught, with a grin of apology, the words he emanated and which he knew would be eventually dissolved. In his last year on earth, Inayat Khan chose to show exactly this, as well remembered and noted by his son Hidayat and by the un-humble undersigned, but only recently digested or experienced.

At such a phase one has no or little right to talk or even appear at meetings where attendants expect the straight teachings of the faith. Except if one is extremely careful in the choice of words—more than most of us can muster. So I have been often wrong in accepting invitations and even more wrong in speaking at these occasions, and thus all became very clear to me at the occasion of your last invitation to your November bash. But when opportunity occurs, I would be delighted to see you and yours.

It seems to me that you, like myself, are diffident, non-elective about life or "death," and that you are extremely well suited to take care of the choice yourself, without any interfering or "healing" from any one except the unseen agencies always at your site or side. As for myself, always ready to go, it seems I have to defer, to renounce any personal wish and let agencies more conversant with the development of the world (energy, economics—these being vital expressions of humanity's spiritual state) make the decisions for me. I don't know if this also be the case with you. Somehow I tend to think so.

All the good things to you in the coming year and all coming years—and to your family.
Shamcher

***

December 7, 1978

Dear Shamcher,

Thank you for your letter of December 2. Yes, we go through many faces in life. We go through many phases in life. The process you describe—when words, teachings, grades, even personalities tend to dissolve into finer and finer stages of spirit—is perhaps a reflection in miniature of what the Hindus call the *pralaya*. It may be that the personality undergoing this change in realization and outlook is aware through some avenue of his unison with the *pralaya*.

It may also be that Inayat Khan entered a kind of *pralaya* state as he neared death. It may be that this *pralaya* state is related to what is called *paranirvana*. Yet, in my limited studies concerning the passing of great souls, I find there is a tremendous effort put forth to congeal all that one has realized through life into that soul's "last words." Certainly the last words of Lord Buddha would suffice for all peoples of all stages. He would satisfy you by his "all component things must ultimately dissolve." He would also satisfy the inner longing of all sentient beings by his "seek thy salvation with diligence."

I do not know what Inayat Khan's last words were. The last words of Nyogen Senzaki were: "Friends in *dhamma*, be satisfied with your own heads. Do not put on any false heads above your own. Then minute after minute watch your steps closely. These are my last words to you."

Anyhow, from the *pralaya* view, you must have been present at our November bash in spirit even though your body may have been occupied elsewhere.

I would agree, Shamcher, that I feel more prepared to meet death as time goes on—though Allah knows best. I too must renounce any personal wish in the matter and pay close attention to the pains and needs of the mureedship with which I have been entrusted. God knows, the most effective means of forgetting one's self comes when a mureed has a pain or need. So in this sense one has many more *fanas* to go through before one may realize in more permanent fashion the *baqa* that leaves no room for the small self.

As always, your words are like a gentle massage to the aching muscles of one's spirit.

May your work be accomplished!
Moineddin

Receiving the Pilgrims (letter 1979)

(Editor's note: This correspondence between W.D. Begg and Moineddin followed the visit of the Ruhaniat pilgrims to India in January 1979. It continues the conversation that began in the letters in "Individuating as a Sufi Tariqa" above.)

Ajmer (India)
29 January 1979

Hazrat Pir-o-Murshid Moineddin Jablonski—
Assalam Alaikum wa Barakatu.

God is gracious, Merciful and Compassionate towards both his devotees and enemies. To be his devotee is awfully difficult in this particular irreligious age of Science & Technology. It was his grace upon me, an insignificant creature, that Murshida Fatima Jablonski, Sheikh Vasheest Davenport and several other dervishes called on me on 25th January, 1979, with your holiness' two inspiring letters after a telegram from Delhi. I cannot express on paper the tremendous happiness I had in receiving and entertaining this devoted party in my bedroom as I am bedridden due to prolonged illness. Their visit put new life in me as I embraced each one of them so affectionately.

They had many visits to the Holy Dargah of our Pir-o-Murshid Hazrat Khwaja Muinuddin Chishti, one of which I personally undertook with them in presenting them at the feet of the holy saint. They are all happy and they left for Agra last night after four days' stay in Ajmer.

I am now perfectly satisfied that so far as Islamic Sufism is concerned, they are on the right path to salvation. Many wars and controversies in this world are due to "misrepresentations" created by middlemen for selfish reasons. I beg you, as a benefactor of the late Murshid Ahmed Murad Chishti, to forget the past arguments I had with you in some of my letters. Magnanimity is the salt of Oriental Sufism, as you know. I am praying here for your holiness' health to guide your mureeds for many many years to come.

I am restricted by my doctors to complete rest and dieting, hence this is only a small and brief letter to thank you for sending your party to see me. God willing, I shall be writing you again in more details. Just now a fourth edition of *The Holy Biography of Hazrat Khwaja Muinuddin Chishti* is in press. It is expected to come out by the end of March. My both books have proved a tremendous success all over the world by the grace of God. I have kept copies of your gracious letters in my office for future reference. With profound regards, best wishes for your health and divine services in the New Year, believe me,

Yours sincerely,
W.D. Begg

February 16, 1979

My Dear Mirza Begg,
Wa-aleikhum as-salaam!
Bismillah, Er-Rahman, Er-Rahim...

Thank you for your kind and magnanimous letter of January 29. It is indeed due to the Grace of Allah that my wife, Murshida Fatima, my colleague Sheikh Vasheest and the party of fine young American dervishes, have been granted the boon of making their pilgrimage to the doors of sacred sites and holy personages throughout the East.

Many unforeseen gates have been opened to further the work of universal Sufism. For instance, when the group visited the chief Sufi Orders in Turkey, they were received with open arms. Sheikh Suleiman Dede of the Mevlevis and Sheikh Musafferedin of the Helvetis were both sympathetic and most understanding regarding the establishment of Sufism in the Western world, and particularly in America. Naturally, the outer forms of Sufism will necessarily be adapted to the new cultures where Sufism is introduced. This is why Hazrat Inayat Khan gave the Sufi Message in such a universal framework. This is why Murshid Sufi Ahmed Murad Chisti gave the practice of Spiritual Dance, based absolutely upon the repetition of Kalama and *wazifa*, as well as upon sacred phrases from the Sanskrit, Hebrew, even Latin and English.

But at the heart of our practice of Sufism is the real Islam, the real surrender to *La Ilaha El Il Allah Hu, Muhammad-ar-Rassoul Lillah*—or as the Indian teachings would say, *Sanatana Dharma*.

My special thanks to you, Mirza Begg, for your unstinting help shown to our group of dervishes, particularly your personal presentation of the group to the holy dargah of Hazrat Khwaja [Moineddin Chishti]. We really cannot thank you enough.

Also, we hope that the photographs you requested will have arrived in time to be included in the new edition of your book, Inshallah. I feel strongly that the inclusion of materials showing the definite growth of Sufism in the West can only bode well for the future of universal brotherhood. Ya Hayyo Ya Qayoom!

With all love and blessings,
Murshid Moineddin Jablonski

[W.D. Begg died shortly after, within a month of his receiving the Ruhaniat pilgrims.]

It's Happening.... (letter 1979)

(A letter to Mansur Johnson, a longtime friend of Moineddin from Iowa and another of the early mureeds of Murshid Samuel Lewis.)

March 25, 1979

Dearest Mansur,

Peace be with you...
It is happening Mansur. One's whole life is passing before one's eyes. The hand of Azrael will not be stayed.
"On the return of Azrael to heaven with the handful of earth, God said he would make him the angel of death. Azrael represented that this would make him very hateful to men, but God said Azrael would operate by disease and sickness.... Moreover, death is in reality a boon to the spiritual, and it is only fools who cry, 'Would that this world might endure for ever, and that there were no such thing as death!'" (Masnavi)
Naturally, one would like and love to feel strong and healthy. I keep up my walking, and now that the weather is warming I am starting to go swimming again. But dialysis patients are afflicted with a number of side conditions that rob one of physical strength: anemia, progressive bone dystrophy, and fluctuations from one extreme to the other in the bodily and mental spheres. The bone dystrophy is perhaps the worst. I used to be able to play tennis for half an hour at a time (two years ago); now the lower back is in such pain that a twenty-minute walk poops me completely. These are not complaints; they are facts in one's life to date.
All indications inner and outer, all intuitions, have only reinforced the overall impression of impending transition from the life on earth. So I am only putting the house in order, and in these last years, or months, or hours, one's whole attention is upon the growth to fullness morally and spiritually of those who must carry on the work which we feel it is our trust to realize.
If Allah chooses to reverse the present process, fine. I am contenting myself with whatever happens. At the same time there is nothing of giving in; actually, I am doing everything possible to maintain the highest level of energy I can, and to maintain all the major concentrations, *inshallah*. Yesterday's *darshan* was the finest yet, and I have made plans to go to Lama in May, to the Northwest Sufi Camp in late summer, and to the Mendocino Camp in between. All of these schedulings require extra

efforts to secure dialysis arrangements away from home, or to operate within severe time limits if I'm only gone for a weekend.

I don't ask you to accept any of this. I only tell it to you so that you will have a picture of this one's view at this time.

'Many a hidden Mansur there is who, confiding in the soul of Love, abandoned the pulpit and mounted the scaffold." (Masnavi)

More later, including Fatima's companions' names and addresses. She is back, alhamdulillah! All is well...

With love and blessings,
Moineddin

A Sufi Life, Part I: Carrying On (1979)

(Editor's note: The following is part one of an interview with Moineddin conducted in early 1979 by Abdul Aziz Bartley, Hafiza Mathieu, Jayanara Herz and Hassan Herz. It appeared in Bismillah: A Journal of the Heart *in volume 4, number 2 in 1979.)*

Bismillah: *I'd like to begin with something that is happening right now, the trip to India and the Middle East. The question has come to my attention recently, of the significance of making this kind of contact with the spiritual orders in the East, why it's important, if it is. Is it?*

Moineddin: Well, I just wrote a letter this morning to a disciple in Eugene, Oregon and remarked that somewhere in the writings of Hazrat Inayat Khan he mentioned that the Message was destined to go from the East to the West where it would have a period of development and flowering and then at the most suitable time it would make its way back to the East in order to give life to that which is dying out in the more traditional forms. So the way I see it is really as part of a general evolutionary pattern in which the whole world is involved rather than just small parts of it.

This pilgrimage to me is a reverberation that was set into motion back in 1967 when there were just a few disciples around Murshid Samuel Lewis, but he kept saying that he wanted to take a group of ten or twelve disciples with him to the orient, formally to commemorate the Gandhi centennial which was to be celebrated in 1969, I believe; but as it happened that never panned out. Now, with Vasheest doing *tasawwuri Murshid* in this respect— he has been responsible for getting this pilgrimage together and being its encourager and guide— I just feel that Vasheest is Murshid. Of course I am very grateful to him. He was able to encourage even a person such as my wife, Fatima, to go along, because she is normally so geared into the work on the earth plane with her responsibilities as a mother and so forth, that it's hard for her to orient her vision toward something that she might consider a little bit too spiritual. You know; she's a much more practical person than that. Vasheest just kept at it and at it and finally just wore her resistance down. As we can see from all the correspondence that's come, especially from Anandashram, the group's visit with Mother Krishnabai (whom Murshid regarded as the most perfected soul he'd ever met on earth) has come to pass. And so I look at it as being a fulfillment of Murshid's original inspiration. He wanted people to see actual God-realized souls on earth.

And he also wanted people to share his own experience visiting the tombs of saints, so that they could partake of the *baraka* that has accumulated over the centuries at these holy sites.

Bismillah: *By having representatives from the Order go through these experiences we're continuing to participate in an ongoing process. Is the idea of confirmation part of this or is that a side result that has a place in some people's minds but is not necessarily a real consideration?*

Moineddin: I don't understand your question.

Bismillah: *When people go to the East, are they being confirmed in some stage of their evolution?*

Moineddin: Confirmation comes from within; it doesn't have to come externally. External confirmations may be of help, and certainly they give a certain impetus if persons are doubtful of their mission or something like that. When Murshida Fatima went to see Suleiman Dede they had a marvelous meeting of hearts, and he did confirm that her work was to carry on spiritually the line of Murshid Sufi Ahmed Murad Chisti. He even remarked to her that he went through a similar period of doubt when it was time for him to assume the formal leadership and responsibility for the order over which he was given charge. Yes, certainly Murshid was spiritually confirmed in his Asian travels. But the real confirmation of one's spiritual station must come from within. Yet at times there may be a need for it to come from without before it blooms from within.

Bismillah: *A need for the individual, or...*

Moineddin: Yes, for instance, Murshid confirmed me to be his spiritual successor, but I didn't have the slightest notion, I mean, I felt like a dunce for years after he died. It just gradually began to unfold; the realization came from within more and more and more.

Bismillah: *So the external confirmation is...*

Moineddin: ...can be very helpful and valuable. But let's take a lesson from Papa Ramas, who said, "Oh, Ram, it's wonderful when you manifest to me in the form of Jesus or Krishna or Shiva or Buddha, but then I feel bereft after the impression is gone. So please don't give me any more of those experiences which are ephemeral, however wonderful they are. I only want You, eternally and permanently."

Now, Papa Ramdas gained much, at least we may infer this from his writings. He went to receive the *darshan* of Shri Ramana Maharshi, and he felt that his cup was filled. And after he received Ramana Maharshi's *darshan* much of his own spiritual progress was given release, was catalyzed tremendously. This happens; this is why spiritual teachers use the glance. This is why *baraka* is cultivated, both on the side of individual effort and on the side of reception of divine grace. Because if it weren't for the *baraka* in the glance and the atmosphere and the other realities of Sufism, what point would there be in seeking for the divine presence through the guidance of a teacher? Sufism is said to be a gradual method of self-realization of God. We don't all start out as illuminated beings. As little children we have a certain degree of illumination, but then it gets covered up. After a certain point when we can't stand all the covers, and start to feel smothered by them, that's when we start to yearn consciously for the reality of our own soul. So we turn, and we turn away from our limitations and we turn toward our perfections.

So, yes, external, internal. In a way they come to a unity. As the Mahayana Buddhists say, "*Nirvana* and *samsara* are one." This would be what the Hindus call *sahaja samadhi*, the natural state. Or as the Sufi poet said: "Only God I saw."

Murshid gave us the example not only of listening keenly for the voice that constantly comes from within, but also of listening for that same voice as if it could come and would come, and does come through others externally. So, he said, "I listen particularly to the voice of a kind father, a loving mother, an innocent child, a helpful friend or an inspiring teacher. Spiritually, in particular, to an inspired teacher." All of these are like mouthpieces of the Divine Voice and if we listen to the helpful friend or kind father or loving mother or innocent child or inspiring teacher, confirmations or guidance can come from outside. It's only our egos which get in the way.

Bismillah: *My question is kind of along the lines of self-realization toward the ideal of God—*

Moineddin: Self-realization *through* the God-ideal.

Bismillah: *Right. It seems that I can remember meeting you in Iowa before you met Murshid. And then seeing Wali Ali when he first came to the meetings, and in a certain sense my impressions of you both at that point, and my impressions of the reality now, it's as if both your natures broadened. Let's say you look at it in terms of color. Somebody begins the spiritual path as say, predominantly red, maybe he needs some blue, and as he goes along the path he broadens his spectrum. Would you comment on the aspect of self-realization that seems to broaden one? For example, I remember Wali Ali as a Jemali man and he seems to have broadened in a different direction. Could you say something about that expansion of personality that seems to take place?*

Moineddin: There are many ways, lines and degrees of development. In one sense you might take the example of the seed, which has to incubate in darkness within the denseness of the earth, perhaps for years, before it ultimately decays enough to send down little rootlets. Then it becomes able to grow upwards and experience life above the surface, to become a tree and bear fruit. And it all started with this tiny little seed. And the fruit in its turn reseeds, and through the play of the elements, through the running stream, a seed can be carried to another area or through the air a spore can be carried afar, so that this seed is regenerated in different places in different times. It just keeps going on and on.

The same process happens with the human soul. In one sense, it's been asked if life has any meaning, because, after all, the soul is always the soul. But a realized soul may assist the evolution on all planes, from the dense earth to the higher planes. In other words, all those planes that occupy what we call time and space may need assistance, and this is the work of the Sufi or the Bodhisattva. And this is the meaning of Christ's words when he said, "I will not drink of the fruit of the vine, until the kingdom of God shall come." The Bodhisattva takes the same oath or vow. He agrees to work in the worlds of becoming, and will not enter into final *nirvana* until his work has been completed to perfection, which is to say, until God withdraws him from those spheres.

So, there is the effort side, which is called *sadhana*, spiritual struggle, and perhaps there is a season for it. I would say there is. Yet I think perfected souls such as Muhammad have given the example that there is always the need to purify one's being more, and even in the midst of spiritual realization, there is always more to be realized. This to me has been an example for Sufis throughout the ages, in the sense that they feel like fulfilling the *Gate Gate* mantra: "Going, going, going beyond, going beyond gone, constantly becoming Buddha."

In other words, keep the balance of your life on earth as much as possible, but at the same time sacrifice as much as you can in order that you may become less concerned with the affairs of the limited self and more concerned with the affairs of the unlimited reality. The more you are able to master the affairs of limitation, the more the affairs of the unlimited can permeate the limited affairs. And this makes one more capable of appreciating the natural state.

Hazrat Inayat Khan was once asked, "Will all souls attain to spiritual realization?" And the answer was, "Yes, of course. It's in the Quran: 'Verily, from Allah we come and unto Him is our return.'"

There's no question. It's just what you might call sooner or later, and Sufis would like to feel that it is going to be sooner. But after they receive *bayat* (initiation), life itself develops through them and in them. What they thought might take a couple of years in their initial hopefulness may take a long, long time. And yet a real Sufi won't mind a bit.

Murshid told a wonderful story once. At one time in his life he was making one mistake after another, really fouling up, blowing it, you know. Finally it got to such a point that God came to him and said: "Well, Samuel.... (he said God used to talk to him man-to-man sometimes). Well, Samuel, you haven't been doing so well. What I'm going to do is add twenty years to your life so that you may work a little harder and prove yourself."

About twenty years later Murshid said he was doing pretty well, objectively speaking, and he said he consulted God about whether he really was doing well or was he just pulling the wool over his own eyes. And God said, "Yes, Samuel, you're doing very well, and as a reward I'm going to add twenty years to your life!" Now, that may have been *our* reward, because part of that twenty years was when we met him, see?

To expand a little further on Hassan's original question— how beings tend to broaden—it's the spirit of sympathy, of love. Love may become overshadowed by the thought of self or pain, or thought of another's pain. Yet what is consideration of another's pain but a form of love? And the more one is able to take on the burdens of others and at the same time keep one's heart clear, the natural result is that empathy begins to grow. But the teacher also has to be awake to the evolutionary potential of each disciple. So you have to be constantly on the lookout for when people start to crack open their shell or begin to turn over in their sleep so you can help bring them to a higher station.

I'm going to be talking a lot about Murshid because he's my exemplar, the exemplar of many of us here.

Murshid wrote a letter to his God-daughter, Khalifa Saadia, and he remarked, referring to himself: "Your Murshid can be the biggest fool on the face of the earth if left to his own devices, but put a mureed who is in need in front of him, and all of a sudden your Murshid turns into a wise man." Now, this is what happens. If a mureed or a disciple comes in some sort of need, the teacher becomes an answer to the mureed. This is why I give darshan once a month, to answer many needs, my own included. A transmission occurs. It just does. As Joe Miller says, you catch it, it's a contagion. And when you catch it you see it was there all the time. But there was something covered up, something had to be seen through before it would connect. So, one is on the lookout, not dualistically on the lookout, one is on the lookout as if one's own being were being brought toward a completion, toward a fulfillment.

Oftentimes it will happen that a disciple has much in the realm of spirit or even in the realm of practical knowledge to share with the spiritual teacher. It happens often. Very often. That's why a real spiritual teacher can never presume or assume anything concerning him/herself, because once you do that there is a dualism, and you become blind to the gifts and talents of other "yourselves."

The lesson that Hazrat Inayat Khan gives is that the real spiritual endeavor is not only to progress as an individual soul, but to progress in a balanced fashion with one's sisters and brothers. This is what led him to say, from his own realization, "What I give to you, you must share with others." This again is the work of the Bodhisattva, and not of the Pratyekabuddha, the one trying to gain something "only for him/herself." It just doesn't happen that way. It's phony, it's false. It cannot be.

Bismillah: *The needs of the disciples around you—in what way do they shape the line of development? Do you feel that the line of development is there and you awaken it, or...?*

Moineddin: Are you talking about the development of the disciples? You see, the actuality is that the disciple and the teacher progress together. That's the actuality.

Bismillah: *But is the line of mastery or sainthood inside the disciple and it just awakens? Can you feel each person's line of development? Do you understand what I mean?*

Moineddin: Yes. I understand what you're saying. There are definite periods of development. They can be gradual and even, or they can be rather extreme. For instance, Sufi Barkat Ali went through what he called a *jelali* phase, and he described his *jelali* phase as spending several months buried up to his neck in the ground, only his head was above the surface. Presumably he had to be fed, or perhaps his spiritual practices nourished him sufficiently, I don't know. He referred to that as his *jelali* period, which you might call making a real effort toward mastery over the lower nature.

And you can see it in the writing of Hazrat Inayat Khan (in volume five of *The Sufi Message*) called "Metaphysics," the head is called *shuhud*, the spiritual aspect, and the body is named *wujud*, the material aspect. So not only symbolically, but actually, his body was buried and his head, the spiritual part, was raised.

You can see it in the growing plant. First the stem, that's *jelal*: straight, linear, upright, "Toward the One." But when the plant has attained a certain growth, then it begins to flower out, and that's *jemali*. It's like the story of Adam and Eve. Adam represents the positive accent and Eve the responsive. And that's the symbolism of the rib: Eve, or the response, is created from the initial accent. It doesn't refer particularly to men and women because there are *jelali* women and *jemali* men.

For instance, Murshida Fatima is basically a *jelali* woman, and Murshid Moineddin is a *jemali* man—usually. But it can change, and it depends upon the need of the moment.

I'm sure Hassan has seen Moineddin in a *jelal* state. I'm also sure many people have seen Fatima in a *jemal* state, particularly in the film *Sunseed* when she's— well, actually it is more *kemal*. But in the sense of following in the footsteps of the Prophet it is *jemal*; in the sense that she stands on her own feet it would be *kemal*.

You know, we could take up much more practical matters. I don't mind talking like this, but there's a lot more in the ocean of life than droning on and on about, you know, "matters of the spirit," as wonderful as they may sound and be.

Bismillah: Well, we do have some practical questions, we do—which I'd like to get to in a bit, but a couple of things have come out of your conversation, and one is that I feel that I heard behind some of the things that you said about jelal *energy, that...*

Moineddin: By *jelal* I mean expressive. I don't mean power as such, although it may incorporate power. *Jelal* is expression and *jemal* is response, that's what I mean.

Bismillah: Maybe I'm trying to analyze it. Let's go on to something else. There are different flavors, methods of study, in Sufism; there are different schools, and Murshid Lewis was initiated into the Naqshibandi and Chisthi Orders?

Moineddin: Yes. Eight or nine dervish orders in all.

Bismillah: Well, my question is this: In the Ruhaniat order here in the Bay Area and the Western states there is a special feeling for the Chishti expression, and I wonder if you would comment.

Moineddin: I can't comment on any of the other schools too much, because my only initiation, which I feel is sufficient, has come at the hand of Sufi Ahmed Murad Chisti.

And while his transmissions involved realization in many schools, he gave me a traditional Chishti Sufi *bayat*, or initiation. Murshid initiated me in the name of Hazrat Inayat Khan and asked if I took "this person," meaning himself, as spiritual teacher, and of course I said yes.

I really don't remember if he named any other holy ones or not. He probably mentioned them. I know he had his heart centered on Christ and Muhammad, perhaps others. I can feel this, but I just can't say for sure.

Murshid received what is called *tanasukh*, or the mantle of transmission, from Khwajah Moineddin Chishti in the same sense that Hazrat Inayat Khan received it years earlier. Like Moineddin Chishti centuries before, they pioneered the "Message" of Sufism in a new country, in a different culture.

The Chishti consider the most effective means toward spiritual awakening and realization are through the use of music, dance, art, singing, poetry. And these were Murshid's gifts. He shared a kind of spiritual drama with us, and even comedy. For real! I mean, the great out-pouring of laughter, such a great outpouring!

When the family meeting was filmed here for *Sunseed*, he said, "You know, we imagine God to be some stuffed shirt up in the sky running the universe. That's wrong. That's not God. In *Lazarus Laughs* by Eugene O'Neill, God is the spirit of eternal life, love and laughter!"

Some Sufi schools concentrate on more formal aspects, like praying five times a day and other features of the *shariat*. We have modes of worship that may not be quite so traditional, but in certain ways they are formal because Hazrat Inayat Khan gave the Confraternity prayers and the Universal Worship.

And some devout Muslims might be very surprised if they came to Noor Mahal to see the entire household praying three times a day. And the prayers even have Arabic names: Saum, Salat, Khatum, Pir, Nabi, Rassoul. It's just that they are said in English, but this is a different culture. So the teachings have been introduced in suitable idioms for this culture.

It's just logical. It's logical and super-logical that the divine Reality should come to reside in the hearts of those who can, will and do appreciate it.

Bismillah: *This brings up a question: At what point does one consider the possibility of manifesting something outside of the school, going someplace and doing something where you are not known as a Sufi per se, or as a spiritual teacher per se?*

Moineddin: That's a question I can't answer, because it's not the role I've been given. It's not part of my experience. I've been assigned to function quite formally, to maintain a post, to be recognized. It is not part of my work to be unknown, except insofar as the operations of the spirit are concerned, operations which belong to the unseen.

However, like Joe Miller says, you can just be walking down the street, and if your heart-atmosphere is strong it's going to have an effect. If a person is open to catch it, they'll catch it, you don't have to say a thing. In that sense anybody can be an unknown.

But I'm talking more about the work of being given a definite outer task to fulfill—like Sufi Barkat Ali gave Murshid a commission to get 50,000 Americans to chant Allah.

And Murshid succeeded, *alhamdulillah*!

You are talking about a path which the Sufis call *rind*, which means unknown, and it is the duty of one who is *rind* to remain unknown, to remain away from the notice of the world as being special or spiritual. And this helps him or her to concentrate better. As far as I am concerned, *rind* is probably at a higher stage than a person like myself. I and others like me may need the outer prop, so to speak, of being recognized, to help in the struggle to achieve along the assigned lines.

Bismillah: *I don't see it as a prop but more as a medium to work in ...*

Moineddin: It's an incentive. It is a medium, but it's an incentive too. Some people disagree with the whole notion of having a school of graded initiations. This is legitimate in a sense, but it's not legitimate in another sense, because I think a person can be helped tremendously by being given a certain degree of initiation, even prior to its realization.

It can serve as an incentive, or as an ideal for one to struggle towards. All I'm trying to do is to stay focused on those mureeds who have asked to be disciples or who have asked for specific protection. That's all I'm trying to do, besides maintaining the same attitude towards my family and household. Oh, and all our initiators, Sheikhs and center leaders of course.

Bismillah: *I feel like I've heard an answer to a question I wanted to ask, but I would like to ask you to develop it further. I see a lot of people continually struggling with daily work and the time and energy it takes, and to still be able to put effort into what they feel they are working toward, the fulfillment of their purpose in life. And I find that the question bears on how to get projects completed. It's a continual struggle. Maybe the outward struggle is just a reflection of an inner struggle?*

Moineddin: It can get that way.

Bismillah: *Well, you asked us if we had some practical questions; I consider that a practical question.*

Moineddin: Ask me the question again.

Bismillah: *Just from my own experience, I'll ask a very specific question. I worked as a sort of handyman for many years, because I didn't feel that I was ready to go out and do something that would involve a more demanding manifestation...*

Moineddin: In other words, you did something to bide your time until you could orient yourself toward a more *dharmic* goal.

Bismillah: *Right. And then it occurred to me that I was spending forty hours a week doing this work—all the time I was putting in wasn't leading anyplace.*

Moineddin: Yes, that's the rat race.

Bismillah: *And one of the solutions that occurred to me was to try to build up from the place that I was in the external world, just to seek advancement from that place rather than to make a big leap into something that was totally different. It didn't particularly work, and it didn't feel like the right thing.*

Moineddin: What do you do now? What is your work?

Bismillah: *My worldly work is pretty much the same thing, only I'm more of a carpenter now than a handyman.*

Moineddin: Are you satisfied? I mean, do you like to "carp"?

Bismillah: *Yes, I do like to carp, but I feel that it's still temporary.*

Moineddin: Well, what do you want to do?....(long pause) ...What do you *really* want to do? This is what a Sufi would ask himself.

Bismillah: *You want me to tell you?*

Moineddin: I'm asking you!

Bismillah: *I would like to feel that I'm continuing Murshid's work in such a way that it may manifest in the world.*

Moineddin: Yes, but you've got to be more specific (slapping knee). Every sincere disciple wants to manifest his or her Murshid. This is natural. What do you desire to do specifically?

Bismillah: *Is the form chosen for oneself?*

Moineddin: Murshid wanted to be a gardener. So he got a job on the highway crew and gardened. And he liked to garden so much that he took courses constantly at the horticultural school. He did what he *wanted* to do...(long pause)...

Shems for instance, didn't know what he wanted to do until we had the Maqbara camp at Lama in May '76. When he went there he realized for the first time in his life that he really wanted to be a *good* carpenter. And he knew that that's what he wanted to do for his whole life. He wanted to become a better and better carpenter, and wanted to be able to take on projects and complete them, and he wanted to be able to instill those projects with *baraka*. And he is now using carpentry as a means to bring the transmission through.

Bismillah: *So, something that...*

Moineddin: You see, disciples come to me and say, "I'm at a loss for what to do." Usually they get into a quandary, because they think they don't know what "God" wants them to do. I don't ask them what God wants them to do. I ask them what *they* want to do, because that has a lot to do with it. It also has a lot to do with what God wants them to do. Because what they really want to do—their heart's desire—will be right. And if they don't have a goal in focus just yet, they can always help Murshid! And it's really something that you know, just opens up before one. But there may be a period of incubation before you can see your way clear.

Now, a funny story concerns Fazl. Murshid asked him what he wanted to do. Fazl said, "I want to be a Pir-o-Murshid." He was totally sincere, and Murshid said: "Well, think of something else, because I'm already the Murshid." But at least he had the innocence and gumption to say he wanted to be a Pir-o-Murshid. I thought that was beautiful.

Bismillah: *For some reason, I'm not sure exactly why, hearing you tell the story of Shems, I feel like that is valuable information. It would be helpful to a lot of people, but how does it get out?*

Moineddin: Well, this is being recorded and it's supposed to be...

Bismillah: *Oh, right! Put it in* Bismillah!

Moineddin: Right. That's where this is going, for better or worse, Inshallah.

Inshallah.

An Exchange: Pir Barkat Ali and Pir Moineddin (letters 1979)

(Editor's note: Following the visit of Ruhaniat pilgrims to his community in Pakistan, Pir Barkat Ali sent Moineddin the following letter to which Moineddin responded. Both letters were published in Bismillah: A Journal of the Heart, *volume 4, issue 3 in 1980.)*

14 July 1979

My Dear Moineddin,

What a joy to pass a hopeful Holy message
From a mind to minds.
It is certain, free from doubt
Not subject to further research.
Come forward.
Try to off the veil a bit.
Mysterious gem discovered.
It is in the
Mine of Mind
Truly and undoubtedly it is in the Mine of Mind.
Mind is a Mountain,
The Gem is in the Mine of Mind.
So far I know this is the fruit of Holy Struggle
Of Sufi-ism.
The goal of man.
The aim of life.
Bind this lesson to thy breast.
Practice
Practice hard
Practice logically
Practice with
peace
faith and belief
strong belief
that
La Ilaha—means nothing exists
Illallah—but Allah.
Belief.

Allah is sufficient for all problems.
Allah must be sufficient for all problems.
Just start a hare over the matter.
Success Success Success.

I think you issue a periodical entitled *Bismillah*. I would like to mention the Holy Pilgrimage visit and this message of a heart to hearts in your journal.

My best wishes, regards, compliments and blessings to you all.

Your own,
Sufi Barkat Ali

***

August 11, 1979

Toward the One, the Perfection of Love, Harmony and Beauty, the Only Being, United with all the Illuminated Souls who form the Embodiment of the Master, the Spirit of Guidance.

Bismillah, Er-Rahman, Er-Rahim. We begin in the name of Allah, Most Merciful and Compassionate.

Blessed Pir-o-Murshid,

Dear Sufi Barkat Ali, *as-salaam aleikhum!*

Our sincerest thanks for your holy message of July 14, 1979. It is indeed a joy to receive such a poetic and prophetic exhortation to "off the veil a bit" and discover the mysterious gem in the mine of mind, as you say. Furthermore, we are grateful for your kindness in sharing with us the practice of *fikr*, along with the diagram showing the details and methodology of the *fikr* practice. (One is reminded of Sufi Ahmed Murad Chisti's saying, "Sufism is based upon devotion and science, or *ishk* and *ilm*.")

However, one feels that it is necessary to explain to you more of our situation with regard to the matter of our Order's curriculum of esoteric studies and the *ryazat* that combine to produce the noble *ahwal* and *maqamat*, through the Grace of Allah.

As you may know, we follow the teachings and example of Pir-o-Murshid Inayat Khan who established the holy Message of Sufism in the West. He was trained thoroughly in the methodologies and realization of the four chief Sufi Schools: Chishti, Qadri, Naqshibandi and Suhrawardi. Hazrat Inayat Khan correlated and systematized the teachings of these four schools into a coherent and integrated curriculum suited to the temperament of human beings living in the Western culture—no small feat!

For instance, our Order contains 12 grades, beginning with the study of lessons entitled *Takua Taharat, Etekad Rasm u Ravaj, Pasi Anfas, Saluk, Kashf, Nakshi Bandi* and *Tasawwuf.* These studies comprise the first three grades and are called the Gathas. The next three grades, called Githas, cover the subjects of *Asrar ul Ansar, Murakkaba, Amaliat, Ryazat, Kashf ul Kabur, Sadhana, Dhyana, Occultism* and *Shafayat*. The third three grades, called Sangathas cover the subjects of *Tasawwuf, Saluk, Khawas, Hasiat, Nasihat, Talim, Ryazat* and *Wasiat*. And the final three grades cover the same themes, albeit they are more advanced studies and require deeper realization for their understanding.

Furthermore, the gradual stages of *ryazat* are vouchsafed to the mureeds as they progress through the grades, grades that require both outward stability and inner experience. In his *A Sufi Message of Spiritual Liberty*, Hazrat Inayat Khan says, "The Sufic method of realization—the study of *shariat, tariqat, haqiqat* and *marifat*, also the practice of *zikr, fikr, kasab, shagal* and *amal* is claimed to be the easiest, shortest and most interesting for spiritual accomplishment." Naturally, we repeat the Kalama, the Salat (in English) that Pir-o-Murshid Inayat Khan gave, and of course the wazifas as required for each individual mureed.

We also follow in the footsteps of our dear Murshid, Sufi Ahmed Murad Chisti. He left a living legacy of epic poetry dealing with the most sublime themes, commentaries on virtually all of the Gathas and Githas of Hazrat Inayat Khan (and on much of the published literature, some twelve volumes of teachings, of Hazrat Inayat Khan). Our Murshid instructed us in the methods of *tasawwuri*, of *akhlak Allah* and, through divine grace, the mysteries of *fana* and *baqa*.

And the phrase "follow in the footsteps" has also been employed most joyously in the very sacred Dances of Universal Peace that Sufi Ahmed Murad Chisti gave to us, so that we might share the same spirit that inspired King David the Psalmist to dance in the presence of his Lord, *Ya Hayyoo, Ya Qayyoom!* —to share that spirit with those whose hearts are awakened through the sacred Dance. There is not one iota of frivolity in these Dances, for they are every one based upon the repetition of the divine Name, upon the Name of Allah who is *Rahman* and *Rahim*.

As you most clearly ascertained during the visit of our pilgrims to Darul Ehsan, our ladies are indeed of "noble birth." But really speaking, all of our mureeds are of noble birth—even all humanity is of noble birth—for all humanity has been created in God's image. Of course, one is hard put to prove the steadfast virtues of a people who trample upon their fellows and bring ruin to justice and modesty and love. But as the Americans say, "There are always a few rotten apples in every barrel."

What I am really saying is that there is a new and resurgent spirit of devotion and mystical/religious seeking in the West today. The pilgrims who visited Khankah Darul Ehsan represent the very best of a new kind of humanity, so to speak. Our Murshid recognized this, and was quick to bring the secrets of Sufism to our hearts and souls. These are human beings who do not feel the separations that divide the larger body of humanity. These are real disciples whose hearts are tender, whose inner faculties are already well advanced at an early age. They would unite with the whole humanity through wisdom and love, yet who also need tremendous care while they grow and mature to completion and even perfection, *inshallah*.

In Sufi Ahmed Murad Chisti's last letter to you, written from his hospital bed, he says, "For I am the first one born in the West to have received the divine Message, and believe to have representatives in all the purity and goodness of which Allah is capable, and which will now be presumed done forever."

So I just want you to know, and I say this with all earnestness and in hopes that you will not consider my words and the sincere feelings behind them as anything but filled with gratitude for your "shelter and care"—that we do maintain our *mujahidas*, that we do our *fikr* and other *daroods* on the breath throughout the day and night, in remembrance of our Creator.

I have personally been practicing *fikr* (the practice you enclosed in your last letter) for some twelve years, under the instructions of Murshid Sufi Ahmed Murad Chisti. In fact, most of our mureeds are taught to practice *fikr* from an early stage of mureedship. Naturally all practices are suited to the individual needs of each mureed. And as mureeds advance they are given the more advanced practices such as *kasab*, *shaghal* and, finally, *amal*. All mureeds join in the practice of regular *zikr* and prayers.

One of the Prayers is called "Pir":

Inspirer of my mind,
Consoler of my heart,
Healer of my spirit,
Thy presence lifteth me from earth to Heaven,
Thy words flow as the sacred river,
Thy thought riseth as a divine spring,
Thy tender feelings waken sympathy in my heart.
Beloved Teacher, thy very being is forgiveness.
The clouds of doubt and fear are scattered by thy piercing glance;
All ignorance vanishes in thy illuminating presence.
A new hope is born in my heart by breathing thy peaceful atmosphere.
O inspiring Guide through life's puzzling ways,
In thee I feel abundance of blessing.

We say this every morning, along with Saum and other prayers. Also, in keeping with our background as Westerners, the men and women are not separated in most spiritual endeavors—the chief exceptions being classes for men which stress the *jelal* developments, and classes for women which emphasize *jemali* developments. There does not seem to be any problem when the mind and heart are focused upon Allah and Allah's Beautiful Names.

As you have asked to be apprised of "the minutes and results" of *fikr*, all I can say is that I find *fikr* to be a means of experiencing the Divine Presence radiating from the heart and filling the whole body, particularly when I do it in a walking manner. I also usually take a couple or three mureeds along with me so that they can imbibe the same sense of realization through attunement and atmosphere. This is exactly what Murshid did for us when he was on earth.

Another practice he trained me in was the *tawajjeh*, or glance. This is perhaps the greatest means of spiritual transmission that I have had the good fortune to share with kindred spirits. As you also are well-immersed in this most beautiful spiritual method, I know you will appreciate the words above. (The photos of you giving *tawajjeh* to the pilgrims are treasured specially.)

Until later, and with all love and blessings, your friend,

Moineddin

P.S. Perhaps I should tell you that my physical condition is not good. For nine years I have been afflicted with a kidney disease, glomerulonephritis. I almost died nine years ago in the hospital, until Murshid came in and yelled at me to get out of there! So I recovered and had a fairly normal life for five years until 1976 when my kidneys failed altogether, and I was placed on hemodialysis, a treatment involving having my blood cleansed by a special machine three times a week, a total of 15 hours. That has been my condition ever since, and honestly I feel that my time on earth is not long.

But I feel ready to respond to Allah's beckoning whenever the call comes. I have prepared for the orderly transition of successorship in our Sufi Islamia Ruhaniat Society, and feel that when I do pass from this earthly sphere, *inshallah*, I can join my Murshid in saying, as he did some nine years ago, "(we) have representatives in all the purity and goodness of which Allah is capable."

One's body gradually weakens, but the spirit is willing and strong, *inshallah!*

Your prayers and concentrations are most gratefully asked for all...

P.P.S. Speaking of *fikr*, my secretary has been sitting and breathing *fikr* for practically the entire writing of this letter! This is the type of mureed I am blessed to have surrounding me. If I started counting I would lose count because I would become lost in the depth of noble qualities in each one.

–Moineddin

III. Healing Heart and Mind

Editor's note

Murshid Samuel Lewis believed that his teacher Hazrat Inayat Khan set qualifications for a Murshid or Khalif, which included the candidate's ability to tune into a state of fana or effacement in one's teacher and produce a "commentary" in some form on the teacher's work. Samuel Lewis produced many commentaries on the written work of Hazrat Inayat Khan in such a state of attunement. These commentaries are not intellectual reflections produced from one's knowledge or learning, but rather an inner conversation with the living being of a teacher who has passed. Whether such a commentary comes in words or in some other form, without some outward "fruit" that benefits others, it is very difficult to distinguish such inner communication from imagination or fantasy.

In addition to creating several Dances of Universal Peace in attunement to Murshid Samuel Lewis, Murshid Moineddin also completed Murshid S.A.M.'s commentaries on Hazrat Inayat Khan's book Mental Purification *(which is published in volume four of* The Sufi Message *series). As he mentions in the second half of the* Bismillah *interview below, he completed these three chapters of commentary while he was preparing to leave his body in 1979. He began the commentaries on the* urs *day of Murshid Sufi Ahmed Murad Chisti, January 15, 1979, and completed them on the 14th day of July, 1979.*

These commentaries show Moineddin effaced in the being of both Hazrat Inayat Khan and Murshid Samuel Lewis. The language itself changes from his more informal mode to one in which only the beauty of some of his imagery shows the unique genius of his soul. At the same time, the subject deals with the most nitty-gritty aspects of being human: how to keep one's heart and mind in a balanced and healthy state while faced with the trials and challenges of everyday life. This commentary, which emphasizes the ways in which Sufi practice can clarify and illuminate the heart and mind "in the light," provides a natural counterpoint to many of Moineddin's writings in the next section, which emphasize the ways of allowing light to illuminate the depths of one's (seemingly) personal shadow.

This section also contains a few other letters and poems written from 1979 to early 1980, as Moineddin anticipated leaving his body.

Life More Abundant: The Power of Thought and Feeling (1979)

(Commentary on Chapter 8, "The Power of Thought" of the Gathekas of Hazrat Inayat Khan on Mental Purification. "Gatheka" indicates the words of Hazrat Inayat Khan and "Tasawwuf" the words of Murshid Moineddin Jablonski.)

TOWARD THE ONE, THE PERFECTION OF LOVE, HARMONY, AND BEAUTY, THE ONLY BEING,
UNITED WITH ALL THE ILLUMINATED SOULS WHO FORM THE EMBODIMENT OF THE MASTER, THE SPIRIT OF GUIDANCE.

GATHEKA: There are some who through life's experience have learned that thought has power, and there are others who wonder sometimes whether this is really so. There are also many who approach this subject with the preconceived idea that even if every thought has a certain power, yet it is limited. But it would be no exaggeration to say that thought has a power which is unimaginable; and in order to find proof of this we do not have to go very far.

TASAWWUF: Many books have been written on the subject of "positive thinking." And the suggestions in some of these books have been helpful to many people, to the extent that they have been able to overcome negative thought-patterns of long standing. Yet even the best books containing the best suggestions cannot enable one—indeed ennoble one—to rise above a certain ceiling which one calls "good."

It takes specific mystical practices, with wholehearted application on the part of the disciple and wholehearted empathy on the part of the teacher, to rise above the ceiling of the mind-mesh, to overcome once and for all the hold of what the Buddhists call *samskaras*.

At the same time it must be said that deep minds, which means inspired hearts, can give verbal keys which—if meditated upon continually—may open one to worlds of meaning beyond doors hitherto closed. In this, the effect is similar to that of *wazifa* or *mantra*, in the sense that *wazifas* have literal meanings in addition to their values from sound-currents—which is a different subject taken up in the Githas on Esotericism [see the Ryazat papers of Hazrat Inayat Khan for Sufi mureeds] and the commentaries thereon.

But these verbal keys, often called aphorisms, must come from the depths of a realized soul for any real value to accrue. The marketplace is filled with books written by commercial and egocentric authors, books replete with suggestions for others, yet there is little evidence that those who read these books become transformed or ennobled in the real sense.

GATHEKA: Everything that we see in this world is but a phenomenon of thought. We live in it, and we see it from morning till evening working just the same through imagination.

TASAWWUF: Imagination is given an important place in all the arts. Yet imagination itself has gradations of importance, of meaning. If the imagination is superficial there is no particular value in it. But when the faculty of imagination is coordinated with noble or spiritual themes, this automatic working of the mind springs from a deeper source. And if artists are able to lose themselves in the contemplation of one or more of these themes, the imagination becomes inspiration.

Too often inspiration is given short shrift in many schools of art and poetics, in favor of a nebulous value attached to imagination and emotion, hailed by artists and critics alike. But again this kind of approach never leads to true art. It is more like the world of fashion, which changes every few months. Yet even fashion has its deeper nature. The Indian sari, for instance, has been worn for untold centuries and even today represents a kind of beauty rarely seen in the West. It may be said that inspiration is the culmination of that imagination which rises from the depths of the heart.

GATHEKA: **Thought** is thinking with willpower behind it; in this way we distinguish between the imaginative and the thoughtful. These two kinds of people cannot be confused; for one is imaginative, which implies powerless thinking, automatic thinking, and the other is thoughtful, which means his thinking is powerful.

TASAWWUF: These two types of mentation are called *jemal* and *jelal* by Sufis. The *jemal* temperament is imaginative, and the *jelal* temperament is directive, powerful. Without *jemal* there would be little refinement and beauty in life and without *jelal* there would be no initiative toward reform and social progress. It is like the Chinese symbol of *yin* and *yang*: there must be a speck of *yin* in *yang*, and there must be a speck of *yang* in *yin* for balanced growth to occur. One devoid of the other may lead to imbalance, even chaos, and we can see this clearly if we only keep our eyes open. This may be a profound theory, but the profundity is not in the words. It is in seeing the actualities manifest.

GATHEKA: When this automatic action takes place in the state of sleep, it is called a **dream**. This is distinct and different from imagination, because while a person is imagining, his senses are open to this objective world, and therefore his imagination does not take a concrete form. But when the same automatic action of mind goes on in the dream, there is no objective world to compare it with.

TASAWWUF: Therefore, the dream state is its own world. It may seem to have norms, or it may seem to have no norms. It is for this reason that the wise of all ages have referred to even the physical world as a "dream" or an "illusion"—because with all its seeming norms and concreteness, the physical world too is subject to constant change and turmoil. But due to the denseness of earth its changes are slower and generally more predictable. The dream-world is much more volatile and often less "logical." All states of mind belong more or less to *samsara*, except for that state which has become quiescent in *nafs alima*. This state is called *amal* by Sufis, and *samadhi* by Yogis.

GATHEKA: The mystic can always see the condition of the mind of a person by knowing how he dreams, for in the dream the automatic working of his mind is much more concrete than in his imagination.

TASAWWUF: There are many ways by which a Sufi perceives the condition of another's mind. The prerequisite is always that one's own being be clarified of any blemish, that one be clear like a polished mirror. Then one may operate through a first impression, through intuition, through a knowledge of the elements and their colors and notes. In the case of very advanced souls, one may operate through what is called *shahud*—or direct and deep sight.

The generic term for all these methods is called *kashf*, or insight. Development of the refined breath and constant vigilance to keep the heart clear of self-thought help more than anything else to develop these faculties of perception.

GATHEKA: There are some who are able to read the character or the future by knowing what a person imagines. They always ask a person to name a flower, a fruit, something one loves or likes, in order that they may find the stream of the person's imagination. From that stream of imagination they find out something about the character of that person and about his/her life. It is not necessary to be a character-reader or a fortune-teller. Any wise and thoughtful person can understand by the way people dress or by their environment how their thoughts run, what their imaginings are.

TASAWWUF: The key here is in the phrase "something one loves or likes." For Sufis are certain of their ultimate return to the bosom of Allah, and they realize that this return is their greatest yearning, their noblest love. They also realize that while the generality may not consciously have this deep love and longing, even the lesser loves and likes of a person indicate clearly the stage of evolution of the person. A Sufi will always trace the direction of a person's positive and developmental nature, and give all encouragement to further development.

The same cannot be said for those who parade a smattering of occult development under the guise of "soothsaying" in whatever form. Yet, with the rise of real spiritual development in this age of expanding consciousness, there are more and more honest practitioners of the occult and healing arts.

Too often an undeveloped occultist will become involved in the lower strata of a person's imaginings, the shadow side. The Sufi's occultism is based upon absolute honesty with oneself and others, and it is this honesty that is at the source of the light s/he is able to shine upon a person's journey toward, with and in God.

GATHEKA: But since the state of dreaming enables the mind to express itself more concretely, the dream is the best way to understand what state of mind a person has. When once this is understood, there is little reason left to doubt whether the dream has any effect upon a person's life and future. Indeed, one does not know, one cannot imagine, to what an extent thought influences life.

TASAWWUF: The dream is not necessarily affected by sense-impressions from the objective world, as is the case with imaginations and day-dreams. And while it is true that there are many types of dreams—some shallow, some deep, some coarse, some fine, some false, some true—they all reveal something to the seer.

Sufic occultism teaches that the time of the dream is important, that a dream in the middle of the night may take a long time to manifest its effect, while a dream just before wakening must be productive of its effect very soon after.

But it should be understood that the best dreams are permeated with a feeling of upliftment. There is a sense of light and other fine qualities associated with these dreams. In such dreams we feel some aspect of our true being, whereas in coarser dreams, which are often shadowy and confused, we feel the falseness. There is no sense of inward satisfaction.

It is rightly said that, "dreams come true," in the sense that they will manifest in some way or other. But this example of how our mind influences our objective lives is really based on the degree of concentration we give to these impressions. If we give fuel, which is to say attention, to nightmares, then we are creating our own hells. But if we concentrate upon the true dreams we will be storing up our treasures in heaven.

GATHEKA: **Vision** can be said to be a dream that one experiences in the wakeful state.

TASAWWUF: This has also been called "open vision," meaning that it occurs in broad daylight as it were. There are other experiences, similar in effect, called "closed vision." They are perhaps more akin to certain types of samadhis described in the scriptures of *dharma*, experiences where one loses consciousness of the objective world totally.

Open vision is more like the *sahaja*-state extolled as most desirable by the gurus. *Sahaja* means "natural." So the wakeful or open vision of the Sufis is very close to the natural, or *sahaja-samadhi* of the Yogis. Generally, the aspirant experiences the closed visions in the beginning, and as he advances the natural state dawns more and more.

GATHEKA: People who are imaginative or capable of imagination are capable of creating a thought. And when this thought that they have created becomes an object upon which their minds are focused, then all else becomes hidden from them; that particular imagination alone stands before them as a picture.

TASAWWUF: This is literally a description of the Sufic science known as *murakkabah* (concentration). In order for the mind to stay focused upon one theme or thought, the disciple is taught to control the thought by feeling, to allow the heart-faculty to hold the usually restive mental atoms in the desired order.

The masters of *murakkabah* may rightly be called master-minds. This means that they have discovered the divine will dwelling deep in their own hearts, and that all particulars associated with the mental sphere stand ready to do the bidding of that will. Even physical atoms may be marshaled by one whose will is identified with the divine will, or as it is said, "The mountain comes to Muhammad."

And although the effects of these masters' thoughts may ultimately seem to come from their mere wish, they had to start at the beginning, they had to go through the many stages of accomplishment in *murakkabah*. When one is close to the divine will there may be little or no difference at all between a wish and a prayer, in the sense that all is fulfilled in the absence of ego.

GATHEKA: The effect of this vision is certainly greater than the effect of a dream. The reason is that the imagination that can stand before one's mind in one's wakeful state is naturally stronger than the imagination which was active in one's state of sleep.

TASAWWUF: In Sufism the emphasis is on development from stage to stage, and the ability to hold a vision in the waking state represents an advancement over dreaming in the state of sleep. However, God inspires and reveals the divine nature in many ways, and we should not reject any grace simply because of some theoretical ideal. It is quite possible that a clear dream may prove to be more inspiring and more sustaining to a sincere beginner than a vision may be to one who assumes s/he is advanced but who is actually filled with self-pride on account of "his" or "her" vision.

GATHEKA: The fifth aspect of thought is **materialization**. And it is in the study of this subject that we find the greatest secret of life. No doubt a person will readily accept that it is by the architect's imagination that a beautiful building is built, that it is by the gardener's imagination that a beautiful garden is made. But generally when it comes to matter and all things that are connected with matter, one wonders how far imagination or thought has power over them.

TASAWWUF: By materialization is meant the spiritualization of matter, also called *alchemy*. Many gardens and edifices have come into manifestation through the combination of vision and effort. The greater the vision and effort, the deeper is the feeling associated with these places, such as the Taj Mahal and its gardens and pools.

But the greatest secret lies not in growing gardens or in building beautiful temples—fine as these undertakings may be, particularly when such growing and building are invested with *baraka*, the blessings that accrue when concentration upon a spiritual ideal is practiced. The greatest secret is in the transformation of selfhood to Godhood, or as the alchemists taught, from the condition of dark earth to purest gold.

Initiates know first-hand the realities of this process, because they have willingly submitted to a master who has him/herself gone through all the purifications and refinements of this highest of all alchemies. The empathy and thought-power of the teacher contribute immeasurably to the progress of the pupil on this path. One might even say that the teacher, or master-mind, builds shrines of individual disciples, constructs temples out of the disciples collectively. In this way are suitable accommodations made for the living God.

And when disciples' development begin to parallel that of the teacher—both through inductive attunement and natural unfoldment—these disciples may be placed in a position of responsibility to their own disciples, thereby becoming teachers in their own right. This is *dharma-transmission*, this is the continuance of the holy chain or *silsila*. But a contemporary Sufi master has declared, "All credit for any greatness of realization belongs to one's teacher, not to oneself." This prevents ego from entering in, as symbolized in the *Gulistan* of Saadi by the donkey passing wind when a murshid started to think how good a murshid he was.

GATHEKA: Nowadays, as psychology is beginning to spread throughout the Western world, people will at least listen patiently when one speaks about it.

TASAWWUF: Even to listen patiently shows an advance in humility—which gives scope for appreciating points of view other than one's own. No matter what may be said for or against modern psychologies, the ability to listen patiently indicates a general evolution in the right direction.

GATHEKA: But on the other hand there are many who take a medicine with great faith, but if they are told that a thought can cure them they will smile at the idea. This shows that with all the progress that humanity seems to have made, it has gone backwards in one direction, the higher thought. For humanity today generally does not believe in the power of thought and it believes still less in what it calls emotion.

TASAWWUF: Despite the seeming sway of materialism, the realities of the mind-world will always prove superior in the end. This is why the Prophet Muhammad spent so much time exhorting his followers to give consideration to the next world. In Sura 9, verse 38, the Qur'an asks, "Do ye prefer the life of this world to the Hereafter? But little is the comfort of this life, as compared with the Hereafter."

The highest thoughts have been given to the world in scriptures, prayers and sacred poetry. What proves the power of these thoughts is their ability to inspire all peoples in all ages. These thoughts have come from such great souls as Jesus and David and other messengers of the living God, and these thoughts can cure all manner of diseases, shortcomings and confusion.

The higher emotions come mostly through sacred music and the arts, including drama and poetry. It may be said that the heart of the spiritual messenger hears an inner music of depth, feeling and meaning.

Echoes of emotion and devotion follow this experience. The echo of these echoes becomes the poem or scripture that person has tried to put into words for humanity, among whom there are always those few who will trace the echo of echoes back to its source in spiritual realization.

But it should not be assumed that the higher thought and emotion come by wishful thinking. The Sufi poet Rumi says that his poetry was born from the deep pain of separation from the Beloved, symbolized by a reed being torn from its reed bed. This reed is none other than the human heart which, even after being torn or exiled, is subjected to further wounds through life, wounds symbolized by additional holes made in the reed. And when God sees that the instrument is suitably tuned to express the divine music, then scripture, prayer, poetry and all divine arts may result. The flute of Krishna has the same meaning.

GATHEKA: In point of fact if one can speak of the soul of a thought, that soul is the feeling which is at the back of it.

TASAWWUF: In other words, the essence of thought is feeling. But the words "the essence of thought is feeling" mean nothing without the actual experience. One must enter into the thought-essence, one must have the deep feeling. When this is accomplished, one has fulfilled the purpose of prayer and has begun the real meditation.

GATHEKA: One sees that people become confused when they hear only words behind which there is no feeling. What makes a thought convincing is the power behind it; and that power consists of feeling.

TASAWWUF: The world of commercial advertising is particularly reprehensible in this connection. Not only are the thoughts shallow, but the *urouj* factor [the desire to acquire things] is exploited to the full. Products are hailed as miraculous cure-alls, or are touted in such a way as to inflate the buyer's ego. From all of this there can only come a fall, a letdown.

The thoughts that really convince come from the heart. Even the voice will convey a certain ring when what is expressed comes from deep within. A shallow voice mouthing shallow thoughts sounds tinny and makes no enduring impression. But as a Sufi master has said, "heart speaks to heart, and soul to soul." These communications, these communions, are enduring, are evidence that we are living the spiritual life.

GATHEKA: The general tendency is to wave aside what is called imagination. When one says that people imagine something it means that they amuse themselves. One may say to a person, "Oh, you only imagine it. It does not exist in reality." But in reality when one has imagined something, that imagination is created, and what is once created exists. And if it is thought that is created, it lives longer, because thought is more powerful than imagination.

TASAWWUF: The tendency to belittle the worlds of thought show the partial decline of *dharma*, and when the universe of feeling is belittled, dharma has fully decayed. It is at such times, when the gravity-pull of mass culture has so degenerated, that a restoration of the divine Message is needed. This restoration does not come cosmetically or superficially. It comes from the deepest springs of humanity, a humanity whose cry for regeneration rises higher and higher until that cry is answered.

And how is this cry answered? It is answered by those who feel responsible, by those who have themselves perhaps gone through a phase of degeneration and have overcome their captivity. A wise guide is very helpful, even necessary, to free captive souls. And the responsible ones, those who have lived life and have gone through test and trial, are the wise guides. As it is said, "when the pupil is ready, the teacher appears." This same principle also works on a collective scale. The appearance from time to time of avatars, prophets and world-deliverers has been in answer to the cry of the whole world.

The thoughts these divine messengers have given to the world are ever-living. For, as Peter said to Christ, "thou hast the words of eternal life" (John 6:68). In another sense, the messenger *is* the Word of eternal life.

GATHEKA: In this way, human beings today ignore that power, which is the only power and the greatest power that exists, calling it sentimentality, which means nothing. It is with this power that heroes have conquered in battle, and if anyone has ever accomplished a great thing in the world, it is with this power of heart that one has accomplished it, not with the power of the brain.

TASAWWUF: To refer to qualities that inspire and awaken humanity from ignorance, and depreciate these qualities as being merely sentimentality, shows lack of character, lack of heart, even lack of thoughtfulness. Again we have the belittling of feeling, the derogation of simple human consideration.

Actually, the power of heart that wins battles, inner and outer, is born of one's character—the greater the development of character, the greater the heart-power. And spiritual unfoldment will always reveal the heart to be like a great sun, while the brain at best will be like the moon, reflective. When through ignorance these functions are reversed, shallow sentiment usurps the real heart-power and thought without feeling prevents the flow of inspiration.

GATHEKA: The music of the most wonderful composers, the poetry of the great poets of the world, have all come from the bottom of their hearts not from their brains. And if we close the door to sentiment, imagination and thought, that only means that we close the door to life.

TASAWWUF: These musics and profound poems often take us above the differentiations of cultures and even of traditional religious forms. While the brain may make much of distinctions and differences, such as we see in theological disputes, the awakened heart seeks only friendship, camaraderie, unity.

Nor is sentiment to be shunned as unworthy. Sentiment is connected with heart but is often also associated with ego. Nevertheless, it represents a beginning of the selfless heart-feeling sought by the devotee. All beginnings must start somewhere. It is development that is important and worthy, it is shallowness that closes the doors to life and meaning. The great poets and musicians have had to dig down to the very depths to find the spring of their inspiration. If we are open, that music and poetry will also deepen our capacity for "life more abundant."

What is more, even a closed person may be suddenly touched or transformed upon hearing a certain phrase of poetry or a passage of music. Neither is closure invariably an attribute of the generality, nor is openness the sole province of mureeds. We are all more or less closed at times, and God is *Al-Fattah*, the Opener of the Way.

GATHEKA: The Sufi sees both the Creator and the creation in human beings. The limited part of the human being is the creation, and the innermost part of one's being is the Creator.

TASAWWUF: Therefore, the Sufi sees both God and human beings, as it were. In this, one definitely follows the example of Muhammad. The Sufi recognizes *zat* (essence) in the Creator, and *sifat* (attributes) in the creation. But this may be too theoretical. When all the veils are lifted, *zat* is everywhere, and *sifat* are open gateways to the *zat*. This spiritual condition so astonishes the Sufi that s/he can only give up the ghost of self unto certain and absolute Unity.

The Bible says that God made the human being in God's "image." The Sufi tries to realize this at all times. The Bible also says that God created the world and saw that it was "good." The Hebrew word for "good" is *tov*—which means good or ripe from God's point of view, not necessarily from a human being's limited view. So the Sufi also practices seeing the creation from God's view. When this becomes reality, the Sufi realizes her/himself as *ashraf-ul-makluqat*, the "crown of creation." Thus is God's image revealed in and through human beings—always through grace (*inayat*), which operates in many ways including devotion, diligence and effort.

GATHEKA: If this is true, then the human being is both limited and unlimited. If one wishes to be limited, one can become more and more limited. If one wishes to be unlimited, one can become more and more unlimited. If one cultivates in oneself the illusion of being a creation, one can be that more and more. But if one cultivates in oneself the knowledge of the Creator, one can also be that more and more.

TASAWWUF: It is the ego-mind, the sense of being separate, that causes and aggravates limitation. All the schools that teach the real wisdom emphasize the eradication of ego-mind. When the sense of being separate has been uprooted and the field of mind has been cleared of the stubble and stones of *samskaras* (impressions), then the process of mental purification has begun.

It is at this point that the depth of mind, the heart, begins to disclose its secrets: inspiration and guidance. This is a wonderful stage on the spiritual path. It is wonderful because one realizes that the guidance one has sought is found in the depths of one's own heart. It is a stage because there are ever-greater stages ahead of the sincere pupil. Muhammad, Christ, Moses and all the great souls have exemplified the striving to go beyond half-way measures, to fulfill the purpose of the Creator.

The more these souls divested themselves of limitation, of being caught in the web of creation, the more they became suns of *ishk* and *ilm*, of the divine love and knowledge. And by becoming suns they were able to shine upon the creation and gradually absorb the lesser and limited names and forms into the *Ramnam*, into the *dharmakaya*—in other words, into God's Name and God's Form. For, as the Qur'an says, "verily, unto God is our return."

GATHEKA: With every kind of weakness, every kind of illness, every kind of misery, the more one gives in to them, the more they weigh one down. And sometimes this can happen even to the extent that the whole world falls on one's back and one is buried beneath it.

TASAWWUF: For this reason one Sufi has said, "Self-pity is the worst poverty." It is the worst poverty because God Himself becomes poor in one's being. And what is the purpose of being rich in self-pity, in misery? This was Christ's theme when he warned against permitting the inner light to be buried beneath a bushel.

GATHEKA: Another person, however, will rise up from it. It may be difficult, but at the same time it is possible. Little by little, with courage and patience, that will rise up and stand upon that world which would otherwise have crushed him or her.

TASAWWUF: This is perhaps the most difficult hurdle to overcome, particularly at the beginning of one's discipleship if one has come to Sufism through what has been called "the school of hard knocks" (and in one way or another many disciples have come this way). There is great initial need for empathy and understanding.

Yet with empathy and understanding, and with the proper practices given by the initiator in whom one has reposed all faith and trust, the bushel that had buried one's light begins to fall away. The culmination of this process comes when one can say with Jesus, "my yoke is easy, my burden is light." For, in this stage the self is naught, and God is All. The legend of Sri Krishna lifting the island-realm of Sri Lanka (Ceylon) upon his little finger has the same meaning: God's power is unlimited, a human being's power is small.

GATHEKA: The former is going down, the latter is rising.

TASAWWUF: The former is going down because one is trying to do everything by oneself and with one's small power. The latter is rising because one has tuned the instrument of one's being to the pitch of love, harmony and beauty. But one does not stop there. One then hands oneself over into the hands of the Player, of God, whose music causes one who is rising to rise even higher.

The complete Sufi Invocation can, with devotion and concentration, affect this rise initially. The first three words of the Invocation (Toward the One), called *Darood*, constitute an excellent general practice for beginners and advanced students alike. It may be repeated aloud as a mantra, or kept on the breath. Its applications are manifold, and its benefits are endless.

GATHEKA: Both depend upon the attitude of mind. It is the changing of this attitude, which is the principal thing in life, either from a material or from a spiritual point of view.

TASAWWUF: All success, whether material or spiritual, depends upon some form of positivity. Sufis stress the positive outlook much more than some other schools, particularly the schools in India where the *chela* is encouraged to repeat, *"neti, neti"* (not this, not this). Sufis try to find God everywhere, as the prayer Salat of Hazrat Inayat Khan proposes: "Thy Light is in all forms; Thy Love in all beings."

So Sufism presents the positive outlooks of Light, Love and Life. And even if there are times when resignation is the only attitude one can take, if the resignation is to God, the success will ultimately increase, although it may not seem so at first.

GATHEKA: All that is taught in the Sufi esoteric studies and by Sufi practices is taught in order to arrive little by little, gradually, at that fulfillment which is called mastery.

TASAWWUF: While the esoteric studies are instructive and uplifting, and while the spiritual practices are aids to our growth, it should not be forgotten that these efforts come from the side of a person her or himself. And a person by oneself cannot compel the descent of Divine Grace.

But one can through instruction and practice overcome, by stages, one's lower nature. And the mystery is that what appear to be one's individual efforts to crush the ego actually constitute a very efficacious form of the divine grace, a form without which it is questionable whether a disciple will ever attain the *baqa*, or salvation. All Sufis of all times have practiced the last words of Lord Buddha: "Seek out thy salvation with diligence." This salvation is not different from mastery.

GATHEKA: Mastery comes from the evolution of the soul, and the sign of mastery is to conquer everything that revolts one.

TASAWWUF: And what revolts one? Limitation. Whether it is limitation in the heart-realm, the mind-world, the moral sphere or in physical disability, the work of the Sufi is to vanquish all feelings of limitation. The greater work of the Sufi is to come to God-realization. This is the real mastery, the real evolution.

GATHEKA: That is real tolerance.
TASAWWUF: Tolerance from the spiritual point of view is based upon the greater and greater accommodation one makes for the indwelling of the divine attributes. Human beings, among all creatures, have this capacity. It has shone most brilliantly in the lives of the holy ones. Through their mastery they were able to tolerate situations that would normally break lesser hearts, to surmount difficulties and trials that would undermine weaker wills.

For, when the divine attributes have been absorbed into human character and personality, the "manner of God" (*akhlak Allah*)—which most certainly includes tolerance—is manifested easily and naturally.

GATHEKA: Souls, which have attained to that spiritual mastery show it not only with people, but even with their food. There is nothing that the soul that has gained mastery would not touch, though it may not like it or approve of it.

TASAWWUF: Although the elementary Gathas [of Hazrat Inayat Khan] teach general rules concerning the foods one should eat and also the foods one should avoid, these are mostly guidelines, not absolute prescriptions. Jesus advised, "Hear, and understand: Not that which goeth into the mouth defileth a man; but that which cometh out of the mouth, this defileth a man" (Matthew 15:10-11).

Much more important than food is one's ability to tolerate the presence of inharmonious influences, of jarring egos. One good way to practice this tolerance is to remember how raw our own egos used to be before entering the path of wisdom, to recall how our own untamed egos would jar against others as well as against ourselves. An even better way to practice toleration is to follow in the footsteps of the illuminated ones, to become illuminated oneself. Then there will be nothing that the soul will avoid as unworthy or separate.

Sri Ramakrishna used to gaze upon the prostitutes as living forms of the divine Mother. Seeing this, many of the prostitutes became transfigured and entered the spiritual path. The glance of an illuminated soul has this power to transform, to raise up those whom the generality regards as untouchable. Toleration of questionable foods is a minor matter compared with the ability to tolerate living human beings of whatever degree of evolution.

GATHEKA: The entire system of the yogis, especially of the *hatha* yogis, is based upon making themselves acquainted with something their nature revolts against. No doubt by doing this they may go too far in torturing and tormenting themselves, and these extremes are not right, but all the same that is their principle.

TASAWWUF: The friction caused by striving against odds, whether those odds be mental, moral, physical or social, generates more strength of will. One Sufi has remarked that the purpose of asceticism is only to develop will power. This is no doubt important, but it represents only one side of inner development, the side of keeping the lower nature in harness. The side of emancipation comes otherwise.

Nor has masochism in the name of whatever sacrosanct tradition ever produced enlightened people. Lord Buddha stressed the "middle way," and Sufis emphasize balance as the key to real development. In this balance is found the secret of the divine will, which is the only will that produces full emancipation.

GATHEKA: It is not the heat that kills a person, but the acceptance of the heat. It is the same with food and medicine, for behind everything there is thought.

TASAWWUF: Sufi poets have written many verses about drinking poison as if it were nectar. This is both symbolic and actual. It is symbolic because the Sufi will accept anything, even the worst unkindness, from the hand of the Beloved and take it as the purest wine. It is actual because Sufis will live through and overcome all worldly tribulations, which they know are from the hand of his God, sent for the sake of their growth.

The negative thought enervates the reservoir of one's limited will. This is called "giving in." The positive thought replenishes personal will, and if the thought is upon the Beloved, upon God, the thought becomes so living that even unwholesome foods and bitter medicines will be counted as blessings. The tradition of eating bitter herbs and unleavened bread by the Hebrews during Passover shows the same wisdom, at least in its origins.

GATHEKA: Even now there are yogis who could jump into the fire and not be burnt.

TASAWWUF: A Sufi might ask, to what purpose? Does one come closer to God by making his body tolerate physical extremes of heat or cold? Does one seek pride or prowess before the submission to God?

Yet, there is a symbolism here, too. It is said in Zen Buddhism that Quan Yin can be found in the deepest hell offering ceaseless compassion to its denizens. This would suggest that the real spiritual teacher will also enter willingly into the flames of hell to assist struggling disciples. It should be remembered that compassion means "to suffer *with*." This may involve visits to hospitals, or mighty struggles in the psychic world. But the teacher will be operating from the standpoint of realization and will not be burnt —except as s/he or God may choose. A higher purpose is always served, whether the teacher manifests fearlessness and indifference as in the case of a master, or accepts wounds and pains as in the case of a saint.

GATHEKA: One will find that intolerant souls are the most unhappy in the world, because everything hurts them. Why should they be so uncomfortable in the house and restless outside? Because of this tendency of disliking, of rejecting, of prejudice. It is this tendency which must be conquered, and when it is conquered great mastery is achieved.

TASAWWUF: Intolerance shows an inability to be in touch with the deeper self—one's own or the deeper self of others. In other words, there is no heart, there is no love. Why was Jesus called "master" by his disciples? Not because he said "Love thy neighbor as thyself," but because he exemplified these words in his outlook and behavior. When one feels the deep unity with one and all, great and small, mastery comes with ease. All disease comes from lack of this unity-feeling.

GATHEKA: I remember my teacher at school telling us that the leaves of the neem tree had great healing qualities. That did not interest me very much, but what did interest me, as he told us also, was that these leaves were so bitter than one could not drink a brew of them. And the first thing I did was to gather some of these leaves (and nobody understood why I did it) and I made a tea of them and drank it. To my great satisfaction I did not even make a face! For four or five days I continued this and then I forgot all about it. [*This story not included in Moineddin's original commentary-ed.*]

GATHEKA: It is fighting against all that one cannot do that gives one mastery. But generally one does not do that. One fights against things that prevent one from getting what one wants.

TASAWWUF: To overcome inner obstacles of long standing may seem impossible at first. But with the teacher standing by one through test and trial, with the teacher showing fortitude when fortitude is called for, or sympathy when only sympathy will help, the disciple must surely progress. And it is by the disciple's realization of his/her own progression that the obstacles, all of them, are eventually overcome.

To fight constantly for one's wants and fancies builds up the ego. To take oneself in hand and deny one's lesser appetites is to crush the ego. This is best done a step at a time, otherwise there can be reactions, particularly when one makes extreme or stringent resolutions. The Christian Lent and the Islamic Ramadan are forms of this self-denial. But mostly people do not take these traditions seriously. They look for loopholes and then proceed to indulge themselves even more than prior to these holy seasons.

GATHEKA: A human being should fight only with oneself, fight against the tendency of rejecting. This would lead one to mastery. As a general principle in life, there is no use in forcing anything, but if we want to train ourselves, that is another thing. It is a process, not a principle.

TASAWWUF: When rejection ceases, one makes an accommodation for unity with self and others. The Sufi Al-Ghazzali has declared, "Sufism is based on experience, and not on premises." Experience alone will satisfy the hearts of humanity, and until one has undergone the process of mystical unfoldment, unity and mastery remain as mere words.

To wish one's own principles upon others shows a kind of tyranny, often unconscious. To force others to adopt one's principles is blatant tyranny. But to adhere to one's own principles can lead to growth, especially that growth called character-building. And when one is content to practice one's own code, and foregoes wishing that code upon others, one has begun a very real training.

GATHEKA: One may say it is a great struggle. Yes, it is so, but there is struggle in both—in coming down and in going up. It is just as well to struggle and come up, instead of struggling and going down.

TASAWWUF: It has been said that life is generally hard. Indeed, life may be excruciating at times. Often one comes to appreciate the life in God, the benefits of the spiritual path, at these moments of crisis. Knowing this, the teacher will ever proclaim the superiority of love over pain as a means to heart-awakening, even if the teacher her/himself is a friend of crucifixion a thousand times over.

For the sign of a teacher is this love, this *agape*, this *karuna*. It is the constant ascent of love over all that would bring pain to the disciples that proves the teacher's struggle most worthy before Allah. Therefore the Sufi teacher emulates Muhammad through whom the Quran declares, "Verily, with difficulty cometh ease; verily, with difficulty cometh ease" (Sura 94: 5-6).

GATHEKA: Whenever a person goes down, it only means that one is feeble in one's thought. And why is one feeble in thought? Because one is weak in one's feeling. If feeling protects thought, and if thought stands firm, whatever be the difficulty in life, it will be surmounted.

TASAWWUF: It may be heroic to save a drowning person, but it is wise to teach a person how to swim. The disciple is trained toward greater ability and greater self-confidence. Then, through life's struggles, the disciple begins to realize that the true self-confidence is based upon deep heart feeling. The increase of this feeling causes faith (*iman*) to awaken. And the increase of faith raises the disciple above the maelstroms of life so that one may calm one's thought, strengthen one's feeling and walk upon the water.

On the Breath: Practices for Healing Mind, Heart and Soul (1979)

(Editor's note: Moineddin made notes on these practices in 1979 during the time that he was writing the above commentary. He compiled and released them as "Some Notes on Fikr Practice" in 1997. As noted previously, fikr refers to the Sufi practice of holding a sacred phrase on the breath, in the heart. The practices below all use some form of either the zikr phrase or of one of the "99 Beautiful Names" of Allah.)

TOWARD THE ONE, THE PERFECTION OF LOVE, HARMONY AND BEAUTY, THE ONLY BEING;
UNITED WITH ALL THE ILLUMINATED SOULS, WHO FORM THE EMBODIMENT OF THE MASTER, THE SPIRIT OF GUIDANCE.

Bismillahir Rahmanir Rahim.

1. The phrase *Toward the One* can be breathed in and out as a foundation practice for the everyday life. It can serve as a background to all one's activities, or it can assume the foreground when more deliberate concentration is required. As a walking *fikr*, concentrating on the feet moving toward a goal, "Toward the One" is marvelous for direction in life.

2. The *fikr* of *Subhan Allah* is excellent for purity in any and every realm; this purity also induces humility. When obsessive thoughts and negative impressions are a problem, this *fikr* is most beneficial.

3. One can inhale *Ya Quddus* and exhale *Ya Tawwab* (with emphasis on the outbreath) to release heavy feelings of guilt or shame.

4. The *fikr* of *Allah Ho Akbar* is used to address conditions of chaos, fear, danger or extremity of any sort. Commonly translated as "God is great" or "There is no power or might except in God," its inner meaning is "Peace is Power." The purpose of this *fikr* is not so much to dualistically defeat

adversaries or conditions as to restore wholeness to one's being and balance to one's world.

5. The *fikr* of Murshid Samuel Lewis is practiced by exhaling *La Ilaha* and inhaling *El Il Allah*. It is recommended for *kemal* conditions as they occur temporarily in the daily life or for periods of longer duration [Kemal *in this sense refers to periods of the breath being in a state of stagnation or stasis, which is similar to the outer situation where two atmospheric pressures collide.—ed*]. Outside of *kemal* conditions, this *fikr* is good for renewing one's heart-life. It is also effective in revitalizing the inner link with one's initiator—especially when performed as a walking *fikr* with concentration upon the heart. When one is in physical or psychic extremity, and nothing else avails, this *fikr* can provide an inner refuge and haven.

6. The *fikr* of inhaling *Ya Hayy* and exhaling *Ya Haqq* is prescribed for increased vigor and life. *Ya Hayy* draws the life-currents upward, while *Ya Haqq* directs the life-currents to the earth and grounds them. Thus, in addition to increasing one's life-force, this *fikr* is helpful in balancing one's energies.

7. Inhaling and exhaling the single phrase *Ya Hayy* can be used to shake off a heavy sleep or to rouse one from any lethargic condition. If there is mild depression, this *fikr* can rekindle one's appreciation of life. Occasionally, the phrase *Ya Hayy* is used as a healing *fikr* for anemia, chronic fatigue and related illnesses, in which case it should be repeated 100 times with the conviction that the disease is becoming nonexistent in the presence of the all-pervading divine life. The healing application of this *fikr* is enhanced if one emphasizes the inhalation.

8. The *fikr* of inhaling *Ya Shafi* and exhaling *Ya Kafi* is used in the practice of the twenty healing breaths [of Hazrat Inayat Khan], and whenever general or specific healing is indicated. It is often helpful to speak or sing the words *Ya Shafi Ya Kafi* over the affected area three, eleven or thirty-three times (depending upon the degree of need) before performing the *fikr*.

9. In cases of extreme emergency, where life-saving more than simple healing is called for, one may concentrate directly and with power from one's soul breathing in *Allah Shafi* and breathing out *Allah Kafi*. If one performs this practice for another, the hands may be extended in the healing manner for added effect.

10. The *fikr* of *Ya Wakil* is used for protection of self and others from danger or harm. One can feel gentleness combined with strength of purpose in this "guardian angel" *fikr*.

11. The *fikr* of breathing in *Allah Allah* and breathing out *Alhamdulillah* is a wonderful way to praise God, the Creator of All of Life.

The Bird Creates Its Nest: Heart and Concentration (1979)

(Commentary on Chapter 9, "Concentration" of the Gathekas of Hazrat Inayat Khan on Mental Purification)

GATHEKA: To gain knowledge of concentration requires not only study, but balance also.

TASAWWUF: The studies in Murakkabah [concentration, in papers of Hazrat Inayat Khan] begin with explanations to the intellect. But the gains associated with Murakkabah come only when feeling takes over, and the mind quiets down. A simile may be drawn in the tuning of an instrument. The mind knows that certain pitches must be set, strings must be stretched or loosened to the right notes, before the musician will be able to play to his heart's content. So there are two steps: the intellectual grasp of how to approach concentration and the actual immersion in the feeling, which is where the real concentration begins, builds and concludes.

These two steps taken together constitute the balance.

GATHEKA: Before touching this subject I would first like to explain what motive we have behind concentration. There are two aspects of life: the audible life and the silent life. By audible life I mean all experiences, all sensations that we experience through our five senses. This is distinct from the life which I would call the silent life.

TASAWWUF: This subject is gone into fully in the book *The Mysticism of Sound* [of Hazrat Inayat Khan], particularly the first chapter entitled, "The Silent Life." The audible life and the silent life are explained also in the teachings of Jewish Kabbalah; each day of the week represents a different plane of the universe, a different degree of vibratory activity represented by one of the seven traditional planets, each with its characteristic note.

Six of the planes (or planetary spheres) are always in varying states of activity, which produce the sounds and lights associated therewith. But the Sabbath day, so named for Saturn, represents the eternity, the silent life. Therefore is the Sabbath called holy, and thus is God said to have *rested* on the seventh day. The motive behind spiritual concentration is to enter into the silent life of the Sabbath.

GATHEKA: And when one asks what benefit one derives from getting in touch with the silent life, the answer is that the benefit is as abstract as the silent life itself.

TASAWWUF: If we substitute the word *transcendent* for *abstract*, the meaning of this statement may be clearer. Often in western culture a pejorative connotation is linked with the term abstract, mostly when referring to a person of artistic temperament. This only shows a lack in our culture, an imbalance where grossness is regarded as normal.

Indeed, practicality is needed, but its excess leads to materialism. The balance of practicality with the abstract life constitutes real spirituality.

GATHEKA: The life of sensation is clear, its benefit is clear. And yet as limited as is the life of sensation, so limited is its benefit. That is why in the end we find all our experiences of little value. Their importance lasts as long as we experience them, but after that the importance of the life of sensation is finished.

TASAWWUF: In the *dharma* teachings, the life of sensation is called *samsara*, the unending cycle of birth, growth, decay and death. The Sufic *nafsaniat* has a similar meaning but may be more instructive in that it refers to definite stages of the ego, definite conditions of the breath—from the coarsest to the very highest. In *nafs alima*, for instance, one transcends all trace of the life of sensation, even all *samskaras* (impressions) good and bad, and enters into the sphere of "immaculacy."

To transcend *samsara*, or *nafsaniat*, is to surpass the archangels who, though perhaps nearest to God, remain outside the bosom of eternity. But the Sufi, realizing *La Illaha El Il Allah*, becomes one with the Beloved God. So a great benefit is gained through entering the Divine Unity. The vibrant love-blessings bestowed thereafter upon the world of sensation and its denizens from a Sufi are known generically as *baraka*.

When this *baraka* permeates the *samsaric* life, all limitations formerly associated with concreteness and sensation are revealed as gateways to ultimate glory. "Thy Light is in all forms, Thy Love in all beings" becomes the norm when hearts awaken. Thus is "messiah" born, thus are *samsara* and *nirvana* become one, thus is the purpose of God fulfilled.

GATHEKA: The value of silent life is independent.

TASAWWUF: We can experience this by going into the forest, the desert or our meditation rooms. Many have reported that nature's cathedrals contain a greater blessing than the edifices built by human beings. Yet, we have the instructions in "Spiritual Architecture" [by Murshid Samuel Lewis] that are most important. We are, after all, not forest dwellers. And when we co-operate with the silent life *and each other*, we can realize that "the Lord buildeth the temple."

It often happens that a period of solitude spent in communion with nature, with the silent life, will charm a person's atmosphere long after he has returned to worldly duties. Silence is first realized as independent, thereafter it is felt as if interpenetrating every thought, word and deed.

GATHEKA: We are inclined to attach a value to something which concerns our outer life. The silent life does not give us a special benefit but a general benefit.

TASAWWUF: Earthly and mental benefits operate through name and form, through the creation. We perceive these benefits through the senses. For instance, we can appreciate foods through touch, sight, smell and taste. Each sense gives a special benefit.

But these particular benefits fade when we enter the silent life. It is as if the silent life has been there all the time in the background. And gradually, or suddenly, the vast reservoir of silence becomes our foreground as well. In other words, the silent life becomes our All. This does not destroy particular benefits, it actually enhances all particulars. For the silent life itself constitutes unity in realization, while its descent into name and form causes appreciation of unity in variety.

GATHEKA: In other words, if there is a minor wound on the body, an external application of a certain medicament can cure it. But there are other medicines that can cure the general condition, and this is more satisfactory than the external cure, though it is less spectacular.

TASAWWUF: The twenty healing breaths and the prayer Nayaz [of Hazrat Inayat Khan] are an example of "other medicines" that tend to cure the general condition. The rise of what is called holistic medicine has produced integrative approaches to disease in which diet, breathing, optimism, activity, repose are all harmonized. And the integration of formerly separate outlooks such as the Western emphasis on circulatory and digestive systems, the Indian Ayurvedic methods, and the Chinese knowledge of the nervous system, show a movement toward synthesis.

Muhammad proposed this thirteen centuries ago when he said, "Seek wisdom even unto China." The organic, integrative or holistic approach to healing shows that our world is coming to wisdom. When this attitude also includes the spheres of art, science and religion, wisdom will have come to the world.

GATHEKA: One cannot say exactly what profit is gained by concentration, but in reality every kind of profit is to be attained through concentration, in all directions.

TASAWWUF: Concentration is considered of utmost importance in Sufi training. Initially, it helps one to overcome chaos and confusion. Ultimately it produces, maintains and promotes integration and harmony. We see this in the solar system: the sun concentrates its energies in such a way as to function as the heart, and the other planets act as auxiliary organs in the body of the system. It is all the planets working together that shows the sun's power of concentration.

The same principle operates in individual beings, in groups, in nations and races, in humanity. From this we see there are many grades in the study of *murakkabah*. The first lessons are presented in the Githas [of Hazrat Inayat Khan] on this subject, although the series of Gathas on Symbology may also utilize concentration.

GATHEKA: There are two kinds of concentration: automatic concentration and intentional concentration. Automatic concentration is found in many people who do not know that they concentrate and yet they do. They concentrate automatically, some to their disadvantage, some to their advantage. Those who concentrate to their advantage are the ones whose mind is fixed on their business, their art, or any occupation they have. They are the ones who because of their concentration can work more successfully. Be it composers, writers, or musicians—according to their power of concentration so will be their success.

TASAWWUF: Automatic concentration upon positive themes shows a natural evolution. Automatic concentration on negative thoughts and feelings shows weakness of will and in extreme cases obsession. Intentional concentration on positive themes shows conscious and willful evolution. Intentional concentration on negative patterns shows self-pity, while the same concentration on evil and wickedness constitutes black magic. The biography of the Tibetan saint Milarepa is particularly illustrative, as he went through a period of practicing the black arts before coming to his guru Marpa who, prior to entrusting Milarepa with the sacred practices, put him through the severest tests of body, mind and spirit, the very severest tests.

A most profound teaching given in concentration is to be found in the words of Jesus Christ: "Seek ye first the kingdom of God and all else shall be added unto you." In other words, concentration of itself is a power, but when God is the object of one's concentration, one becomes selfless. This results in the realization of God as all power, wisdom and love, and all virtues follow naturally in the wake of this realization.

GATHEKA: I once had the pleasure of hearing Paderewski in his own house. He began to play gently on his piano. Every note took him into a deeper and deeper ocean of music. Any meditative person could see clearly that he was so concentrated in what he did that he knew not where he was.

The works of great composers that will always live, that win the hearts of men, whence do they come? From concentration. So it is with a poet, so it is with an artist. It is concentration that brings color and line, that makes the picture.

TASAWWUF: Again it must be repeated that concentration is accomplished when *feeling* holds and orders thought. Hearts are won only through heart, through depth of feeling. When concentration has penetrated through to the depths "the moonlight penetrates through the waves, reaching the bottom freely and easily," in the words of a Zen poem. The spring of inspiration is discovered. All real art, music and poetry come from this spring. As the spring is eternal, so the works it inspires become immortal.

GATHEKA: Naturally, whether it be an artist or a writer, a musician or a poet, or somebody who is in business or industry, in the absence of concentration one can never succeed.

TASAWWUF: Concentration creates order and harmony, and makes a way for the heavenly condition to be reflected upon earth. Lack of concentration in life leads to limbo, purgatory or hell, depending upon the degree of this lack. The pains associated with these regions, these experiences, often are sufficient to cause renewed efforts to center one's being. So even in chaos is hidden the seed of mercy.

GATHEKA: Sometimes concentration works to a disadvantage. There are some people who always think that they are unlucky, that everything they do will go wrong, who think that everybody dislikes them, that everybody hates them. Then some begin to think that they are unable to do anything, that they are incapable, useless.

TASAWWUF: Muhammad has said, "Every child is born a true believer in the One God." And the sayings of Jesus include the statement, "Verily, I am with little children unto the age of seven years." These remarks indicate that souls come into the world clear, fresh and pure—not only innocent of denseness but also immune to it for the time being.

The second half of Muhammad's saying is, "... but the child's parents and society turn it from the true belief." This indicates that the coverings the parents have allowed to veil their own souls eventually cast a shadow over the soul of the child, and that the denseness associated with life in the world also contributes its share of shadows. The child is so accepting by nature that it takes all reflections—including those which would cover its light.

If no moral training has been given, if worthy examples have not been set by the parents, it may not be too many steps before the child adopts questionable ways of thinking and behaving. Once a soul has inwardly given up hope of taking a positive approach to life, or has begun to give more and more scope to negative habits—and this process is most subtle in its beginnings—that soul becomes unlucky, bitter and inharmonious. But most of all that soul becomes lonely, and longs unconsciously for its original being.

Very often disciples come to the spiritual path from this kind of background. It is most important to restore positivity and hope to the struggling soul. That is why we pray constantly to know God "as a loving mother, a kind father, an innocent child, a helpful friend, an inspiring teacher." With proper concentration, these examples are no less than powerful medicines to an ailing soul. These examples have power to heal.

GATHEKA: Others out of self-pity think that they are ill. In that way even if they are not ill they create illness. Some by concentration cherish illness and always think of it. No physician could be successful with them. An old physician once said, "There are many diseases, but there are many more patients." Once a person has become a patient through concentration, he is difficult to cure. And there are many such cases of automatic concentration to the disadvantage of a person.

TASAWWUF: Once one has permitted self-pity to enter one's consciousness or has allowed the suggestion of disease to take root in the ground of one's thoughts, the ways of illness stand open. Unless the self-pity and loneliness are taken away, unless hope, faith and love are restored—really restored—the impression of disease will be difficult to uproot.

It is for this reason that "mental purification," with all its methodologies, is regarded as the pharmacopoeia of Sufism—the divine wisdom whose adherents in another age were called *Ikhwan-i-Safa* or the "Brethren of Purity." The mental purification is based on *fana*, or self-effacement. The more the limited self is effaced, the more the shadow-impressions associated with disease are erased. And when the blessing of heart awakening comes to one, especially when this state can be maintained, the entire field of mind and heart becomes clarified of all the roots and stubble and stones of disease.

This can lead to a restoration of health on all planes.

GATHEKA: Intentional concentration is taught by thinkers, philosophers, and meditative people. The whole of mysticism, of esotericism, is based upon the idea of concentration.

TASAWWUF: Seekers of whatever persuasion have found—and continue to find—the object of their seeking through definite and diligent concentration. This would indicate that keeping centered on a goal opens a way toward one's object. Keeping centered inwardly tends at the same time to attract the object sought to the seeker. Ultimately, concentration is a key that opens the door to the merging of subject and object, which is the purpose of all mysticism and esotericism.

GATHEKA: This mystical concentration can be divided into four different grades. The first is **concentration**, the next **contemplation**, the third **meditation**, the fourth **realization**.

TASAWWUF: The very suggestion of grades shows that Sufism is not only devotional, nor is it solely scientific. Sufism is a school of training that takes into account all aspects of human nature, and through a combination of science and devotion, gradually develops the human nature toward self-realization through the ideal of God.

GATHEKA: The definition of the first grade is the fixing of one's thought upon one object.

TASAWWUF: This is gone into and explained thoroughly in the Githas on Murakkabah (concentration). But the mere reading of the lessons will be of no avail. One must practice concentration, often for many years, in order to advance from grade to grade. Nor is it ever wise to presume a constant advancement. It often happens that the advanced students, being burdened with more responsibilities, will stumble under the weight of numerous concentrations, will become scattered and nervous. This is a definite sign that the students need to come back to the simplest forms of concentration upon one object. The only sin, so to speak, is to rely upon the power of one's small self. The virtue is realized when we rely on the life and power of God.

GATHEKA: One should not concentrate upon just any object that comes along, for what one concentrates upon has an effect upon one.

When one concentrates upon a dead object it has the affect of deadening the soul. When one concentrates on a living object, it naturally has a living effect. The secret of the teachings of all prophets and mystics is to be found in this.

TASAWWUF: To focus upon objects or events that bring thoughts of destruction, of degeneration, of enervation, by the process of reflection produces a lessening of the life-force—or rather a lessening of the capacity to keep the life-force centered and orderly. This can bring ossification and inertia to one's spirit if such indulgence is prolonged.

On the other hand, all symbols of all religions, all signs associated with the various divine messengers, e.g., the ark of Noah, the "living waters" of Ezekiel, Moses and the burning bush, Jesus and the bread and wine, Muhammad and the "night journey," can bring an influx of life, of spirit, if concentrated upon. Greater still is the influx of life when one concentrates upon the being of the messenger him or herself, but the greatest of all life comes when we concentrate upon the One whom the Messengers themselves know as the living God.

As Sufism is a school of gradual spiritual unfoldment, so *murakkabah* is also a gradual training. One may remain in a certain stage for a long time, yet it frequently happens that once the initial stages are accomplished, the more advanced degrees follow swiftly. It would not be too surprising if one were to start by concentrating upon the Cross, then merge with the heart of Jesus Christ, and at last experience the life of resurrection (*baqa*).

More often human views of time-processes just get in the way and impede the actual spiritual progress that is taking place.

GATHEKA: This **concentration** is achieved in three different ways. The first way is by action. One makes a certain movement or performs an action, which helps the mind to concentrate on a certain object.

TASAWWUF: The Walks of the divine attributes [begun by Murshid Samuel Lewis] are examples of this kind of active concentration, as are the Dances of Universal Peace. The movements associated with each attribute assist the concentration and help to bring inner feeling outward so that "Thy will be done on earth as it is in Heaven."

GATHEKA: Another way is with the help of words. By the repetition of certain words one learns to think automatically of a certain object.

TASAWWUF: This includes the ways of prayer and wazifa (mantra). When we add movements to prayer or wazifa, we are putting psychic law into practice. That is to say, we are experiencing how principles operate when feeling, thought and action are coordinated, are harmonized. Action alone can sometimes bring the proper thought and feeling needed to complete the experience, but in the absence of action there can be no actuality, no grounding of the experience.

The spiritual Walks and Dances are really based upon the repetition of sacred phrases *with* appropriate movements. It has even been said that the sacred phrase is fundamental and the action secondary in the practice of Walk and Dance. Yet both are necessary to complete the experience.

GATHEKA: The third way is with the help of memory. Memory is like a builder's yard. From this the builder takes anything he likes: tiles, pillars, bricks, whatever he wants. Those who concentrate in this way do the same as children who have bricks to build toy houses with. They collect things in their memory and with them they compose objects in order to concentrate on what they wish.

TASAWWUF: Ordinary memory is what we recall from our experience of the past. But there may be a super-memory that belongs not to the past alone. The super-memory may belong to eternity, which would include the realms of past, present and future, as well as transcend these realms. The vision of life built by a prophet would utilize materials from ancient times, from the contemporary world, and would also project the needed elements forward to insure proper foundations for the future humanity.

Yet even ordinary memory is often special. If it were not special we would not remember it. There are stories of composers who heard a phrase of music during their childhood, and so meaningful and memorable would that phrase become during the course of their lives that whole symphonies would emerge—just from one little line of music. It is like one little seed yielding a whole forest.

But what is memory? Is it not simply the castle we build around a moment sacred to our heart? The castle is only the body of the memory, but the beautiful princess who dwells therein is the soul of that sacred memory. Castles will be built and castles will fall into ruin, but the princess is forever. This is symbolic.

With the help of *zikr* (remembrance), Sufis try to perfect their memory of the divine presence.

GATHEKA: As to **contemplation**, it is only when a person is advanced enough that he can contemplate, because contemplation is not on an object, it is on an idea.

TASAWWUF: Concentration is like sculpting a block of marble; the sculptor holds the thought of the desired object with the power of his feeling. Yet when the sculpture is completed the artist begins to see the spirit of his creation. The idea that was hidden in the block of stone has become realized.

A Sufi poet has said, "First do your duty, then behold beauty." Concentration is associated with duty, contemplation is associated with the beholding of beauty. And, though it is taught that concentration precedes contemplation, there is also need to consider that some form of contemplation, some inspiration or ideation, precedes the work of concentration. Thus, in any true artistry there is a marriage, a balance, of these two processes.

GATHEKA: No doubt one may think that one is ready to do anything and that after concentration one can contemplate. But the nature of the mind is such that it slips out of one's hands the moment one tries to hold it. Therefore before one really starts to think, the mind has already thrown off the object of concentration like a restive horse.

TASAWWUF: Successful concentration may demand special ability, and this ability often comes only after long and arduous self-discipline. In many schools the mind is likened to a great body of water with waves, tides, whirlpools and eddies. In other words, the mind—like the ocean—is in constant motion. It is the work of the disciple to still the waves and turbulences of the mind. When this is accomplished the mind becomes like a clear mirror able to reflect the noble themes of the heart-sphere which arise naturally. This is the beginning of contemplation.

GATHEKA: Mind is not always so unruly. It proves to be unruly when it wants to rule itself. It is like the body: one may feel restful sitting naturally, but as soon as one keeps quite still for five minutes, the body begins to feel restless. And it is still more difficult to make the mind obey.

TASAWWUF: In the Gathas on Everyday Life (entitled Takua Taharat, from Hazrat Inayat Khan) for first-year students, lessons are given to help refine and harmonize the physical body, and second-year students are taught to purify the mind. Often it happens that bodily ablutions tend to refresh the mind, and a purified mind in turn reflects life and vigor to the body.

Today all Sufis are given the twenty purification breaths as their foundation practice. This practice involves the breaths of the elements as a means toward the revivification and purification of "body, heart and soul"—so beautifully expressed in the healing prayer Nayaz [of Hazrat Inayat Khan].

When the disciple establishes the regular practice of the twenty purification breaths and repeats the Nayaz with all wisdom and devotion, the body will become radiant and healthy, and the mind will become balanced and obedient, even inspired. The regular practice of these breaths also creates an accommodation for the more advanced practices of *kasab* and *shagal*, which are given at the time of the 4th and 7th initiations respectively [in the system of initiatic grades given by Hazrat Inayat Khan].

GATHEKA: Mystics therefore find a rope to tie the mind in a certain place where it cannot move. What is that rope? That rope is breath. It is by that rope that they bind the mind and make it stand where they wish it to stand.

TASAWWUF: Sufis attempt to center in and with the breath. And while the elemental breaths are used to start the day, the rhythmic practice of Darood [breathing the phrase "Toward the One"] or *fikr* [the practice of *zikr* on the breath] may and should be used throughout the day. These practices are not restricted to periods of seclusion or to one's private daily devotions. These practices are meant to be integrated with one's work in the world, for it is thus that the divine attributes are infused into the practical and earthly spheres.

But these *thoughts* are not mental purification. The *practices* of *fikr* and Darood are *processes* in and toward mental purification. As one Sufi teacher has said, "You can live without thinking, but you cannot live without breathing." And if the initial endeavors to calm the mind may seem elusive, after a period of regular practice the methods of breath will certainly prove their sufficiency.

GATHEKA: It is like the bird which uses its saliva to make its nest. So is it with the mystic who out of breath creates atmosphere, creates light and magnetism in which to live.

TASAWWUF: Some mystics make an atmosphere as if only for themselves; they are called *Pratyekabuddhas*—adepts who would gain the enlightened condition solely for themselves. But there is a real question whether enlightenment can be so limited.

Sufis would not be in harmony with such an approach. The Pir [Hazrat Inayat Khan] who established the Sufi teachings in the Western world declared: "What I give to you, you must share with others." Who are these others? They are ourselves.

Therefore the Sufi teacher will create a nest, an atmosphere, in which his mureeds are placed like so many eggs. The warmth of his or her attention helps the process of incubation within the shell, and assists the growth out of the shell. The teacher strives every moment of life to give a worthy example to the fledgling disciple so that the disciple in turn may continue and develop the lines of transmission when s/he reaches spiritual maturity. This process is called in Sufi terminology the "chain of *baraka*," and it is living, real.

GATHEKA: One characteristic of the mind is that it is like a gramophone record: whatever is impressed upon it, it is able to reproduce. And another characteristic of the mind is that it does not only reproduce something, but it creates what is impressed upon it. If ugliness is recorded, it will produce disagreement, inharmony. The learning of concentration clears the record, makes it produce what we like, not what comes automatically.

TASAWWUF: The learning of concentration and the development of willpower go hand in hand. Even when one concentrates upon an object outside of oneself, the effect sooner or later will be toward a greater inward stability on the part of the disciple. This inward stability, coupled with depth of feeling, ultimately tends to center in heart, and it is in and with the stable heart-centration that the power of will begins to reveal itself.

When the power of will is developed sufficiently, the mind becomes the willing servant of the heart. As lack of heart-feeling, combined with an inability to keep centered, produces inharmony and ugliness, so full heart-centration—ever expanding—creates all virtue and beauty. It is far more important to practice and realize the means toward virtue and beauty, than to worry overmuch about a momentary and passing inharmonious thought.

GATHEKA: In this world one is so open to impressions. One goes about with eyes and ears open, but it is not only the eyes, not only the ears that are open. The lips are open to give out what the eyes and ears take in, and that is the dangerous part.

TASAWWUF: The prayer Rassoul [of Hazrat Inayat Khan] begins, "Warner of coming dangers ..." We do not generally like to consider coming dangers. It is like skipping certain parts of scripture, because to face the parts we skip over would require facing ourselves, even God, directly. We accept the surface comfort rather than face pains and problems.

It is one thing to allow coarse impressions to gain a foothold in one's consciousness. It is quite another thing to thoughtlessly broadcast an unbecoming or harmful impression into the atmosphere at large, the same atmosphere we share with those near and dear to us. If we are thoughtful we will not permit unworthy impressions to take abode in our minds, and if we are conscientious we will never allow such impressions to pass our lips and assume the form of speech.

This is a hard yet very basic lesson in the culture of morality. Once the impulse to speak noisily and unrestrainedly has been quelled, the tendency to commit to speech every little unimportant thought has been governed, then we may witness the improvement in ourselves and in the atmosphere. Sometimes, in particularly difficult cases it is necessary to remind the disciple that the ancient Sufi schools enforced absolute verbal silence upon all neophytes for the first three years of training. But this is a new day, and there is an advanced human evolution. If one only looks for it, one will discover it.

This discovery, however, requires a deeper sight, a special listening, because the impressions of everyday are always there to deter us from our real purpose. But when we listen for "thy Voice which constantly cometh from within," when we seek the disclosure of "thy divine Light," we will overcome dangers and at the same time we will consciously assist the evolution of humanity to the higher wisdom.

GATHEKA: The third part of concentration is **meditation**.

TASAWWUF: This subject is taken up in lesson form in the fifth grade of the Sufi Islamia Ruhaniat Society's esoteric program. Called *dhyana*, which is Sanskrit for meditation, the lessons show how the methods of *wazifa, zikr, fikr* and *kasab* may all lead to the goal of meditation.

And what is meditation? A Vedanta swami was asked what he thought about "transcendental meditation." He answered, "All meditation is transcendental." Therefore, meditation is a process that overcomes the seesaw of opposites and raises us above the denseness of earth. And if these words are not sufficient indication—and they are not—there is always the practice itself.

GATHEKA: In this grade one becomes communicative. One communicates with the silent life, and naturally a communication opens up with the outer life also. It is then that a person begins to realize that both the outer and the inner life—everything in fact — is communicative.

TASAWWUF: Thus is experienced unity in variety, and "heart speaks to heart, and soul to soul" becomes the norm. This is a heavenly condition and represents the capacity of its bearer to "make earth a paradise"—as suggested in the prayer Nabi [of Hazrat Inayat Khan]. Or as Shakespeare has written of those whose lives are "exempt from public haunt, (they) find tongues in trees, books in running brooks, sermons in stones, and good in every thing."

GATHEKA: Then a person begins to learn what can never be learnt by study or from books, that the silent life is the greatest teacher and knows all things. It does not only teach, but gives that peace, that joy, that power and harmony that make life beautiful.

TASAWWUF: When the angel Gabriel appeared to Muhammad and commanded him to "Read!" he was beseeching the prophet to perceive all life, inner and outer, as being pervaded by the silent life, the Name of Allah. Now Muhammad was illiterate in the worldly sense, yet the more he began to *read* in the mystical sense the more he realized the All-ness of his Lord, and the more he became the repository and proof of the divine *sifat* [qualities]. As mercy and compassion are the chief qualities of Allah, so too are Rahman and Rahim foremost among the perfections attributed to the Holy Prophet.

GATHEKA: No one can claim to be meditative. For a meditative person need not say it with the lips. One's atmosphere says so, and it is the atmosphere alone which can say whether it is true or false.

TASAWWUF: A meditative person *need* not say it aloud, but a meditative person *may* say it aloud. Much can be given as *baraka* in the form of sound—and if there are limitations inherent in the nature of speech and verbalism, there are not those limitations upon sounds which can be uttered by the teacher, sounds that resonate from the heart and ring from the soul. At the same time it is true that those who have realized this power of sound also possess more life and love in their silent atmosphere. It is generally the *line of development* of a given teacher that determines whether sound or silence will predominate in his or her teaching, but s/he will be proficient in either if God wills.

We have the example of Moses and Aaron. Moses usually kept silent, and Aaron usually spoke. But patterns and rules are made to be broken just as idols are broken. And Moses certainly stood up to Pharaoh with inspired words *and* the power of atmosphere.

GATHEKA: Once I asked a spiritual teacher what was the sign of knowing God. He said, "Not those who call out the Name of God, but those whose silence says it." Many go about looking, searching for something worthwhile, something wonderful, but there is nothing more wonderful than the soul of a human being.

TASAWWUF: "The still, small voice," "the voice of the turtle," "the peace which passeth all understanding," are all synonymous with the ring of the soul's silence. Too often we find so-called religious people, even some who pose as representatives of God, mouthing the name of God or the name of a favored messenger. But what they are actually saying is, "Do it our way or be damned to hell."

The real religious people will strive all their lives to discover the silence of the soul, and when they discover it they will pronounce God's name with all their being. Their most eloquent pronouncement may be through the deep silence of their atmosphere, indeed some paths require this silence as prerequisite to the work at hand. But the sounds and even literal words of anyone who has realized the soul will also be eloquent, will be most effective in teaching, in the bestowal of *baraka*, in all matters pertaining to spiritual awakening.

Sufis practice *wazifa* and *zikr*, which have sound-values and literal values, Sufis also practice *fikr* and Darood, which are silent and utilize the refined breath. Sufis join in group practices that involve sacred phrases recited or sung aloud, and Sufis join in group silences. But individually or in group, the main thing for Sufis is balance. "What is the sign of your Father in you? It is a movement and a rest" (Gospel of Thomas).

GATHEKA: **Realization** is the result of the three other grades. In the third kind of experience man pursued meditation; but in this, meditation pursues man. In other words, it is no longer the singer who sings the song, but the song sings the singer.

TASAWWUF: All these gradations are illustrated in the ten ox-herding pictures of Zen: everything is there including the pursuance of meditation and the being pursued by it. The Christian "stations of the cross" also illustrate this process of gradual awakening to the reality of the soul.

An American Sufi master once remarked to an Indian audience, "The Bhagavad Gita (the song celestial) is the flute of Krishna turned into poetry...." The reality of all sacred scripture can be ascertained when we see the prophet or messenger as the inspired *vox humanum* [human voice] of the divine song.

GATHEKA: This fourth grade is a kind of expansion of consciousness. It is the unfoldment of the soul; it is diving deep within oneself. It is communicating with each atom of life existing in the whole world. It is realizing the real "I" in which is the fulfillment of life's purpose.

TASAWWUF: In short, one who reaches this stage has fulfilled the urging of St. Paul to "put on the mind of Christ." Its extent is as great as God, its unfoldment embraces all in utter *agape*. The sea of this love has neither been fathomed as to its depth nor has any shore ever been sighted. Every atom is a living being on a journey from the corpus of the first Adam to that of the second Adam, and the "I" with which one is identified is the Only Being, the All-Being.

One may write spiritual poetry or utter scriptures from this realization, in which case one functions in *nafs salima*. Or, one may keep steeped in the silence of this realization and be in *nafs alima*, the heart of uttermost repose, the mind of omniscience, the parenthood of God.

Love, Relationship and Bayat (letter 1979)

(Editor's note: From a letter to a mureed.)

June 16, 1979

Beloved One of Allah, as-salaam aleikhum!

Thank you for your recent letter. Your news of various workshops being given, covering a wide spectrum of themes, is most welcome. More and more one sees real initiative being taken by those center leaders in whose hand our work is entrusted.

It is concerning the couples seminar that I wish to address myself. The subject of marriage, or living together in sincere and mutual respect and love, or any number of permutations of the above, has come to the point of needing more definition in this time of general stress and strain. Even among the so-called strong relationships there is need for more and deeper introspection. There is need to dig through much mud before the treasure of pure and life-giving water may truly be said to be found.

Take, for example, my own situation. For many years I approached Fatima's and my marriage not exactly as an endeavor separate from the path of spiritual initiation, but I did tend to contrast the relation with my spouse to my relation with Murshid. This tendency to contrast came largely from some of the Sufi lessons in which the bond between Murshid and mureed is idealized as the highest manifestation of love possible to a human being.

At the same time, Murshid always down-played any particular love or reverence or awe toward his being, and definitely gave indications that the important thing was to find the true love with a husband or wife if one were married. In fact, he seemed quite intent in his prayers that his single mureeds find partners in life. This may be due in part to Murshid's own experiences in never finding a permanent partner—and his consequent compassion for the loneliness he had known firsthand and saw in his disciples, mostly the single ones but also in some of the married ones.

Yet, I always tried very hard to feel that my marriage vows were equal to the vow of *bayat*. I always tried to see that Fatima, and in due time my children as well, *were Murshid* in different bodies. Indeed, as time went on, I tried to see Murshid in all the mureeds—and this is where things stand at present, *inshallah*. And I think this outlook is in keeping with the gradual realization taught by Sufi murshids generally.

Somewhere in the lessons it is said, "Love is the divine force of attraction focused upon a single being; affection is the same force divided amongst many." It would seem that we are caught up presently in undoubted sincere feeling, but that it is more on the side of affection than on the side of love. I am talking here about the general condition and not about specific relationships in which true love may indeed be foremost.

It seems to me that if we would transcend affection for the greater love, we must endeavor to keep the focus upon a single being—yet to enlarge the capacity of heart so that our focus may include more and more beings in that same grace that heretofore was directed more or less exclusively toward our Murshid or spouse or child. (I know this is just a lot of words, but I am really trying to say something that I feel is important.)

Now that my physical condition is becoming less and less, and the normal physical energies and drives are gradually fading, one begins to see certain things. One begins to see that the teachings concerning the relation of mureed and Murshid are indeed true; this relation is foremost. *But* to take this teaching only literally and surficially is to miss the whole point. For when one has dug through all the mud of one's limited views, and has bathed one's eyes in the treasure of pure water, one sees truly that the *fana-fi-sheikh* is only real when the spirit, the *agape*, the light of Murshid is apprehended in every being.

"Whatsoever ye do to the least of these, my creatures, ye do unto me."

At a certain point one cannot look back. This is taught in the parables of Lot and his wife, of Orpheus and Eurydice. It is at this point that the realization of "the spirit quickeneth, the flesh profiteth nothing" becomes clear.

There is so much here that I am not saying—despite the plethora of words already written. And what I have not said can be found in that silent realm of the soul where the feeling for the Beloved is so tender and profound that one would accept "poison for nectar with felicity" (Diwan of Hazrat Inayat Khan).

> That living and dying in love
> are but one I have proved.
> This only know I,
> that I live by the sight of
> the beauty of her, the Beloved,
> for whom I would die. (Ghalib)

There are those who would live to see their ideal accomplished, and there are those who would die to see their ideal fulfilled. The signs of mastery and saintliness can be traced to these modes. Yet in the end they are one.

All love and blessings,
Murshid Moineddin

A Sufi Life, Part II: Effacement and Facing Death (1979)

(Editor's note: This is part two of the interview conducted by Abdul Aziz Bartley, Hafiza Mathieu, Jayanara Herz and Hassan Herz. It appeared in Bismillah: A Journal of the Heart *in volume 4, number 3 in 1980. The first half of this session reveals Moineddin in a state of what the Sufis call* fana—*effacement to his teacher and the lineage, clearly bringing through teaching and wisdom for everyday life. In the second half Moineddin pushes the interview in the direction of his expected impending death due to kidney failure. This is one of the most remarkably honest interviews with any spiritual teacher. Life still had more surprises for him, however.)*

One on the path of mastery cultivates success. One on the path of sainthood does not cultivate failure, but he cultivates resignation to God's will. The master cultivates identity with God's will and presents it in a masterful fashion so that it becomes the norm. The saint works in a different way. One of my sayings from a few years ago is, "Mastery involves power as such, sainthood involves power not as such."

That reminds me of a story. Murshid generally was the master. But there were times, and everybody who lived in this house (Garden of Inayat) knows it, when Murshid would become ill. He would get real quiet, he didn't do much. He tried to keep up a certain amount of work, but there were times when he just rested. And one morning I was in the office and Murshid was in there and so was Mansur. And Mansur said, "Murshid, I know right now that you are not feeling very well, and usually you are a master, but right now I look at you and I see a saint. What is the meaning of this?"

And, I don't remember exactly what Murshid said, but it was something along the lines of "The saint can't say anything. In this condition I can't say anything. I just can't." It didn't mean he was any less in tune with God. It just meant he wasn't in a state to be *jelal*, expressive. It wasn't his normal condition, but Murshid could be anything. That was why he was an *Abdal*, a changeling. Murshid taught the women how to walk like Mary.

Murshid also taught that the Prophet said, "There are three chief things I love: womankind, scent and prayer." Western interpreters have held that he was just a rogue and a rake because he had an eye out for women. Nothing of the sort. His love for womankind was due to the tenderness of feeling that the *jemal* qualities produced in his soul. In other words, he saw womankind reflecting the beauty and perfection of *jemal*, which is a divine quality. So it was an enlargement of his spiritual realization to be able to appreciate womankind. And that wasn't done very much in his time. They used to bury female infants alive. Can you imagine having to deal with that kind of evolution?

O.K., Jayanara, how about a question?

Many of us were raised along very strict orthodox religious lines of one sort or another.

Right, tell me about it.

We drew away from that, and later went on our own paths of seeking. In relation to having our own children, how formal or informal do you feel one's point of view in terms of spiritual development, of Sufism, should be?

Well, you know, sometimes spiritual teachers, particularly the advanced ones like a *Nabi* or a *Rassoul*, will give a code. The Mosaic code was given by Moses. It was a development or an updating of the Egyptian codes, which had gotten way out of hand. I think there were some fifty-two prohibitions that had to be balanced against the feather of divinity in the Court of Osiris before one could enter the land beyond the earthly denseness. So Moses in a sense epitomized the Egyptian teachings by putting them into the Ten Commandments. He went up to Mount Sinai and received these commandments—which may be historically true—but you might also say he entered a high state of consciousness and following divine guidance clarified the Egyptian teachings, teachings he was thoroughly trained in. A very similar theme—that of clarifying the teachings for the new generations—was initiated by Hazrat Inayat Khan and by your Murshid. This is what is happening today. Please give out the real teachings. Take the teachings to those who are waiting, who are ready. You see?

So, there's a code side, which is designed to apply to the multitudes. And something is happening in Iran right now with the Ayatollah Khomeini. He wants to establish modes of life, presumably Islamic, though I will put that word "Islamic" in quotes, because I don't think these modes have anything to do, in many cases, with what the Prophet Muhammad exemplified or gave. For instance, the veiling of women. That came two centuries after the Prophet Muhammad; two full centuries after the demise of Muhammad the veiling of women came in as a cultural adjunct to Islam. But as Murshid said, "What has Islam become? The Five Pillars have become five thousand." And it's more important what finger you eat your food with or whatever than if you realize that Allah is closer than the jugular vein. I mean, any child can see through such foolishness.

So to answer your question I feel that it has to be on the individual merits of each child. Hazrat Inayat Khan says in the Bowl of Saki that each person's religion is his or her own. When we are on the path of our soul's yearning, then we are religious. When we are off that path, then we are irreligious. And to me being a Sufi parent involves the ability to perceive what that child needs physically, mentally, emotionally, morally and spiritually. Yes, all these things have to be taken into account. Each individual has to be considered—because each individual is at a different stage.

I'm doing follow-up work on Murshid's commentary on [Hazrat Inayat Khan's book] *Mental Purification*, and it has become clear that we are not all at the same stage of evolution. There may be backgrounds that are similar, and that is why birds of a feather flock together. We can appreciate the backgrounds, and our sympathies tend to bind us.

That is why we are Ruhaniat people. That is why we have embraced a certain outlook. Some other outlooks we have moved away from—for instance, "church-ianity." We have departed from church-ianity, but we have not departed from the spirit of devotion. There may be those who benefit by more formal approaches. There are others who benefit from less formalism. There will be times in a person's life when formalism may mean a great deal. There will be times in a person's life when a sense of liberty means much more to her or him.

Now the balance may be seen in the work of the spiritual hierarchy. In one sense, this hierarchy may work as an army in which they drill constantly, and practice. And each individual needs this because it's part of discipline. On the other hand, there may be times when that army, far from directing force towards the lower spheres, will permit their spirits to look upward and rise, and this is what you have in the instance of the illuminated souls dancing—not marching, not regimented for a certain cause—but dancing for what may be the ultimate purpose.

See what I'm saying? There has to be balance. That's why Murshid would constantly say and demonstrate, "If things get too serious, you've got to bring in the comic side. If things get too comic, you've got to bring in the serious side. You've got to keep that balance." This is why I don't always like to give too much emphasis to stories about Murshid busting people. Sure, it's humorous to tell an occasional story about somebody or even oneself being busted by Murshid, but Murshid had no fun doing it. It was no fun for him to have to do that. It's just like kids talking about the trips they went through with their parents. "Oh, boy, did I really get it that time. Ha. Ha. Ha. Ha. You know, the time I got caught chewing tobacco in the barn, or smoking behind the garage." We're all little children. And I think that this age is one in which freedom of thought, freedom of outlook, and fullness of insight are going to count more than the formalisms of the past.

But there will be aspects of formalism that will be necessary. For instance, we meet on Thursday evenings for a spiritual class. Now that's a rhythm that Murshid adopted that has been established among the Sufi brotherhoods for centuries. Thursday night spiritual meetings. And Murshid instituted that in our group. Not only that, he introduced rhythm into the lives of people who had lost all sense of rhythm and had become used to a kind of euphoric chaos.

If you wake up in the morning, and the first thing you do is light a joint and turn on some rock and roll, it's hard to be clear about what's going to happen for the rest of the day. Who knows who is going to show up on your doorstep? It's just that there's no element of planning in such a life. And Murshid introduced this aspect of planning, or God as the divine architect or God as the stage manager, the actor, the set manager, everything. And he gave the example of seeing, foreseeing, overseeing. And that's what a Sufi does.

You mentioned earlier the process of covering that children go through.

Yes, this is very...I mean I can almost mark the day when it happened to me.

Do you feel that this is an essential process or is it an accident?

It is a normal thing. And I think it will happen regardless of the efforts, even the best efforts, on the part of parents and society. It is a natural phase of life that the light that the infant brings from the angelic spheres gradually becomes covered. Jesus Christ said, "Lo, I am with little children unto the age of seven years." I asked Murshid what that meant. And he said, "Well, it's as if God gave each individual soul a certain number of breaths. And that number of breaths would represent the length of time that that soul would be able to bask in a type of spiritual resilience. The light would always be there for them to go back to. It would never disappear for that span of seven years or that time of so many breaths. Once that number of breaths had been used, then the covering process would gradually set in."

So the shadowing is a natural process. I think it is partly social and cultural, and partly from the parents' own thought-forms of what is right and wrong. All of these things create shadow impressions that tend to cover up our innate light. But the point is that we've been given the means to overcome these shadows through the spiritual practices. And the practices cover such a multitude of life's areas. There's not one single area of life that the 112 Shiva practices in *Zen Flesh, Zen Bones* don't cover.

One of the first things I ever asked Murshid was, "Murshid, we live in Bolinas, and our only source of heat is a wood stove, and I do a lot of wood-chopping. Is there something that can help me do it without getting fatigued?" He said, "Oh, that's a very good question. Yes, when you take the axe say 'El Allah Hu' and say 'Hu' when the blade strikes the log. And when you are sawing logs say 'Allaho Akbar' in rhythm with the strokes. You can even do it on your breath." Totally practical, totally practical.

Hazrat Inayat Khan, in the Sangathas, certainly gives an indication when he says that Sufis of this grade of study should always be doing *fikr* with their work, whether one is an engineer, carpenter, anything. Unite your physical activities with the breath, with the God-thought.

So returning to your question, what I'm saying is that our children can be raised in love, and our own maturity is going to have a deep-felt influence on their children. Sure, they're going to go through many of the loop-the-loops that we all went through. That's part of it too, but I think they're going to be more resilient and ultimately less covered.

But I don't feel that those acting in the capacity of Sufi initiators should take on children as mureeds at too young an age. Hafiza's daughter, Atha, was initiated into the Ramnam. In Murshid's letters toward the end of his life, he wrote this to Anandashram: "I'm accepting children into the Ramnam, but they have to be sixteen before they can be initiated into Sufism." There is a certain stage—call it "glandular"—that a person must be past before they are able to take on something so serious as the study of Sufism. This is not to separate the Ramnam from anything. The Ramnam really is pure enjoyment for children and adults alike.

So little children shouldn't be doing other types of practices?

They don't need it! They may be encouraged to join—we ask Noah and Nooria to join in prayers, but they come of their own accord usually. They just realize, "Oh yes, prayer-time." And this is part of the rhythmical process. And by golly, even Noah knows the prayers, every single word. True he may not understand them. But I can say for certain that since my upbringing as a Catholic, from the age of seven until I was nineteen, I have found those initial prayers and sacraments to be most valuable, because I can tune right back to those days when I was a Catholic and making efforts without really knowing how, just making my own personal efforts toward coming to some sort of realization after having received the wafer of Holy Communion. I knew I was supposed to feel something. I knew I was supposed to try to feel something. And even in the absence of feeling something, now I can see what it was I was supposed to feel. For in Sufism one experiences the reality behind the form.

Do you feel that the unfoldment you've experienced since you met your teacher is something that you "remember" from before you went on the spiritual path formally? Do you feel like it was something that was not previously recognized but was there just the same?

When I first met Murshid, I said "Murshid, I was raised Catholic, and you're teaching us these Sanskrit mantras. Are they similar in effect to the Gregorian chants?" He said, "O absolutely." I said, "Well, that's great, because I have a background in Latin plainchant, and I really like to sing it." He said, "Sure, just center in the heart, and the singing will have a marvellous effect."

I ask because sometimes I have a feeling that when we try to leave everything behind we end up fighting what is supposed to be brought out.

I think I get your drift. To that I would definitely say yes. The deeper the experience spiritually, the more one realizes one's own soul, and one's own soul is an activity of the light of God, the intelligence of God. That's the beauty of the divine intelligence. So naturally when we have these experiences in the higher states, the higher mystical states, we naturally remember that this is what we *are*, not what we were, not what we will become, but what we *are*. And what we are can never help but augment and enhance all of the processes of growth. I don't know if that's an answer to your question.

Well, it is. So thinking about dealing with children again, in their development, could it be helpful to take the attitude when raising very young children and realizing that they are probably going to go through the experience of becoming covered, is it possible to try to provide them with keys that will help them to re-awaken at a later time?

The only safeguard—yes, and the best safeguard—and the most golden key is to shine oneself. To give a worthy example at all times. That is what Murshid did for us, that is what Murshid does *right now*. He *was* here in form, and he *is* here both in form and not in form. As the tenth lesson in the Self-Protection Githekas that Murshid channelled from Hazrat Inayat Khan teaches, "You are indeed blessed to see me in vision or *hal* but, if you wish to really concentrate on Pir-o-Murshid, look at your fellow mureed. If you then see me you are blessed, and if you act toward your fellow mureed as you would to me you are blessed a million times." And the same thing with children: look at them and behold "the first in the Kingdom of Heaven."

So that whenever they remember the light of their ideal...
We give them something to remember, and ideally not even to remember, because it will be happening all the time. It's the forgetfulness that is the shadow, and as Murshid says somewhere, the shadow isn't real, forgetting isn't even real. The forgetting is just the preoccupation with self.

Now the self has needs, and we have to attend to them, but it doesn't have to be a big trip. In one sense it can be, as Hafiza knows, and Fatima Roberts, because they come to Noor Mahal several times a week to help me dialyze. It's a big job just to keep one's physical body in order. But everybody has tests, everybody feels the weight of the physical world in some way—the denseness of the earth as it is called—to one degree or another. Murshid teaches that life is generally difficult, but Muhammad declares in Quran: "Verily, with difficulty cometh ease." And if it were not for difficulties in life there would not be much realization. But there is realization, and it comes through the link of Murshid and mureed, through the chain of *baraka*.

The chain of *baraka* is open to everybody. The chain of *baraka* is everybody, and this is the realization of the Rassouls. There is nobody that is not themselves. There is no thing that is not themselves. There is no event that is not themselves, there is no state that is not themselves. There is no stage of being upon which their own being does not act with full understanding. Lord Buddha said, when he finished his meditation under the Bo tree: "I see now all sentient beings have perfect illumination, only they do not know it. I must teach it to them."

So how about a practical question now? I feel that the practical questions lead to spiritual awakening. I mean, isn't that the ultimate practicality? I don't mind talking about Murshid or about Fatima.

Well, here's a question. Murshid Lewis seemed to really enjoy the intellectual understanding of the sciences. There's a lot of his writing that I've studied and just been unable to follow. It's so deep and technical. With Murshida Fatima in mind it occurs to me it's possible to grasp these ideas of the universe and their manifestation just through love, no?

The Sufis have two terms: *ishk* and *ilm*. *Ilm* means the divine knowledge, which is probably identical to the Sanskrit *jnana*. *Ishk* is similar to the Sanskrit *bhakti* or *parabhakti*, which is translated as love. Papa Ramdas pointed out that while Sri Ramakrishna was externally a *bhakti* yogi, he was inwardly a perfect *jnana*. Yet his chief disciple Swami Vivekananda outwardly was a *jnani*, but inwardly he was a pure *bhakti*.

Now that's an interesting way of looking at it, because you really can't have one without the other. The divine will contains love and knowledge, and it is for us as seekers of the divine wisdom to experience these realities, both the love and the knowledge. I think it has truly been said that the knowledge is not real if it doesn't come through love, and the love isn't real if it doesn't come through the light of intelligence. There is such a thing as knowledge of God, and this is what is meant by *jnana*, but the knowledge leads to the love, and the love leads to the knowledge.

Now that's too theoretical. What you were remarking on was Murshid's aptitude in the sciences. He had encyclopedic knowledge. He had mystical knowledge, or *kashf*, which is another kind of knowledge—the ability to penetrate through surfaces directly to process, function, operation, which is more in keeping with essences, what is called causal knowledge. I confess to being very deficient in that area. Mostly it is lack of interest. I'm just not interested in being a "brain." But Murshid had this scientific bent. He told us on several occasions that he was engaged at one time in his life in some scientific endeavors, perhaps roughly similar to what Einstein was working on. And he said that God came to him and said, "You're 200 years ahead of the human race. You must stop this work." Murshid said, "I stopped."

Who said he was 200 years ahead?

God said he was 200 years ahead of the evolutionary standard of science. It wasn't the time for it. The world wasn't ready.

I'm not totally satisfied with this yakety-yak, but this is an interview. That's what we're here for.

Are there certain subjects you would like to be questioned about?

Just look at me and I think you'll get some ideas. I mean, I'm going through certain things. And I do certain things.

Do you have a daily routine of work?

I do, as a matter of fact. I get up every morning about 6:30. And if it's one of the three mornings after a dialysis treatment I get up at 6 and take a bath and shampoo. If it's Thursday, Fatima Roberts and

I jointly produce breakfast, usually scrambled eggs or something. On other days, at 7: 05 I blow the conch, which is the sign that there is five minutes for everybody to get to the chapel at Noor Mahal for practices. We do the twenty purification breaths and the healing prayer. Then we have a reading from Swami Ramdas, *Ramdas Speaks*, two or three paragraphs. Then we do the practice of *kasab*. And then we finish with the Confraternity Prayers [of Hazrat Inayat Khan]. And since the beginning of the Ruhaniat pilgrimage, the day after Christmas, we've been doing Ya Wakil, God is the Protector, eleven times for the protection of the pilgrims. Then we go to the dining room, we say the blessing and read the Bowl of Saki and Murshid's Commentary on the Bowl of Saki for that day. Then we eat.

After breakfast, ah well, when we first moved to Noor Mahal I wanted to make a worthy impression, so I took on certain tasks of washing dishes and cleaning up the table, but I realized that even those menial chores were sapping energy that could be better placed in areas in which I was expected to function such as the commentary work and interviews and correspondence with mureeds—you know, spiritual work. So I have exempted myself from all those tasks, much as I don't like not doing them. I would rather be in a condition physically where I'd have sufficient energy to give a good example. But the physical energy is not there, and I've done my best to maintain a modicum of energy just to make it through the work patterns of the day.

We start immediately after breakfast with correspondence or commentary. I generally take a walk around the block once a day as a constitutional—using sacred phrases. I try to get to the post office. I just try to get out, you know? Thank God we've had an early spring, and when the sun comes out we take a dip in the swimming pool, which is excellent as a physical exercise. I try as much as possible to maintain a rapport with my wife and children and with the mureeds in my household, but at times it is difficult, for we have the example of Murshid before us.

His energy was so tremendous that even at his advanced age he could outdo physically most of his strong male mureeds. I mean his tremendous *baraka*, whether he said it was due to Hazrat Inayat Khan's yelling at him during the "Six Interviews" or due to his practice of actual yoga—he could say anything and you would believe it because all of it was true. Or whether it was from catching the chewed-up food that Haji Baba Abdul Aziz spat into the air before it hit the ground, you know? Or whether it was due to the transmission he received when he had the vision of the prophets dancing, with Elijah bestowing the robe. Or any of those myriad experiences. Or whether it was due to the devotion and awakening of disciples. That has a lot to do with it: "It is the mureeds who make the Murshid."

So as I started to say, one of the most difficult things for me at this period of life is being unable to do *tasawwuri Murshid* in that vigorous sense. One has anaemia, and one's physical level of energy is reduced at least by half and probably more compared to a normal person. And this cuts out most of life, much of what people regard as life. It just cuts it out. On the other hand, the cutting out of certain portions of life permits what you might call a kind of reservoir function to take place on other planes. I am constantly being surprised by letters from mureeds that say, "Oh, Murshid, I had the most wonderful experience. You were in this dream, and...." It's a surprise to me totally. I'm not aware of these things, but they're happening on some level. And people are feeling some sort of blessing or benefit from it. Because it shows another side than the denseness of the earth. And apparently this is what is happening with one's being. One is in gradual fashion being released from the physical bonds. Everyone goes through this, is going through it. That's what age is, going from one station to another physically. It just seems that the process is accelerated in my particular case.

So this is part of the difficulty. One might prefer to practice *tasawwuri Murshid* in the fullness of spirit and life and vigor and laughter that Murshid Samuel Lewis manifested as part of his everyday life. And yet one realizes that, at this point, one's "friend" is a kidney machine. Or as I remarked recently while holding hands with the gathering of Ruhaniat leaders, "You are my real life-support system."

At one time, I think, you were considering some sort of transplant from a member of your family. In the past year or so has your feeling changed?

Yes, my sister offered to donate one of her kidneys, but when she came here for her hospital work-up, the doctors determined that she was hypoglycemic, and it would have been a tremendous risk to her life if she were to undergo major surgery and give up one of her kidneys. Because the kidneys regulate the body's chemistries particularly with regard to the blood sugar. And as it turned out, less than a month later she had a modified radical mastectomy. That would have meant two major surgeries in a row, and I don't know that she would have lived through them.

So I feel the verdict of Allah in this matter is dialysis. I've had absolutely no indications otherwise, despite the best intentions and wishes of many mureeds who remind me that they are constantly praying for my health. People tend to overlook the fact that I've been through nine years of healers, acupuncture, diets, herbs and the like. We must realize that Allah may have His own ideas about some things.

You spoke earlier of the path of the master and the path of the saint. My feeling of your relationship with this illness would that be the path of the saint, or the path of resignation?
Yes, I would tend to agree. Resignation, yes.

Did you feel that throughout the—when you first had the kidney trouble—did you go through a period of wanting to...
...master it...
...right.
Absolutely. And that was the indication that Murshid gave me, because he knew that I would. You see, what was causing me to die in the first place, when the kidneys began to atrophy back in 1970, was a process in which I saw myself as an old man. And well, you and I lived at the Garden of Inayat at the time, so you may have been conscious of it or perhaps unconscious of it, but it was certainly in the atmosphere. That's how I saw myself, and it had to do partly with a sense of *tasawwuri Murshid* because I saw Murshid as an ancient, or an old, person. And I wanted to be like him. But that wasn't right. It was the wrong rhythm to adopt, the wrong example to follow, because it led to certain things, and they weren't particularly...well, who can say what is and isn't beneficial? I mean, I could say this thing has been intended from the beginning.

But anyhow, I felt like an old man, and this disease set in. I did almost die in the hospital. The doctors had given up hope, and they called Fatima. Fatima called Murshid and said, "Murshid, you'd better get over there and give him what you've got to give because the doctors have lost hope." And I didn't know anything. All I knew is that I had had one stomach operation, and they said the day afterwards, "Oh, it's a great success. We got all the infection out." Two days later they said, "The infection's back, we have to operate again." And at that moment I sank. At that moment I lost it. I mean I gave up totally. I didn't realize I'd given up, but I lost it totally. It was the straw that broke the camel's back. I couldn't take any more. It was just too much to have lived through one operation and then to have another one two days later.

So I guess I got the other operation. Murshid came in, and I wept the whole time he was there because there was nothing else to do. He just ranted and raved. As Frida Waterhouse would say, he gave me "holy hell." And the moment he left I realized that I had hit rock bottom. I didn't realize I had been dying. I didn't know what had been happening until

Murshid left the room. Then I realized that that was as low as I could possibly go. I don't know if other people have experienced that or not, but I felt for the first time in my life that I had hit bottom totally, and that the only place to go now was up.

So when Murshid left I knew there was nothing else to do but employ some real will power. I can't say it in any other terms. When he left I had a sense of what will power was. Before that visit I had a sense of what struggle was, but I didn't know what will was. And it has never left since, the constancy of an adamant will, always there, never absent, inshallah. So from then on it was simply a matter of applying the knowledge that I had a will, and that it could be a tremendous force for overcoming obstacles.

For the next five years, I had what is called remission. That means that the disease was there latently but not really manifest. I had to watch my diet. I couldn't drink too much liquid, stuff like that, but the kidneys were functioning. I was urinating. It only takes about 10% kidney function for a person to get along almost normally. But then in July of 1976 my kidneys totally gave out. And again I didn't realize it, but when they were going out, which was a progressive stage, I was getting sicker and sicker. My system was getting filled with toxins which affected my thinking. I was going off my nut. I bought two motorcycles, of all the dumb things. Blowing my family's savings account. Just dumb stupid things. So then, when I realized that my urine level was going down, I went to see a doctor and he said, "Good God, you'd better get into a hospital right away. Your function is nil." In less than a week I had a cow's vein sewed into my arm so that I could be dialyzed, and then that same month I started dialysis treatments.

Now, hemodialysis patients as a rule become physically weakened. And this is what has happened. I've had to make major adjustments in terms of physical mastery. There are just some things I do not do. I cannot walk very far now without getting tired, just can't. So—

I don't know if this is of interest to you—it's just sort of a personal insight into what one has dealt with these past nine years, and one continues to deal with it. But this lack of strength on the physical plane permits the strength to accumulate on more subtle planes, and one is able to operate with more strength on those planes. This is what I see happening.

As far as one's physical longevity goes, it's totally up to God. I'll just keep doing what I'm doing for as long as I can keep doing it. As Reverend Deborah from the Church of MANS once said, "Yes, it's called *carrying on*."

Has there been a change in the last few months? I mean, I feel a certain change has been...
Yes. And I don't know exactly how to put it. There has been a change. That's why I can't say a thing about physical longevity, because I just don't know. I strive against assuming or presuming anything, because there's too much of the person that can slip in, too much ego can get into that type of thinking. I think it's best for all concerned if I just leave the matter entirely in God's hands and continue to do what I can do and forget what I can't do. I don't want to get too speculative about it. The body is mostly felt as a burden.

I want to ask for others who may have briefer but still intense periods of illness or discomfort, how do you maintain a respectful and kindly attitude toward the body when it is a burden?
You try to maintain the practices: *fikr*, Darood. Darood unites one with one's teacher and with the chain of Murshids and thereby the Spirit of Guidance. *Fikr* unites one with the divine presence and can give full release from denseness. *Zikr* can enhance all the vibrations, the dance of the physical and subtle atoms, particularly when it is accompanied by God-thought and a feeling of unity with One and All. Ya Hayy is a most wonderful practice for a person who, perhaps more than healing, requires simply an influx of life. So consequently I do a lot of Ya Hayy. But the ability of my physical frame to store and maintain the vibrations of the spiritual practices is not great. This is the wonder of physical health—that it represents a capacity to store the benefits of spiritual practice. And a weak physical frame has not this capacity or at least not this capacity over an extended duration. So you see me in dialysis feeling pretty good for the first few hours, but the last two hours get to be very hard and painful.

You've been with me, Hafiza, in that condition. I don't take phone calls, don't give advice, and try not to assume much responsibility at those times, because it would be wrong. I would actually be less responsible to mureeds if I were to offer advice or if I were to converse with them in such a state. As Jesus Christ said: "Whoever has in his hand, to him shall be given; and whoever does not have, from him shall be taken even the little which he has."

Can you relate any of this to the conditions surrounding Murshid's passing?
Yes perhaps. Murshid was conducting nine classes a week, plus his commentaries, correspondence and interviews, even gardening. He was

getting more and more nervous, and he was at his wit's end as to how to proceed. And I was feeling every bit of it. I sensed that he was going, and all I wanted to do was go with him. And there was Fatima's dream a little earlier: it was six months before Murshid's passing, and he had us all gather at the Mentorgarten, and said, "Well, I'll be leaving pretty soon. I just want you to know. You'll carry on and flourish." Fatima told me that I answered in the dream, "Well, if you're going, then I'm going too." And I flung my head off, and it went rolling down the street. Fatima said, "Oh, no you don't!" She ran after my head and picked it up and whacked it down on my shoulders. "You're not going anywhere!" And that's what happened.

I'll never forget that last Christmas eve at the Garden of Allah. Frida [Waterhouse] was there. She was still blind. And she said, "Samuel, how are you?" I overheard this. And he said, "You really want to know?" She said, "I asked, didn't I?" And he replied, "My nerves are jangled." It was like he just didn't know what to do. But we never realized what tremendous capacity he had for overcoming his own feeling of limitation. And then someone showed this film footage of Sri Bhagawan, which was later put in the film *Sunseed*. Bhagawan was a very beautiful soul, but I thought we were there to honor Murshid. Somehow I never did feel right about that film footage, but that's off the subject.

Anyhow, I felt Murshid was being overlooked. Inwardly I felt he was leaving, and to give attention to other teachers at a time when our own Murshid was preparing to be withdrawn from the world was a slight. And then I saw his mastery and his love for his disciples. I don't know how it happened, but either he said, "Well, is there anything anybody wants to do?" Or somebody said, "Murshid, I have a request." However it happened, one of the ladies asked, "O Murshid, would you do the Krishna Dance?" What I saw was a flicker of great effort in his expression. It was like he was ninety-nine percent gone already. But he geared up and felt "I've got to do it." And then he did the Dance. I think it's the one in the picture in *Toward Spiritual Brotherhood*. The *ishk* in that dance was so potent, so real. These are the things we should remember, and try to bring to the world. *Mashallah*.

A Spark Borrowed From the Blaze: Will, Wish and Desire (1979)

(Commentary on Chapter 10, "The Will" of the Gathekas of Hazrat Inayat Khan on Mental Purification)

GATHEKA: Words such as wish, desire, love and their like mean more or less the same thing, but the word "will" has a greater importance than all those other words. And the reason is that will is life itself.

TASAWWUF: The themes of will, wish and desire are taken up in the published literature [volume eight of the *Sufi Message* volume series of Hazrat Inayat Khan], but will is so important that its connections imbue all of the Sufi teachings, published and esoteric.

The Qur'anic phrase *kun faya kun* ("be, and it became!") shows that the command of God originated existence. In this sense, the attribute *Al-Bari* (the Maker out of Nothing) becomes clear. Whether we speak of God or of a human being, the one who possesses this will, this power of command, is one with the fullness of life, both temporal and eternal.

The American Sufi poet Murshid Samuel L. Lewis (Sufi Ahmed Murad Chisti) illustrates this principle in his epic poem "Saladin" when he speaks in the voice of Sri Krishna: "So I sing the universe unbounded, and electrify the universe which is bound...."

GATHEKA: The Bible calls God love. Love in what sense? Love in the sense of will. The Creator created the universe by what? By love? By will; love came afterwards. Love is the will when it is recognized by its manifestation. Then it is called love, but in the beginning it is will.

TASAWWUF: Will is *zat* [divine essence], love is *sifat* [divine attribute]. They are inseparable. Only in the worlds of multiplicity do we recognize an apparent dual principle. A will without love could not possibly be ascribed to God, and as we have been created in God's image, our own wills are essentially replete with love. The realization of this is the chief attainment of Sufis.

GATHEKA: For instance, the Taj Mahal, the great building at Agra, is said to be the token of the love that the emperor had for his beloved. At the same time when one looks at it objectively, one cannot call it an expression of love. One would sooner call it a phenomenon of will. For the beginning of the building at least, one may look at the spirit, the impulse which started it, as a phenomenon of the emperor's will. After it was finished one can say it was the expression of his love.

TASAWWUF: The Welsh poet Dylan Thomas wrote: "The force that through the green fuse drives the flower...." This force of creation is the will behind the goal represented by the flower. It is not the force we love, ordinarily speaking, it is the flower we love. Yet it is the flower that shows that love was there in the force from the very beginning.

It may be said that love for an object is the first stage of love, but when that object reveals its soul to the lover, then the lover perceives the divine will that gave it life. It is the perception of the divine will that leads to absorption in the destination of love: peace—vibrant with immaculate unity.

GATHEKA: When a person says "I desire it," "I wish it," it is an incomplete will, a will that is not conscious of its strength, a will that is not sure what it wills. In that case it is called a desire, a wish. But when a person says "I will it," that means it is definite. A person who never can say "I will it" has no will.

TASAWWUF: An incomplete will is a shallow will. Strength of will comes from the depths of heart. A desire or wish may be regarded as lesser degrees of the complete, deep will, but really speaking the complete will is transcendent in relation to all degrees. For the complete will is God's will.

When one becomes identified with the complete will of God, one may disclose it verbally, as in the case of Mansur Al-Hallaj. Or one may reveal it through the power of miracle (*karamat*) as in the case of Jesus Christ and others. Or one may simply abide in God's presence and manifest the Beautiful Names through the course of everyday life, as in the case of Muhammad who is the exemplar for many Sufis.

Nor should we assume one mode of behavior to be less instrumental than another. Al-Hallaj's declaration that he and the Truth were one was for a definite purpose. The orthodoxy of the time had to be shown that spiritual realization is always pre-eminent over so-called religious views devoid of devotion to a living God and sympathy toward humanity. Thus he was crucified. Jesus Christ's example of self-sacrifice was the very means by which the power of miracle was able to operate, for when the ego is crushed the will of God may immediately work through the hand of humanity. The miracles were for those who needed them, in one way or another. But the lesson of crucifying the limited self that the unlimited Life may be realized is for all times and all peoples.

Sufis generally idealize Muhammad because his life shows the perfection of balance, of a deep and comprehensive spirit, of completion—all this in the midst of human enterprise. But all the holy ones have come to earth with the message of divine perfection. And as Holy Qur'an says, "We make no distinctions or differences among them (the prophets)."

GATHEKA: From this we may conclude that will is the source and the origin of all phenomena.

TASAWWUF: The Divine fiat *kun faya kun* has already been commented upon.

GATHEKA: Hindus have called the creation a dream of Brahma, the creator. But a dream is a phenomenon of the unconscious will, when the will works automatically.

TASAWWUF: Too much regard for such interpretations of the creation may actually produce cultures where lack of a general direction has become paramount, such as we see in late 20th century India, despite the influences of Gandhi and Sri Aurobindo, despite national independence.

GATHEKA: The will is the action of the soul. One can also call the soul the self of the will. The difference between will and soul is like the difference between a person and his action.

TASAWWUF: And when the soul has shed its coverings and becomes united with the divine spirit, all its actions produce pure, sweet and wholesome fruit. A realized soul will always commend the fruits of his or her labors to God—for seed, sunlight, rain, air and earth—*all* contribute to the great harvest.

Without the divine will there would be no seed, and without the elements there would be no growth, no fruit, no harvest. In a very real sense, the harvest is a symbol for the soul's return to its source—for as Qur'an declares: "Verily, to Allah is your return."

The soul itself is the action of God. "What is the soul?" one of the companions asked the Prophet. *"Amr-i-Allah,"* answered Muhammad, "an activity of God."

GATHEKA: There is a difference between the thoughtful and the imaginative person, and the difference is that the one thinks with will, the other thinks without will. When once a person knows the value of will, that person then recognizes that there is nothing in the world that is more precious than will.

TASAWWUF: It is those souls who have united with the divine will who form the embodiment of the "Master, the Spirit of Guidance." It is the Master who possesses willpower in its greatest degree, and it is the unity of Masters working together that constitutes the spiritual hierarchy. This embodiment of illuminated souls represents the very order of God, an order inconceivable to the mind of humanity, but which may be glimpsed by an open heart and clearly seen by an awakened soul.

Human effort, human will, is a spark borrowed from the blaze of the divine will. Its instrumentality to effect change for the better should never be underestimated, yet its power is small in comparison to the blaze from which it has been borrowed. Therefore Sufis strive to annihilate their limited egos by entering the all-powerful, all-loving, divine will—as the moth becomes naught by entering the lantern. When this stage is reached one may rightly be called "a torch in the darkness," as suggested in the prayer Nabi [of Hazrat Inayat Khan].

GATHEKA: Naturally, therefore, the question arises in the mind of the thoughtful person, "Have I will in me? Have I a strong will or have I a weak will?" And the answer is that no one can exist without will. Everyone has a will.

TASAWWUF: The various degrees of will, from weak to strong, which we see operating through the humanity show clearly that there is either direction or lack of direction in people's lives. It is those with direction who prove their understanding of willpower, and it is those who lack direction who evidence ignorance of willpower.

One of the first duties of the spiritual teacher is to kindle the heart of the disciple so as to awaken the sense of will. Often a disciple is looking for direction in life, a feeling of order and rhythm, but until the will is awakened one does not experience much ability to direct one's affairs. In this regard, the teacher must be a living example of the purity, power and unity of the divine will. The living example is the greatest of teachings, the distillate of all that is worthy of God and worthwhile for humanity.

GATHEKA: The automatic working of the mind produces imagination, and the value of imagination depends upon the cultivation of the mind. If the mind is tuned to a higher pitch, then the imagination will naturally be at a higher pitch. But if the mind is not tuned to a high pitch, then naturally the imaginations will not be at a high pitch.

TASAWWUF: Prayer provides a cultivation that can include concentration (upon sacred themes), postures and movements based upon psychic law and devotion. In this way thought, action and feeling are united, and the whole being is involved in willing surrender to God.

And while prayer may bring the benefits of sobriety, this sobriety does not necessarily bring the consciousness of unity. God and humanity may remain as if separate. Thus Sufis have held sessions called *sama*, musical and poetic gatherings where the highest expression of devotion is in the sacred dance. The tendency of these gatherings is to produce types of ecstasy unknown to the generality, but certainly known to heart and soul—even to the body.

Yet one will find that most of these gatherings—where poetry, music, singing and the sacred dance take place—are preceded and concluded by prayer. So all ranges of imaginative and devotional thought and feeling are experienced through the combination of formal prayer and modes of bliss. This is a kind of balance outside the ken of orthodox, narrow or fixed outlooks, but it is a balance that the Sufi holds to be of immense benefit in life—not because it sounds good in theory but because the Sufi knows it through his or her own experience.

GATHEKA: Imagination has its place and its value. But when? At that time when the heart is tuned to such a pitch that the imagination cannot go anywhere else but into paradise. The heart that is so tuned by love, harmony and beauty, without willing begins to float automatically. And in this automatic movement, it reacts to whatever it touches or expresses it in some form. When it is in the form of line or color or notes, then art, painting, music, or poetry is produced. It is then that imagination has value.

TASAWWUF: It is this imagination that has been called "the symphony of emotions." All artists and lovers are familiar with this symphony, with this pitch of imagination raised high by the fire of devotion and made pure by the tears of revelation. This is the state that may come to the purified heart of the devotee, yet it is not the *state* that is sought by the Sufi. The Sufi seeks only God, who discloses and veils its Being according to the divine plan.

States (*ahwal*) are important in spiritual development, because they remove the sight of the self from one's eyes. But unity with God is supreme because then one's self is God. This is the goal of all spiritual longing and endeavor. As Jesus Christ has taught, "Seek ye first the kingdom of God, and all else shall be added unto you."

At the same time one should certainly practice art, poetry or music—or any special talents that inspire one's heart—as avenues of seeking God, in addition to the practices given by the teacher. This will result in more God-realization on the one hand, and the production of greater beauty through all art forms on the other hand, *inshallah*.

GATHEKA: But when it comes to business and science and all things that are connected with our everyday life and the world, it is better to leave imagination aside and work with thought.

TASAWWUF: That is to say the will should be active rather than passive. Thought with will should be goal-oriented. Yet it often happens that the solution to a problem in science or other field of mental or material endeavor will occur when the mind is passive, even in a dream or when one is going to sleep.

GATHEKA: As both night and day are useful, as both rest and action are necessary, so both thinking and imagination have their place in our life. For instance, if poets used will to direct their imagination, it would become a thought and would become rigid. The natural thing for poets is to let their minds float into space; and whatever they happen to touch to let their hearts express it. And then what is expressed is an inspiration.

TASAWWUF: Poets must be passive to the higher worlds of imagination, yet positive with regard to the world of humanity, which they desire to impress with the seal of their inspiration. It is easier if, as in the case of Muhammad with the Qur'an and Rumi with the Masnavi, the prophet or poet can be uttering the revelations as they come and leave the recording to the amanuenses. It is harder if the poet must also be the instrument of writing, for this brings the consciousness more into the physical realm and the inspirations may be slower or less spontaneous in coming. Yet it should not matter too much, for Sufis learn the lessons of balance, which is to say Sufis master the ability to function at all levels, often at more than one level at a time.

The spiritual teacher is in much the same circumstance. One must be passive to God and the spiritual hierarchy, and one must be positive to the disciple. If the teacher is truly selfless before God and hierarchy, there is no question that the disciple will be selfless before the teacher. As Hazrat Inayat Khan has taught, "Devotion to a spiritual teacher is not for the sake of the teacher, it is for God."

GATHEKA: But when people need to attend to a business affair, they must not let their hearts float in the air. They must think of the things of the earth, and think about figures very carefully.

TASAWWUF: Strength of will is built by facing the problems of earth directly, by keeping one's feet on the ground and learning how to stand firmly in the midst of disagreeable situations and especially severe trials. Those who lack will tend to run away from earth plane responsibilities. Those who possess will always combine wit, skill, and optimism in meeting difficult persons or events. An even greater mastery is gained when one faces the enemies in one's own self and overcomes the forces associated with ego and lower mind. This has been symbolized in the picture of Saint George slaying the dragon.

GATHEKA: Then we come to the question of how we can maintain our will. The nature of the life we live is to rob us of our will. Not only the struggle we have to undergo in life, but also our own self—our thoughts, our desires, our wishes, our motives—weaken our will.

TASAWWUF: The will is like a sturdy and healthy tree. But when ivy, mistletoe, fungus or other parasitic growths attach themselves to the tree, the strength of the tree becomes increasingly sapped. The tree becomes robbed of its full share in life. This is how our own will becomes less through life: by little attachments that grow large if we let them.

If people would maintain their will through life, they must cut away, even uproot, the attachments that become like parasites, preventing the trees of their being from bearing proper fruit in due season.

GATHEKA: The person who knows how our inner being is connected with the perfect Will, will find that what makes the will smaller, narrower, more limited, is our experience throughout life. Our joys rob us of our will as do our sorrows. Our pleasures rob us of our will as do our pains, and the only way of maintaining the power of will is by studying the existence of will and by analyzing among all the things in ourselves what will is.

TASAWWUF: Youth is a time in life when there is seemingly a surfeit of willfulness, even to the point of rebellion. The candle is burnt at both ends, as the saying goes. Youth does not recognize as a rule how the inner being is connected with the divine will, although Sufi parents and guardians will try their utmost to make such matters clear to their children of teenage years.

Usually it takes a trial or sudden blow in life to catalyze a recognition of will, will in its own element as contrasted with the unconscious willfulness of youth. When one is thus awakened to the real nature of will, he or she will begin to understand the processes of steady growth and maturation. There will be more attention paid to maintaining one's center, one's will, one's life-force. And this very attention will serve to sustain and improve the will—if it is not overdone.

GATHEKA: It might seem that motive increases willpower, but no doubt in the end we will find that it robs us of willpower. Motive is a shadow upon the intelligence, although the higher the motive, the higher the soul, and the greater the motive, the greater the person.

TASAWWUF: This is to say that motive is associated with the ego personality of a person, and is thereby limited. As one's ego reinforces the sense of separation from one's fellow human being, so one's motives can overshadow the light of the divine will, the perfect will that is ever ready to give of its inexhaustible wealth.

But as one's ego becomes more refined and harmonious, one's motives move that much closer to the impulses of the divine will. It is in the refinement of self as it moves nearer to the perfect will that the living progress of the spirit is experienced. This is the true *sadhana* [path of attainment in everyday life].

GATHEKA: When the motive is beneath the ideal, then this is the fall of a person; and when one's motive meets one's ideal it is his rise. According to the width of motive a person's vision is wide, and according to the power of motive a person's strength is great.

TASAWWUF: If the motive falls short of the ideal, it is often due to fatigue, inharmony of thought, loss of rhythm and tone. And if one becomes guilty or defensive because of these shortcomings, he or she will only double the weight of the burden. This is the real "fall" of humanity, which if not faced with will and optimism eventually results in the entrapment which we call self-pity.

The antidotes to these shortcomings are proper patterns of activity and rest, hygiene and self-discipline. But these are only the skin and bones of mystical seeking. Our ideal is to dwell in the presence of God. The Sufi Invocation [of Hazrat Inayat Khan] proposes that the God ideal can be realized through the perfection of love, harmony and beauty. When we seek God through these avenues, we may feel our motive most worthy. This is surely humanity's rise, a rise that depends not alone upon skin and bones but upon the faculties of heart and breath. These come through devotion and training and diligence.

Perfection in *fana* [effacement] leads to the complete *baqa* [soul-expression]. Thus, the symbol of the cross is used to promote breadth of vision (the horizontal arm) and fullness of purpose and will (the vertical arm). When one becomes the cross, it is as if the intersection of the lines produces effacement of self and revelation of soul simultaneously. This is seen in the Rose Cross, the rose signifying the heart of Christ. One must become the cross for the rose to bloom.

GATHEKA: Furthermore there is an English saying, "Man proposes, God disposes." One is always faced with a power greater than oneself that does not always support one's desire. And naturally a person with will, faced with a greater power, must sooner or later give in and be impressed by the loss of his or her own will. This is only one example, but a hundred examples could be given to show how one is robbed of one's will without realizing it.

TASAWWUF: That will that can be taken away from one is the limited will of humanity. For this reason disciples in Sufism pray, "To Thee do we give willing surrender." For complete and wholehearted surrender to God (*fana*) leads to absorption in and expression of God (*baqa*). When one possesses the divine will, or rather when the divine will possesses one, it can never be taken away for its source is inexhaustible.

This realization led Hazrat Inayat Khan to declare, "Can anyone break me? No. By doing so, he may as well prepare to break God. Neither I nor God can be broken. But the one who would wish to break me, he is broken" (from the sayings in *Nirtan*).

GATHEKA: Very often people think that by being active or determined they maintain their will, and that by being passive they lose their will. But it is not so. Where there is a battle there is an advance and there is a retreat. By a retreat one is not defeated and by an advance one has not always succeeded.

TASAWWUF: The following commentary may not be easily understood. There must be power in one's advance, and there must also be power in one's retreat. A real general knows this. If one is a great general one knows that the maintenance of power in retreat is often more important than power in attack. For power in retreat prevents the scattering of one's forces, keeps one's forces united and whole. This is true even if one must hide for tactical reasons.

It is a challenge to face an enemy in battle. If the battle is outer, the general must have the wisdom and will to know when to advance and when a retreat is indicated. But the real fortitude of the general comes when s/he is challenged by, and overcomes, the host of internal enemies—loss of hope, fear, confusion and so on. This fortitude is really the strength of optimism, and it must be realized inwardly and practiced in the world at large. All forces, whether internal or external, rally to optimism and power of purpose.

The story of Abu Bakr and the Prophet Muhammad is well-known. The two comrades were hiding in a cave, and the enemy horde was seeking to kill them. Abu Bakr said, "What are we to do?"

Muhammad replied, "Allah is among us a third!"

Not only did they manage to elude the enemy, but as history has recorded the Prophet of Islam became a light and a guidance to friend and foe alike. Many former enemies willingly entered the ranks of the Muslims. In the words of Hazrat Inayat Khan, "The true sword of Muhammad was the charm of his personality."

Toward the end of his career as a military man, Muhammad gathered his people and said, "We have succeeded in the lesser *jihad* [struggle], now let us undertake the greater *jihad*." But the truth is that Muhammad had long since succeeded in the greater *jihad*. It was his supremacy in the inner struggle that led to victory on the battlefields and to friendship beyond the battlefields.

GATHEKA: A person who exerts his will all the time, strains it and exhausts it very soon. It is like being too sure of a string that one has in one's hand while rubbing it on the edge of a sharp stone. Very often one sees that people who profess great willpower fail much sooner than those who do not profess it.

TASAWWUF: A tragedy occurred recently. Two mountain climbers were scaling a sheer rock face. They were using brand new equipment and their rope was the best available—a type of nylon guaranteed at a tensile strength of several thousand pounds. Unknown to the upper climber, the rope was thrown over a sharp outcrop of rock. The constant back and forth motion of the climber cut and frayed his lifeline. Finally the rope broke and the man fell to his death. Fortunately, his partner survived.

Like the rope, the will of a person may test at a certain strength. Through proper training, chiefly *murakkabah* [concentration], a person's willpower may increase greatly. But one of the fundamental aspects of such training is in knowing how and when to relax one's will, one's efforts. If one keeps the will in a constant state of exertion and force, it is like fraying one's lifeline against the sharp rock.

There are similitudes with two elementary principles of physics: kinetic energy and potential energy. All activity, speech, profession and exertion belong to the kinetic mode—which is the *usage* of, and in extreme cases the *wastage* of, the vast reservoir of potential energy. Repose, silence and non-expression can lead to baptism in the reservoir of potential energy. When this occurs, one experiences the source of true will. It is after this baptism that the Sufi begins to learn what is the real balance in life. There is no failure for one who practices this balance.

GATHEKA: There is also always a battle between willpower and wisdom. And the first and wisest thing to do is to bring about a harmony between wisdom and willpower. When people say, "I wish to do this, I will do this," and at the same time their sense says, "No, you cannot do it, you must not do it," then even with all their willpower they either cannot do it or they will do something against their better judgment.

TASAWWUF: The principles of *yin* and *yang* in Chinese philosophy and of *jemal* and *jelal* in Sufism denote the conditions of responsiveness and expressiveness. The former is related to wisdom, and the latter is related to willpower. The harmony and balance of these two faculties are essential to understand life better. It is wise to first listen, and if one's impression is in harmony with one's conscience, then one may employ the willpower and commit one's efforts toward a purposeful result. Again one is simply practicing the balance mentioned above—not thinking too much about it but actually practicing it.

GATHEKA: This also shows us life in another light: that those who are wise but without will are as helpless as a person with willpower but without wisdom. There is no use keeping wisdom at the front and willpower at the back; nor is there any use in keeping willpower at the front and wisdom at the back. What is necessary is to make the two as one, and this can be done by becoming conscious of the action of both in all one does.

TASAWWUF: The founder of Sufism in the West, Hazrat Inayat Khan, instituted an esoteric lodge known as Ziraat—with rites and lessons based upon the model of agriculture. In Ziraat the heart is regarded as the field to be cultivated, the field from which all roots, stubble and stones must be purged before the seed of the divine ideal can be sown.

The plough used in Ziraat is equipped with two wheels, one representing the *jelal* force, and the other representing the *jemal* force. If only one wheel were to work at a time, the blade would not open the soil deeply, nor would it make straight furrows. But with both wheels working together the blade will plough properly, opening the heart's soil for inspection (and introspection).

In the sense that all endeavor, inner or outer, may be regarded as a kind of "ground-breaking," the symbol of the plough—with the two wheels operating in balance—proves to be most valuable in life.

GATHEKA: At the same time one can practice it in one's everyday life, depriving oneself of things one likes. If people always have what they like to have, no doubt they spoil their will, for then their will has no reaction.

TASAWWUF: That is to say, when one makes sacrifices, tiny or great, for the sake of one's ideal; when one quits habits that stand as obstacles to the fuller functioning of one's *dharma*—then the benefits of wisdom and willpower alike accrue to the pupil. And whether one is formally a pupil or a teacher, it must be remembered that we are all pupils of God, the only Teacher.

GATHEKA: A stimulus is given to the will when one deprives oneself of what one desires. Then the will becomes conscious of itself, alive; it wonders why it should not have it.

TASAWWUF: This very wondering, this questioning, brings the wisdom of *listening*. One can almost hear, nay, one *can* hear the "Voice which constantly cometh from within"—in other words, the indications of the divine will.

There is a tendency to become abstracted in the listening aspect. This is good and necessary in the beginning stages of the spiritual path. But it is only the first half of progress. If this aspect is indulged in too much it can become a definite hindrance, for then one starts to "receive" impressions for anybody and everybody. This can result in the worst kind of presumption and self-delusion.

For the complete experience one needs the listening and the purposeful action both. This is the ideal balance. The Zen *prajna* and the Sufi *kashf* tend to unite these two apparently separate functions into one simultaneous, and ultimately practical, process. When one reaches this stage, then one's impressions become revelations. Thus are the eyes of the Bodhisattva opened—not the slight faculties of self-presumed psychics, but the grand sight of one whose being is identified equally with God and humanity, with Heaven and earth.

GATHEKA: For instance, a person wants to have peaches, but at the same time very much attracted to the flower of the peach. One thinks the flower is beautiful, and then the idea comes: why not let it remain on the plant? That will make the person decide not to pick it. This gives him or her a stimulus, because first desire wanted to take hold of it, then sense wanted to work with it; and as light comes from friction, so also does will come from friction.

TASAWWUF: Desire may be natural, but its friction with sense and conscience produces that light that is the divine intelligence operating as will. The cross is an excellent example of both light and friction. The friction caused by depriving one's being of the false ego results in real light, real will, and the discovery of one's true nature.

GATHEKA: The power of will is in controlling, in contrast with imagination, which works without control for if one wants to control it one spoils it. Nothing in the world, either in the sphere of the mind or on the physical plane, can move without the power of will. But while with one thing the power of will is in absolute control, with the other it is working automatically.

TASAWWUF: Examples of the will in the modes of absolute control and of automatic working can be experienced in the Sufi practices of *tasawwuri Muhammad* and *Akhlak Allah*. In *tasawwuri Muhammad* one makes a deliberate, devotional and willing effort to identify with the being of the Prophet, usually in the form of Walk. This practice requires considerable concentration, even a certain tension, for the perfection of control (and perhaps the control of perfection) to manifest. The tension, the sobriety, the control all result from the striving to maintain absolute spiritual poise in the midst of *nafsaniat* [consciousness of the individual self], of *samsara*.

The *Akhlak Allah*, which is to say the practice of living and moving and having our being in Allah directly, is much more automatic and spontaneous. There is no one way to describe *Akhlak Allah*, for each soul has its unique means of rapport with and expression of its creator. To quote a familiar saying, one "lets go, and lets God." Yet even in the *Akhlak Allah*, with all its ecstasy and freedom, one begins with *willing* surrender. What may begin as a dance of *fana*, may culminate in a dance of *baqa*. And while the initial will to surrender may seem imperfect or even awkward, the more one practices the letting go of self in God's presence, the more one experiences the perfection of will— replete with purpose, plan, and all manner of blessings.

It is often wise to follow the *tasawwuri Muhammad* practice with that of *Akhlak Allah*, for in this way one learns the actual values and effects of sobriety and tension on the one hand, and of bliss and ease on the other hand. Even the generality is coming to realize the wisdom of relaxation after effort.

GATHEKA: There is another enemy of willpower and that is the power of desire. Sometimes this robs willpower of its strength. Sometimes willpower, by a conflict with desire, becomes strong.

TASAWWUF: By giving in to excessive desires, by indulging every habit and whim, one's power of will is weakened. A kind of dry rot invades one's fiber. When one deludes oneself that one can coast along smoothly in *nafsaniat*, one has certainly pulled the wool over one's own eyes.

But when one fights the excess and indulgence of desires and questionable habits, one is practicing the battle of life faithfully. This striving to overcome the attachments and habits that drag one's spirit downward is one aspect of the "middle way" preached by the Lord Buddha. One neither pampers oneself nor does one become blind and fanatical in the fight. One keeps progressing towards the ideal of God, of truth, and finds life's balance in so doing. In this balance is real strength of will.

GATHEKA: The self-denial taught in the Bible generally means the crushing of desires. It should not be taken as a principle but as a process. Those who have taken it as a principle have lost. Those who have taken it as a process have gained.

TASAWWUF: This means that those who merely philosophize against ego attachments, without employing practical efforts to this end, are self-deluded and lost. But those who actually embark upon a course to crush the ego and its nonsense are those who gain the victory.

GATHEKA: The enemy of sense, of wisdom, is the lack of tranquility of mind. When the mind is tranquil it produces the right thought, and wisdom naturally rises as a fountain.

TASAWWUF: We have sense, and we have wisdom. Sense is the ability to make decisions that will promote practicality and benefit the everyday life. Wisdom, which begins with impression, advances to intuition and culminates in insight (*kashf*), is the spirit of guidance and the reliance thereupon. This wisdom is the so-called "fountain of youth," which Ponce de Leon failed to find in Florida. If he had sought it in his own heart, he might have found the reality.

GATHEKA: The Sufis have therefore taught different exercises, both in physical and in meditative form, in order to make the mind tranquil, so that the wisdom that is there may spring up as a fountain.

TASAWWUF: The value of certain postures, of prayer, meditation and concentration, are all presented fully in the early chapters and commentaries of this work. In fact, the original commentator did not stop with simple postures but also brought the values of spiritual Walk and Dance to the attention of the reader. The Walk and Dance bring the rewards of active devotion, as contrasted with the rewards of the more reposeful arts of *hatha yoga* and *zazen*.

A careful study of the world's different religious cultures will show why certain forms of practice predominate in the Far East, while other forms are practiced in the Middle East. Much of traditional practice is just that: tradition. It may or may not produce the desired result, depending on certain factors, chiefly the presence of a realized teacher who has the power of spiritual transmission.

In the Western world today and particularly in America, there are many representatives of the various Eastern schools, some quite tradition-bound and some others less so. It's one thing to recognize that there is an advanced human evolution in the West, especially among the young people, and yet to apply traditional but possibly inappropriate disciplines. It is wisdom to fathom the real needs of the actual people involved, and to provide the practices that will awaken bodies, hearts and souls to the divine presence.

No doubt there is need for both active and passive endeavor. The wise teacher will know what to give to individuals and to groups to produce the balanced unfoldment. For the wise teacher's wisdom has its source in that person's superior ability to be a pupil. It is this earnest ability that keeps the fountain of wisdom flowing.

GATHEKA: It is not in disturbed water that one can see one's image reflected; it is in the still water that one can see one's image clearly. Our heart is likened to water, and when it is still, wisdom springs up by itself. It is wisdom and will together that work toward successful outcome.

TASAWWUF: So much of real spiritual practice is solely for the purpose of stilling the mind, calming the emotions. Once this is accomplished, there is really not much more to do except to await the favor of Allah. But who is doing the waiting? When we become perfected in the tranquility, there is only Allah. And then we realize who has been waiting for whom.

GATHEKA: Willpower is systematically developed by first disciplining the body. The body must sit in the prescribed posture. It must stand in the place it is asked to stand in. The body should not become restless or tired by what is asked of it, but it should answer the demands of the person to whom it belongs.

TASAWWUF: The postures and movements connected with the Islamic *nimaz* (daily prayers) were given by the Prophet Muhammad in order to restore a certain wisdom that had been lost through the decay of previous traditions. This wisdom has been called "movement in accord with psychic law," which is to say movement that unifies one's body, mind and attitude into a devotional whole.

Modern Sufism has reaffirmed this approach with the introduction of the Walks of the Divine Attributes and the Dances of Universal Peace, all incorporating movements which accompany a divine name or phrase. The integration of these movements with the sacred phrase can attract very high and noble forms of magnetism from the space, and at the same time can impregnate the immediate and not-so-immediate atmosphere with these magnetic qualities.

No doubt the movements associated with certain forms of *zikr* also follow the same principle. But as a contemporary Sufi Murshid has declared, "What must remain is the sacred phrase. This, the sacred phrase and not the form, is the foundation of development along this line." While the divine phrase may be all-sufficient, still the combination of phrase with proper movements can augment the instilling of *baraka* upon earth.

Regular practice of these devotional methods in the same room or space can result in the accumulation of *baraka* to such an extent that centers of living-love-magnetism are established. These centers were known as *thebes*, or arks of refuge, in ancient Egypt. Our own meditation rooms today may serve the same purposes of sanctuary and shelter from the vicissitudes of life, and lead to the purification, revivification and healing of body, heart and soul promised in the prayer Nayaz [of Hazrat Inayat Khan].

When we praise Allah through the Beautiful Names using the right movements, we are positive-izing the space and at the same time feeling the exaltation that heartfelt praise to Allah must bring. This positive side is most important, for sooner or later all human beings recognize their need before Allah. It is the presence of *baraka* that will refresh and restore when, in our need, we come in willing surrender to these places of refuge.

Muhammad has said, "Praise Allah in times of prosperity, and surrender to Him in times of adversity." When this becomes our practice, we may be assured of meeting all the demands of life.

GATHEKA: The moment Sufis begin to discipline their bodies, they begin to see how undisciplined it always was. Then they find out that this body, which they have always called "mine," "myself," and for whose comfort they have done everything they could, that this infidel seems to be most disobedient, most faithless.

TASAWWUF: The overcoming of physical desires such as eating, drinking or sex passion—particularly to excess—requires effort, often repeated effort and sometimes great effort. But if one keeps up the effort, and relies more and more upon the aid of God's Name, (and less and less upon personal strain), the ability to keep the body under control of one's will comes with surprising swiftness.

It is most important to inculcate with positivity and cheerfulness the vocal or mental repetition of God's name in all of life's endeavors, even in situations of ease! The rhythm of God's name as a background to all we do can be a protection and a sustenance. And when we bring God's name to the foreground, or the divine name comes to the foreground of itself, the sunshine of devotion and purity scatters the dark clouds of excessive bodily desires. This experience of overcoming the restlessness and faithlessness of the body is well known to the spiritual student. But in this overcoming, the "infidel" of the body becomes a "believer."

In the Hebrew Bible the psalmist sings, "The earth is the Lord's and the fullness thereof." In the Christian Bible it says, "The body is the temple of the spirit." Both of these teachings indicated that the complete spiritual realization must penetrate and enliven every atom of the body. It is this condition that led the companions of Muhammad to exclaim, "He cast no shadow in the noonday sun!"

GATHEKA: After that comes the discipline of the mind. This is done by concentration. When the mind is thinking of something else and one wishes it to think on one specific thought, then the mind becomes very restless. It does not want to remain in one spot for it has always been without discipline.

TASAWWUF: As the body benefits from the discipline of certain postures, so the mind benefits from concentrating on certain themes. In the Buddha's *jhanas* [a practice also called the *mahamudra*—ed.], the themes of love, joy and peace are presented. When an individual or group performs the *jhanas* with wholehearted concentration, not only are individual minds benefited but the group mind is unified and benefited.

And as postures for the body are of little value without consideration of the breath, so the practices involving visual or mental concentration are of little value without some degree of breath-consciousness and heart-consciousness. But when concentration is practiced with breath and heart-feeling, unity comes, calm comes, discipline comes. And while these realizations constitute life-giving hope for beginners, advanced students considers such practice indispensable for their work.

GATHEKA: As soon as one disciplines it, it becomes like a restive horse that one has to master. The difficulty starts when one tries to concentrate. It begins to jump, while at other times it only moves about. This happens because the mind is an entity. It feels as a wild horse would feel: "Why should I be troubled by you?"

TASAWWUF: Despite the mind's quicksilver-like nature, it is much more readily concentrated, calmed and unified when the appropriate divine attributes are given. The *jhanas* of Lord Buddha have been mentioned above, and all religious traditions have forms of concentration upon themes deriving from heart and soul, from God. The Ninety-Nine Beautiful Names of Allah are especially beloved by the Sufis. Yogis chant the sacred *mantrams* in Sanskrit, and Hebrew is regarded as a sacred language. While all languages may not be "mantric" as such, all sincere praise in any language helps to concentrate the mind toward an appreciation of the inner life, toward the treasures of heaven.

The wise teacher will give positive and appropriate themes to disciples to concentrate upon. The wise teacher, like the prophet Isaiah, believes that "comfort ye my people" is best for spiritual progress. Therefore, the teacher will not demand that pupils sit in painful postures nor give themes for concentration that are not in accord with the pupil's purpose and direction in life.

This is much better than forcing any kind of discomfort upon body or mind and expecting positive results therefrom. Such tyranny would make even a tame horse rebel. Life has enough pains as it is, and the characteristics of the teacher presented in the prayer Pir [of Hazrat Inayat Khan] are sufficient for balanced heart awakening. Only in the most critical cases do teachers of Sufism employ seemingly harsh methods, and they never like to be that way.

GATHEKA: But the mind is meant to be an obedient servant, just as the body is meant to become an obedient tool to experience life with. If they are not in order, if they do not act as one wishes them to, then one cannot hope for real happiness, real comfort in life.

TASAWWUF: The Buddhist considers that mind and body are as one, and the Sufi would not disagree. Indeed, the Sufi—realizing the heart awakening—discovers the bliss and peace of the inner life only when the mind and body repose in the divine presence, either passively as in *zazen* or other forms of silent *yoga* (union), vocally as in mantric endeavor, or actively as in spiritual Walk, Dance or *Akhlak Allah*.

All such practices help bring life to body and mind, and healing to the spirit. More could be said, but it is practice—and not philosophy—that brings the blessing.

GATHEKA: The will can become so strong that it controls the body, making it perfectly healthy. But one may ask, what about death then? Death is not something foreign to willpower. Even death is caused by willpower.

TASAWWUF: Taken from the mystical point of view, the adept indeed attempts to bring the pearl of immortality up from the depths of life's ocean. In other words, s/he "dies before death" to realize the life everlasting. This mystical "death" is caused, at least in part, by the adept's power of will.

But the relative roles of the adept's will and the descent of divine grace in the achievement of spiritual illumination must remain among the secrets of the "great mystery." One Sufi teacher has said, "It is all divine grace, but we should act as if it came through effort."

GATHEKA: One thinks one does not invite one's death. Indeed one does not, but the personal will becomes feeble and the greater Will impresses this feeble will, turning it into itself. For the smaller will belongs to the greater Will. Sufis call the former *Kadr* and the latter *Kaza*. *Kaza* reflects upon *Kadr* its command, and the latter unconsciously accepts it.

TASAWWUF: To make a long story short, life is a series of stages like the different movements in a symphony. The final note in that symphony is sounded, or silenced, at the moment of our physical death. But the final note here is the first note of life in the Hereafter. All aspects of life, from the seen to the Unseen, lead sooner or later to the source and goal of All whom we call God.

It is the command of *Kaza*, which is indicated in Holy Qur'an: "Verily, unto Him is our return."

The initiate strives to merge with the command of *Kaza* wholeheartedly and consciously. At the same time one attempts to fulfill all one's responsibilities on earth, considering them as a most sacred trust given by God. Thus, the life of the initiate requires tremendous balance, often accompanied by pain. But the awakening to the light of love makes the path of initiation and discipleship the most worthy pursuit in this world or any other.

It is the ordinary person who remains unconscious and blind through life and whose return to God is beset with adversity, limitation and inertia—all from ignorance of the divine teachings, which are for everyone.

GATHEKA: On the surface a person may still want to live, but in the depth one has resigned oneself to die. If one did not resign oneself to death, one would not die. In the depth of one's being one becomes resigned to death before one's life is taken away.

TASAWWUF: In the depth of a human being is found the life of God, of the soul. The spheres of mind and heart do not reach to this great depth. Therefore it is said that man (*manas*, mind) is resigned to death. In other words, all phases of the temporal existence must eventually give way to eternity.

Qur'an says, "All is perishing except thy Face." And Jesus Christ declared, "Heaven and earth shall pass away, but my words shall not pass away."

There may be surface residues which, like honey, can cause temporary adhesions both from stickiness and from addiction to its sweetness. But this does not go on forever. At a certain stage in one's evolution, one begins to lose one's taste for the sweetnesses of the physical life. All that one once held near and dear begins to fade in its importance. This is not to say that love disappears, for God is love and abides everlastingly. It is rather to say that *loves* disappear. It is like Orpheus who had to leave the love of Eurydice's form behind in order to achieve the love of her essence—for essence calling to essence is to experience the perfection of love, the *agape*, the Holy Communion with one and all.

GATHEKA: Resignation of the human will to the divine will is the real crucifixion.

TASAWWUF: This resignation is none other than the willing surrender given for the sake of living the life in God, of God.

There is a *hatha yoga* posture called the "corpse position" that represents involuntary surrender, but Sufis and devotees of Christ can practice the "cross position" in which the arms are out-stretched instead of at the sides. This represents the voluntary surrender to the divine will, the willing sacrifice of the limited being to the Unlimited.

GATHEKA: After that crucifixion, follows resurrection.

TASAWWUF: This is considered of such importance that the theme is iterated twice in succession in Holy Qur'an: "Verily, with every difficulty cometh ease; verily, with every difficulty cometh ease."

The real difficulty is the crucifixion of our falseness. The real ease is the rebirth into the holiness of eternity and truth.

GATHEKA: One can come to this by seeking the pleasure of God, and it is not difficult once one has begun to seek the pleasure of God. It is only when one does not begin to try that one does not know what the pleasure of God is.

TASAWWUF: To begin with we must never take the name or names of God for granted. It is God's pleasure that God's name be called upon with all devotion and concentration and love, and never as in Aesop's tale of the boy who cried, "Wolf, wolf!" Yes, it is God's pleasure that we strive, that we put forth effort in our work—for effort is a form of grace that cannot be denied. But even more important than effort, which is mostly confined to the earthly and mental spheres, is the awakening to love. This is so beautifully given by Christ when he says, "consider the lilies of the field; they toil not, neither do they spin."

To reach this stage is more than pleasure, it is ecstasy. Yet if one does not try, one may wait for the ecstasy world without end.

GATHEKA: But apart from this there is another lesson that the Sufis have taught: to seek the pleasure of one's fellow, and this is the very thing that one usually refuses to do. One is quite willing to do the pleasure of God, but when one asks one to seek the pleasure of one's fellow, she or he refuses.

TASAWWUF: There is no better way to seek the pleasure of one's brothers and sisters than to efface one's self entirely, than to look at the situation as God is seeing it—with all the possibilities of love, harmony and beauty ready to be brought from latency to manifestation. This may seem like a "tall order," so to speak, but really speaking there is no more viable way to see the work of God accomplished than to lose the self in the divine glory. Real spiritual unfoldment may begin with the awakening of the so-called individual heart, but it culminates when we awaken to universality, to all-ness. And like the Good Samaritan in the Gospels, there will be no one we can refuse for everyone will be an immanence of Christ.

GATHEKA: In either case, however, one is seeking the pleasure of one and the same Being.

TASAWWUF: The first American Murshid, Sufi Ahmed Murad Chisti, was once asked by a group of Shias (Muslims who revere Ali), "Was Ali as great or greater than Muhammad?" The Murshid replied,

"Ali was always aware of Allah. Muhammad was aware of Allah and of humanity as well. Thus he was the Perfect Human Being." The Shias accepted this explanation.

We also have the poetry of Jelaluddin Rumi: "Whether you have loved a human being or whether you have loved God, if you have loved enough you will be brought in the end into the presence of the supreme Love itself."

And in the Sufi Invocation given by Pir-o-Murshid Inayat Khan, the opening lines of the two stanzas are *"Toward the One"* and *"United With All."* Realization of these phrases awaken one to the knowledge of the Only Being.

GATHEKA: One begins with resignation, but once one has learnt to be resigned in life and when one is tuned to the divine will, one does not need to be resigned for one's wish becomes the divine impulse.

TASAWWUF: This resignation is not different from the *La illaha* of *zikr*. It is transmitted as philosophy in the Prajna Paramita Hridaya Sutra: "All things are in essence empty." But this does not mean empty of essence; the emptiness is of all limitation.

The shadows of limitation teach us resignation to the Light of the divine presence, in which no shadows ever were or are. The lesson of this resignation is taught over and over again until we finally see, become and manifest that Light forevermore. Thus is achieved the *el il Allah* of *zikr*, wherein the attunement to the divine will is made perfect.

This is the end of "mental purification," in which is fulfilled the purpose of the human being, of the individual. Then begins the fulfillment of the purpose of God.

The latter purpose is the unceasing work of the spiritual hierarchy.

The Ultimate Season (poem 1979)

The Tree of Life has dropped another leaf.
Into the eddying stream it falls—
A gaily painted raft
Curling at the edges,
Moving swiftly toward the great river.
If this leaf-life makes it past
The ox-bow,
The ocean of perfection
Will be in sight!

About Effacement and Nirvana (letter 1979)

(Editor's note: From a letter to Mansur Johnson concerning the difference between the Sufi state of fana or effacement and the spiritual practice of tasawwuri, a type of Sufi "gestalt" exercise in which one actively imagines that one is inside the breath, atmosphere and body awareness of a teacher.)

September 12, 1979

Dear Mansur,
As-salaam aleikhum!

I can only agree wholeheartedly with everything you say concerning *"fana* Inayat." Your comments are balanced and clear—yet there is a sense of limitation too, which I am sure you realized as you penned each word. I could respond, but it would only be of the same nature: limited by the very words the mind would use in its attempt to clarify principles, remembrances and deep feelings based on one's realizations.

Murshid used to say, "I am the proof of Hazrat Inayat Khan." But even if all Murshid's disciples were to relate all their experiences and realizations, inner and outer, it would only be a thimble full of water compared to the ocean.

In a similar vein, I overheard Murshid tell Allaudin about a notion the American composer Henry Cowell had: "No matter how perfect and seemingly complete a musical composition may be, at best it can only serve to show the infinitude of perfection and completion that was not expressed." It's rather like Murshid's lesson with regard to kinetic and potential energy.

So rather than launch into a tome of commentary on your words concerning aspects of *fana*, allow me to quote a few words of Elisabeth de Jong-Keesing from her new book, *Inayat Answers*: 'Fana may be compared to the Buddhist term for the ultimate goal, *Nirvana*, in that it represents an annihilation of the individual's limited qualities, and fusion into the Whole. This fusion is reached through graded experiences. First the individual personality, then the spirit, then the innermost being, the soul, accomplish *fana* on their own plane of being...."

And a quote from Hazrat Inayat: "In this condition of *Nirvana* or highest consciousness, however, one is conscious all through the body as much as of the soul. During this experience a person lives fully."

Nor should we forget that it was Pir-o-Murshid's yell at Murshid during the "Six Interviews" that gave our Murshid the key to mastery in this life. Wali Ali will attest to that.

Like I say, instead of responding with a tome (which I seem to have already begun...) let me simply enclose a copy of Murshid's paper called "Risalyat." I haven't even read it recently, but it does take up matters involving the stages of *fana*; and one's first impression upon reading your letter was to send you the Risalyat paper. Perhaps you already have the paper; but you may not, as my secretary only found it last year in the Mentorgarten files after much rummaging around. I consider Risalyat to be a Sangitha-level lesson.

One's various concentrations in many realms have been dropping away one by one as the body continues to deteriorate. Last night I gave what may be my last public Sufi meeting; and while I plan to inaugurate this year's Githas tomorrow night, I have slipped several notches physically and mentally since your visit, so I may drop the Githa class too unless some dramatic turn-around takes place. I do plan, *inshallah*, to carry through with my *darshan* set for the 22nd of this month; but even *darshan* is almost too much. The only factor in my favor is that *darshan* is given in the mornings—a time when one has a modicum of *urouj* [initiating, "up"] energy. But evenings are proving to be just too damned rough.

It is difficult to convey to a healthy man the vicissitudes of mind and body that one struggles to live through, but the above should give you some idea.

On the subject of your vision of a shrine for Murshid near Navajo, Arizona, let me be frank. No, I feel no connection whatever with your concentration there—though I can certainly appreciate my friend's vision. To be even more frank, I am somehow reminded of the day Murshid died, and without apparently asking anyone present about supper arrangements, you went ahead and bought Chinese food and brought it back to the hospital for people to eat. It pained me to see that no one wanted it. The ironic thing is that most of us ended up going to the Starview *[a Chinese restaurant near the Mentorgarten in San Francisco]* for supper that evening. In a way, I see the seeds of your long-standing dissociation from the Ruhaniat having been planted in such wise.

But, God bless you, you have worked and loved hard to fulfill more than a narrow *tasawwuri Murshid* based more or less upon raw initiative. The promise of love, harmony and beauty has been borne out, *alhamdulillah!* I think all of us have experienced the journey from Murshid's rugged and radioactive exterior to his heart-of-hearts. A real

Murshid contains all the *fanas* and is able to impart them, through grace, to capable disciples as they advance from capacity to greater capacity.

In answer to Pir Vilayat, I would remark the words of his blessed father: "There is one Teacher and that is God; we are all His pupils."

With love and blessings,

Moineddin

P.S. Mansur, just as I lay down for my afternoon nap, shortly after finishing the preceding letter, I realized something. When you said "...the feeling was, even in the being of Hazrat Inayat Khan, one of limitation—like a painter, say, who can reproduce Van Gogh's perfectly..." I realized that you weren't talking about *fana*, but about *tasawwuri*. *Tasawwuri* can lead to that feeling, in my experience, because the attunement itself is limited to the limiting factors in the mind and heart of the practitioner. *Tasawwuri* is mostly based on the effort of the disciple.

But real *fana* is something else. It's all grace, and there is no limitation as we conceive it or even feel it. If one is in *fana-fi-sheikh* one experiences everyone one encounters as the very image and being of their sheikh, all veils stripped away, no obstructions. And if the being of one's sheikh has also been bathed in the reality of Rassoul, then *fana* in one's sheikh can also manifest in the disciple seeing his or her divine ideal in everyone—or even as Murshid says in his poem "Crescent and Heart"—"The stones were my Avatars, each blossom, my Prophet, my Rassoul." And so on. That's *fana*; the other is a stage of *tasawwuri*.

Last Poem (1979)

A solitary, aging pine
enters winter.
Snow bends limb
and bough, while dreams
of springtide stir
in the needles.
Here—the fragrance
sought by the journeying
caravans.

—November 23, 1979

Releasing Negative Impressions (letter 1980)

(Editor's note: From a letter to a mureed.)

February 22, 1980

As-salaam aleikhum!
Thank you for your letter of February 18. We will miss you on Thursday nights, but it will make your Murshid very happy just to know that you will be by your husband's side instead.

Your concern with the negative impressions left as a residue from certain slide presentations in two of your art courses is really one of the greatest problems facing Western "culture" and American "culture" in particular. This is not to say that the problem lies with art courses—or even with the more outrageous insults that bombard us every day in the ads for sleazy films, and perhaps even more insidious use by Madison Avenue of what are called "hidden persuaders" rampant in all phases of advertising.

Yes, one does have very strong feelings about this subject; and one has only been able to overcome such impressions through the grace of his Murshid and through the use of certain wazifas, notably *Subhan Allah*. (*Allaho Akbar* seems to work better in situations where actual physical danger is apparent, such as a bad accident or natural disaster.) Mostly I use these phrases on the breath, but vocal repetition is never wrong.

I am going to quote the first paragraph from a chapter called "Overlooking" found in volume eight of *The Sufi Message* by Hazrat Inayat Khan:

"There is a tendency which gradually manifests in a person who is advancing spiritually, and that tendency is overlooking, or *darquza* as the Sufis call it. At times this tendency might appear to be negligence, but negligence is not overlooking; negligence is not looking. In other words, overlooking may be called rising above things. One has to rise in order to overlook; the one who stands beneath life could not overlook anything even if he wanted to. Overlooking is a manner of graciousness, it means to look and at the same time not to look...not to be hurt or harmed or disturbed by something, not even minding it. It is an attribute of nobleness of nature, it is the sign of souls who are tuned to a higher key."

Now in my second paragraph I stated that the problem did not lie with the apparent manifestations of reprehensible "art" or advertising.

No, the source of the problem is to be found in our own weak areas, those areas where we have not attained sufficient concentration to overcome and master these negative impressions which occasionally find an echo in the less awakened strata of our being.

Therefore I would recommend the words of His Holiness, the present Dalai Lama, with regard to *dharma*: "The meaning of *dharma* is to have compassion for *karma*."

All love and blessings,
Murshid Moineddin

The Kidneys of Our Hearts (letter 1980)

(Editor's note: From a letter to a mureed in May 1980, written just before an attempted kidney transplant operation in July.)

I tried to do my first Thursday night class last week but had to ask Fatima to take over because I got nauseated. I did manage to concentrate on the mureeds in the afternoon however, and that has been the high point of my week.... It is funny, now that I want to live, I feel instead the slow dissolve of faculties, and worst of all the inexorable trend toward actual physical paralysis. One can barely navigate the stairs anymore.

I tell you all this not to add to the already considerable weight you are shouldering for your community, but to let you know that all pain is but the blink of an eye. Allah is the Cherisher and Sustainer of all the worlds. Murshid is ever-present, even more so in what we erroneously perceive as his "absence."

There is nothing but Love, and if we feel the brief crucifixions that improve our *fana* let us keep Allah foremost in our heart-breath. It is all a process, at once enlightened and eternal, and also a gradual awakening according to our innocence, strength, purity and love. But until these latter become entirely of Allah, instead of "ours," there will be more need for some little pain.

Also, the world's condition is being poured through the kidneys of our hearts. Why should it be otherwise? We asked for this before the beginning of time.

Now let us be who we are.

A Large Golden Key (letter 1980)

(Editor's note: From a letter to Mansur Johnson.)

Noor Mahal
August 5, 1980

My dear Mansur,

As-salaam aleikhum! I am very glad we were able to see each other shortly after my transplant operation. (Murshid was forever telling us that the usual result of his encounters with other holy men was: "Let's have some tea!" Do you think we qualify?)

I returned home from the hospital—sans kidney—on August 1. I had started to lose any sense of having either an anchor or rudder. I felt adrift in an atmosphere increasingly not my own. I simply needed to come home. So I insisted on it and, despite their wish for me to remain longer, Moineddin got his way, inshallah.

As it turned out, practically the whole household were attending the annual Mendocino Camp. This is exactly "what the doctor ordered." I had three days with no one here but my kids, Ananda (out from Boxwood Lane Farm [Virginia] to watch the kids while Fatima was at Camp), Hridaya (a very faithful helper and disciple, though a non-resident) and Salaman and Christine Coy. Those three days enabled me to recoup all my nebulous energies until I felt whole again. I really feel that a kind of small miracle happened—for which all praise is due to Allah. Atmospheres can teach us so much if only we would listen keenly and with peaceful hearts.

Mostly one is taking this present time to let things sift and clarify. A major decision will have to be made sooner than later regarding one's physical condition. My bone and joint pain has increased somewhat since I entered the hospital, and I also lost three more pounds. This loss of weight not only decreases one's strength. It also increased the aforementioned pain plus rendering more difficult any type of treatment requiring intramuscular injections.

If I do choose to attempt another transplant, inshallah, they will no doubt need to use a new experimental drug, which is given by injection. So, I am trying my best to regain some of the weight I lost. Gosh, Mansur, do you realize that I weigh less than at least two of the women in my house?

All right, enough of this.

Nooria painted me a beautiful watercolor. In the foreground are prison bars, but beyond them lies a many-colored land with a large golden key. The painting is entitled "Freedom."
Good luck with your many concentrations, and much love from us all...

Om Sri Ram Jai Ram Jai Jai Ram!
Moineddin

IV. Depths of the Self and Soul

Editor's note:

As Moineddin describes below, his life's journey after his successful kidney transplant in January 1981 took him from impending death into uncharted territory—resurrection and new life.

The section begins with an interview from 1992 in which he describes the outer and inner changes that led him to move to Hawaii and remarry. With the help of the Rev. Frida Waterhouse, one of Murshid S.A.M.'s colleagues, and later Harvey Grady, Moineddin begins to "illuminate the shadow" that his spiritual practice had not previously touched. He also begins a personal counseling practice in Hawaii and gradually articulates a way of working that he later termed "Soulwork."

This way, which has much in common with the native Hawaiian mysticism of Huna as well as with other "inner dialogue" techniques, became for Moineddin an evolving inner story, with various characters that appear and disappear, enabling him to articulate in archetypal language the non-rational, instinctive side of life. This is nothing other than the unity of purusha (life energy) and prakriti *(creative body) in Hindu terms, or of* zat *(divine essence) and* sifat *(divine activity in form) in Sufi ones. This interplay also features in all great folkloric and mythic stories of humanity, which is one of the reasons that Moineddin avidly began to tell fairy tales and Sufi stories. In this sense, his "Soulwork" was never meant to be a cognitive psychological "system." For him, that would have meant putting the logic, discursive mind back in charge. Instead, Soulwork became for him a language, an unfolding story in which the further adventures of all the characters were always towards greater integration and health.*

Because his own health (as well as the Ruhaniat's finances) did not permit him to travel widely in space, he travelled inwardly more intensively, with a view to healing qualities within himself. By so doing, he used the Sufi practice of mushahida *(inner witnessing) to also heal the community that he held in trust. This practice of holding one's outer community or region in one's heart-awareness as part of one's inner work features heavily in the paper on mastery of Murshid Samuel Lewis, quoted earlier. Moineddin also found inspiration in the work of Hermann Hesse and C.G. Jung. In one of the books Moineddin mentions in a letter from 1984, Jung is quoted:*

> "If the archetype, which is universal, i.e., identical with itself always and anywhere, is properly dealt with in one place only, it is influenced as a whole, i.e., simultaneously and everywhere. Thus an old alchemist gave the following consolation to one of his disciples: 'No matter how isolated you are and how lonely you feel, if you do your work truly and conscientiously, unknown friends will come and seek you.' It seems to me that nothing essential has ever been lost, because its matrix is ever present with us and from this it can and will be reproduced if needed. But those who can recover it have learned the art of averting their eyes from the blinding light of current opinions and close their ears to the noise of ephemeral slogans."
>
> —From Miguel Serrano, C.G. Jung and Hermann Hesse: A Record of Two Friendships.

Letters, poems and articles from this period follow the initial interview, culminating in Moineddin's final review of his life's inner process in Soulwork terms a year before he passed, entitled "Uniting the one to the One."

All during the period of 1981-2001 Moineddin, as the Pir of the Ruhaniat community and as a Sufi guide for individual mureeds, continued to handle the same types of questions and challenges that he did previously. This is described in the next section. What changed for him was his deeper attunement, intention and understanding of his whole self, which were born from difficult inner work. While one can never really separate a person's inner process from her or his outer one, the writings in this section provide the "roots" from which to view the "fruits," the outer activity described in the next one.

We find some of Moineddin's best writing from this period in personal correspondence with mureeds and colleagues, some of which is excerpted here and in the following section. In one letter, he emphasizes the honesty that had enabled his own personal healing and which he tried to maintain throughout the rest of his life. This honesty, which sometimes saw him being "not nice," was often misunderstood by his colleagues and fellow students of Murshid Samuel Lewis, many of whom subsequently went through similar inner and outer experiences in life, only not so publicly. The picture that we have of Moineddin in much of this section is of an "extra-ordinary ordinariness," a very human life, lived in small, but with much, much wider influence. It is simply because of his honesty that we know as much about it as we do.

In this sense, Moineddin tried to follow the words of Jesus in the Gospel of Thomas:

"*If you bring forth what is within you, what is within you will save you. If you fail to bring forth what is within you, what is within you will destroy you.*"

Ferment of the Earth's Evolution: "We Are All Becoming Bridges" (1992)

(Editor's note: This is part two of the interview with the Sound newsletter conducted via email in 1992. The first part can be found in section one, "Meeting the Teacher." In this half, Moineddin recounts the story of how he found his life changed after 1980. The interviewer was Vasheest Davenport, another mureed of Murshid Samuel L. Lewis.)

THE SOUND: Over the past decade there has been much contrasting of the disciplines of mysticism and psychology. In your view, how do these disciplines relate to one another?

Moineddin: The relationship between mysticism and psychology is the story of my life. Because it is a story, I must give you a wide-ranging and deeply personal answer. I believe it will be an answer that will resonate in the bodies, minds and hearts of many readers.

I was raised in the Roman Catholic Church and had faith in everything I was taught about God, morality and sexuality. Now, along with the rest of society and its institutions, the Catholic Church has undergone dramatic change and growth since my formative years in the 1940's and '50s. But what I was dealing with as a teenager—Elvis had just hit the charts with "Heartbreak Hotel" and "You Ain't Nothin' But A Hound Dog"—was a Church that told me I would go to hell if I masturbated or had premarital sex.

Naturally I rebelled. Despite the painful burden of guilt I carried for "violating" my religion and "sinning" against God, the joyous sexual feelings I was experiencing began to teach me about Nature herself. I was terribly split inside, but I would not, could not, return to a religion that spoke against my direct human experience.

Through my early twenties, I paid little attention to psychology and none at all to mysticism. My initially enthusiastic rebellion had degenerated into heavy drinking, partying, and one-night stands. I was basically sleepwalking my way through life. The only bright lights in my world were my love for folk music and an active participation in the civil rights and peace movements.

Little did I realize the surprise in store for me one hot summer evening in 1965, when one of my friends handed me a small white pill and said, "Try this, it's called LSD." I thought it would be like the uppers or downers or tranquilizers I had taken before. Like I say, it was quite a surprise. The whole world changed before my eyes.

I immediately joined the psychedelic revolution. The various inner experiences my friends and I had throughout that year transformed us inside and out. The flower of our idealism burst open and we became truth seekers. Many of us became mystics. All we wanted was union with God. Nor were we alone. Our whole generation was beginning to "tune in, turn on and drop out."

Who would become our most articulate spokesperson? None other than the Harvard psychologist Richard Alpert, one of the founding editors of our dog-eared bible *The Psychedelic Review*. A year later he would travel to India, meet his Guru, and return to this country as Baba Ram Dass. So for us there is this connection between psychology and mysticism from the outset.

But before we go further, let's define our terms. It has been said that a mystic seeks to find God hidden in light, and that a psychologist seeks to find truth hidden in shadow. Another definition: the mystic seeks union with God through love; the psychologist seeks integration with Self through knowledge. Are these the same or different? Clearly, both disciplines require deep inner intelligence and feeling if they are to succeed.

Sufism—divine wisdom—teaches that mysticism and psychology are inseparable. The mature mystic will always have a profound knowledge of psychology, and the mature psychologist will always have a profound love of God. The enlightened Hazrat Ali said, "Know your Self, and you will know God."

In the heyday of the psychedelic revolution however, psychology and religion were both shunned as unenlightened tools of straight society. Mystical seeking became a way to reject the values of our parents and the "establishment" on the one hand, and to embrace our newfound freedom in higher consciousness on the other. In this way, the spiritual nucleus of the hippie counterculture or "love generation" was born.

A quarter of a century has passed since then, years filled with the rise of many socially and spiritually significant consciousness-raising movements. Eastern gurus flocked to America to lead the truth-seeking young people beyond psychedelics in their search for God. Hippie activists demonstrated *en masse* to end the Vietnam War. The women's movement challenged, and continues to challenge, obsolete patriarchal models of God, religion, politics and gender roles throughout society. The sexual revolution freed people to express themselves fully and without guilt. The gay liberation movement brought gay men, lesbian women, and bisexual women and men out of the closet and into society's mainstream. The human rights movement monitors government brutality against human beings wherever it occurs. The civil rights movement, routinely undermined by the Reagan and Bush administrations, has nevertheless grown to include the rights of indigenous peoples and racial and ethnic minorities everywhere. The newest of these revolutions is the environmental movement—but the politics of a sane ecology is only the surface of a larger planetary consciousness now emerging. Human sensitivities are deepening every day, every year, every decade. We are moving rapidly toward conscious multi-dimensional rapport with the vast global and spiritual being of Earth—whose healing is our healing, whose evolution is our evolution, whose illumination is our illumination.

All of these movements are direct manifestations of a "new age" of humanity and consciousness. They are vivid and life-affirming expressions of deep-felt needs in the growing planetary psyche.

At their burning core, these revolutions draw from truths so real and self-evident that they are compelled to challenge, defy and overturn prevailing social, religious and governmental norms in order to bring their truths to light. This is the ferment of earth's evolution, and we are its inspired harbingers.

Beloved Ones of God, we too are worlds. Inside each one of us the drama of healing, evolution and illumination is being played out. In the last twenty years we have discovered many old and new psycho-spiritual systems to help us in our unfoldment. We have found the subconscious dimension of our personalities to be home to highly creative and sometimes highly destructive "inner selves." We have found the superconscious dimension of our personalities to be hosted by wise and loving "high selves" whose service is inner guidance.

When we ignore the signals of our inner selves, denying their vital role in our personal and spiritual growth, we reap a harvest of inner conflict, depression and ill health. But when we relate openly and as friends to our inner selves, regarding them as equal partners in our growth process, we experience a living connection with our high selves at will and reap the fruits of love, harmony and beauty.

Now I would like to go on with my story...

When I met Murshid S.A.M. in January of 1967, I had already stopped taking psychedelics. I had experienced *satori* on LSD a few months earlier, and the message I got from that experience was to find a teacher who could lead me to enlightenment through practices, not drugs. I was deeply convinced that this would happen.

A month after I met Murshid, he initiated me into Sufism. Two weeks later he gave me a paperback copy of *Zen Flesh, Zen Bones* and told me, "I'm too busy now to give you regular Sufi practices. In the meantime, take this book and look in the chapter on 'centering.' You'll find 112 meditation practices given there. Read through them and pick one or two that strike you. Do those for your practices until I can properly sit down with you."

I read through all the practices, but only one jumped out at me. It was a meditation that involved breathing in my forehead as I went to sleep. I did the practice faithfully every night for two years. Then one night it happened. I entered a state of spiritual realization. It absolutely transcended all my previous psychedelic experiences, yet at the same time was "nearer than breathing, closer than hands and feet." I had become one with God.

Why, then, after such an awakening, was I still fearful—especially of my own sexual feelings? Had I not just experienced my entire being as utterly and profoundly divine? The answer to that question would come by slow and painful degrees. I did not realize that the patterns of guilt and self-condemnation I had internalized from my Catholic upbringing would soon manifest in my physical body.

In June of 1970 I was diagnosed with kidney failure, and I spent the next five months in the hospital. At one point, close to death, Murshid came and gave me "holy hell." That, and a similar visit from Wali Ali a short time later, had the effect of restoring my health to normal until 1976, when finally my kidneys failed for good.

I spent the next four and a half years on dialysis.

Now you'd think after all that, I might begin to see the light. But despite my spiritual experience, I still subconsciously held the belief that God had divided the universe at my beltline: everything from the chest up was holy; everything below the belt was dark and unworthy. I was sitting on top of a powder keg, and it was about to explode.

In 1980, my body deteriorated to the point where a kidney transplant became mandatory if I was to survive. The physical and psychic burden of my health care weighed heavier and heavier upon my family. I received a transplanted kidney in July of that year which failed. I returned home to a failed marriage. I thought I was going to die and made plans accordingly.

But my slate of lessons was not yet full. In October my transplant surgeon called and said he had a plan that might save my life. I was to receive three months of intensive X-ray treatments at Stanford Medical Center to render my immune system incapable of rejecting a new kidney. When a kidney became available I was to return to San Francisco for the operation. So I moved to the Palo Alto khankah [*the Sufi community nearest to Stanford*] and carried out my doctor's plan. On January 28, 1981, I was summoned to San Francisco to receive the kidney of a young woman who had died of a brain hemorrhage.

The operation was a success. After a slow start, my kidney would last for ten years, opening all the possibilities inherent in a second chance at life. Indeed, I fell in love again, started a new family and returned to the Sufi community a deeply changed man. Instead of dying, I came back to life. But in the beginning I found that life was a lot harder to handle than the slow death I had been living. There was hell to pay, and I was going to pay it.

It began in the hospital one week after the operation. It was February 5, Hazrat Inayat Khan's urs [*anniversary of his passing*]. I was being treated with an experimental drug with powerful side effects. My kidney hadn't started to work yet. I was heartbroken over the breakup of my family. The eight-year-old Hispanic boy on the dialysis machine next to mine died without warning. My mom telephoned to say that my grandmother had just died. The next day my dad called to tell me that my uncle had been killed in a bicycle accident.

WHAT WAS HAPPENING???

Suddenly, all the denied grief, tension and repressed feelings of a lifetime erupted in massive confusion and chaos. Psychologically, I was having a nervous breakdown. Mystically, I was entering a "dark night of the soul." I believed I was going totally and irreversibly insane and closed my eyes...

> *Humpty Dumpty sat on a wall,*
> *Humpty Dumpty had a great fall;*
> *All the king's horses and all the king's men*
> *Couldn't put Humpty together again.*

I called to Murshid S.A.M. to help me. The chaos intensified. I cried to Inayat Khan for healing. The delirium increased. I wept to Allah in heaven to save me. The lid flew off Pandora's box, and the hosts of hell tore me apart.

I opened my eyes and the room was swirling. This is getting serious, I told myself. I'd better ask the nurse for a sleeping pill. I tried closing my eyes again. The demons clamored for my soul. I opened my eyes and asked the nurse for a pill. She gave me a Dalmane, and I swallowed it in the vain hope that relief would come.

Ten minutes passed. No change. Eyes open, purgatory. Eyes closed, hell. An hour passed. I was reaching critical mass. I couldn't hold on any longer. I was going to close my eyes and enter the living hell of eternal damnation. I closed my eyes and surrendered myself to madness.

But instead of spiraling into insanity, I saw a horizontal frame appear. It was like a movie screen that filled my mind. Within the frame, I saw—from behind and from the knees down—the hem of a gray skirt and two legs walking. "What is this?" I asked. Then I realized that the legs belonged to Frida Waterhouse. There was nothing dramatic about this discovery, just peaceful acceptance of seeing her take one step after another in quiet succession. My breath seemed to follow her steps. I was receiving the vision of my own "next step." I was being saved.

A week later my new kidney would kick in.

With that the first half of my life came to a close, and the second half began. It seemed like the turning of an age. It was the turning of an age. Nevertheless, the "dark night of the soul" was not finished with me. It became the womb within which my new life would take shape.

In the spring of 1981, I moved to Hawaii and fell in love with Mei-Ling. The months that followed were a jumble of intense lesson-learning: culture shock, passionate sexuality and bottomless grief all vied for the privilege of shattering my old ego to pieces. Mei-Ling was a powerful healer for me, but we were lovers subjectively involved in our own process, and it was not fair to burden her with my need for treatment. I went into therapy locally, and made plans to see Frida Waterhouse later that year in San Francisco.

To make a long story short, Frida initiated me into the mysteries of spiritual psychology. She taught me how to communicate with my inner selves as the key to personal integration, and with my high self as the key to spiritual integration. She called it, "Uniting the one to the One." She said, "Moineddin, this can be a healing adjunct for you in your Sufi work."

My vision of Frida in the hospital had come true. I followed her footsteps and was healed. In so doing I became a bridge, uniting in my own being death with rebirth, past with future, male with female, above with below, Piscean Age with Aquarian Age, mysticism with psychology, traditional Sufism with the never-ending message of the soul.

Now we are all becoming bridges. Many will cross over *us* into their own light, and become bridges in their turn. "All these things, and greater things, shall you do."

Murshid and Frida are dancing in my heart as I write this. It is a wedding dance they are doing, a joyous wedding dance in a sunlit meadow. They are laughing and singing, telling me something. Their shouts rise above the music.

"Bring more guests! We need more guests!! This is a happy occasion!!!"

Snapshots from Maui (letter 1981)

(Editor's note: From a handwritten letter to friends in the SF Bay area.)

Maui, Hawaii
August 23, 1981

As-salaam aleikhum...and Aloha...

Listening to Richter play "Pictures at an Exhibition" after seeing the movie "Arthur," Mei Ling & I write letters and send pictures to dear friends. It is 9 pm & our light is from a kerosene lamp & candles. And we are happy....
It is (like) learning how to live all over again.
Somehow I wish I were writing this with a conductor's baton.... I would command the finest grace notes to sparkle through these words & lines to you... But why command? The notes are sounding so softly, so brightly, just now!

Let us listen to them together....
All love,
Moineddin & Mei Ling

PS. Snapshot shows the boy [*Moineddin himself*] tying the beanpoles together. Kitchen windows in the background, garden beneath.

***

(Editor's note: From a letter to a mureed.)

Haiku, Maui
December 23, 1981

I have resumed my practices each morning and evening, and it is helping now.
The dog and cats usually join me as I sit on the bench of the picnic table out by the ironwood sapling. The cats like to rub up against me, and Toge (pronounced Toggy, Tibetan for *tiger*) noses me sometimes.

It all feels like home....

Thinking About Getting a Milk Goat (letter 1982)

(Editor's note: From a handwritten letter to friends.)

Maui, Hawaii
July 19, 1982

Dearest Friends,

Aloha! Thanks so much for the exquisite wedding pictures. They make our hearts sing again & again.

The weather here has been lousy for 3 straight weeks...lots of rain, wind & mud. We're hoping it will be back to normal by the time my kids come here for a visit next month. I'm building a swing between two eucalyptus trees to celebrate their arrival. Kids will be here Aug. 17 – Sept. 5. Hope yours are healthy and growing in all ways!

I've been busy around the house lately. Plumbed in a new lavatory in the bathroom; put in some plywood panels between the two different levels of our roof to keep the next winter's rains out. Thinking about getting a milk goat. What do *you* think?

By the time you get this, the Mendocino Camp will be over *[the annual Sufi Camp organized by the SF Bay area Ruhaniat community]*. Let us know how it felt this year. Mei Ling & I are tentatively planning on attending next year's. *Inshallah.*

Keep well dear friends.
As-salaam aleikhum!
Moineddin & Mei Ling

Renewing, Rebuilding (letters 1983)

(Editor's note: From letters to a mureed.)

Haiku, Maui
March 29, 1983

I am working in Iman's [*Howden*] office here in Wailuku every morning, mostly renewing my correspondence. However, the more I work here, the more an atmosphere is being built up; and impressions have been coming for me to start both a Dance meeting and a Gatha class.

This has nothing to do with my will. Nevertheless, I am looking forward to the Gatha class first and foremost, then we'll see what develops in terms of Dancing every week on Maui.

***

Haiku, Maui
October 21, 1983

Lama was a tremendous opening for me.... I conducted a session of practices at the Maqbara every morning before breakfast, usually Walks of some sort, circumambulating the grave, or Dances on the dance ground, in addition to the 20 Breaths & Nayaz.

We began each session with a form of *sijda* that Murshid showed me: start with forehead to ground, then roll up till the crown center is the point of contact & EMPTY OUT on the breath (out) following the spine.

"The Message is in the Sphere" (letter 1983)

(Editor's note: From a letter to a mureed.)

December 29, 1983

There is resistance on the part of many [*in the Sufi community*] to accepting a personality structure divided into three distinct parts. This may be an echo of Murshid's strong adherence to the Islamic insistence that God is ONE, and his speaking against the Trinity of the Christians.

But the more I study psychology, whether it is the type that posits *id, ego* and *superego*, or subconsciousness, consciousness, and superconsciousness, the more these functions of awareness are being recognized each in their own way. And I can also quote Murshid in his eighth Lesson on the Walk entitled "The Use of Centers" (meaning chakras, or psychic doors as Frida refers to them):

"Differentiation and evolution and advancement all go together. This would suggest that there is a centering in abdomen, a centering in head, and a centering in thorax near heart, and each has its purpose."

Perhaps it would be better to say that God is ONE, and the Human Being is three.

The enclosure of the chapter on chakras by the tantric Swami is self-explanatory. I personally found it very helpful, confirming many feelings, and also opening some new doors. In particular, I was interested in the different layers of karma housed in each particular chakra, or psychic sphere. It also brought a new appreciation of Inayat Khan's dictum: "The message is in the sphere."

Ever since my transplant operation I have struggled with unleashed forces that have seemed to overwhelm an ego often helpless to deal with them. This has forced me to do three things: one, to accept all of my shit that the basic selves bring up to consciousness to face, stuff that I kept down with an iron heel for forty years; two, to build an ego-consciousness that attempts to deal with life on a more rational basis than previously; and three, to give it all up, so to speak, and rely on the guidance coming through the High Self, once a day hopefully as discipline.

With this program, appropriate responses seem to be manifesting more and more as the days pass.

Love, Moineddin

Beginning Life Counseling (letter 1984)

(Editor's note: From a letter to a mureed.)

Maui, Hawaii
March 20, 1984.

I'd like to let you know that my work in what I am calling "Life Counseling" is going well. I am charging $35 per hour, so now I am functioning as a legitimate professional. A "professional" in my understanding is one who suspends ego desires during his or her time of applied channeling. One who acts "unprofessionally" is one who is somehow at odds with what he or she professes to be doing. This may be one reason why Murshid S.A.M. used to say that for a Sufi, hypocrisy was the only sin.

It would seem that the "dues" I have paid (and of course continue to pay, as lesson-learning goes on all the time) have paved the way for this new endeavor in counseling.

Little did I know at the time the personal holocaust was overwhelming me, that the very things I was going through would prepare me to help others negotiate their own similar passages.

Abandon Tension... (letter 1984)

(Editor's note: From a letter to the Rev. Frida Waterhouse.)

June 22, 1984

Dearest Frida,

Aloha from sunny Maui!
This is just a note to share some impressions from my meditations this past week.
"ABANDON ALL TENSION YE WHO ENTER HERE" (from the poem "Saladin" by S.A.M.)
"Much of our work with the basic selves is to practice relaxation in areas which hold onto tension. Hopefully, and gradually, we will reach our goal of full relaxation in the Spirit of Peace."
"The whole point of working with the Three Selves is to remove the blocks which prevent unconditional love from flowing freely."
"The feminine basic self can use 'Toward Wholeness' as a *darood*. But the masculine basic self must lose his ego-self. Therefore, his *darood* will be 'I am not, Thou Alone Art,' and this should become a reality in his feeling. To feel the 'Thou' as *Above* and/or *Within* can help greatly here."

I am not prepared to say that the latter is generally applicable, since it was given to me to work with as an individual. But it *may* have more general validity as well. For instance, in mulling over the spiritual paths with masculine orientations by and large, it seems to me that the necessity to bring the ego to naught is overbalanced in terms of realizing the necessity also of wholeness in one's existence.

Even though they may lead to the identical spiritual realization, the getting there is certainly not always as stable a process as it could be.

When I meditate on my masculine and feminine basic selves together, I perform (actually) the mudra of Moses, right index finger pointing upward and left hand cupped to receive. Then it is that the "pillar in our midst" can be felt [*a reference to the pillars of smoke and fire that led the Israelites in the desert*].

Hopefully just sharing, Frida, and not making grand pronunciations.
Love, & see you at camp or before,
Moineddin

Messages from the Inner Community (letter 1984)

(Editor's note: From a letter to a mureed.)

August 26, 1984

I've been reading books by Mircea Eliade, a Romanian professor of the history of religions at the University of Chicago. Very intellectual but intellectual in the same way Fritjof Schuon or Ananda Coomeraswamy are. In other words, intellectual for the sake of formulating precise reflections of real cosmic processes in the mental sphere. (Sometimes, of course, a steady diet of this type of thing can result in headaches!)

Enclosures speak for themselves. The notes from my meditation are in the raw, first draft stage. They usually go through a revision or two before I call them OK.

Again, our best wishes are with you.

Moineddin

High Self: "We are here to answer needs, not to cater to wants."
Mary: "The work (as in alchemy) is to purify one's wants until the essential need is all that remains. It may be that all our wants are but covers over an even deeper need. We need to discover our real need. Then God's Presence may come as an answer, for as Hazrat Inayat Khan has said, 'Verily, a deepfelt need is itself a prayer.'"
"It is the spirit itself that cuts and tears the flesh of the body, and at a deeper level lacerates and stabs the heart. It doesn't have to be this way, but given the resistances and fixations of body and mind, the soul has no recourse but to force an issue. As Holy Qur'an says, 'Verily, from Allah we have come, and to Allah is our return.'"
Rama: "The force and will and penetration of the masculine principle is only really effective when it brings the human being face to face with his or her unknown feminine side. Once this has been accomplished with real willing surrender, the feminine in concert with the masculine can take one into that Presence which otherwise defies the presumptions of the masculine-on-its-own."
Ungrownup self: "The *hara* center (navel plexus) is often felt to be a kind of 'snake pit' with its denizens writhing and knotted in a poisonous and impenetrable darkness. But Krishna and Shiva each had a way of

untangling the serpents, of turning their poison into nectar, of bringing light into the darkness of the pit. When we can call upon the Krishna or Shiva in us, we too will experience the transformation of the poisonous serpent into a creature of wisdom."

Metamorphosis (letter 1984)

(Editor's note: From a group letter to several friends and mureeds. The story Moineddin mentions is included in Appendix II.)

November 1, 1984

Dear Friend,
Aloha!

In my recovery from a thorough-going breakdown a few years ago, the writings of Hermann Hesse helped me to go on. *Demian, Narcissus and Goldmund,* and *The Glass-Bead Game* are some of the titles I recall.

However, during that time I also came across a small volume by a Chilean writer, Miguel Serrano, called *C.G. Jung and Hermann Hesse: A Record of Two Friendships.* Mr. Serrano somehow managed to capture the rare spirits of these two beings in his little book.

During the past week I have been re-reading the section on Hesse, and this time around it is much clearer. The clouds of depression have largely lifted and dispersed. One's understanding is now more conscious.

Because of the daring spirits of Hesse and Jung, our thoughts and feelings of what it can mean to be human are increased tremendously. We can experience the storms of life with greater equanimity, and we can also recall our own childhood moments of anguish and delight with an attuned sympathy.

But I am digressing...

Really, I just want to share the enclosed tale called "Piktor's Metamorphosis" [*from the Serrano book*]. It may be helpful to those of you who are studying the possibilities of cooperation and union between the feminine and masculine principles operative in each of us.

At the every least, "Piktor's Metamorphosis" is a story of wonder and deep delight.

With love,
Moineddin

Celebrate the Search (letter 1984)

(Editor's note: From a letter to Allaudin William Mathieu, fellow mureed of Murshid Samuel Lewis and director of the Sufi Choir.)

December 20, 1984

Dear Allaudin,
Aloha!

Thanks for the invitation to join in with the Sufi Choir (in all its myriad ancient and more recent incarnations) as we celebrate Murshid's *urs* next month. It was especially heart-warming to hear that Stan, Shirin and Kathryn would be there as well as everyone else you mentioned on the phone.

I won't be able to be there this year, as plans have already been made for the second annual celebration of Murshid's *urs* here on Maui. I'm committed to a three-hour stint of *darshan*—always a challenge in the sense of "letting go and letting God." Hopefully, my friend Malik (who attended the June Jamiat weekend) will have returned from China by then so he can lead some dancing. The rest of the program will consist of pigging-out on *ono*-licious foods and desserts.

I recall fond memories of Mansur Johnson, speaking of drawing together the loose ends of our many journeys, exiles, prodigalities, what have you. Back in the mid-sixties he wrote some prodigious acid poems, i.e., "Blue Monday," "Ithaca," and others. They were all gathered under the title DON'T SEARCH, CELEBRATE.

As intoxicating as this dictum was to us "realized" acid-heads, the sobriety of Muhammad's "We have not known Thee as Thou shouldst be known" has proven to be a maturer view.

Therefore, let us now CELEBRATE THE SEARCH!

With love,

Moineddin

No Escaping Anymo' (letter 1985)

(Editor's note: From a letter to a mureed.)

Haiku, Maui

January 7, 1985

I can empathize with you about not having the juice to write, etc.
Family life is all-consuming, one goddamned demand after another. No escaping into "spirituality" anymo'!
This is it, and if it *ain't* it, it just plain hurts!

Honesty (letter 1987)

(Editor's note: From a letter to a Sufi colleague.)

June 26, 1987

Aloha from Maui!

I found your remarks re: the Ruhaniat organization interesting. I especially wonder at the statement, "I want very much to please you...." Truly, the greatest pleasure I experience, bottom-line, is honesty—from others *and* from myself.

I don't get a clear ring from you honesty-wise, despite your use of the word, when you say, "I honestly cannot define where my sympathies lie in respect to the present or future agendas of SIRS."

Isn't this because you may possibly *not* have sympathy for what you perceive as my initiatives with the organization?

Inayat Khan experienced heartbreak when he found that Western egos could not take in the music he came to bring. He healed his heartbreak by developing a musical dimension to the Message he was constrained to present verbally.

My own heartbreak, not so recent now, has become healed through an ongoing process in which honesty plays the key role. I suppose Inayat's "sincerity leads straight to the goal" is not different from this honesty, but honesty leaves no room for unseen and surreptitious motives whereas "sincerity" can be the refuge of *poseurs,* as I well know from firsthand experience.

No doubt honesty is important to me, because due to an unconscious inner split in myself for my first 40 years, and because this inner split was reflected outwardly as a "betrayal" in my first marriage, I now am enabled to reach down into and touch those parts of myself that were rejected for so long. Those rejected parts have now become cornerstones for the new cycle.

Perhaps you were at the Thursday night class at the Garden of Inayat when someone asked Murshid, "What does it take to reach enlightenment?"

Murshid's response?

"Great love. Or great pain. Usually both."

With love and respect, Moineddin

Beseeching the Breath (poem 1988)

(Adapted from a Zuni prayer)

>Beseeching the breath of the Divine Ones,
>Their life-giving breath,
>Their breath of many seasons,
>Their breath of waters,
>Their breath of seeds,
>Their breath of fecundity,
>Their breath of power,
>Their breath of abundant blessing—
>Beseeching the breath of the Divine Ones,
>O, into my body drawing their breath,
>I add to your breath
>That you may live happily!

Look to the Source (brochure 1989)

(Editor's note: From an informational brochure at Moineddin's counseling practice in Maui, Hawaii.)

Three-Self Work

Three-Self work is the distillate of all transpersonal psychologies, from ancient shamanic models (including Huna) to modern integrative therapies such as Psychosynthesis. It brings together the Three Selves—divine, human and basic—into a cooperative and mutually supportive process whereby our inner life may be fully realized and shared.

Along the way the personality is clarified of obstructive belief-patterns ("the male is superior to the female," etc.), conflicts between *anima* and *animus* are resolved and our inner child is healed of every wound. Each step forward results in greater awareness of our wholeness as we experience the "sacred marriage" of feminine and masculine principles, and the merging of deep feeling with clear light.

Three-Self work is initially conducted by a facilitator who calls forth in turn to our high self, basic selves (female and male), and inner child. The conscious self is voluntarily placed in neutral gear, awake yet transparent to the process. Each self is honored with respect and love and is encouraged to voice its present reality and need. As the work unfolds, emotional traumata from painful, numb or rigid places in the psyche are released and blessed.

Our growing rapport with Three-Self work opens inner pathways of spirit, and we no longer see ourselves "through a glass darkly, but face to face." Ultimately, Three-Self work moves us to the stage where we can process and heal ourselves, either solo or via co-counseling.

All Three Selves have their origin and destiny in the Oneness of Being we call God.

Thou art That, my friends. May we perfect our Remembrance.

—Moineddin Jablonski

Source of Spiritual Counseling

My late teacher, Frida Waterhouse of San Francisco, believed that the fountainhead of the Kahuna tradition arose "from the Ancient of Days of Babylon and Ur." She added that the Polynesian cultures that developed the Kahuna truths, in names and forms unique to their Pacific island heritage, trace their holistic worldview to this earlier time and place.

Our universe—and the human psyche that mirrors it—was seen as comprised of three primary dimensions of being: superconscious, conscious and subconscious. Further insight revealed that powerful inner personalities served the creative intention within each dimension. In the order of nature these personalities were identified as goddesses and gods; in the psyche they were called the "three selves."

The ancient Kahunas were spiritual therapists as well as skilled navigators of the divine mind. Today this is known as "Three-Self Work." We call the three selves by the names high self, conscious self and basic self, to reflect their purpose in the universal design of our growth in and toward God, the Only Being.

Nana I Ke Kumu! Look to the Source!

Moineddin Jablonski is a Three-Self counselor living in Haiku, who works as an associate of Grace Clinic.

Grief (essay 1989)

You swore you would never let your heart be broken again. Once or even twice was enough, but a third time, never. Or perhaps this is your first time getting to know Humpty-Dumpty after the Great Fall? At any rate, here you are, brought to your knees by having lost what you loved most in life....

The grieving process is an eclipse of the conscious mind by the emotional mind in reaction to a great personal loss. Painfully characteristic of this eclipse is the loss of control normally experienced by the conscious mind. Inner chaos suddenly displaces years of hard won but ultimately fragile self-possession. One feels crazy, alien, exiled from life.

The unclaimed and shattered feelings encountered in the abyss of grief can disembowel one's identity so completely that hell becomes a living reality. It is important to reassure persons in grief that what they are going through is indeed a healing process and a natural response to the holocaust of loss.

In no particular order, one is numbed by *denial*; obsessed by *anger* and *rage*; in the *bargaining* phase one sells one's soul in exchange for personal survival; one's *depression* ranges from neurotic to psychotic. When one has traversed these stages with blood, sweat and tears, the challenge of *acceptance* calls one to cross the threshold of pain into a new life.

Short of acceptance, a crisis of personal identity is potentially dangerous. Because one has suffered ruin at the level of one's most basic feelings—and remember, feelings are always held sacred—the primal survival instincts can go haywire. One may feel like killing oneself or someone else in answer to one's loss. Help should be sought from a competent source.

It is imperative to show the grieving person that these raw and inflamed feelings need acceptance and honor. Rejection aborts the embryo of sanity seeking to be born. Acceptance heralds the new birth, betokens healing of the broken heart. *Take a giant step toward wholeness: be at one with your pain.*

There is a tendency to want to return to the way things were before the Great Fall. But counterfeit innocence can never stand up to authentic experience. *There is no way out but through.* New life will only come when one finds the courage to step into the unknown. The unknown often involves embracing that which has been regarded as unacceptable, such as a nice person with repressed feelings having to become a real person with real feelings. All these challenges brought forth by the grieving process are variations on one inescapable theme: *will you choose life or death?*

Pain of loss brings all of us to our knees sooner or later. The passion play of personal crisis serves to create the human being anew, to move the soul a step closer to its spiritual purpose. Thus it has been, thus will it be. Let us start from our knees for a change, and pray that we become instruments of the divine compassion.

Beloved, Thou diggest into my heart deeper
than the depths of the earth...
Thou changest my flesh into fertile soil;
Thou turnest my blood into streams of water;
Thou kneadest my clay, I know,
to make a new universe.

—Hazrat Inayat Khan

The Big "D" (poem 1990)

(Editor's note: For a friend going through divorce)

Your coyote-part howls for a moon
gone out of your sky.

Your bleached skeleton crawls
through one hot desert after another
seeking a sign of Khidr,
the green man who would declare
an end to this waste land.

Alas, bless the passing
of your life's brightness
with heartfelt curses. Rue
the day you were born
again and again, until your cries
reach the invisible Throne.

Let your coyote-part mourn
the empty sky.

Pray through the darkness
for a new moon.

Cry the tears of Isis
and clothe your naked bones
with living flesh.

Winged Kidney (letter 1990)

(Editor's note: A letter to family and Ruhaniat leaders.)

August 8, 1990

Dear Family and Friends, Aloha!

This is an update to my letter of May 5 in which I shared with you the news of the impending failure of my transplanted kidney. My hope then, as now, is that a new kidney would become available before the present kidney gives out. If the present kidney were to fail completely before a new kidney became available, I would be required to go back on hemodialysis for the interim.

Yesterday I had a blood test to evaluate the creatinine level, a general indicator of kidney function. The result showed a creatinine level of 6.3 compared to 5.1 a month ago. This means that my kidney function is slipping faster over a shorter time span than previously. Unless a new kidney shows up fairly soon, it appears inevitable that I shall have to go back on hemodialysis.

Already I am experiencing the stages of grieving the news of my test results from yesterday. First came shock, then denial and depression, and today I feel anger. Real acceptance has not yet come, probably for the reason that hemodialysis, should that prospect come to pass, will bring a major change in lifestyle for me and my family. Since Mei-Ling is the breadwinner in our family and works full-time to support us, childcare for the children and transportation for me to and from the dialysis clinic will present real challenges, challenges that as I see it must be met with the help of our friends.

In addition, I will personally be unable to meet the demands of answering Sufi correspondence and seeing mureeds and clients for counseling as I do now. I will be operating from a much lower energy level physically besides having to dialyze three times a week, which will cut seriously into the amount of creative time I can devote to my family and the spiritual community.

I'm telling you this so you can prepare yourselves for the changes ahead, those of you who will be affected by the change in my health status. For those in the spiritual community who have come to depend on me, this will be an opportunity for you to learn self-reliance and take a mature initiative in terms of aligning with your inner guidance. This will help all of us as the community itself moves into a new level of understanding and support for each other.

I visualize a "winged kidney" flying to me, as some of you have suggested I do. Overall, however, the image of a butterfly is closest to my heart. I imagine that I am now entering into a cocoon, and that after my new kidney is received I will become a butterfly.

Love and blessings,
Carl/Moineddin

P.S. Please share this with your classes.

Writing Through the Pain (letter 1991)

(Editor's note: From a letter to a mureed.)

March 15, 1991

Aloha!

Thank you for your letters and poem. I'm watching your developments with interest, but find myself wishing for more news of the home front. Heaven can take care of itself; everyday life we are responsible for.

I have some good news. I am in process of being placed on the University of Pittsburgh's transplant list. Those are the people who are using FK506 in clinical trials. So there is some positive movement despite the limbo of being on dialysis.

Enclosed is a poem I wrote recently. As you can see, I am writing my way through the pain.

Love, Moin

Shiva (poem 1991)

I admire the skulls and bones
you wear so easily around
your neck, my Lord.

Contrariwise, my thoughts
make for me a briar-crown.
The failure of an organ
brings the dance down.

Balance limps away
from the hallowed ground.

What did you lose?
you asked, kind.

It's not what I lost.
It's what I'm losing.

Breaking the Spell (poem 1991)

The people are in profound denial.
But in a box in a drawer in a dream
I find sticks for fire,
stones for light.
The ancient fear of death
vows to be my ally.

Dressed in black, we approach
with utter stealth the dark
usurper of children.

Crucifixion (letter 1991)

(Editor's note: From a letter to a mureed. Moineddin received a new kidney in June 1991.)

August 12, 1991

Crucifixion is one of many Mysteries. In my opinion, it is deeply valuable to have crucifixion as a model suffered by one of the Masters of humanity to relate to when undergoing a similar experience.

Integrating it into an overall picture of self-realization shows that vulnerability to universal process is also essential for coming to wholeness and compassion. Victimhood is when you take pain and suffering and deal with it only on an ego level.

My two cents worth.

Love ya,

Moin

Illuminating the Shadow (essay 1996)

(Editor's note: Moineddin wrote this article in April 1996 as a presentation for the annual Jamiat Khas leaders' meeting of the Sufi Islamia Ruhaniat Society.)

"Shadow is created by light interfering with light—different gradients of light interfering with each other. The higher the grade of light, the more it is able to resolve in itself the interferences associated with denser grades." (Samuel L. Lewis)

"It is said of Muhammad: 'He cast no shadow in the noonday sun.'" (Hadith)

What we call "the shadow" or "the dark side" of our personalities is that portion of our being that operates below the threshold of normal waking consciousness. In other words, our "shadow" or "dark side" consists of those parts of us that are unavailable to our conscious mind. For example, we have all experienced the frustration of having something important to say—it's right there on the tip of our tongue—yet we cannot bring it to mind. Maybe we are tired, and after getting a good night's sleep the forgotten phrase is easily remembered. This is one of many common instances of the shadow-play of consciousness. We generally accept such momentary frustrations, and their eventual resolution, as part of life.

Well, most of us accept these instances of forgetfulness as normal, nothing more than minor inconveniences that quickly pass. But some Zen masters have not found these lapses of memory acceptable. Here is a story from the book *Zen Flesh, Zen Bones* [by Paul Reps and Nyogen Senzaki] called "Every-Minute Zen":

> "Zen students are with their masters at least ten years before they presume to teach others. Nan-in was visited by Tenno, who, having passed his apprenticeship, had become a teacher. The day happened to be rainy, so Tenno wore wooden clogs and carried an umbrella. After greeting him, Nan-in remarked, 'I want to know if your umbrella is on the right or left side of your clogs?' Tenno, confused, had no instant answer. He realized that he was unable to carry his Zen every minute. He became Nan-in's pupil, and he studied six more years to accomplish his every-minute Zen."

This Zen parable illustrates how the enlightenment process—in the Soto school compared to the slow maturation of a peach growing on a branch, until it falls, plop, on the ground ready to be eaten—and in the Rinzai school likened to a sudden bolt of lightning that electrifies one's whole being with the spirit of compassion—irradiates the denser layers of the psyche with full consciousness, remembrance and insight. The practice of Zen, based on the foundational experience of Shakyamuni Buddha, is one way of "illuminating the shadow."

Nyogen Senzaki, Murshid S.A.M.'s mentor and friend, shared the following Zen poem with Inayat Khan in the blink of an eye:

No living soul comes near that water—
A vast sheet of water as blue as indigo.
The abyss has a depth of ten thousand feet.
When all is quiet and calm at midnight,
Only the moonlight penetrates through the waves,
Reaching the bottom easily and freely.

Nyogen, which means "no such person," had compassion for every level of his being, and every level responded with "no obstruction."

As mentioned, most of us accept instances of forgetfulness as minor blips on the radar screen of life and move on. But when patterns of forgetfulness, confusion, depression or other imbalances emerge to such an extent that the quality and continuity of our lives is seriously compromised, then it is time to take a closer look at what is going on. Chances are that certain hidden yet very real aspects of our consciousness are feeling neglected and unappreciated, and are "taking it out on us" in order to get the attention, love and respect they need and deserve.

Sometimes the neglect and lack of appreciation on the part of our conscious minds toward the parts of us that live in shadow becomes so pronounced and prolonged that our so-called dark side reacts to this tyranny by creating a steady stream of accidents, illnesses, psychological disorders, or other intensive disruptions, until we wise up and begin to include our shadow in the personal equation. If things are allowed to slide beyond this point, the disintegration of our personal lives may lead to career failure, destruction of family and friendship bonds, and can easily escalate to become a matter of life and death.

That is what happened to me. A brief sketch of my early years will give clues to later developments. I was raised Catholic at a time when the

IV. DEPTHS OF THE SELF AND SOUL

In Iowa City, 1966. Photo: Mansur Johnson

church taught, among other things, that you could go to hell by having premarital sex, masturbating, or eating meat on Friday. I was quite gullible and believed every word. As a fairly normal teenager, I wasn't particularly interested in eating meat on Friday, but I was interested in premarital sex and masturbation. Pretty soon I was well on my way to hell—on roller skates, as the saying goes. The only way I could save myself from the eternal damnation I believed in was to go to confession and feign repentance for acts that felt intrinsically wonderful. I would promise not to do them again, but that was a lie because I knew I would do them again. My guilt, inner conflict and rebellion quickly compounded. I left the church when I was eighteen.

Unfortunately, the church didn't leave me. As the founder of General Semantics Alfred Korzybski wrote: "God may forgive your sins, but your nervous system won't." The impressions of church authority and its teaching that people deserved to suffer eternally in hell for exploring their premarital sexuality had been stamped indelibly in my heart. The part of my shadow that fed on judgement grew large. I took up drinking and one-night stands to numb my loneliness and pain. During this time I began to raid medicine cabinets at parties, making cocktails of uppers, downers and beer. It wasn't long before I was arrested for breaking into a restaurant, jimmying the cash register and stealing thirty-five cents.

Clearly, I was an unsuccessful thief. But I was also crying out for help in the only way I knew how: by getting myself into so much trouble that someone, anyone, would have to rescue me. And I was rescued. Every evening my dad and mom would come to the county jail, stand on the lawn outside the window and talk to me through the bars. I was grateful for their support. And still having a few smarts left, I asked that the judge who I used to deliver newspapers to as a kid be my court-appointed attorney. Remembering me, he reluctantly arranged to get me off on one year's probation, on condition that I live at home, get a job and see a psychiatrist regularly for six months.

Bear in mind that I am sketching only the shadow aspects of my youth, and not the sunnier features. Above ground, so to speak, I was taking classes in poetry writing at the University of Iowa Writer's Workshop and was involved in the resurgence of folk music, especially the songs of Pete Seeger, Odetta, Woody Guthrie, Joan Baez and Bob Dylan, many of which I would sing at local hootenannies. The civil rights and peace movements attracted me with their strong messages of social justice and human survival. I was a member of the Socialist Discussion Club on campus and marched in numerous demonstrations for a variety of causes. In August of 1963, Darwesh Walker and I hitchhiked to the nation's capital to attend the march on Washington in which Martin Luther King gave his "I have a dream..."speech. One year later, at the age of twenty-two, I took the bus to McComb, Mississippi and spent the summer working for the Student Non-violent Coordinating Committee, registering black people to vote.

The lights and shadows of my life were intertwined and happening simultaneously, as they do in everyone's life, but I was not very reflective then and was not able to view my personal psychology with any real depth or clarity. Moral philosophy and social activism were jumbled up with bodily appetites and "the pleasure principle." And in the confusion of continued drinking and partying, I was unaware that it was possible to have peace of mind, or that peace of mind could help me understand life better.

Unaware, that is, until the summer of 1965 when LSD hit town. After that, things began to happen fast. First of all, I discovered that the universe I lived in was multidimensional and not confined to the constipated and fearful mind-set of the "establishment." Next, I realized that God was not dead, but living and real in the here-now. Finally, after coming across a book on Zen, I understood that the real religion of my heart and purpose of my soul were never lost at all, but could be found in the Bodhisattva ideal, which is rooted in the enlightenment experience of the Buddha: "I now see all sentient beings have perfect enlightenment, only they don't know it. I must show it to them."

As you can see, my initial connection to direct spiritual experience was through LSD and other psychedelics. One of the insights I had while using psychedelics was: "If I can have mystical experiences by ingesting substances outside of myself, surely I can have mystical experiences by doing spiritual practices relying on my own efforts." It was just a hop, skip and a jump from there to reading books on Zen. After an unusually clear satori experience on LSD in November of 1966, I made up my mind to give up psychedelics and begin the search for a Zen master. My belief that I would find a Zen master was very strong. Two months later I met a man named Sam Lewis.

Shortly thereafter, I asked Sam Lewis if I could be his disciple, and he said yes. He initiated me, not into Zen (though he was a Zen master), but into Sufism, which he assured me was more in keeping with the love-nature of the young people now coming to his door. Sufism or Zen, it didn't matter to me. Being with Sam was the important thing. I was absolutely certain I would attain enlightenment under his guidance—and in one sense I did. And in another sense I didn't.

A few weeks after my initiation, he said, "I don't have time right now to sit down and give you Sufi practices. In the meantime, take a look at the "centering practices" in the back of *Zen Flesh, Zen Bones* and pick one or two that strike you. That should hold you for a while." I followed his instruction, and sure enough, one of the practices seemed to jump off the page at me. I showed him the practice and asked if it would be all right if I went ahead and did it. He said yes, do it. I did the practice every night for two years—"with the persistence of a mosquito trying to sting an iron bull" as an old Korean Zen manual puts it—and experienced many subtle effects but never the enlightenment I was looking for.

Then one evening in late February of 1969, I felt a special buoyancy and tingling in the atmosphere. The message seemed to be: "Go to your room early tonight and do your practice." So I said good night to everyone in the TV room at the Garden of Inayat, retired to my room and entered my practice. It felt as if there were helping spirits everywhere around me, yet the practice would depend upon my own will and skill for it to be successful. An hour or so later, the mosquito's efforts paid off. The iron bull turned out to be the cosmos itself, and I entered it and it entered me, I becoming it and it becoming me until there was only Oneness. I had found the enlightenment I sought.

But this was only the beginning, a backdrop for the symphony of realization that would be played. Without going into the procession of *samadhis* with various messengers of God, including the Divine Mother and her Divine Child, let me say that the experience began by becoming one with Lord Buddha. His steadiness of concentration and ability to bring consciousness back to one-pointedness whenever it would waver, made everything else possible. The entire revelation was a result of effort and grace. One without the other and there would be nothing to report.

One final comment, for what it may be worth, is that the *samadhi* with Muhammad was deeper—not higher, but deeper—than the others, in the sense that he was able to open my lower chakras to the flow of healing *baraka* and grace more than the other messengers. Since I had been stuffing my sexual fears and guilts in the bottom chakras seemingly forever, this unanticipated blessing to parts of myself I had been taught to regard as unworthy was so profound as to constitute an additional and unique illumination—"Light upon Light!" To experience the lower chakras as pristine and clear instruments of spiritual presence was a proof of God's mercy beyond anything I dared hope for.

Okay, enough on that. That is the sense in which I did attain enlightenment under Murshid's guidance. The sense in which I *didn't* attain enlightenment is also part of the story, and verges directly upon the problem of "illuminating the shadow."

Uniting the one to the One (essay 2000)

(Editor's note: Moineddin subtitled this article, written about a year before his passing, "Notes on the Practice of Soulwork.")

Part One

"Uniting the one to the One" is a phrase that was used by the late Reverend Frida Waterhouse to indicate the sacred marriage of one's human consciousness—with its vital underpinnings in the psyche and body—to universal divine consciousness. It represents the merging of the personal self with the spiritual Self, or Soul.

Before I go further, I want to acknowledge with love and respect the debt of gratitude I feel toward my mentors Frida Waterhouse and Harvey Grady in the study and practice of spiritual psychology. Frida introduced "Three-Self Work"—meaning the coordination of the (1) instinctive, (2) conscious, and (3) divine realms that comprise the human spirit—to the Sufi community in the early 1970's. More recently, Harvey Grady's discovery of the Astral and Mental Judge Selves has added a crucial dimension to the mapping and understanding of the human psyche. Although they never met, Frida and Harvey both studied with Drs. Wayne Guthrie and Bella Karish of the Fellowship of Universal Guidance in Los Angeles, where they learned the basics of Three-Self Work. Each in their own way, Frida and Harvey expanded the scope of what they learned with Wayne and Bella. Harvey now calls his work "Self Integration."

I refer to my practice as "Soulwork," because it takes the myriad forces projected by the Soul into the human psyche, body and personality and melds them into a functioning unity or whole. This constitutes the first stage of Soulwork: to integrate the various conscious and subconscious aspects of the personality into a harmonious family of "selves," which in devotional practice becomes a prayer circle.

The second stage of Soulwork is to coalesce the integrated personality self, or prayer circle, with Higher Consciousness. In other words, to repeat Frida's maxim, "to unite the one to the One."

In brief, Soulwork is Three-Self Work, plus acceptance of and work with the Judge Selves [*explained below*]. In my experience, the befriending of each of one's subconscious selves is essential in Soulwork. It is the Bodhisattva ideal transposed to the world of one's own psyche.

Along these lines, Hazrat Inayat Khan says, "Psychology is the higher alchemy, and one must not study it only without practicing it. Practice and study must go together, which opens the door to happiness for every soul" (Gatha 1, Series II, "Insight").

Perhaps the best way to proceed would be to share my personal experience with the Soulwork process. It began in the fall of 1980 when I entered my fifth year of hemodialysis due to end stage renal disease. Illness and debility had convinced me that I would soon die. I had undergone a kidney transplant operation earlier that summer, but my body rejected the kidney, and after a week the transplanted organ was removed. On top of my health problems, I was going through a painful divorce. I was deeply depressed and emotionally numb. It was a time that felt marked by an absence of hope.

Curiously, a part of me must have held some hope, because I had taken the initiative to move from my home in Petaluma to the Palo Alto Khankah to receive thrice-weekly inputs of X-radiation at the nearby Stanford Medical Center over a period of three months. My transplant surgeon believed that a radical protocol involving massive doses of X-radiation would render my immune system incapable of rejecting a new kidney. The doctor, so sure the protocol would work, told me I would be at the top of the list when a kidney became available.

In December 1980 toward the end of the three-month protocol, I returned to Petaluma to spend Christmas with my children. On my desk was a letter from Frida Waterhouse. In her inimitable concise style she had written:

> *It is my reality that each of us has a Male Basic Self and a Female Basic Self, as well as an Inner Child, that live in the psyche. These Selves can, and often do, cause difficulty in our lives—especially if we don't honor them and give them their due. If the neglect is pronounced, the Basic Selves can cause illness.*
>
> *Please consider the possibility that you have neglected to acknowledge and honor your Basic Selves, and that this may be why you are having such a hard time. I offer myself as an instrument of the Most High, and am willing to help if you are interested.*
>
> *With love,*
> *Frida*

Something in those light-filled lines caused a stir within me. I returned the letter to the envelope and made a mental note to read it again after my protocol and transplant operation were over.

I don't mean to dwell on my past medical history, but to use it as an example to illustrate how a medical or other personal crisis can precipitate needed life changes. Many of us "plateau out" at levels comfortable to us, which can result in stagnation and lack of growth. When such a status quo persists for too long, High Selves will graciously provide stimulation, whether we like it or not, for further learning and growth.

After the Christmas holiday, I returned to Palo Alto to conclude the weeks of the X-radiation protocol. Toward the end of January 1981, I received a 2 am telephone call from the University of San Francisco Medical Center saying that they had a kidney for me. A few hours later, I received a kidney from a 22-year-old female student who had died of a brain aneurysm.

With the introduction of the new kidney, my body experienced a dramatic improvement. But my mind, which faced a divorce upon my return home—not to mention the challenge of having to learn how to live instead of die—began to disintegrate. While in hospital, I experienced several episodes of psychogenic distortion and breakdown. My surgeon attributed the episodes to the effects of the X-radiation combined with powerful immunosuppressive drugs.

One night in early February 1981, as my mental condition worsened, I believed I was descending into madness. What I was actually descending into was the chaotic state of my own psyche. At the moment I was about to give up hope of ever being sane again, a remarkable thing happened. Frida Waterhouse appeared to me in vision. She didn't say a word, she just walked, putting one foot in front of the other. The rhythm of her walk set my whole being in order, and the mental chaos disappeared—temporarily.

Over the coming months and years, I would be forced to deal with the painful realities of a shattered mind, a broken heart and a grief-stricken spirit—all housed within a fragile body that was now destined to stay alive. Like the jumbled pieces of Humpty Dumpty after the Great Fall, these were the elements that would require more grace and healing than "all the king's horses and all the king's men" could muster. My Male Self, with whom I was primarily identified and who had been running the show for the first 40 years of my life, was now utterly broken. He had believed himself capable of Olympian feats, especially in the spiritual realm. But he had forgotten how to willingly surrender his ego, so now the universe was graciously crushing it for him.

He had also forgotten the importance of the Feminine Principle in his life: a loving presence rooted in connection to all of Life—"Thy Light is in all forms, Thy Love in all beings." She would prove to be a nurturing, healing presence, a presence whose very vulnerability would confer a strength and resilience that my Male Self, in his arrogance, could never know.

"All the king's horses and all the king's men" were going down to defeat. The death-knell of the patriarchy and its one-sided imperatives was tolling, the funeral procession was trooping through my psyche. It was the end of the world as I knew it. It was also a revolution. The inner voices that had been suppressed for ages, beginning with the voice of my Female Self, would now speak. Not only would they speak, they would be heard. No longer would they be taken for granted. And as is typical of revolutions, the "good" would be thrown out with the "bad."

This thoroughgoing psychic purging was a necessary prelude to the slow, laborious and painstaking process of grace and healing that must come, that would come. Indeed, grace and healing came through Frida, my teacher and friend, and through Mei-Ling Chang, my life partner. Grace and healing also came through my own need to be an ordinary human being—not special but just ordinary—replete with faults, feelings, lusts and longings.

As Hazrat Inayat Khan declares in *Gayan*, "Hail to my exile from the Garden of Eden to the earth! If I had not fallen, I should not have had the opportunity of probing the depths of life."

Inayat Khan's tale of Usman Haruni Chisti and his mureed Moineddin Chisti, bowing before the image of Mother Kali, influenced me powerfully during this time. Equally important in my healing process was the myth of Isis journeying through Upper and Lower Egypt, collecting the various parts of Osiris's body that had been butchered and hidden by Set. Isis gathered the scattered body parts and breathed new life into them, and made Osiris whole.

The divine and earthly Feminine Principle was being restored to my psyche and personality. The mystery of healing and the magic of feeling were becoming paramount in my life. Darkness was discovered to be the sacred soil for learning and growth, and my grieving process was a potent compost. I was being reborn.

Now, how does all this relate to the specifics and practice of Soulwork? Let us return to Frida's letter. What was it that she said? Oh yes, I was interested. I was more than interested. My life and sanity depended upon Frida's wise help. Her inner plane appearance to me in the hospital was a clear confirmation of that. After years of avoiding and resisting her, I was now surrendering to her.

My first Three-Self session with Frida took place in her San Francisco home in the fall of 1981. She began with her usual Kabbalistic Invocation:

Holy art Thou, O Lord of our Universe.
Holy art Thou Whom Nature hath not formed.
Holy art Thou, O vast and mighty ONE,
Lord of the Light and of the Darkness—
For Thine is the Kingdom and the Power
And the Glory forever. Amen.

Frida asked my conscious mind "to place itself in neutral gear, awake yet transparent to the process," and then proceeded to call forth with love and respect to my "Male Basic Self." No response. After three tries, she moved on to my "Female Basic Self." No response. Next she called forth to my "High Self." No response. My confidence level was rapidly nose-diving. I could not properly surrender.

I had two more sessions with Frida over the next several months, both with the same result as the first session. Was I cut out for Three-Self Work? In my limbo-like state I seriously wondered. Yet there was something in Frida's presence and atmosphere that kept me coming back to try again.

Finally, during my fourth session in late 1982, the opening occurred. Frida had called forth to my Male Basic Self, and from somewhere in my belly region came a timid, frightened voice: "My name is Rutherford." Naturally, my conscious mind was shocked to hear this unacknowledged and fearful part of myself take the stage. In fact, my conscious mind's first reaction was to think, "What kind of weird name is Rutherford? I don't know any Rutherford. And I don't want to know any Rutherford."

Thank God, Frida was more understanding and compassionate than my conscious mind. She accepted Rutherford unconditionally, and stated clearly her appreciation for all the work he had done on my behalf twenty-four hours a day, seven days a week, three hundred sixty-five days a year, year in and year out. As Frida continued to treat Rutherford with love and respect, and as her ministering words brought him partway out of his shell, I began to settle down and accept him as a valid and real part of myself.

Yet in spite of Frida's light and kindness, Rutherford was badly damaged. His rage toward me was surpassed only by his rage toward God, whom he held ultimately responsible for his pain, fear and shattered state. He became recalcitrant and vindictive. He shared his hellish reality freely with me, sending suicidal thoughts and repeatedly causing sore throats and other ailments to grab my attention.

Over the next year, it became clear that Rutherford was unwilling and unable to relate in a harmonious way with the other members of his inner family of selves, much less with me (the conscious or "outer" self), despite consistent and respectful work with him. During my next session with Frida, she suggested to Rutherford that his healing might be better served by a return to an inner plane where he would be with others like himself and where he would receive needed help. She explained that his need for healing was so pronounced as to prevent him from assuming the normal Basic Self responsibilities of serving the development of the personality.

After gentle but firm persuasion by Frida, Rutherford reluctantly agreed to be removed to an inner plane for healing, to be temporarily replaced by a "Missionary Basic Self"—Frida's term—an advanced Basic Self from an inner plane repository whose capability is suited for emergency situations. Frida performed the replacement through the aegis of my High Self, the guiding Solar Angel in charge of a person's earthly and spiritual evolution from lifetime to lifetime until one's graduation from the schoolhouse of Earth. She said I could expect to perceive the arrival of the Missionary Basic Self within 24 to 48 hours.

Two days later, I became aware of the presence of an androgynous Basic Self who said "his" name was Gabriel. He located himself just below my heart chakra. Gabriel's presence would harmonize my psyche and stabilize my personality to a much greater degree than I had previously experienced. In fact, I developed a heartfelt friendship with him and came to appreciate his steady and bright influence. Six months later while doing my spiritual practice, Gabriel said, "It's time for me to leave you now. My work is done." I thanked him from the bottom of my heart and wished him well in his future work. I never saw or heard from him again.

As these changes were transpiring, other equally important developments were taking place. During a session a few months after Rutherford's first appearance, Frida called forth to my Female Basic Self and asked her to state her name and emotional age. I was very moved to hear a little voice say, "My name is Mary and I am four years old."

Mary's emergence from subconsciousness to consciousness marked the beginning of a major phase in my personal and spiritual growth, a phase that would last ten years. As it happened, Mary felt like she was four years old because Rutherford, who had long dominated my psyche and personality, had overshadowed and prevented Mary from growing up and assuming her rightful role in my life.

But with Rutherford's departure, the little four-year-old would have the psychic space necessary to grow. And grow she would! After two more sessions and much homework between those sessions, Mary matured to the emotional age of nineteen. In another year, Mary would grow to the age of twenty-eight. During this time, she manifested primarily as a compassionate and efficient nurse, assisting my immune system to prevent major infections and generally upgrading my overall physical health and mental outlook.

Mary also helped me descend consciously into the deeper layers of my psyche, into my very roots. She showed me how the Feminine Principle is identified with primordial creative energy. At one point she appeared to me as a dragon, much like the Chinese depiction of the dragon as the vehicle of Quan Yin. Eastern religions regard the dragon as the sign of life, even as life itself, whereas in the West the dragon is seen as a diabolical beast to be opposed and slain.

My "bible" during this period was Erich Neumann's *The Great Mother*, a lucid and sympathetic presentation of the divine Feminine Archetype throughout its many expressions in different cultures stemming from prehistoric times. Neumann was one of the pioneers of depth psychology, and I recommend *The Great Mother* for anyone interested in gaining greater insight into the full range of the spirit and forms of the Feminine Principle.

The fact that my body had received the kidney of a female college student also figured prominently in my awakening, especially my emotional awakening, to the importance of the Feminine Principle. Nothing that was happening to me was imaginary or theoretical—it was all very real. Inwardly, my psychic reality consisted of deeply meaningful and often dramatic growth. Outwardly, I identified with feminist political initiatives—something that was previously anathema to me when Rutherford was pulling the strings.

As I mentioned earlier, these developments took place over a ten-year period. A carefully timed plan orchestrated by my High Self was underway. First the old regime marked by the domination of the Male Self had to go. Next the Female Self would gain ascendancy—*karmically* as a counterbalance to the years of Male Self imperative and control, and *dharmically* because she must embark on a journey of self-discovery and awaken to her own highest purpose.

Frida died in 1987, an expected but nonetheless painful exit after an extended illness. The process of her passing was quite initiatory for the inner circle of women who helped with her care during this period. For Mei-Ling and me, Frida's departure left a significant hollow in our lives. Her death naturally threw me back on my own resources in terms of my inner work.

As part of the above-mentioned, carefully timed plan, my transplanted kidney began to fail in early 1990. By December of that year, I had to begin dialysis treatments again after a decade-long hiatus away from the machine. The female student's kidney had served me well, and I thanked the soul of the young woman for the sacrifice she had made so that I and others who had received her organs might continue to live, grow and prosper.

I used this "down time" to review my health needs and explore my options. I wrote poetry during this period as a creative way to move through the depression associated with kidney failure. Having heard that the University of Pittsburgh Medical Center was sponsoring clinical trials of an effective new immunosuppressive drug for transplant patients, I traveled to Pittsburgh for an evaluation and was placed on their transplant list. A few months later in June 1991, I received a telephone call asking me to fly there at once. "We have a kidney for you, Mr. Jablonski." The voice on the other end of the line was music to my ears.

After the transplant operation, plus ensuing complications that required three additional surgeries, it took the entire summer to recover. The new kidney, a priceless gift from an eight-year-old girl, kept me going through the hell and high water of my hospitalization. Frida had told me ten years earlier, "Moineddin, you have cut a wide swath through your karma." Apparently, I was still "mowing the lawn." In any case, I am happy to say that the kidney continues to function as well as the day I left Pittsburgh. I continue to thank the young girl for her gift of life.

Along with the ascendancy of the Female Self throughout most of the 1980s, my Inner Child also came forth to consciousness. Frida often called the Inner Child the "Ungrown-up Child." In my Soulwork experience, the Inner Child does have two sides. One side is generally happy, innocent and sunny; the other side is often emotionally arrested at a certain age due to a traumatic event that might range anywhere from physical violence to sexual abuse to perceived neglect resulting from the birth of a sibling.

When working with a subconscious self that is wounded—whether that self is the Inner Child, or the Female or Male Basic Self, or the Body Self, or one of the Judge Selves—it is important to guide the self back to the time, place, circumstances and participants in the traumatic event that disrupted the self's integrity. Once these factors have been identified, the work of understanding, forgiveness and healing can begin. The integrity of the self can be restored, the rent in the fabric of the psyche repaired, the personality given a new lease on life.

Most of the problems that exist between one's personality self and one's Inner Child are attributable to nothing more than lack of proper attention. Because the adult world is filled with responsibilities and deadlines, the personality self frequently gives itself the excuse that it is "just too busy" to pay attention to the needs of the Inner Child. When the personality self gives time and care to the Inner Child, improvements are dramatic and immediate—if the personality self is sincere. All subconscious selves are good at knowing whether the personality self is genuine and sincere in its intentions.

If an Inner Child perceives that the personality self is insincere or unreliable, he or she can retreat into a shell of unhappiness, confusion and distrust of the personality self and of the adult world in general. In some cases, a mistreated Inner Child will "act out" and sabotage one's relationships, or cause obsessive and inappropriate relationships. A neglected Inner Child can also be at the root of depression.

However, when one's personality self shares "quality time" with the Inner Child on a regular basis, listening to its hopes, wishes and needs, and is willing to engage in playful activities, the Inner Child tends to become a truly happy member of one's inner family of selves. The Inner Child will often leap-frog into new levels of growth, to the surprise and delight of the personality self!

During this time, my Male Self was making increasingly frequent visitations to my psyche. His rehabilitation in the inner plane where he had been sent had apparently been successful. He was now tentatively feeling his way back to a more balanced and caring role in my life, with due respect for Mary, the Female Self, and with affection for the Inner Child, whom he regarded as a younger brother.

Recovery from the multiple operations of my Pittsburgh summer was not without intense personal effort. The months spent in a hospital bed had reduced my physical strength to nil. I had to will myself to exercise. I walked my way back to health, adding ten more steps every day to increase my strength. The will to heal was due in large part to the rapport I had established with my Female Self and my Inner Child. They, and I, welcomed the new kidney with open arms, regarding the kidney as a special "self" who had come as a gift and a blessing to assist in the unfoldment of one's being.

Part Two

It is now 1992. I sense that something is coming, but I don't know what it is. There is a feeling of presentiment, unease and reckoning. A new challenge with opportunities for further deepening and growth is being triggered in the lower, and previously inaccessible, strata of my psyche. I am about to make the acquaintance of my Astral Judge Self.

Around this time a close friend writes that she has begun to do healing work with a man named Harvey Grady of Scottsdale, Arizona. She says that he has discovered the presence of an entity called the Judge Self who inhabits the basement, or more accurately in some cases, the dungeon of the human psyche.

Harvey's research will eventually reveal that the Judge Self has two dimensionalities of operation, one in the Astral Plane, where desires, emotions and drama are the norm; the other in the Mental Plane where thought, imagination and reason are exercised. Negative or afflicted Astral Plane activity can result in addictions and delusional glamours. Negative Mental Plane activity spins a web of grandiosity, illusion and attachment to "being right." The higher aspect of the Astral Plane produces symphonic and inspiring chords of universal feeling. The higher aspect of the Mental Plane is where the luminous imagery of the divine ideal is spontaneously conceived.

I enter into my spiritual practice with renewed effort. Daily I intone the sound "Hu" in each of my chakras, starting with the root chakra at the base of my spine and proceeding upward until the halo center above the crown chakra is reached. I use the musical scale to do this, beginning with the lowest note and concluding with the highest note of the octave. The practice has a cleansing and purifying effect, and allows me to perceive the shadowy energy associated with my lower chakras clearly and in a non-judgmental way.

One morning as I am sitting in silence after my practice, I hear a voice speak to me from the area of my second chakra: "Everything you hate is me." Hearing this voice for the first time, as I try to "grok" the tragic message it conveys, hits me like an earthquake. "Who are you?" I ask. The voice replies, "My name is Agrippa."

Stunned by a resonance both familiar and alien, I look up the name in the dictionary. Here is the meaning I find: "Agrippa—Latin. 'born feet first.' The name of a first century Roman client king, the son of Herod." In other words, the name my Astral Judge Self has given indicates that he considers himself to be like the son of the Roman king who ordered a slaughter of all male infants to ensure that the Christ child, whom he feared as a threat to his rule, would also be killed. In addition, "born feet first" suggests a generally resistant, rebellious and oppositional nature.

All of these negative qualities are initially borne out as I begin to work with Agrippa. I am familiar with hard and arduous personal effort, but work with this seemingly intractable being, who knows no other home than the gross vibrations of the lower Astral Plane, is very difficult indeed. Agrippa is angry, fearful, resentful, distrustful and unable to give or receive love. The power of his fear is immense. Yet as I consistently give him respectful attention and assure him that I accept him as a creative and vital part of myself, he begins to melt like wax. His level of fear diminishes dramatically. As Agrippa and I become conversant—not so much in the verbal realm as in a mutual interchange of feelings—I notice that my ability to extend consciousness deep into my pelvic bowl increases.

Agrippa is proving to be an ally in my journey of personal and spiritual discovery. He seems to have an innate capacity to connect with the golden light of the High Self. As he gains confidence in linking the fields of feeling and light, he is guided to empathetically impart his feelings of well-being to the rest of my psyche. Agrippa begins to experience joy as he returns to the spiritual path. He feels blessed with an ancient memory of freedom as he consciously aligns with the Spirit of Guidance. Now, however, it is freedom balanced by a sense of responsibility.

In a few months, Agrippa will, upon request, share these transformative feelings with the Astral Judge Selves of mureeds who come to me for Soulwork counseling. These feelings are shared less through conversation than silently through a powerfully focused intention and resonance—in short, through an industrial-strength attunement. In this process of attunement, tides of deep emotion are mediated back and forth until an equilibrium of mutual understanding is attained.

We cannot underestimate the importance of accepting and befriending our Judge Selves. This is how Judge Selves awaken, learn and grow. This is how they release their impressions of hell-worlds created by fear, pain, anger, confusion and despair. This is how Judge Selves move beyond feelings of shame, blame and unworthiness to find refuge and healing. This is how Judge Selves rediscover their Souls.

My work with Agrippa will last six years. When I undertake similar efforts with my Mental Judge Self in 1998, I begin to see a pattern emerge. The pattern is one of coherent, planned unfoldment. Earlier I mentioned that a "carefully-timed plan orchestrated by my High Self" was underway. I now begin to fathom the spiritual intelligence working behind the scenes to effect these evolutionary changes in sequential stages.

Shortly after my work with Agrippa began in 1992, my Mental Judge Self came forth and announced his name as Bernard. Bernard, however, seemed content to let me devote the lion's share of my time to Agrippa. Thus, while I included Bernard regularly in my Soulwork practice, my ongoing primary attention was given to Agrippa.

But there were occasional exceptions. From time to time, physical health problems would come up that had to be dealt with. I went through a yearlong period when my blood pressure could no longer be controlled by the medication I had been taking. It took months of appointments with my doctor to find a new combination of medications that would control my hypertension. Naturally I had to pay attention to my body's needs.

Consequently, my Body Self also emerged to consciousness. As I write, I have an image of a crocus flower popping up through the snow. Yet unlike a flower, the name my Body Self gives at the time is Peter, which means "rock." This has significant meaning for me. It says that Peter, my Body Self, will be slow to change, much like my Capricorn nature. Capricorn, which means "goat horn," also suggests a kind of rocklike hardheadedness and rigidity. Yet I am taking seriously in the present moment the image of the crocus flower. My impression is that fragility and vulnerability can contain great strength. This can be an important lesson for Peter. Murshid Samuel Lewis says in his epic poem Saladin, "A tiny sprig, gathering dust, can split a precipice."

The crocus pushing through the snow becomes a symbol of breath-essence renewing and transforming the physical body. In his "40 Lessons on Breath," Murshid S.A.M. states, "When breath is in the body, life is in the body; and when breath is not in the body, life is not in the body."

Peter has struggled to survive again and again during this lifetime. Many times when the light seemed about to go out, he rallied and came back. I sometimes refer to him as a "veteran of many campaigns." Peter has been and continues to be one of my greatest teachers. My work with him is constant, because my health concerns are constant. Twenty years of Prednisone and other medications has resulted in extremely thin skin and fragile tissue. Any little knock or bump can cause bruising or laceration. Peter has had to learn to develop an almost extrasensory awareness of where physical objects are located, especially objects like coffee tables that have sharp corners.

Obviously, Peter has experienced a great deal of help from the transplanted kidney he received in 1991 from the eight-year-old girl. It took him awhile to get used to the idea of accommodating the new organ. When I explained to him that without it he would be forced to return to a lackluster life on dialysis, Peter was quite happy to accept the kidney.

One morning several years ago as I was doing my Soulwork practice, I was moved to thank my new kidney for restoring me, and Peter, to a normal life. In gratitude, I christened the kidney with the name Hilal, which is Arabic for "new moon." Not only is the kidney crescent-shaped, the name itself resonates with a sense of renewal and growth in the light. Hilal is a God-send.

During these developments with Agrippa, Bernard, Peter and Hilal, my Male Self returned as a full-time member to my inner family of selves, who collectively welcomed his long-awaited homecoming. He says his name is Christopher, which means Christ-bearer. He no longer feels like Rutherford, nor does he carry any scars from that former incarnation. His healing in the inner plane where he was sent seems to have been accomplished.

Although Christopher's emotional maturity can range freely all the way from being a playful lad to being a wise elder, depending upon the circumstances, he prefers to manifest primarily as a teenage youth. All the positives and negatives of adolescence are present in Christopher's being, but the main element he now contributes to my personality is his zest for everyday life and work. When called upon, he is quite willing to become the Christ-bearer signified by his name. This is how Christopher renders divine service.

Another change that occurred in the 1990s was that Mary, my Female Self, changed her name to Mariam. It is interesting to note that the names of my inner selves relate in some way to the life of Christ. These names identify the inner selves who constitute the foundations of one's personality and spirit. Many people I work with have psychic structures that contain names similarly grouped around a central theme. Some names draw from various cultural and spiritual traditions, others are seemingly ordinary and conventional, while yet others are otherworldly or fantastical. Each name is unique, even magical, in that it carries the vibrational signature and something of the inner secret of the self it identifies.

The High Self oversees the implementation of the divine plan for each person, and for each inner self within each person, initiating psychic and spiritual development in carefully sequenced states and stages. At times, we are touched by grace and given glimpses of our essential oneness with the universe. Not a single one of these peak experiences is random.

Each is exquisitely choreographed into a design that serves universal compassion and purpose.

No less compassionate and purposeful are the times marked by personal challenge, trial and pain. The phrase "you get right down to the real nitty-gritty" is quite apt. Each inner self is required to balance its karmic accounts. When a self has sufficiently cleansed and cleared its slate, and attained a certain level of competence and balance, the scene shifts and another self becomes the principal focus of one's inner work. During these periods of transition, the outer personality self often undergoes adjustments that are confusing and difficult. It is important at such times to call upon the guidance of the High Self to be assured of the focus and direction of one's work.

When my work with Agrippa concluded in 1998, Bernard, my Mental Judge Self, came forth with unanticipated acrimony. I had assumed that Bernard was a fair-minded and compatible member of my inner family of selves. But Bernard, the "inner critic," had other ideas. Now that Agrippa had been placed on the back burner, Bernard would be pleased to take over and run things his way. "Be reasonable—do it my way" was his motto.

According to Harvey Grady, who pioneered the work with the Judge Selves: "The Mental Judge Self is normally in hiding, extremely alert and sensing, in the distance, for possible threat. This situation occurs because the Mental Judge Self lives in a state of self-imposed isolation, seeking to preserve its own existence. The average person is as yet unaware that he or she contains a Mental Judge Self. In that state of ignorance, the Mental Judge Self has established a position of power. As part of the human shadow, it prefers to remain in hiding because there it can manipulate, sabotage and control much of the action of the personality with impunity."

The Mental Judge Self's great fear is loss of control. Control equals survival. It is a consummate trickster and will do anything to stay in control. Impersonating the High Self, or even God, is one of the tricks up its sleeve. Thriving on reactivity, the Mental Judge Self is highly skilled at causing mental and emotional agitation. It knows how to instill confusion and pain, often resorting to cruelty and sarcasm as part of its modus operandi. These behaviors are directed not only toward other human beings but to one's inner family of selves as well. Reinforcing low self-esteem is a favorite pastime of the Mental Judge Self. It will zero in on and aggravate any and all weaknesses. It regards the personality self as a lesser being of little or no consequence.

Given this background, how does one proceed to work creatively with the Mental Judge Self? One very productive way is to turn the tables on it. Its expectation is that no one will choose to accept and befriend it. It cannot conceive of that possibility, because being friendless is normal. To befriend Bernard, who carried these attitudes and saw me as an insignificant pawn in his game, was not going to be easy. First I tried to extend heartfelt love to him. He didn't buy it. "That's strange," I thought to myself, "Agrippa responded quite well to love." "Well, I *ain't* Agrippa," Bernard fired back, "you'd better try something else."

Every step of the way, Bernard set up stumbling blocks. This turned out to be a good thing. It forced me to appreciate the subtle dynamics of the lower mental plane. I couldn't hatch secret plots to mollify and redeem Bernard; he was telepathic and knew my thoughts immediately. So I decided to ask the High Self for help. The High Self suggested simple acceptance and listening as a basis for working. Ask what Bernard's needs are. Negotiate agreements based on those needs, with the understanding that cruel attitudes and harmful behaviors are no longer acceptable. Encourage Bernard to open up to the Golden Light of Grace.

This proved to be wise advice. What Bernard really needed was to be respected as a self and valued for his work. Once I could respect and value him, he in his turn could respect and value me, thus transforming a duel into a duet, as a poet once said. I proposed that he expend less energy being an exacting taskmaster and put more energy into serving the divine mind, which is discriminating yet inclusive and compassionate too. As Bernard made the shift to more harmonious interaction, I began to notice a shift in my own manner. Our mutual suspicion grew into mutual appreciation.

Instead of inducing avoidance, Bernard now actively encourages me to engage in daily spiritual practice. He was experiencing firsthand the benefits of softening and surrender as stepping-stones to radiant freedom and goodwill.

Bernard also gained insight into divine purpose: each self in its turn is given opportunity to consciously move "Toward the One," to become liberated into the larger universe of its sponsoring Soul, to become one with the Only Being.

It is now January 2000. My work with Bernard remains the current focus of my Soulwork practice. I am pleased to note that for the first time in years, Bernard did not generate a spell of mid-winter depression. I kept waiting for it to happen, anticipating the month-long period when the bottom would fall out, and I would descend to face my inner discord and darkness. Instead, I witnessed an inordinate upsurge of personal crisis and conflict in the lives of others. My own relative stability this winter has allowed me to assist a number of persons with their problems instead of focusing on my own.

My inner family of selves join me in thanking Bernard for his steady growth and harmonious support. We congratulate him for his progress. No longer insistent on being isolated and devilish, he is choosing a path of regeneration and connection.

The Gospel of St. John states, "And the light shone in the darkness, and the darkness comprehended it not." This was true in the Piscean Age. Now we are moving into the Aquarian Age. What is true now is that our darkest shadows are beginning to comprehend the light.

This is the work before us.

Epilogue

We now return to our original theme: uniting the one to the One. Each inner subconscious self is given opportunity to become conscious. As each inner self becomes conscious, it is encouraged to release and heal old hurts, and to accept and respect the other members of its inner family. The inner selves are invited to connect with each other and with the guiding light of the High Self. This is the basic pattern of psychic and spiritual evolution according to the Soulwork model.

It is a process of continual mergence with states, and emergence into stages, of expanded awareness and spiritual consciousness. All the mystical traditions of the world teach: return to the Source. In the Source we find the compassionate love that illuminates every heart. In the Source we discover the "morning star" of every soul.

Sir Edwin Arnold's poem "The Light of Asia" concludes with this description of the Buddha's enlightenment:

The dew-drop slips into the Shining Sea.

The one unites with the One.

A further realization comes when the "Shining Sea slips into the dew-drop."

Thus is born the spirit of Rasoul, the Sufi Ideal.

***

A note, and suggested references:

The phrase "the Shining Sea slips into the dew-drop" was a spontaneous remark shared by the late Joe Miller, pal of Murshid Samuel Lewis, friend of the Sufi Community, Bodhisattva.

A Little Book on the Human Shadow by Robert Bly.

Self Integration and *Explorations with Monitor* by Harvey Grady

Soul Without Shame: A Guide to Liberating Yourself from the Judge Within by Byron Brown.

Why Me? by Frida Waterhouse, privately published. Available online at: http://www.sufimovement.net/files/WhyMe_byFridaWaterhouse.pdf

V. An Evolving Sufi Path

Editor's note:

Depending on how one defines it, Sufism in its many worldwide varieties dates from at least fifteen hundred years ago. Yet the challenge of adapting it for Western modernity only began with Hazrat Inayat Khan about a hundred years ago. Before this time, historical Sufi tariqas either followed the way of retreat and quietism—refusing to engage with Western culture—or, as often as not, were in the forefront of resistance to Western colonialism and neo-colonialism.

During Hazrat Inayat Khan's short time in the West (1910-1927), we see the beginnings of a personal approach to the Sufi mystical path, one suited to the increasingly more individualistic nature of Western culture. After

Hazrat Inayat Khan, the path began to evolve in a direction that emulated Western psychotherapy, with mureeds meeting with their guide in sessions that approximated the "therapeutic hour" of psychotherapy.

Hazrat Inayat Khan's own Sufi training in India was very different. One did not have "sessions" with one's sheikh or guide, listen to lectures or attend workshops. As Hazrat Inayat Khan described it, he learned through the way of inner silence and attunement. Through intuition one communicated "on the inside" to the teacher and tried to receive the wordless wisdom through his or her atmosphere. Hazrat Inayat Khan tells some form of the following story more than a half dozen times in his memoirs and lectures:

> "When first I became initiated at the hands of my spiritual teacher in India I was eager as any man could be to assimilate, to grasp, as much as I could. Day after day I was in the presence of my Murshid, but not once did he speak on spiritual matters. Sometimes he spoke about herbs and plants, at other times about milk and butter. I went there every day for six months to see if I could hear anything about spiritual things. After six months the teacher spoke to me one day about the two parts of a personality, the outer and the inner. And I was overenthusiastic; the moment he began I took out a notebook and pencil. But as soon as I did this my teacher changed the subject and spoke about other things.

> "I understood what that meant; it meant in the first place that the teaching of the heart should be assimilated in the heart. The heart is the notebook for it; when it is written in another notebook it will remain one's pocket, but when it is written in the heart it will remain the soul. Besides one has to learn the lesson of patience, to wait, for all knowledge comes in its own time. I asked myself further if it was worth while to come to a place after a long journey, and go there every day for six months to hear of nothing but trees and butter. And my deepest self answered: yes, more than worthwhile, for there is nothing in the whole world more precious than the presence of the holy one. His teaching may not be given in theories, but it is in his atmosphere. That is a living teaching which is real upliftment" (from "Mental Purification").

During the last hundred years, some Sufi tariqahs or orders around the world have remained village or community-based, essentially extended family systems. In many of these, the sheikh or pir—the head of the family—is literally the "father" of his community; he serves social and welfare needs mixed together with religious-spiritual ones. The lineage is then passed from father to son in a hierarchal (and patriarchal) way. Concerns with Western ideas about gender, ethics and privilege were and still are seldom heard. Some Sufi lineages brought the same models of spiritual authority with them when they came to Europe and America in the period since World War II. Part of Hazrat Inayat's Khan's many-sprouted lineage was understood in the same fashion.

After the passing of Hazrat Inayat Khan, Murshid Samuel Lewis had a very conflicted relationship with the Sufi Movement, the legal organization that his teacher left behind and which quickly splintered into multiple groups. That story is told in the book Sufi Vision and Initiation. Murshid S.A.M. resisted organizing his own group—the Sufi Islamia Ruhaniat Society—until just before his passing. Of the hundred or so mureeds who were with him when he passed in 1971, the three who had been with him the longest—Moineddin, Fatima and Mansur Johnson (author of the autobiographical work Murshid about his time with Murshid S.A.M.) had spent only a bit more than five years in S.A.M.'s presence. Most of those who surrounded Murshid Samuel Lewis during his lifetime left the Sufi path for long periods of time, or permanently, in order to discover their own sense of human purpose and "illuminate their own shadow."

Moineddin did this while at the same time shepherding a nascent tradition of Sufism that was linked to its historical past but actively involved in adapting to a very different world from medieval Persia or even early 20th century India. In the years since Moineddin's passing, many Sufi orders and tariqas have undergone massive transformation around the world—from actively engaging in government as political parties (for instance, in Bangladesh) to working hands-on for ecological balance (try googling "green Islam in Indonesia").

This section collects letters and other documents that reveal how, while engaged in his own personal healing, Pir Moineddin struggled with the changing nature of an historical mystical path like Sufism. With loving stewardship and adamantine wisdom he helped it evolve into a living 21st century tradition and transmission.

Mureeds Rights (letter 1984)

(Editor's note: A hand-written letter to all members of the Ruhaniat Jamiat Khas, the group of senior teachers, dated March 14, 1984.)

To the Members of the Jamiat Khas,
My Dear Sisters and Brothers,

Aloha!

Last month during my visit to the [San Francisco] Bay area, I met with a large gathering of mureeds at the Mentorgarten [the home of Murshid Samuel Lewis in San Francisco]. At one point, after referring to several recent disclosures of abuses by teachers toward their disciples, I proposed that a list of "Mureeds Rights" be drawn up, to be read alongside the 10 Sufi Thoughts and the 3 Objects of the Sufi Movement [*of Hazrat Inayat Khan*] at the time of future *bayats* [*the initiation of a person as a Sufi mureed*]. A veritable cheer went up.

Friends, if we expect to be regarded with credibility by mureeds, either singly or collectively, for the living experience and experiences we have presumably had, then we must respect the most basic rights of the body, *and bodies*, of our sacred charges.

We ask our mureeds to accept willy-nilly our presumptions of the aristocracy of spirit. Do we at the same time respect the actual requirements of the living spiritual democracy to which we belong? This is not some separate elitist clique or country club we have entered by virtue (or vice) of our ancestors. This is a gathering of *souls* who have *earned* their realizations, who will continue to *earn* by hard and sincere training the vision and reality of the integration of self and the unity with all.

If we cannot commit ourselves to the deepest motives of THE ONLY BEING—at a pace commensurate with our own growth and balance *as determined by the Spirit of Guidance*—then we have no business being here as obstructers of the real work of the Jamiat Khas!

We are here to serve as *instruments* of the Divine Mother and Father. How hard are we trying to clarify and make ourselves whole as instruments? I'm not talking about compulsive behavior here. I'm talking about a whole program of healing and accomplishment.

When we are sought out by our mureed, any mureed whomsoever, we may *and we must* join with that spirit who informed St. Francis:

"Lord, make me an instrument of Thy Peace..."

I want your help, people. Please ask your mureeds at your various classes to begin thinking about the kind of rights any and all disciples deserve and should expect throughout the course of their sacred relationship with each of you.

I'll try to have something ready for each meeting to keep the ball rolling.

Peace be with you!
Moineddin

Sufi Practice, Psychology and Gender Issues (letter 1984)

(*Editor's note: In summer 1984 under Moineddin's influence, the annual Sufi retreat camp in Mendocino, California began offering private one-to-one counseling alongside the usual classes that focused on Sufi practice. From his own experience, he began to recognize that doing intense spiritual practice in any tradition had psychological effects. Victoria Tackett, a Psychosynthesis practitioner, was asked to serve as the first counselor. She was overwhelmed with the response and wrote a letter to Moineddin asking him how to distinguish issues that arose from spiritual practice at the camp from those that related to emotional issues that a person brought from his/her "everyday life." The following was Moineddin's response, which was copied to Frida Waterhouse, the camp director and a few other senior mureeds.*)

October 29, 1984
Dear Victoria,

Aloha! And thank you for your group letter. You ask, "What is really different here (camp situations) from everyday life as we experience it?"

Saadi [Klotz] has written an article for *The Journal of Somatics* in which he says, "Students are encouraged to feel the [Sufi] movement practices in a way that synchronizes ideas, emotions and action; that is, they feel that 'all of them' is acting. In itself, this initially distinguishes movement practice from movement in everyday life in that during the latter, one is often divided in one's attention: one moves to pick up something, go somewhere or otherwise manipulate the environment, often at the same time thinking and feeling something unrelated. Rarely does one take the opportunity to move simply for the sake of movement, with one's feeling and intention fully engaged, except in the case of moving toward or with a loved one."

I think Saadi's insight is right on the mark. In everyday life there is no general agreement as to a common focus. That is why Psychosynthesis and other types of Three-Self work are so important: at least we can be cooperative and focused within ourselves. It gives a real meaning to the word *integrity*.

Thank you for sending the data on statistical differences between men who abuse children and women who do the same. I am in general agreement that it is the male ego which is mostly at fault—and here I am speaking of the "male" in both female and male bodies. But I can see also that there are probably some unredeemed types of female egos involved in abuse too. Erich Neumann's study *The Great Mother* goes into detail about the "Terrible Mother" and other similar archaic manifestations.

I also agree with you that it is our sisters who are beginning to seek and receive help. My [counseling] work is 80-90% with women. But a few men do come, and they do receive help. Mostly it is a matter of getting them to: 1) admit that they have a real problem, and 2) begin to face that problem in practical ways, both inner and outer. To keep it practical, directive and focused and yet to allow oneself to be vulnerable to one's lack of direction and malaise from time to time. As Hazrat Inayat Khan says, "One should not try to be too good, for if one becomes too good, one can become too good to live."

You say, "Action occurs spontaneously from Self, is blocked in self-absorption." If you mean not to capitalize the s in self-absorption, then I agree. If you mean "is blocked in Self-absorption" then I disagree. *Nirvakalpa* and *Sahaja* states (in Sanskrit terms) are like the systolic and diastolic beats of the heart. Or the inhalation and exhalation of the breath. Oftentimes it is our absorbed experiences that lend vitality, credence and real wit to our human endeavors. Otherwise, why meditate at all? In God-realization there is never blockage as such—despite apparent active and passive appearances.

I think it would be interesting to tackle the 50/50 responsibility issue [for one's action and what happens to one] *beyond* the stalemated point. I have been taught by both Murshid S.A.M. and Frida Waterhouse that "We live in a universe of absolute justice." However, this type of work could only be done through a totally clarified instrument, one who is open to the complete stories of all the lives (and past lives) involved. It would certainly necessitate a radical shift in our views of what is called *innocence*.

Without total clarity and openness, it is better to simply fine-tune our already existing laws. But some people will be ready for the "total responsibility" journey, and they will be drawn to the appropriate instrument(s) for their unfoldment.

It reminds me of Hazrat Inayat Khan's story of the madzub he met. Inayat asked the madzub, "Are you a thief?" And the madzub replied, "Yes." H.I.K.'s explanation was that in God-realization, there is nothing and no one whom you are not.

Thank you again for sharing your view and growth insights with me.

I too am glad to be here on the planet with the rest of us, even with my new-found rosy persona—complete with thorns!

Peace!
Moineddin

Jamiat Agenda I (letter 1985)

(Editor's note: From a letter to a mureed preceding the spring 1985 leaders' gathering of the Ruhaniat.)

January 16, 1985

Aloha! I wrote to the Jamiat coordinators with the following three suggestions for the agenda:

1. That women chairpersons share equally as to number and time with the men (who are usually dominant) during all discussion and practice throughout the three days we are in session.

2. That there be a presentation of the Feminine Principle by all women who feel they have something to say on the subject. This panel would hopefully represent a spectrum of views. I think such a presentation, with plenty of give and take among the panel and between the panel and everyone else, would be valid and valuable for our growth toward more mature outlooks.

3. That we resolve definitely to establish a national newsletter for our work, perhaps upgrading and enlarging *The Sound* for the purpose.

4. That we begin to call the "Brotherhood Work" the "Sister/Brotherhood Work." I place the Sister designation first for two reasons: one, because chivalry demands "ladies first," and two because there is legitimate ground for redressing the millennia of patriarchal dominion with its vaunting of male prerogatives and depreciation of the feminine values and rights.

5. I wouldn't mind participating in Hidayat [Inayat Khan]'s confederation [a group proposed to link all of the lineages deriving from Hazrat Inayat Khan] as long as we have someone who could give it proper concentration.

6. Re: grades of initiation, use of the study circles. In my class on Thursday nights we begin with a chapter from Robert A. Johnson's *We: Understanding the Psychology of Romantic Love.* Then we read two of Inayat's Gathas (also publicly), and conclude with a few lessons from

"Fana-fi-Sheikh" (for mureeds only) [a paper of Murshid Samuel Lewis]. Most of my non-mureed students are mature people in their 30s and 40s who have been through many many of the various spiritual scenes. At any rate, I tend to gauge my presentations according to Jesus' "Let those who have ears to hear, hear." It seems to work here on Maui.

Naturally, I will call into question the use of initiatic grade to bolster personal power while demeaning the "half who is equal." Speaking for myself, this problem is more tenacious at subtle levels. It requires much focus to even see that subconsciously we tend to hoard our troves of power, much like the dragon guards hers. Our work on that level is to befriend our "beasts" within so that they will become gradually transfigured. As a result of our respect for the light that sources all shadows, our more basic parts will feel free to share the *mana* [Hawaiian Huna term for life energy] and depth that are naturally theirs.

The work of resolving dichotomies in the outer world begins and ends much closer to home.

7. Re: the Jamiat members getting their hands dirty. Why not have a Jamiat Work Party, with mureeds assigning all the chores?

See you in a few weeks.
Love,
Moineddin

Funding the Work (letter 1985)

(Editor's note: A letter to Ruhaniat leaders.)

May 6, 1985

Dear Mureeds and Colleagues,

Aloha! *As-salaam aleikhum!*

Dues this year are down one-third from last year. This might not be so bad except that 1984 was down a third from 1983.

This being the case, it makes it hard to carry on the normal work-load of our order, particularly the secretariat functions. Besides leaving us with no cushion for emergencies, it limits our scope in getting Murshid's work into the world effectively.

So, I am putting out the word to each of us to pay the dues our order depends upon to continue the work. For some of us this may seem like an impossible step to take.

Such is the path of initiation.

I also take this opportunity to ask all Sheikhs and teachers to begin tithing ten percent of net earnings from camps, seminars and workshops back to the order. This is a policy that used to be honored, but through time and the decay of resolve has been allowed to lapse.

I base this reinstatement on two hard facts:

> 1) We are not the originators of what we present as teachings.
> 2) The Sufi Islamia Ruhaniat Society must represent for us the best of Murshid's efforts for the cause of God.

Thank you for bearing with me.
With respect,
Moineddin

Moths (letter 1985)

(Editor's note: From a letter to a Sufi colleague.)

May 22, 1985

Thank you for your reply re: dues and tithing.

I appreciate that you are "working like blazes." This intensity of your commitment to your craft and students has always provided you with a rationale not to part with a few bucks from a billfold that at least has a few bills in it. Most of us open ours and see moths fly out.

Neither am I surprised that you believe my draft letter is not "the right tack." While I cannot speak for you or anyone, but only for myself, I can let you know that to date the mail and phone calls are running seven-to-one in favor of my proposals.

The "strenuous, active, imaginative, consistent, hierarchal, inspired and demonstrative leadership" that you claim the Ruhaniat lacks—to the effect that "dues are down, down"—may be linked to unfinished grieving on your part for a vanished Murshid S.A.M. who displayed these qualities, as do you, in spades.

One of our colleagues who phoned to encourage me said she thought the reason dues were down is a direct result of a mureedship which sees the Sheikhs and Jamiat members generally behaving as a privileged elite that tends to set itself apart from, and possibly above, those who form the mass of a less financially and spiritually developed type.

Ha!

Could our colleague be possessed of a different kind of knowing than yours, albeit equal?

Finally, I would like to reply to your statement that "SIRS is but one manifestation of it (Murshid's legacy), perhaps a minor one."

If you were in my shoes you would not dare to say it. Nor did, and does, Murshid feel that way. Not that you may not be right, but if you stood in my shoes you would not deign to say it.

Aloha!
Moineddin

Continuing the Conversation (letter 1985)

(Editor's note: From a subsequent letter to a Sufi colleague.)

June 12, 1985

Aloha!

Thank you for your reply of May 29, especially for sharing underlying feelings. I feel more open to your input as a result.

You write: "...leadership of SIRS is not my transmission that I have any inkling of. But at the same time I was sad and mad that these qualities of spiritual fire which you and Wali Ali possess in fine were not brought forward. The moment seemed like a clear vignette of the SIRS stalemate."

Back in 1971 or '72, Krishnadas [*another early mureed of Murshid S.A.M.*] came to the Wednesday night meeting in Sausalito Art Center and announced, "I just returned from Colorado, and when I was there someone asked me who Murshid's successor was. I said, 'We all are.'"

Krishnadas was right then, and his words are right now. If you see and feel a need to bring a certain energy into the group sphere, but don't, you cannot blame others—no matter how much *you* feel *they* should be doing it.

One of the tragedies of Murshid's life, then and now, is that his disciples refuse to become his colleagues.

At any rate, I respect your process the more you share it with me.

If you feel moved to suggest a "decent salary" for Wali Ali and/or me, by all means let the sisters and brothers in the Jamiat know your idea. Mention it to your mureeds. Speaking for myself, it would be very helpful if I were enabled to join with everyone (the mureedship no less than colleagues) more often than the once or twice a year now possible.

With love and respect,
Moineddin

An Open Letter to Moineddin (letter 1986)

(Editor's note: The following letter was sent by 23 members of the Ruhaniat Jamiat Khas to Moineddin.)

March 6, 1986

Dearest Moineddin, Beloved Brother,

As Salaam Aleihkum and Aloha!

We are writing this letter to express our common group feeling.

We feel much love and appreciation for your having taken on the role Murshid offered you and for the many years of gracious service.

During your illness and for years after you were out of touch with us and the group at large and now find yourself 4000 miles away.

At this point we no longer have trust and confidence in the structure of our organization. Just as your main topics for the Spring Cleaning Meeting deal with democracy versus hierarchy and abuse of power, we feel our antiquated By-Laws need to be addressed to protect the continued life of S.I.R.S.

We are asking you to restructure the organization toward democracy and away from hierarchy, that we will all be answerable to a democratic process and no one will have autonomous rule and power.

We, who can attend, would like to meet with you when you come in April at a Jamiat for this purpose at your convenience. Let us avoid a volley of letters but just meet face to face, heart to heart and try to help S.I.R.S. be an effective tool of the Message.

With Love and Respect,

Bottom of the Milk of Life (letter 1986)

(Editor's note: From a letter to a mureed.)

March 24, 1986

Aloha!

I am willing to participate in a cleansing and clearing process with the other original mureeds of Murshid. The June 1984 Jamiat was a step in the direction you suggest, but it stayed mostly on the "top of the milk of life" side and didn't really deal with curdling or dregs. My only problem would be airfare and scheduling, but with willingness on the part of others, this could be overcome.

I'm making no predictions as to the outcome of next month's Jamiat Ahm, and that goes for both the Saturday and Sunday sessions. I haven't made any hard decisions regarding hierarchical or democratic changes, and am more than willing to begin discussions toward a more workable framework for our efforts.

At the same time, I am not attached to the prospect that some may walk away, or even many may walk away if they don't "get their way." I don't feel particularly sentimental about sharing my energies with people who seem to be plugged into a social status quo more than the sincere wish to grow according to the dictates of the soul.

Love to you,
Moineddin

Reconciliation, Guts and Guidance (letter 1986)

(*Editor's note: From a letter to a mureed.*)

April 15, 1986

Aloha! Thank you for your supportive notes, letters and comments. I agree that a meeting of S.A.M.'s original mureeds, more or less, is a good place to start with much needed emotional clearing. Hopefully, this can come about in the next several months.

I have received the advice: "I would if I were you make a decision on the purpose and direction of SIRS now. I would give the Sheikhs and Khalifs a time to review it and then start sailing my ship with or without them." Naturally, I am prepared to move ahead with as many or as few as are willing to work with me. But until we can determine the main priorities of the *whole group*—which I hope will come out at the Jamiat Ahm—I cannot in all fairness assume that my limited vision covers all bases.

We are a very plural group, and I would not be operating honestly if I were to unilaterally present an ultimatum to those with titles. Furthermore, it may be time for the direction of the Ruhaniat to include the input of the increasingly mature (both as to physical age and psychic evolution) mureedship. Certainly this was the feeling developed at the Spring Cleaning meeting.

What I am saying is it is time to emphasize a spirit of reconciliation. Within this context, it will be necessary for me me to concede that my shenanigans have not exactly paved the way toward love, harmony and beauty. And I expect others to come clean, too. If after the Jamiat Ahm there still remains hardness of heart on the part of some toward my willingness to open up the Ruhaniat's future to a consensual type of participatory democracy, with mureeds sitting side-by-side with teachers, then and only then should we be prepared to say some alohas, is my feeling.

I want to give reconciliation every possible chance to emerge and grow. Yes, we do need some real changes. Some will be effected simply by people admitting faults and a willingness to work on those issues on a personal nature in their meditations. Others will come about only through the blend of guts and guidance from *each person in the circle speaking their most deeply felt and illuminated mind.*

Love and see you soon, Moineddin

The Making of a Sufi Teacher (letters 1986)

(Editor's note: Traditionally, the Pir, or head sheikh, of a Sufi tariqah made all of the decisions regarding who could represent the lineage as a teacher, sheikh or khalif. Murshid Samuel Lewis used one form of Hazrat Inayat Khan's guidelines for this process, recognizing that a teacher needed to function from effacement and transmission in relation to her/his living teacher (fana-fi-sheikh), to the teachers who had passed (fana-fi-pir or fana-fi-rassoul) or in Allah (fana-fi-lillah). In the following excerpts from letters to mureeds, Moineddin talks about his own experiences with these states in relation to how teachers are recognized in the Ruhaniat. On this subject, see also the letter in Section III entitled "About Effacement and Nirvana.")

December 10, 1986

Re: Advanced initiations. As you know, my usual practice when considering someone for such an initiation or confirmation is to consult with two or three experienced initiators and get their feedback before making any final decision.

The looseness with which initiatic links have been regarded in SIRS in recent years shows our failure to come to grips with the shadow side of democracy. Related to this is the history, beginning with my illness in late 1976, of too many SIRS Sheikhs taking off on their own with little regard for the principles of cohesion which a monthly Sangitha (teachers) class could have salvaged. Ego agendas took precedence over the *mujahidas* (heart-clearing) required to become selfless instruments for the Spirit of Guidance.

Anyhow, my point in telling you this is to begin to explore the balances incumbent in having an order and a society, in having aristocracy and democracy together. It is my conviction that in exploring the possibilities of a sacred marriage between these "opposites," we may be enabled to enter the universal evolution more fully.

Also, I want to open up discussion on the whole subject of God-realization, however defined or conceived, as essential to the 10th initiation (Sheikh or Khalif). This is properly the need of Sangitha students, and should you choose to convene a monthly Sangitha class for the Bay Area initiators, discussion of this theme could accompany the lessons and practices of Hazrat Inayat Khan.

Your reply is awaited with alacrity!

Happy holidays, and love,
Moineddin

***

December 23, 1986

"Light upon Light: Divine Spirit and Human Psyche" (Lama Foundation, August 22-28, 1987)

Exploring the ways in which the Spirit of Guidance answers the needs of the human psyche for balance and healing. Long symbolized by the star and crescent, spirit and psyche will be approached through Sufi, Jungian, Huna and Neuro-Linguistic models of consciousness—with special attention to recalling the Divine Feminine from the Depths of Life.

(A retreat with Moineddin Jablonski, Mei-Ling Chang, Ana Perez and Jaffar Baugh).

Aloha!

Thanks to each of you for your letters. The above is the blurb for the 1987 Lama retreat we're doing.

I am in general agreement with your outlines for admission to the 9th degree. My direct experience with Murshid S.A.M. consisted of several visions of him covering a range of manifestations. Sometime in the winter of 1968 Murshid had two or three of us in the Garden of Inayat [Novato, California] office with him, and he asked Mansur Johnson to write down the grades of each disciple on the list he had. Most were placed in the first three grades, a few were placed 4th or 5th, but it was a total surprise when he came to Moineddin and said, "9th." I think Akbar Simmons may have been 9th too, and Wali Ali and Amin 6th at that time.

But I never had an experience of *fana-fi-pir* in the sense of being effaced in Inayat Khan. Everything was S.A.M., except for one experience on LSD two months before I met him that included what I consider an archetypal experience of Muhammad followed by an extended *satori* or *kensho* after reading a Ko-an and looking at a drawing by Hakuin Zen-shi in the book *The Zen Ko-An*.

Fana-fi-lillah (or *Amal* or *samadhi*) didn't come until a few months later. After telling S.A.M. that I had an experience of "infinite space," he replied, "Oh, God bless you, that means you are to be Khalif." Then he paused a few seconds before continuing, "But we must wait six months to see if it is real." About two or three months later I lay down for a nap on the couch in the Garden of Inayat office and had a vision of Akbar sitting in Murshid's chair at the dining table. Everyone was seated as if for a meal, when Akbar all of a sudden stood up to full stature and looked directly into my eyes. Rose-colored waves of *baraka* poured from his heart into mine, and I passed away into bliss before awakening to ordinary consciousness a few moments later. When I reported this to Murshid, he said, "God bless you, this confirms that your first experience was real." After that, he began to make plans to initiate Akbar and me in Pir Vilayat's presence later that summer—which he did in July, although Akbar was late so got his robe on the sidelines a little later. Pir V. was pretty bent out of shape by the whole thing, which he later told me was nothing less than a *fait accompli*. Nevertheless, he went along with it ultimately.

I'm only relating this to show that my experience with Murshid was dealt with *flexibly* in terms of Hazrat Inayat Khan's criteria concerning the 12 grades and the stages of *fana-fi-sheikh, fana-fi-rassoul* and *fana-fi-lillah*. I *didn't* have an experience in *fana-fi-pir*, yet was admitted to the 9th grade in the Order. I *didn't* have an experience in *fana-fi-lillah*, yet was confirmed to the 9th. But what Murshid called the "Great Awakening" *was* the one criterion he used for admission to the 10th degree, esoterically speaking. Khalifa Sa'adia [Murshid Samuel Lewis' mureed and goddaughter in Pakistan] referred to the same experience as the "Grand Night."

In spite of jumping the gun with several persons to whom I have given the yellow robe [10th degree], I now feel that the 10th degree *must* be preceded by an experience of effacement in The Only Being—what Pir Vilayat calls being "alone with the Alone." Other factors will necessarily enter in, such as psychic balance, balance on the earth-plane and so forth. Consultations should wisely precede such confirmations too, as well as a thorough examination of the candidate for the 10th degree.

So there you have some of my thoughts on the same subject. I certainly agree with Wali Ali [*Meyer*]'s advice that *hal* [a spiritual state of consciousness] must be integrated into *makam* [the stage of one's everyday life] before a confirmation properly takes place. It is also important, and this is certainly related, to take into account the teaching of Hazrat Inayat Khan on the subject of reception, assimilation and manifestation—which seem to correspond to the tri-grade divisions of the four Study Circles, each grade representing reception, assimilation or manifestation in terms of the spiritual stage actualized by a given Study Circle.

I agree that the 10th is only for those who *will* give personal time and energy to being teachers, or rather selfless instruments for the Spirit of Guidance/Only Being. There are too many possible nuances to have a discussion about "God-realized doctors, etc." who may not be titled. Each case will have to be on its own merits.

Actual consultations and examinations should be carried out by persons who themselves have had God-realization proven by balance in everyday life, it seems to me. This will require the questioning of [Sangitha] class members as to their realization, but after all, we want life to be interesting, no?

I agree with everything you propose about the spring [1987] Jamiat, down to details. I sincerely hope that the petition signatories will let their hurt feelings dissolve in the vision of the work ahead of us. I have no real wish to process what essentially is unresolvable beyond an "agreeing to disagree" situation. I mean, in one sense what we have is a bunch of conservatives masquerading as democrats trying to hold Moineddin hostage to their emotions. I tend to get very one-pointed in such a situation. I refuse to quit the responsibility that S.A.M. indicated, and as far as I can tell, is still indicating.

Also, I want to write an article about the [San Francisco] Bay area *not* being the center of the universe—in the same spirit as Hazrat Inayat Khan's, "the sun shines and the rain falls elsewhere than Suresnes" [the headquarters of the Sufi Movement in Paris, France toward the end of Inayat Khan's life]. At the same time, each and every merit will be noted.

Got to run and pick up the kids from the sitter....

Love,
Moineddin

Winged Apple? (letter 1987)

(Editor's note: From a letter to mureed.)

Haiku, Maui

February 5, 1987

Today being Inayat Khan's *urs*, I thought I'd read some selections from his autobiography to the class tonight. Also some stories from his *Tales*.

People were starting to complain that I didn't conduct enough practices during class, so last week I began with a practice Murshid gave me early in my discipleship: *sijda* [full prostration]—but moving from the forehead up to the crown center, with emphasis on relaxing the whole being and releasing all tensions out through the crown center into the ground on the outbreath. The in-breath would start at the base of the spine (the highest part of the body during *sijda*) and continue until the crown—like a playground slide—and then the out-breath through the crown.

Murshid even told me at the time that this was more for psychological benefit than for devotional exercise. It has been a mainstay every since. It is excellent as an opening practice for any undertaking or sufficient by itself.

After the *sijda* practice, we did a *zikr* practice that Pir Vilayat introduced during a seminar at Oak Street in the early 70's. It's the same as the regular spoken Zikar except that instead of saying *'illa* in the heart, it is said in the various chakras starting with the *muladhara* at the base of the spine. We said the *zikr* three times in each chakra, then moved up to the next one. By the time we got to the crown center, things were starting to sparkle.

I should also mention the variation we did: instead of visualizing a circle and then breaking into the center on the *'illa*, we visualized a sphere (our self) and saw the axis as our line of entry to the inner world. We felt ourselves to be the crescent moon in each of the chakras, receiving the light of the star from the North Pole, so to speak. Call it winged heart or winged globe, it's the same thing.

(Actually I wouldn't be surprised if the heart symbol came from a culture where the apple was regarded as the "fruit of immortality." The witch's poisoned apple given to Snow White was in reality a poisoned heart.)

Winged apple, anyone?

One Ceaseless Ko-an (letter 1987)

(Editor's note: From a letter to a mureed.)

February 9, 1987

You are aware of my regard for the role Murshid formally indicated to me spiritually as head of the esoteric order, and legally as Permanent Member of the SIRS Board of Trustees. You are aware of my wish to evolve as a group without me sticking out like a sore thumb in either a hierarchical or legal context.

Yet despite my wish, people act now the same as people acted when Murshid was in the body: with disregard for his presence as a person and carelessness for his role as a Murshid. It was at such times that he manifested the fire of demanding a reordering of priorities, instead of the light of blessing.

In a similar sense, Inayat Khan has offered the teaching, "Act as a master, but feel as a servant to your mureeds."

The whole challenge of handling this role with humor and balance is like taking on the little and big stresses, the creaks and strains, the sudden impulses of growth—in short, every dynamic that affects the inner and outer behavior of the Ruhaniat Society—as if they constituted one ceaseless Ko-an.

Ethical Standards for Teachers (letter 1987)

(*Editor's note: Under Moineddin's leadership, the Ruhaniat became one of the first Sufi tariqas worldwide to institute ethical guidelines for teachers and a grievance procedure for mureeds. This was and is an important part of Sufism's adaptation to not only the so-called Western world, but the modern and post-modern world in general.*

The Quran enjoins all believers to the work of sister/brotherhood: the consideration and caring for and about others usually called morality or ethics. Sufi philosophers and teachers from Imam Al-Ghazali to Hazrat Inayat Khan have written extensively about what this type of sister/brotherhood would look like in an ideal society that recognizes the reality of tawhid, or unity with Reality

Over the past fifty years in modern Western culture, the field of psychotherapy developed insights about the nature of the therapeutic relationship, and the ways in which mental projection affects both parties in it, especially when there is, or is perceived to be, an imbalance of power. The terms "transference" and "counter-transference" refer to this effect, which Hazrat Inayat Khan called an aspect of the mind world's "palace of mirrors." Over the same period, several professional associations of doctors, teachers and psychotherapists have developed codes of ethics and models of peer supervision to help provide a "reality check" for professionals in these difficult areas, which usually involve the issues of money, touch, sexual behavior and power.

Beginning already in 1984 (see the letter entitled "Mureeds Rights" above) and here, Moineddin took a step toward a code of ethics adapted to modern Sufism, which was instituted soon after this letter was written. He also required every active Ruhaniat initiator and guide to have a living guide as a "checkpoint," even if their original teacher had died.)

February 25, 1987

To: the Board of Trustees of the Ruhaniat

Aloha!

I have some suggestions for the proposed packet:

1. There should be clear information concerning the Ombudsperson, who s/he is, how s/he is elected by the mureeds, length of tenure in

office, how to lodge a complaint, etc. (I hope we can work out some definite proposals re: the above in committee at the Jamiat in May, to place before a general meeting of mureeds sometime after that. After the mureeds vote in a definite policy then we will have something definite for the packet.

2. There should be a list of guidelines concerning the standards we expect of all Ruhaniat initiators toward their, or anyone's, mureeds.

After the stories surfaced about Baker Roshi, Muktananda, Chogyam Trungpa, et al. it became necessary to examine our own denial of the Ruhaniat's dark side. What we found was a pattern of dope-dealing and sexual manipulation, physical and psychic violence, personal greed and also subtle, and not so subtle, power-tripping. Presumably these patterns belong mostly to the past, but if we, or at least I, do not insist on professional behavior on the part of all Ruhaniat initiators we simply continue the denial.
This is a delicate area for everyone, but with guidance and skill the right words to frame such guidelines will come.)

Love,
Moineddin

The Path of the Ruhaniat (letter 1987)

(Editor's note: From a letter to a mureed.)

Early morning dream of March 8, 1987:

It was not a typical dreamscape so much as an area of focus. My gaze was drawn to a table top where a new book had been placed. The title of the book, *The Path of the Ruhaniat,* was a total surprise.

Everything was in full color, and the book was a combination of ivory, gold and green. Upon closer examination, the name MOINEDDIN JABLONSKI began to pulsate upon the title page as if written in light. I was deeply touched to see that my inner faith was supported by the author of the book, whoever he or she might be. I turned the book over to see if there was a photo and biographical sketch of the author.

There was a clear picture in profile of a young blonde woman who, although I could not identify her as anyone I knew in life, nevertheless seemed familiar as one of my mureeds. I mused on how wonderful it was that someone could have written a book on the Ruhaniat order, and my role of learning to become a Pir, and keep it secret until it was completed.

It was like a confirmation of one's purpose, and an illumination in the midst of struggle and darkness. I woke up while musing in this fashion.

—Moineddin Jablonski

Jamiat Agenda II (letter 1987)

(Editor's note: A letter to Ruhaniat leaders.)

Dear Jamiat Friends, Aloha!

The decade of the 1980s has brought much healing to the collective human psyche. As individual souls we will recognize the following discoveries as our own:

- The Goddess re-emerging to consciousness...
- The Child within receiving acceptance and love...
- The taboo against spiritual seekers as sexual beings lifted forever...
- The belief in ego-bashing as a ticket to heaven discredited as a lie...

In the vision of wholeness vouchsafed to us, we have come to honor and respect the roles played by our egos in the human and divine dimensions:

- Conscious coordination of the various levels, or selves, of our beingness...
- Willing surrender—the ability to become transparent—to the Spirit of Guidance...

In this way we have found the *makam* of psychological depth and quality to be an evolutionary basis of coalescing the *hal*, or revelation, we may receive from the spiritual world.

This uniting of one to the ONE is at the core of our Sufi training. We invite you to share in the practice and spirit of this work at the upcoming November Jamiat. The program will include:

- Darshan workshop for initiators...
- Original zikr Dances of Murshid Samuel L. Lewis...
- PeaceWorks...
- Teachings and discussion of the *rind* (independent) and *salik* (initiatic) paths in Sufism...
- New expressions of the Universal Worship ideal...

Please register soon. Childcare will be provided free. It is important to let us know your plans and needs now, so that meals and childcare can be properly organized.

Ya Hayyo! Ya Qayoom!

Moineddin

New Directions in Universal Worship (letter 1988)

(Editor's note: This is from a letter directed to the then-head of the Universal Worship concentration in the Sufi Order in the West. The Universal Worship is a form of religious ritual that honors the major religions of humanity together on one altar, originally begun under the influence of Hazrat Inayat Khan. In his time, it included six traditions: Hinduism, Buddhism, Zoroastrianism, Judaism, Christianity and Islam, plus the "Spirit of Guidance" for "all those, known and unknown to the world, who have held aloft the light of truth through the darkness of human ignorance.")

June 15, 1988

Aloha! Thank you for your letter of January 17, plus the Universal Worship materials. You seem to have developed a comprehensive program for the training and ordination of Cherags [ministers in the Universal Worship], including a journal to keep everyone interested and interconnected. Keep up the good work!

Our own program is small-scale in comparison, besides being less formal. The "small is beautiful" approach allows us the flexibility to experiment with new/old realities. For example, in 1977 we inaugurated the Flower Service, which is identical to the original Universal Worship except that it is based on water instead of fire [watering flowers instead of lighting candles]. The Flower Service, in addition to normal use, has proven beneficial during times of drought and forest fire, showing that earth-plane concerns need not be excluded from the religious ideal.

In 1983 we began to include the religions of the Great Mother on the altar of Universal Worship, since Hers was the universal way of worship before Her sons the patriarchs entered the picture. We now place Her religion first to reflect actual history. Inclusion of the Goddess religion does much to heal a denied part of patriarchal culture, and affirms for women and men alike the reality of the Female Principle so necessary to very life.

The Native religions, direct descendants of the Goddess tradition, have also re-emerged to take their rightful place as keepers of the "sacred manuscript of nature." They show us the "tree of creation" and point out the pathways between root and branch.

Women and Natives have systematically been excluded from white versions of religion, and what is called the New Age is seeing the return of these denied peoples into, and as, the whole humanity.

We are entering an era of being honest with ourselves. We are realizing the truth of Jesus' teaching: "The first shall be last, and the last shall be first."

Our senior ministers and I function as a council, so you can network with any or all, as you like.

Take care, and thank you again for writing.
In service to The Only Being,
Moineddin

The Link of Initiation (letter 1988)

(Editor's note: a letter to the Ruhaniat Board of Trustees.)

July 19, 1988

Dear Trustees, Aloha!

In going over the Board minutes of June 17, I note some question regarding the status of Ruhaniat mureeds who are not currently working with an initiator. The rules of our Order require that each mureed be formally linked with an authorized initiator. However, at the 1987 Spring Jamiat in Pescadero [California] we decided that there would be three categories of membership in the Sufi Islamia Ruhaniat Society:

1. Mureeds of Ruhaniat initiators.
2. Mureeds of non-Ruhaniat Sufi initiators.
3. Extended family.

These categories make it possible for a wide range of persons to participate in the community life of the Ruhaniat, but our esoteric classes are open only to categories 1 and 2, and the initiatic privilege with respect to a Ruhaniat initiator is only for those in category 1. Category 3 or extended family is comprised of those who support our work through active sympathy without esoteric involvement. All three categories are expected to contribute to the financial well-being of the SIRS.

I have gone on record that any mureed who finds him/herself unable to work with his/her initiator may trust me to stand in until he/she finds another initiator. If a student's intention is not to seek eventual connection with another Ruhaniat initiator, that student automatically falls into category 2 or 3. It is the initiator's responsibility to keep current and straight with each mureed in these matters, including assistance in transferring a mureed to another's guidance if that is clearly indicated.

Whatever special connection a student may feel with Murshid S.A.M. or Hazrat Inayat Khan or other illuminated soul on the inner planes, if that student is not duly committed via the sacred pledge of *bayat* to a Ruhaniat initiator, then he/she is not regarded as a Ruhaniat mureed, strictly speaking, though he/she would be a Ruhaniat Society member of category 2 or 3.

Unless a student is willing to commit to an earth-plane representative of the God Ideal—which all Ruhaniat initiators are expected to be— that student is not following the footprints of our founder, footprints made by a realized yet fallible human being walking on earth.

Without this commitment to another human being, things stay nebulous, and nobody—mureed or initiator—has a living reference for growth.

Also, for semantic reasons it would be appropriate to call the proposed Mureeds Camp a Members Camp, unless those attending have truly committed themselves to the path of initiation and discipleship.

In service to the Only Being,
Moineddin

Ancestry, Death and Dying (letter 1990)

(Editor's note: From a letter to a mureed—another agenda item for a Jamiat leaders gathering.)

May 8, 1990

Aloha!

There's a bee in my bonnet that keeps buzzing about ancestry. Last Sunday we went to a Native Hawaiian ceremony in Honokahua, the site of a recent battle fought between resort hotel interests and Hawaiians trying to protect the honored memory of their ancestors. The site is an ancient Hawaiian burial ground containing ancestral bones dating back 1700 years.

Nobody expected the handful of Hawaiians to make much of a stand against the Ritz-Carlton developers, but the issue of ancestral bones—which in Hawaiian belief are said to contain the essence of one's spirit—turned out to be a rallying point for Native Hawaiians not only on Maui but from all the other Islands as well.

The Hawaiians won. The hotel relocated away from the burial mound and reinterred the bones. The ceremony was held to honor the final resting place of the Hawaiian forebears. As each Island's representatives carried their *ho'okupu* (gifts to the spirit) to the burial *piko* (life connection), I became aware that this was the same to the Hawaiians as the Maqbara [the grave of Murshid Samuel Lewis at Lama Foundation in New Mexico] is to us. When I realized that, I understood why the Hawaiians won.

Now there is a legal precedent guaranteeing the respect of Native Hawaiian burial sites, which developer interests must heed.

The whole reality of spiritual guidance, it would seem, is based on a recognition and connection with "those who have gone before." The spiritual teacher (*kahu*) is "one who has gone before," before actually dying.

In any event, I would like to ask you to consider presenting the theme of ancestry, with your researches and experiences as jumping-off points for discussion and practice, at the next Jamiat which has been set for November 10 and 11, 1990. We are entering the stage of life where death is more common among us. Murshid died twenty years ago. Frida died much more recently. Jemila Pinckley, our young Sufi sister, joined them a couple of years ago.

To take up the matter of ancestry would focus some needed light on an area presently shrouded in mystery in our spiritual community. Your own work in the interface between life and death ("I came to the circle where two lines cross, the line of nothingness where two planes meet..." from Murshid's poem "Crescent and Heart") could significantly help our understanding and realization, *inshallah*.

Bodhisattvas, unite!
Moineddin

Jayanara Herz, Moineddin, Fatima, Murshid, Zeinob Burnham at the Garden of Inayat.

A Spiritual Switzerland? (letter 1990)

(Editor's note: The following letter was sent to the Lama Foundation about its plans for remembering the 20th anniversary of Murshid Samuel Lewis' passing in 1991.)

August 28, 1990

Dear Lama Foundation,

Aloha!

Thanks so much for your letter of August 22nd. The possibility that Lama might dedicate its 1991 summer program to Murshid S.A.M. sounds wonderful, and certainly has Mei-Ling's and my full support should you decide to do that. In fact, I can see Murshid dancing with delight.

Murshid was drawn to Lama in life and in afterlife, because he discovered at Lama a spiritual community that *practiced* the ideals that his teacher Inayat Khan had laid down in theory for the Sufi Movement fifty years earlier. Murshid S.A.M. saw in Lama's work and prayer manifest proof that a real new age was not only possible but had arrived.

In its attempt to maintain a neutral stance in relation to the many paths to the One, Lama is very conscious of its responsibility not to play favorites—recalling perhaps the painful period in the 1970s when one Lama resident subverted the principles upon which Lama was founded by insisting that everyone adopt Islam. Ram Dass, in his article "The Breath of Lama" in the Spring 1990 Lama Newsletter, is careful not to mention either Murshid S.A.M. or his own teacher Neem Karoli Baba in connection with Lama Foundation.

Is it necessary to bend over backwards to be "a spiritual Switzerland," I wonder?

No doubt there is a middle path here. It is my feeling that a middle path would allow for Lama to delight in its spiritual history and to celebrate the many teachers, past and present, who have played a role in developing Lama's reality. Certainly the being of Murshid S.A.M. is one of these. I don't believe he wants to be left up on the hill to be remembered solely by a handful of retreatants. His blessings are meant for the whole of Lama, not to mention the whole world.

S.A.M. celebrated his teachers. May Lama claim its inheritance and do the same. Let S.A.M.'s 20th anniversary of passing be remarkable for his universality of spirit, and celebrate him by celebrating all who have guided Lama thus far.

Love and blessings,

Moineddin

Ancestry, Part II (letter 1991)

(Editor's note: From a letter to a mureed.)

April 5, 1991

Aloha!

In recent Three Self sessions with some of the more advanced Maui mureeds, I have called through their High Selves for spiritual personalities such as Murshid S.A.M., Hazrat Inayat Khan and Frida Waterhouse to join in and participate. I only do this when the connection with the High Self has been established and is flowing.

By doing this, we are building up a stronger and more effective link with our eternal, and our more immediate, ancestry at the High Self level. I know I'm not telling you anything new, but it nevertheless feels good to share it.

When I got home the following phrase came through: "The Murshid is the soul of the personality."

In speaking with Frida, she affirms that the Three Self Work is destined to move into a co-counseling mode, but that timing is all-important in each individual case.

Murshid S.A.M. advised: "The Bay Area is in a stage of growth similar to a shoot or a bud. It needs to be fertilized more for this new growth to bloom. You need to help fertilize it."

Not only is personal growth helped greatly by bringing in our teachers to augment High Self direction, but the sense of community, of *sangha*, is brought in with real depth and scope.

Good luck with the Jamiat and accompanying benefit *"Say I Am You."*

Love and blessings,
Moineddin

Relations with Lama Foundation (letter 1992)

(Editor's note: A letter to the Lama Foundation Board of Trustees.)

October 21, 1992

Dear Lama Foundation Trustees, Beloved Ones of God,

I am writing on behalf of the Sufi Islamia Ruhaniat Society Trustees, to open a discussion with you as to how we might create a bond of mutual understanding between Lama Foundation and the Ruhaniat Society that would ensure our continued practical and spiritual relationship into the future.

Ever since the original Lama residents invited Murshid Samuel Lewis to teach Sufism and the Dances of Universal Peace at Lama Foundation in the summer of 1969 and again in 1970, we of the Ruhaniat community have felt a deep and abiding connection with Lama.

This connection was profoundly strengthened when those same Lama residents buried Murshid S.A.M.'s body in the frozen earth of Lama mountain in the winter of 1971. The gravesite became known as the Maqbara, and since that time the Maqbara has added a silent dimension of peace and power to Lama Foundation as a whole.

For most of the past twenty-two years, Ruhaniat teachers and mureeds have played important roles at Lama. We have been Lama residents. We built the Maqbara pilgrim's hut. We mounded the grave with white quartzite rocks from the surrounding mountainside, and developed the immediate site into an area suitable for meditation and walking practice. We created a large, level Dance ground nearby. We have maintained and upgraded the trails to the Maqbara and pilgrim's hut every few years as needed. And we have held camps annually as part of your summer programs.

On all of these projects, we have worked in mutual cooperation with the Lama residents, with the tacit understanding that Lama and the Ruhaniat have a shared working relationship "in perpetuity."

When some of our teachers came to Lama in August for the annual Dance Teacher's Training Camp, they were surprised to learn that the current Lama residents knew little or nothing about the Maqbara, Murshid S.A.M., or the Ruhaniat. It took considerable effort on their part to build new friendships and re-establish an understanding of our common connections.

We would like to work out an agreement with you, the Lama Foundation Trustees, to formalize a "covenant of understanding" between Lama and the Ruhaniat. This covenant would ensure that we would have reasonable access to the Maqbara for pilgrimage and upkeep indefinitely into the future, as well as to enhance our mutual and ongoing concord with the Lama community.

In addition, the Ruhaniat will donate a complete set of Murshid S.A.M.'s books and cassettes to the Lama library; and a copy of *Dance To Glory*, the 30 minute video of Murshid S.A.M., will be donated to Lama's video library.

The possibility of a small explanatory posting near the Maqbara telling about Murshid S.A.M.'s life could be explored with the Lama community. It has been mentioned that the plaque at the head of the Maqbara needs repair; we would be happy to pay for this. But at some point I would like to see a new plaque created that would replace the word "men" with the word "people," so that the saying of Muhammad would read, "On that day the sun shall rise in the West, and all people seeing will believe." This would be more in keeping not only with the spirit of the times, but with the spirit of truth.

Finally, and most important, would be the establishment of a liaison person or persons from the Ruhaniat to work with the Lama community on an ongoing basis to keep our mutual relationship vital and growing. The liaison person or persons would be responsible to lead, coordinate or otherwise arrange for an annual winter retreat for the Lama residents. The Ruhaniat would pay all expenses for this. With such a liaison or liaisons, other projects of practical and spiritual interest to both communities could evolve spontaneously in the coming years.

We look forward to your reply.
Toward the One,
Moineddin Jablonski

Another Step in the Dance (email 1995)

(*Editor's note: From a letter to a mureed about a plan for all of the Ruhaniat areas of concentration to participate in a joint camp at the Lama Foundation in June 1996, the one hundredth anniversary of Murshid S.A.M.'s birth year. The camp did occur, with all the Ruhaniat concentraitons participating, just after a fire that destroyed many of the Lama buildings in May 1996.*)

25 April 1995

Aloha!

Heck, I agree with everything you say about everyone. But honoring one's "psychic scars," while initially necessary for personal healing, eventually erects walls—which to a Dervish are non-existent.

Every one of us has sustained significant personal loss. Many of us have been through divorce and lost custody of our children. Death has stolen loved ones. Things like these tend to sour our innocence and make us more clever than wise in dealing with life. I am reminded of the bumper sticker that reads, "Ever Since I Gave Up Hope, I Feel Much Better."

But we do have work to do. "Agreeing to disagree" is a powerful tool for moving on. It just takes someone who is brave enough to take the first step and communicate with "those ass-holes who make life miserable for me."

We're all insecure somewhere inside. That's what makes us manipulate situations so that we can stay in control. I believe that this stuff is coming up now so that we can look at it, run it through our personal processors and come up with ways to honor (or at least tolerate) our differences with each other. When being "right" further divides us from our fellows, it may be better to be wrong.

Murshid wanted us to be better, not busier, just better than he was. I don't know if that is possible, but we can give it our best shot.

Can you open lines of communication with [various Ruhaniat Sufi leaders] re: a Silver Jubilee Reunion at Lama in 1996, and propose an integrated camp in which Dance and Walk, Healing, and other streams are honored each day, instead of holding separate camps for each concentration? Coming from one who heads up a complete transmission, as you do, will carry a certain weight.

Mother Krishnabai drank dog vomit. That was her way of practicing the Shiva Principle: internalize whatever is most revolting to us, in order to include it as simply another step in the Dance.

Moineddin

A Southwest Sufi Community (email 1995)

(Editor's note: Beginning in 1994, Moineddin began to engage mureeds in a vision of a wilderness land community. After an extensive search, property was found and purchased near Silver City, New Mexico. The Ruhaniat Board of Trustees raised the question of whether to sell part of the property established as Khankah S.A.M., around Samuel Lewis' home in San Francisco. In the following email, Moineddin wrote to the Board about his vision for the way the city and rural communities might complement one another. The Southwest Sufi Community was established and thrives today as a center for native seed preservation. It became the location of Moineddin's dargah.)

10 May 1995

Aloha Fellow Trustees,

I would like to share a few of my thoughts and feelings with you.

Khankah S.A.M. (which includes the Mentorgarten and formerly 416 Precita as well) has been through the normal series of ups and downs that every family experiences. I have had the good fortune to be on the receiving end of Khankah S.A.M.'s hospitality throughout its existence.

In the late 1970s when I was ill with end-stage renal disease and in and out of San Francisco General Hospital on a regular basis, Khankah S.A.M. provided a live-in room for me at 416 Precita, then the home of Wali Ali and Khadija Meyer upstairs, and Nizamuddin Robinson downstairs.

In 1982 when Mei-Ling and I were married in a ceremony at the Mentorgarten by Saadi Douglas-Klotz and Kamae A. Miller, followed by a reception in the dining hall at 65 Norwich, we were given the little apartment at 63 Norwich for our honeymoon. Merrice Hoppe lived there at the time and was kind enough to move to the even smaller guest room at 65 while Mei-Ling and I stayed at 63.

All through the 1980s I was given the Dharma Room to stay in during my biannual trips to attend Jamiat gatherings. And twice a year through the present decade, Andalieb and Ali Qadr have graciously given me their large apartment at 65, while they moved into a bedroom down the hall.

As you can see, I have a positive emotional history and bond with Khankah S.A.M. and its stream of residents. I have no wish to see any of the Khankah S.A.M. houses sold—not simply because it is like a second home to me, but because as Wali Ali has pointed out, "This is a functioning Khankah with a spiritual history and a place in a critical American city."

As I write, Silver City, New Mexico is attracting more and more Sufis to live there and participate in the birth of a new Sufi community. Already there are regular Dance meetings and Gatha classes. The people who live in Silver City are not necessarily the people who will live on the Bear Creek land that we hope to *inshallah* buy in the coming month. The city community and the rural community will support and depend upon each other. Although geographically separate, the Silver City community and the Bear Creek community are forming a spiritual whole known as the Southwest Sufi Community. This is not theory, it is happening right now.

It is like Wali Ali said, "Murshid insisted on living in the city four days a week, and in Marin three days. Retreat is to be balanced by involvement. In this way we can and should maintain both concentrations from a holistic perspective."

In a similar way, the SSC and SIRS can also provide mutual support for each other. We are one people. Let us unite our minds and hearts and souls to purchase the Bear Creek land. Together we can do it.

Love and Ya Fatah!
Moineddin

***

22 May 1995

Dear Friends of the Southwest Sufi Community Project,

A counter-offer was presented yesterday to the SIRS Board of Trustees by the seller of the Bear Creek land. The SIRS Trustees voted in favor of buying the land. Qayyum Klein will fly to Silver City in June to close the transaction.

The securing of suitable land was our first objective, and now, *alhamdulillah*, this has been accomplished. Our second objective will be to create a master plan for the land and, step by step, begin the process of providing infrastructure, common buildings and housing for community living.

A permaculture evaluation of the land will be an essential component of the master plan.

The latest SSC Newsletter will go out next week. The SSC fundraising brochure is on its way to the printer, and will be sent out soon too.

Your prayers and support for the success of the SSC project are most appreciated!

Ya Fatah! Ya Fatah!! Ya Fatah!!!

Moineddin

An Inclusive Spiritual Path? (email 1997)

(Editor's note: From a group email to mureeds who were focusing on the establishment of the Southwest Sufi Community in New Mexico.)

What is an "Inclusive Sufi Order or Spiritual Path"?

by Moineddin Jablonski

On one hand, an inclusive Sufi order is one that does not require its members to belong to a particular religion, or to any religion, as a precondition for admission. On the other hand, an inclusive Sufi order respects all religions, including pagan, native and shamanic traditions, and its members often belong to one or more of them. In contrast, there are a number of traditional Sufi orders that insist that its members belong to the Islamic religion as a precondition for mureedship (initiatic training).

Hazrat Inayat Khan, the Pir (Sufi teacher) who brought the Sufi Message to the West from India in 1910, called Sufism a "Message of Spiritual Liberty," a Message of "Unity, not uniformity."

"The true religion to the Sufi," he said, "is the sea of truth, and all different faiths are as its waves." He added, "Sufism has never had a first exponent or a historical origin. It existed from the beginning, because human beings have always possessed the light which is their second nature. And light in its higher aspect may be called the knowledge of God, the divine wisdom—in fact, Sufism. Sufism has always been practiced, and its messengers have been people of the heart."

An inclusive spiritual path is one whose adherents practice a "live and let live" ethic in relation to their fellow human beings in matters of religion and spirituality. Like Sufis, persons treading an inclusive spiritual path will respect all religions and spiritual traditions as having a divine origin. Normally, such persons will be linked with a spiritual teacher from whom they receive practices and direction, and to whom they are accountable for their personal and spiritual growth.

Examples of inclusive spiritual paths are universal forms of Zen, Vipassana and Vajrayana in Buddhism, Vedanta and Tantra in Hinduism, and schools of universal realization in Taoism, Judaism and Christianity. Students of these and other inclusive spiritual paths will practice a deep-felt toleration for all forms of truth-seeking, since spiritual experience reveals the same divine essence in the heart of all beings.

However, some spiritual seekers are of the "natural type" described by Inayat Khan. These persons take Nature itself as their primary teacher, and may not be formally linked in a teacher-disciple relationship. Sometimes this can be problematic, because there is no one to whom they go to have their personal and spiritual growth reality-checked, nor are they accountable to anyone in matters of personal behavior and self-control. In such cases, a community representative must take on the role of advisor and reality-check, and if the seeker wishes to belong to the community, he or she must be willing to accept this kind of appropriate oversight.

Mature seekers of the natural type often prove to be invaluable builders of land-based spiritual community, due to their rapport with the rhythms and cycles of the earth, kinship with plant and animal life, practical hands-on approach to getting things done, and general willingness to accept responsibility in a group setting. Ideally, all members of the Southwest Sufi Community will possess a heartfelt attunement to Nature, because stewardship of the Bear Creek land will be a spiritual practice in itself, a way to increase life, virtue and unity-consciousness in the world.

As we prepare to come together for this experience in holistic living, remember that we are living in a time of rapid change and intensive growth—a process that brings out the worst and best in each one of us. Everywhere people are challenged to stick to their ideals in a world of fearful emotions, which too often lead to abusive words and violent acts, even in our own homes. Our work is to root out these imbalances in ourselves so that our hearts can become havens of safety, peace and refuge for each other.

Practicing thus, we develop individual spiritual capacities which, when transposed to the level of intentional community, create greater potential for harmlessness, compassion and loving-kindness to arise planet-wide.

These are some of the things that spring to mind in considering the meaning and importance of inclusive Sufi orders and spiritual paths in our lives.

The Voice of the Turtle (email 1998)

(Editor's note: The name that Moineddin received in vision for the Southwest Sufi Community wilderness retreat center at Bear Creek was "The Voice of the Turtle." From earlier correspondence, it seems that he was focusing on this name as early as the mid-1970s.)

30 August 1998

The Voice of the Turtle

When Murshid S.A.M. says, "Where the Holy Spirit echoes as the Dove," he is referring to the sound "Hu," which is regarded as the universal sound current by Sufis, hearing which is to realize that God and Self are one.

However (and this is a subtle distinction), he says "echoes as the Dove." This indicates that there is an even deeper "Voice" that produces the echo. This deeper voice is the very Silence itself, symbolized by the turtle withdrawing its head, legs and tail into its shell, in the same way that the Sufi practice of *shagal* allows one to withdraw all the senses within by closing the eyes, ears, nose and mouth with the fingers and thumbs.

Shagal is an important retreat practice and permits one to enter the Silence. As I indicated in my first email about the Voice of the Turtle, the name has definite mystical overtones, which resonate well with the theme of a retreat center and retreat practices generally.

Regarding turtle myths, I've seen a couple of children's books with turtle myths. You might want to check out the children's section of your local bookstore.

Bismillah and Buddhism (email 1997)

(Editor's note: From a letter to a mureed).

31 August 1997

Bismillah, as far as I know, means "In the Name of Allah." Murshid S.A.M. added "We begin [in the Name of Allah]," to enlist the power of the human will to effect engagement, devotion and depth in our spiritual practice. Sufism is POSITIVE, he said.

The usual approach of Buddhism, to dissolve the personal ego in the Absolute, is based on the Buddha's enlightenment experience, so beautifully summed up in the final line of Sir Edwin Arnold's poem "The Light of Asia": "The dewdrop slips into the shining sea." (*Fana* in Sufism.)

The Bodhisattva attains this experience, then becomes a vehicle for teaching, practice and enlightenment-transmission so long as sentient beings struggle to free themselves from illusion in the temporal spheres, including the illusion that they have an existence separate from the whole.

This phase is summed up in: "The shining sea slips into the dewdrop." (*Baqa* in Sufism.) The shining sea is *nirvana*; the dewdrop is the soul of the Bodhisattva.

The Bodhisattva knows from direct experience that God/*nirvana* is the Only Reality, but elects to perform the role of savior in the drama of creation. The vow of St. Peter is essentially not different from the Bodhisattvic vow.

Joe Miller used to point to his body and say, "Hey, THIS is only temporary!"

Love,
Moineddin

For the Murshids Circle... (emails 1997)

(Editor's note: In the last five years of his life, Moineddin established a circle of Murshids with whom he could consult on the decisions and challenges confronting a Pir. He would mainly communicate with this group by email, with in-person meetings coming at the time of the annual Jamiat Khas.)

10 September 1997

Dear Murshids,

I'm currently proofreading "Instructions for the Pir" and making it gender-inclusive. Going over Lesson Eight just now, I happened upon the following words of Murshid, which are very much in the spirit of our earlier discussion this morning.

"On the path of the Pir...it is not so much the stage (*makam*) of development as the state (*hal*) one maintains which is important. By keeping in the state of heart-awakening, one is in rapport with the Spirit of Guidance. At the same time, the heart has to overflow with love, and this love must be life itself. When there is this state, the very presence of the personality awakens in another a momentary purity and holiness and arouses inspirations. Some souls thus coming to a Pir are enlightened for a short period but do not maintain their condition. Nevertheless, they may come again and again, and as they fulfill the conditions which permit interviews and always respond most excellently, it becomes the duty of the Pir to make use of such people while observing their limitations. The work of the Pir is not moral purification but spiritual enlightenment, and if sympathy is awakened in the heart of another for a moment, for an hour, for a lifetime, then there is success for all concerned."

Love, Moineddin

***

12 September 1997

Dear Murshids,

The enclosed "Self-Evaluation for 11th Degree Candidates" is designed to assist our assessment of those who have been nominated for possible inclusion in the Sufi Islamia Ruhaniat Society's 11th degree initiators'

(Murshids) circle. If any of you have input you would like to share, please send it during the coming week. I'd like to send copies of the Self-Evaluation to the candidates we discussed last April in Charlottesville, as soon as possible. The questions will need to be answered in time for us to read them before the Portland Jamiat Khas.

We can give consideration to these questions as well.

Ya Fattah!
Moineddin

* * * SELF-EVALUATION FOR 11th DEGREE CANDIDATES

"I...believe to have representatives in all the purity and goodness of which Allah is capable..." (Murshid Samuel L. Lewis)

Beloved One of Allah,

This is, at base, a job application. If for any reason you are not interested in applying for the job of Murshid or Murshida in the Sufi Islamia Ruhaniat Society, please say so and there will be no need for you to proceed further at this time. If you are interested in applying for this work, please be emotionally honest in your responses, keeping them brief, clear, and to the point.

1. How many mureeds are you currently working with?
2. Have any of them attained spiritual illumination?
3. What is your greatest challenge in working with mureeds?
4. Speaking personally, what benefits do you offer, and what risks do you pose, to the order?
5. Do you have any mental, emotional, or physical health problems?
6. Do you have any addictions?
7. Are you willing to work within the parameters of group process and teamwork with the 11th degree circle?
8. Describe the nature of your personal spiritual path.
9. In a couplet or quatrain, describe the depth of your insight into the heart sphere.
10. What spiritual figure(s), living or dead, do you most strongly resonate with/emulate in your work?
11. What level(s) of inner surrender have you achieved:
    A. *Fana-fi-sheikh* (with whom? and describe briefly)
    B. *Fana-fi-rassoul* (with whom? and describe briefly)

C. *Fana-fi-lillah* (describe briefly)
12. What is your vision for the future of Sufism?
13. In the event of my death or incapacitation, Wali Ali Meyer is my successor-designate to become Pir and Permanent Member of the Sufi Islamia Ruhaniat Society. Do you feel you can work harmoniously with him in the spirit of Love, Harmony and Beauty to spread the Message of God far and wide?

Your responses are deeply appreciated, and will be kept confidential among the members of the 11th degree circle.

If you have any questions, or need any assistance in responding to these questions, please feel free to call or e-mail me. Thank you most sincerely for sharing your heart.

Love and blessings,
Moineddin

***

21 September 1997

Dear All,

Perhaps it will be helpful if I give some background on how the Self-Evaluation questions came into being.

I was sleeping in Ramabai and Bob's guest room in Portland [Oregon]. I was awakened from sleep at 4 am with a series of "seed impressions" for an 11th degree Self-Evaluation form. I was reminded of Murshid's inability to sleep due to his reception of the Dances. This was a similar experience insofar as these impressions would not leave me alone until I had gotten up and written them down. This process continued until 6 am when all the impressions had been received. Then it was time to waken the kids and get packed for the trip home to Maui.

Being wakened from sleep is sometimes the way things come to me. For example, this is how the Flower Service came through after our break with the Sufi Order. This is also how various inspirations, including "Job's Tears" [*a collection of his aphorisms later included in the book* The Gift of Life] and some spiritual names for mureeds, have come through.

I frankly don't know if the Self-Evaluation for the 11th Degree is a good idea either. But at this point I would like to try it and see what happens. For all I know, it may now be time for us to approach advanced initiations with candor and emotional honesty as a matter of "continuing adult education" in its truest sense. Certainly, we will gain insights from having people evaluate themselves, instead of us attempting to evaluate them in a one-sided manner.

Again, if any of you have further input, please get back to me soonest. I want to get the Self-Evaluation questionnaire out to the candidates tomorrow, *inshallah*.

Love,
Moineddin

Support for the Dances of Universal Peace Network (letter 1997)

(Editor's note: A letter to all Ruhaniat mureeds.)

Fall Equinox, 1997
Ha'iku, Maui, Hawai'i

Dear Fellow Mureeds,

I am writing to you on behalf of the PeaceWorks International Network of the Dances of Universal Peace, to inform you of important developments both historic and current, and to encourage you to support the Dance Network by becoming contributing members (more on this later).

In 1981, ten years after Murshid S.A.M.'s death, the Dances of Universal Peace had become widespread as a result of efforts by Ruhaniat leaders in regional centers throughout the United States, Canada, and Europe. There was no Dance Network then. All aspects of the Message work, including the Dances, were being managed by the Sufi Islamia Ruhaniat Society.

During that increasingly busy time, Moineddin had moved to Hawai'i to recuperate from a kidney transplant operation/nervous breakdown/depression, while Wali Ali was heading into a divorce and personal burnout situation at Khankah S.A.M. In other words, the two primary leaders of the Ruhaniat had their own demons to face and were unable to provide vital leadership at that time.

It was against this backdrop that Murshid Saadi (then a Khalif) undertook two intensive retreats, one at Murshid's Maqbara at Lama Foundation. During the course of those retreats, Saadi experienced visitations from several Rassouls who gave him instructions for future community and world developments, including the Aramaic Lord's Prayer zikr (Jesus), and the setting up of an autonomous Center for the Dances of Universal Peace (Murshid S.A.M.). I'm probably embarrassing Saadi by saying this, but that's all right; we are an Order whose reality is based on direct spiritual experience and transmission. The spiritual government of the world has an ongoing program of love, joy, healing and peace, which it imparts to humanity through dedicated and surrendered instruments—and those instruments, my dear sisters and brothers, are you and me.

Clearly, the transmissions imparted to Saadi have taken root and borne fruit here and abroad, as Murshid foresaw. The Dances of Universal Peace have touched more than half a million people in North and South America, Europe, Eastern Europe, the nations of the former Soviet Union, Japan, India, Pakistan, Australia, and New Zealand. In addition to the 1996 Summer Olympics presentations, significant healing work was conducted via the Dances this past year in Croatia. As I write, the Dances are poised to spread to the Middle East and South Africa as well.

Further recent developments include the marvelous video production *Eat, Dance and Pray Together* by Anahata Iradah, and the beautiful book *Wisdom Comes Dancing: Selected Writings of Ruth St. Denis on Dance, Spirituality and the Body* by Kamae A Miller. Both of these efforts represent years of sacrifice and concentration on the part of Anahata and Kamae and their helper-friends. The *baraka* in each of these offerings will reach out to increasing numbers of people around the globe in coming years.

In another recent development, the Sufi Islamia Ruhaniat Society turned SIRS Publications and its inventory over to PeaceWorks for future publication, marketing and distribution. SIRS Pubs had been languishing due to a lack of personnel and funding, so its acquisition by PeaceWorks has been a positive move assuring greater availability of Murshid's writings to a world audience.

These are some of the many things happening in the overlapping spheres of PeaceWorks and the Sufi Islamia Ruhaniat Society. It is, moreover, important to remember that a majority of Ruhaniat mureeds have come to the path of initiation and discipleship through the door of the Dances of Universal Peace. So very many of you became mureeds by first being touched by the Dances.

In the spirit of this living connection between the Ruhaniat and PeaceWorks, I ask you to support the work of the International Network of the Dances of Universal Peace, through your prayers, and through your pocketbook, for its continued success.

"On, on with the Sacred Dance!"—Murshid Samuel L. Lewis.

Thank you, and love,
Moineddin

Time to Descend (email 1997)

(Editor's note: An email sent to all mureeds in the Ruhaniat.)

19 December 1997

Dear Sisters and Brothers, Beloved Ones of Allah,

This is a reminder that we live in a world of seasons. The season we are now entering (in the northern hemisphere) is a time to "descend within." All of Nature follows this seasonal pattern.

Human beings sometimes ignore or resist this natural invitation to "enter the dark time of the year." Indeed, popular commercial culture has a vested interest during the solsticial holy days in keeping people's attention focused on the surface of life in an epiphany of advertising and marketing.

Yes, the seed of light, the promise of the New Year, will be born. But there is more to the Hanukkah and Christmas stories than Santa Claus and shopping. The events we now commemorate at Hanukkah and Christmas were times of great human distress and suffering, before the light could be brought forth.

Hanukkah and Christmas are truly modest celebrations. Their beginnings were accomplished in simple homes, and in a stable, respectively. These are reminders of the original simplicity of our heart.

I encourage each one of you not to be afraid to "descend within" at this time of the year. There are parts in all of us that routinely suffer rejection or avoidance. This is the time to visit those parts of ourselves in a spirit of acceptance and friendship.

By comforting "the least of my creatures," you express the real meaning and deeper understanding of the birth of the light.

God bless you,
Moineddin

If You're Going Through Hell... (email 1998)

(Editor's note: From a letter to a mureed.)

9 February 1998

Yes, Murshid said that Inayat died of heartbreak over the problems and dissension within the organization [*the Sufi Movement*] that he had poured his heart and soul into. The frontispiece picture of Inayat in volume twelve [*Sufi Message* series] shows the deep sadness that overwhelmed him, perhaps even killed him.

Shamcher used to say, "Inayat Khan suffered more than Jesus on the cross, knowing what was coming to his daughter, and seeing the enmity between his sons."

Having lived through deep sadness, the kind of sadness that makes one want to die, I have a different view than I used to. It's a view which makes me comfortable with the fact that there are now three orders instead of one order. I, like many in the Ruhaniat, am a child of divorce thrice over: once when my parents split up; again when we broke with Pir Vilayat, and again when Fatima and I went our separate ways.

As painful as those experiences were, they led to important types of growth that would not have been possible if my parents, or SIRS and the Sufi Order, or Fatima and I had stayed together. It's hell on wheels when it's happening, but as Winston Churchill said, "If you're going through hell, keep going."

The karmic sadness you mention has already lifted considerably between SIRS and the Sufi Movement.

So I humor myself with the idea that "Two out of three ain't bad!"
Moin

The Invocation (email 1998)

(Editor's note: From a letter to a mureed.)

17 April 1998

Many thanks for sharing the Sufi Invocation in German, with the word "master" in the feminine form. In my own practice, I have alternated using "who form the embodiment of the Master" with "who form the embodiment of the Message"—depending upon my need for more personal mastery, or more connection with the message in a brother-sisterhood "united with all" sense.

The option to use *message* instead of *master* came as an inspiration to Najat Roberts, a Ruhaniat Sheikha from the Los Angeles area, several years ago.

All best, and Allah bless you,
Moineddin

Sacred Vowels (email 1999)

(Editor's note: From an emal to a mureed.)

14 May 1999

At tonight's Gatha class we intoned the divine name I-A-U just as Murshid did thirty years ago. The energy in ourselves and in the room shifted into a higher vibration.

Then we talked about *Yahuvah* as a divine name. The *Yahu* part of the name corresponds exactly to I-A-U, which energizes the inner vibration of the person intoning it. The *vah* part of the name allows the practitioner to give back to the Universe—*vah* energizes the immediate external space, blessing the creation.

In other words, Yahuvah doesn't just illuminate the practitioner, it moves the practitioner into the sphere of the Bodhisattva. The *vah* is the bestowal of blessing beyond one's own person.

Love, Moin

Happy Birthday, Murshid (email 1999)

(Editor's note: From an email sent to all Ruhaniat mureeds.)

18 October 1999

Dear Friends,

Today, October 18th, marks the 103rd anniversary of Murshid S.A.M.'s birth.

Murshida Vera Corda, in the book *In The Garden*, describes him this way: "If you met him and looked at him in the spirit, then you would understand that here was a man who had a divine work to do, and no obstacle or life situation could stop him."

The Reverend Frida Waterhouse said, "The greatest gift you can give to a spiritual teacher is your own realization."

Here are the last two paragraphs from Murshid S.A.M.'s "Ten Lessons on Meditation":

"Initiation is the beginning and perfection is the end, the making complete. But where is the beginning and where is the end? They are both in silence, in God. In silence we were born, and to it we return.

"Therefore, the perfection of meditation is meditation. It is the perfected souls who continue ever in meditation, being absorbed in meditation, creating from their meditation, and living in that meditation. The spiritual life is the drawing of sustenance through the breath from God. It is a life of praise, yet of sobriety and balance, a life of fullness and emptiness both, being empty of self and filled with God. This is the true purpose of initiation and spiritual training, from the moment the mureed takes *bayat* until the eternity of eternities, time without ending."

Happy Birthday, Murshid! Thank you for your living example and spirit.

Love and blessings to all,
Moineddin

Thanksgiving (email 1999)

(Editor's note: An email to Ruhaniat mureeds on the American holiday of Thanksgiving.)

25 November 1999

Dear Wayfaring Pilgrims,

Here is a quote from the Sufi poet Sa'adi on the theme of giving thanks:

"Every breath which is inhaled prolongs life, and when exhaled quickens the body. Thus in every breath two blessings are contained, and for every blessing a separate thanksgiving is due" (The Gulistan).

Toward the One,
Moineddin

A Federation of the Sufi Message (emails 1996–2000)

(Editor's note: During the last five years of his life, Moineddin spent a great deal of time in communication with leaders of two other Inayat Khan-linked Sufi lineages—the Sufi Movement International and the Sufi Order International. This concerned the formation of an umbrella organization to help all branches achieve a greater sense of community with one another. The organization that he formed together with Pir Hidayat Inayat Khan was eventually called the "Federation of the Sufi Message." The following excerpts, selected from Moineddin's emails during this time, culminate in the first formal gathering of the group in April 2000. Annual meetings continue, see: http://federation-message-hazrat-inayat-khan.blogspot.co.uk)

March 3, 1996

Dear Pirs Hidayat and Vilayat, Beloved Ones of Allah,

Last month, Hidayat, you wrote to me: "My dream is to have once again one united Sufi Organization which represents my father's work." More recently you drafted a proposal to create a federation called The United Sufi Movement and Sufi Order, which you sent to Vilayat.

Looking the proposal over, Vilayat along with his Board and Jamiat Khas decided not to accept your proposal, citing his claim to be the rightful successor to your father's Pir-ship and stating the opinion that there cannot be an organization with two captains.

No doubt there are strong feelings between you and Vilayat regarding the issue of sole successorship to your father's mantle. Two brothers equally beloved of their father, and equally committed to carry the Message of their father into the world, would naturally feel they received an equal share of spiritual inheritance, opportunity and blessing.

Perhaps part of this issue can begin to find resolution by going back to impressions received by your parents as they contemplated the qualities of your respective souls on the way toward manifestation. At birth, you were given the name Hidayat, indicating a personality who would grow in association with the Spirit of Guidance; and your brother was given the name Vilayat, indicating a personality who would grow in association with the Spirit of Mastery. These are distinctive themes that have set your lives on their highly individual courses.

Even if the two of you aren't always aware of the profound effects your names have had upon you and the organizations you represent, they are quite clear to those who have eyes to see.

Be that as it may, it is important now to move into the present tense. Grand organizations with Great Men as leaders are rapidly becoming like the dinosaurs that disappeared in an earlier age. Shared power, shared responsibility, and teamwork are the modes of operation that will carry the Message forward into the new millennium.

Speaking on behalf of the Ruhaniat, I reiterate our readiness to work with both of you if you are willing to work with us—meaning neither over us, and certainly not under us, but WITH us.

This is my sense of your father's Message.

Opening the various Gatha classes to attendance by members of the different orders would be a simple and elegant beginning. From there we might consider ways to unify the activity now variously called the Universal Worship, the Church of All, and the Service of Universal Peace.

Finally, permit me to quote something Murshid S.A.M. used to say: "There will be no peace until each side learns to say, 'I concede....'"

This from the man who received a simple peace plan from Jesus Christ: "Eat, dance and pray with each other."

Love and blessings,
Moineddin

***

15 September 1999

My Dear Pir Vilayat, Beloved Elder Brother-in-Allah,

Bismillah er-Rahman, er-Rahim...

Thank you for your heartfelt email message, which I received late last night. It is encouraging to me that you are attempting in a sincere and deep way to come to grips with the problem of how to bring the Sufi Order International, the Sufi Movement International, and the Sufi Islamia Ruhaniat Society closer together organizationally at top levels. I say top levels, because it is my experience "in the field" that there is already considerable interaction and harmony among the respective mureedships of each order at grassroots levels.

To me, this is the future of the Message, and the future is happening now. I see the attempt to achieve similar results among the leaders of each order as a form of playing "catch-up." In other words, I believe we have much to learn from our mureeds.

Let me state clearly where I am coming from. I really am embarrassed by people calling me Pir Moineddin, or for that matter Murshid Moineddin. I much prefer Moineddin, or as most of my colleagues and mureeds know me, simply as "Moin."

However, where the question of standing on an equal footing with other Sufi orders is concerned, then I insist for the sake of the order I represent (and not for me personally) that if the leader of one order is called Pir, then the leaders of the other orders be accorded the same respect.

Outside of that, I have never claimed to be a Pir, nor do I wish to be referred to as such.

The only credentials I have for such recognition are:

1. The requisite spiritual experience;
2. The fact that my teacher wrote a series of 32 lessons for me and for all Pirs of all orders entitled "Instructions for the Pir";
3. The Reverend Joe Miller began calling me Pir Moineddin in 1977, shortly after you wrote your Declaration;
4. Your brother, Pir-o-Murshid Hidayat, the current head of the Sufi Movement International, has recognized me as a Pir.

Re your statement: *"That Murshid S.A.M. claimed to be an Abdal I must say came as a shock. No Pir in the East would take that seriously and that certainly does not fit into the practice according to which the Pirs nominate their successors in their capacity as a Pir."*

Murshid S.A.M.'s claim to be an *Abdal* was not an open claim made in public. He asked a handful of his close disciples to swear that we would not reveal what he was about to say until after his death. We swore that we would abide his wish. He then proceeded to tell us that he had eaten locusts. That was the preamble. Then he told us of the inner plane work he did as part of a team headed by Abdul Qadir Jilani, to carry the souls of the Jews who were being gassed by Hitler into the next world. At that point, he said he was an *Abdal* in the spiritual hierarchy, and that his responsibilities as an *Abdal* were "not fun." He said, "An *Abdal* has to be prepared to sacrifice personal preferences and to change one's state from moment to moment in order to fulfill the divine will."

Beloved brother, I would not ordinarily say these things to you. But you asked in our recent telephone conversation if Murshid S.A.M. had ever claimed to be a Pir. I replied, "No, he never claimed to be a Pir, despite the fact that he authored a series of lessons called 'Instructions for the Pir.' But he did claim to be an Abdal."

It is only because you asked that I disclosed his claim.

Where do we go from here? That is up to you, Pir Vilayat. I will continue to work with Pir-o-Murshid Hidayat and my other Federation colleagues, as well as with the leaders and mureeds of all three orders, relying on the truth of Christ's teaching, "By their fruits you shall know them."

United in the Message of your father, and in the spirit of your sister Noor Inayat,

I remain yours with love and blessings,
Moineddin

***

(Editor's note: An email to Zia Inayat-Khan, the son of Pir Vilayat Khan.)

17 September 1999

Dear Zia and All,

Thank you, I appreciate your response. The ground rules you suggest for continuing our discussion seem reasonable and sound, and are acceptable to me.

Thank you also for providing Ibn Arabi's comments on the beings called *Abdal*. I had not read his interpretation, though I did come across a quite similar description of hierarchical functions in the introduction to "Futuh al-Ghaib" of Abdul Qadir Jilani in the late 1960s.

Your quote from Hazrat Inayat Khan about "the initiation of the higher orders" is apt. I would question the exclusive use of the male pronoun re: "...when one [*Abdal*] passes on, he mysteriously transmits his role to someone else..." It seems to me that women could function equally as well as men in the hierarchical structures of the orders of the Unseen (as well as be Pirs in the orders of the seen).

Murshid S.A.M. said the [*Semitic language*] root of the word Abdal is *"bdl,"* which can be found in the Bible as the change-stone called *bdellium* in Genesis 2:12 and Numbers 11:7. He often compared his mercurial nature to bdellium. Interestingly, Smith's Bible Dictionary says that no one can say whether "bdellium" denotes a mineral or an animal production or a vegetable exudation.

I do have a couple of questions that seem relevant to this discussion:

1. Was Shams-i-Tabriz a Pir who in turn initiated Jelaluddin Rumi as a Pir? Or was their relationship outside the structure of the Mevlevi Order? If the latter, how did Rumi become a Pir?

2. Was Hazrat Inayat Khan initiated as a Pir by Abu Hashim Madani? Or did Hazrat Inayat Khan install himself as the Pir-o-Murshid of the Sufi Order within the Sufi Movement that he founded?

In other words, are there precedents to becoming a Pir that don't conform to the usual rules?

Love,
Moineddin

***

24 September 1999

Dear Zia and Everyone,

Thank you for your thoughtful email of 9/19. I too was buoyed by Wali Ali's heartfelt letter. I would have replied sooner, but had to meet deadlines on a couple of projects. You bring up three interesting points:

1. "What if...we...try to identify the distinct paradigms of spiritual authority that are competing for currency in our negotiations?"

2. "Like the early Muslims, we are attempting to come to terms with the absence of our charismatic founder figure."

3. "[Pir Vilayat's] pattern, the pattern of the Sufi Order International, is one of person-to-person transmission through initiation, in accord with traditional Chishti practice."

Let me respond to your points one at a time.

PARADIGMS OF SPIRITUAL AUTHORITY. I can only speak for the Sufi Islamia Ruhaniat Society, and even so whatever I say will only be partially true since a spiritual family is composed of the voices of all of its members and not just one member. If there is one identifying factor in the make-up of the Ruhaniat it is the importance of the grassroots aspect of its being. My dictionary defines grassroots as: "People or society at a local level instead of the political center."

While there is an operational hierarchy in SIRS, the leadership has taken care to honor and listen to the grassroots. The Ruhaniat takes seriously Hazrat Inayat Khan's teaching "It is the mureeds who make the Murshid." As well as the teaching of Christ, repeated often by Murshid S.A.M., "I am the vine, and you are the branches thereof."

In other words, we are all one.

THE ABSENCE OF OUR CHARISMATIC FOUNDER FIGURE. You are speaking no doubt of Hazrat Inayat Khan, yet only his sons Vilayat and Hidayat among those of us engaged in this conversation have experienced firsthand the loss of his personal presence. Apart from the fact that he died at a relatively young age, I have not personally experienced Inayat Khan's absence from the physical plane as anything tragic or unusual.

Nor do I experience the absence of Murshid S.A.M. from the physical plane as particularly challenging. Great ones depart in order to permit great growth among their successors, and when I say successors I mean all of us, including the grassroots.

Murshid S.A.M. emerged from a coma on January 2nd, 1971 (he died 13 days later) to say, "Praise be to Allah! This has been a glorious exit, and one which will go down in history, a sign of all the beauty, truth and goodness in the universe.... For I am the first one born in the West to have received the divine message, and believe to have representatives in all the purity and goodness of which Allah is capable and which will now be presumed done forever."

Perhaps Abu Bakr Siddiq had the right idea when he declared, "Those of you who worshipped Muhammad, know that Muhammad is dead. But those of you who worship Allah, know that Allah is Ever-Living and Eternal."

PERSON-TO-PERSON TRANSMISSION THROUGH INITIATION. The policy statement that appears on the inside front cover of every issue of *Heart-Beat*, the Ruhaniat journal, says, "The path of initiation and discipleship is the central theme of the Sufi Islamia Ruhaniat Society. The relationship between teacher and disciple exists for the purpose of providing training that leads to realization of the divine essence in each human being and to leading a life of service to God and humanity."

My experience with mureeds and leaders of all three orders is that the path of initiation and discipleship is alive and well in each order. Of course, there are nuances, notes, flavors, hues, and a general character unique to each order, but the processes of transmission and illumination that constitute the core of Sufism continue to deepen and unfold without exception in all three orders.

Given this reality, does it not behoove us to share our energies and work together for the sake of the Message?

Having said all this, I return to Pir Vilayat's concern that Pirship in the Ruhaniat, in his eyes, lacks credibility. And although Wali Ali mentioned the example of Allauddin Sabri, my questions from an earlier email still remain to be addressed:

"Was Hazrat Inayat Khan initiated as a Pir by Abu Hashim Madani? Or did Hazrat Inayat Khan install himself as the Pir-o-Murshid of the Sufi Order within the Sufi Movement that he founded? In other words, are there precedents to becoming a Pir that don't conform to the usual rules?"

Thank you for your consideration.

Love and blessings,
Moineddin

***

27 September 1999

Dear Pir Vilayat, Beloved Brother in the Message,

Peace be with you, and thank you for your email of 9/26. Your reflections are very much respected and appreciated. Permit me to respond to the following comments:

"Indeed the branching out of the tree opens up a wider spectrum for the bounty in the Message than if it is confined to one organization. Our fragmentation does present an advantage over its disadvantage."

Yes, we do seem to be part of a global trend toward decentralization, signaled by a rise of participatory governance at local levels. This is in contrast to the strong solar models exemplified by Hazrat Inayat Khan and other great personalities of his era. The very Pir-ship of our respective orders reflects an orientation to the solar model, so we as leaders are challenged to retain the noble character and example of this model (aristocracy) and to release the aspects that no longer work as we move into a more cooperative sphere (democracy).

In "The Problem of the Day" your father says, "The difficulty has been the adjustment of the new idea of democracy to the foundation of aristocracy on which it was based.... Democracy is the fulfillment of aristocracy...[and] means recognizing the possibility of advancing just as others have done, trusting in that possibility, and trying to advance to the same level as that of the others."

I believe that the triune branching of the tree of the Message planted by Hazrat Inayat Khan can be looked at not so much as fragmentation, but rather as an organic growth-process toward fulfillment. In the literature, your father speaks of the creation of a *raga* as melodic lines branching from, and returning to, the main trunk of the tree. This is the thought I hold in my heart regarding the Sufi Order International, the International Sufi Movement, and the Sufi Islamia Ruhaniat Society.

"To find cooperation we need to honestly call bygones bygones, and cease to entertain incriminations on all sides and cease to justify our respective positions or to inquire into these. By recognizing there has been pain, forgiveness emerges out of the heart."

Murshids Wali Ali, Karimbakhsh, and Shabda have spoken eloquently to this point in their recent email contributions to this discussion. Without exception, they have expressed a willingness to forgive and forget, and to move toward harmony and healing. I know that this is also the wish of your brother Pir-o-Murshid Hidayat, and my wish as well.

"Our interrelationships need to be as was the initial inspiration of the Federation, loose, respectful, but if we tried to make them more committal that is where we run into problems."

To me, the initial inspiration of the Federation of the Sufi Message breathes through the official statement to which member organizations subscribe. Bylaw number three clearly extends the hand of friendship and welcome to you and the Sufi Order International:

"A place shall be reserved for a third Chair representing the Sufi Order International."

And I agree with you that our interrelationships should be loose knit and respectful. Our commitment is to the Message of Love, Harmony and Beauty, in a heartfelt and truly cooperative spirit.

Apparently, the only problem that needs resolution concerns the matter of whether or not Pir-ship in the Sufi Islamia Ruhaniat Society is, in your eyes, legitimate. I certainly recognize and accept you as the Pir of the Sufi Order International, and your brother Hidayat as the Pir-o-Murshid of the International Sufi Movement—and will respectfully leave off further speaking at this stage of our conversation.

Finally, I sympathize with you having to meet the publisher's deadline for your new book, and wish you godspeed and success in bringing it to birth.

And while we can, via email, continue to prepare the soil for sowing the seeds of the Message in the coming era, we will all need to meet face-to-face at some point to really bring our efforts to fruition. I know that all the principals from the Sufi Movement and SIRS will be together in Charlottesville, Virginia next April for a Federation Leaders Retreat, followed by the SIRS Spring Jamiat Ahm the weekend of April 14, 15 and 16, 2000. If you and Zia will be in the general area, perhaps that would be a good time for us to get together to feel each other's hearts and see how we might proceed.

Love and blessings,
Moineddin

***

5 October 1999

Dear Zia and All,

Thank you, Zia, for your email of 9/28. You are gracious to call us *Qibla*, and I feel your honor and respect in doing so. It would seem that you are not prepared at this time to address the matter of mutual recognition of Pir-ship, one order to the other, but would prefer to study and discuss the sociological patterns unique to each order as a basis for further understanding.

You state: "...there may be significant variations in our respective approaches to questions of transmission, organization, hierarchy, and authority, which, in not receiving sufficient clarification, may account in large measure for our failures to achieve amongst ourselves the harmony our Master would have hoped for us."

Well, yes, but in the view of the Federation of the Sufi Message these variations are honored and valued from the outset. The very existence of the Federation stems from a mutual acceptance, appreciation, and sometimes even forbearance for our distinguishing characteristics.

Because we do differ, the Federation has come into being to achieve the very harmony you speak of.

You also say, "I see the wisdom of my father's recognition that a process of canonization, with far-reaching implications for several generations to come, is underway."

Can you elaborate on this, Zia? I'm not sure what, or whom, you are talking about.

Finally, you bring up the matter of "legitimate authority in a spiritual Order (or Orders)."

One of the strengths of the Federation is its recognition that each member organization accepts and respects the legitimacy and *raison d'être* of the other. That simple act of acceptance and respect nips feelings of "we're legitimate, therefore they're illegitimate" in the bud.

In the all-inclusive heart of Inayat, not a single one of us is misbegotten.

Love and blessings,
Moineddin

P.S. For a third time in this discussion I ask: In the annals of Sufi history, even recent Sufi history, are there precedents to becoming a Pir that do not conform to the usual rules? Specifically, was Hazrat Inayat Khan initiated as Pir by Hazrat Abu Hashim Madani, or did he institute himself as a Pir? Obviously, we all accept him as the Pir-o-Murshid *par excellence* in our time, but what are his actual credentials in the traditional sense? I ask this because I do not know. I would truly appreciate some feedback.

***

16 October 1999

Dear Pir Vilayat and Friends of the Message,

Thank you for taking time out from writing your book to respond so clearly to my request for your current thoughts and feelings about the Federation of the Sufi Message. Your sharing is most helpful and appreciated.

There is, however, one point which I would like to clarify simply as a matter of information.

You state: "According to the customs of traditional Sufi Orders in the East, Murshid S.A.M. was one of the Khalifs of Hazrat Pir-o-Murshid Inayat Khan and you are one of the Khalifs of Murshid S.A.M. Since the Ruhaniat does not consider itself to be part of the Sufi Order or Sufi Movement founded by Hazrat Pir-o-Murshid Inayat Khan, it is up to Ruhaniat to decide upon its Pir-ship and to deal with the question whether it's endorsed by the official Sufi Orders."

This is only a partial view. In his letter to you of May 19, 1969, Murshid S.A.M. wrote: "I should like to see both Moineddin Jablonski and Akbar Simmons officially instituted as Khalifs. They have shown all the signs of spiritual awakening but I have been holding it off hoping that in your presence it could become more official. I have full authority from both the combined Chisti-Qadri-Sabri Orders in Pakistan and the Islamiyya Ruhaniat Society of Islamabad to select and ordain Khalifs, but should prefer to work in unison."

In fact, Pir Dewwal Sherif of the University of Islamabad told Murshid S.A.M. that if for any reason he ever needed to organize his work in the West, he should call it *Islamiyya Ruhaniat Society*. When in 1970 it appeared that you were reluctant to officially recognize the Khalif and Sheikh initiations initially proposed and later carried out by Murshid S.A.M., he did indeed, with Wali Ali's assistance, organize his work in the West as advised by Pir Dewwal Sherif, with the word *Sufi* added before *Islamiyya Ruhaniat Society*.

Of course, after Murshid S.A.M. died you did officially recognize his Khalif and Sheikh appointments as valid in the Sufi Order, and as a result we were able to enjoy many years of mutual and harmonious working together. That was a wonderful chapter in the history of modern Sufism.

Now, with the formation of the Federation of the Sufi Message, a new chapter has begun. Murshid S.A.M.'s work has been officially recognized and accepted by the Sufi Movement, and his words "I should prefer to work in unison" are being fulfilled.

The Federation is our sincere attempt, as Hazrat Inayat Khan said, "to bind ourselves together in one strength." We would so very much welcome your participation.

With love and blessings,
Moineddin

***

(Editor's note: An email to Karimbaksh Witteveen, the General Secretary of the Sufi Movement.)

21 October 1999

Dear Murshid Karimbakhsh,

Thank you for your email about the ongoing correspondence with Zia.
Re: *"I understand why you ask that question [about our Master's Pirship]; but it seems to me really irrelevant."*
I believe it is important to respect the concerns that Pir Vilayat and Zia have expressed regarding authenticity of Pir-ship. They want some assurance that Pir-ship in the Ruhaniat has been recognized by a traditional Sufi order, so that should the Sufi Order International choose to join the Federation they won't be seen as lacking credibility in the eyes of the traditional Sufi world.

That is why I recently sent Pir Vilayat an excerpt from a letter Murshid S.A.M. wrote to him in 1969 stating that he (Murshid S.A.M.) had "full authorization from the combined Chisti-Qadri-Sabri order to select and ordain Khalifs." I also shared with Pir Vilayat that Pir Dewwal Sherif of the University of Islamabad had told Murshid S.A.M. that if he ever needed to organize his work in the West he should call it *Islamiyya Ruhaniat Society*. And when Pir Vilayat was reluctant to recognize Murshid S.A.M.'s initiations of Khalifs and Sheikhs in 1970, he (Murshid S.A.M.) and Wali Ali did indeed set to work on incorporating the [Sufi] Islamia Ruhaniat Society.

I also mentioned that Murshid S.A.M. wrote a series of 32 lessons called "Instructions for the Pir" in the months before he died. I wrote a 33rd lesson to be added to the series last year.

And of course Pir-o-Murshid Hidayat has publicly stated that he and the Sufi Movement recognize the authenticity of Pirship in the Ruhaniat.

All of this is by way of establishing the Ruhaniat's spiritual credentials so that Pir Vilayat won't be embarrassed if he joins the Federation. My correspondence with Pir Vilayat and Zia has been written solely for this purpose. If we're truly interested in welcoming the Sufi Order International into the Federation I believe this conversation does have real relevance.

That's one aspect.

The other aspect is the fact that Hazrat Inayat Khan himself does *not* appear to have been a lineal successor in any of the branches of the Chisti

Order. In other words, he established himself as the Pir-o-Murshid of the Inner School of the Sufi Movement based purely on the will of God as dictated by his inner realization, vision and guidance.

The logical extension of this is that other great souls might also have the direct blessing of God to establish a spiritual school based on divine guidance, as Murshid S.A.M. in fact did.

The important thing to remember is that Murshid S.A.M. never wanted to incorporate separately. He always wanted to work *with* the various successors and representatives of Inayat Khan's Sufi Message. Now that the Federation has become manifest, this is finally happening. Praise God it is finally happening.

The subject whether Hazrat Inayat Khan is a *Rasul* is not something I want to get into. Pir-o-Murshid Inayat Khan himself did not make such a claim, and asked his mureeds not to make claims for him, encouraging them at every turn to let their work speak for itself.

That's all for now. I look forward to seeing you and Murshida Ratan soon.

Love and blessings,
Moineddin

***

(Editor's note: An email to Murshid Nawab Pasnak of the Sufi Movement.)

7 November 1999

Dear Nawab and Everyone,

I was sorry to have missed the Federation Council meeting. My leg injury is slowly healing with the help of antibiotics.

Thank you for responding to Devi's as well as Zia's questions regarding membership in the Federation, which I believe you have addressed quite clearly. I am in general agreement with the Discussion Points that you copied to the participants in this email conversation—with the exception of statements made in Point #1 and Point #4.

The last sentence of #1 states: "Some of the above mentioned organizations had lost contact with the Sufi Movement, which is in fact the original creation of Hazrat Inayat Khan in 1923."

Speaking for the Ruhaniat and Murshid Samuel Lewis, it is mistaken to characterize the Ruhaniat as having "lost contact" with the Sufi

Movement. In fact, it was quite the reverse. Following the death of Hazrat Inayat Khan, Samuel Lewis spent decades trying to establish contact and a viable working relationship with Sufi Movement headquarters and leaders. Instead, the efforts of Samuel Lewis were snubbed, and he was personally rejected, by the leaders of the Sufi Movement. There is no way that this can be construed as having "lost contact" with the Sufi Movement. It would be more accurate to say: "For reasons of their own, some of the above mentioned organizations found it necessary to incorporate separately from the Sufi Movement, which was originally created by Hazrat Inayat Khan in 1923."

The opening sentence of #4 states: "There is no official link, nor historical link, nor transmission link between the Federation and the Chistia School in India." And the last clause of the final sentence states: "...therefore it is quite clear that the transmission of the Sufi Movement is a direct link with Hazrat Inayat Khan, founder of the Sufi Movement and bringer of the Sufi Message, as of the creation of his new initiatic line."

I neither outright agree nor disagree with these remarks. However, I believe that the following words of Hazrat Inayat Khan, taken from the "Book of Instructions for Murshid" that he left with Murshida Rabia Martin, and which came into the possession of Murshid Samuel Lewis, deserve some consideration. This is from the chapter called "Initiation" and follows several paragraphs of detailed instructions and practices that were supposed to precede the ceremony of *bayat*:

"From this time, I initiate thee in the Chisti Branch of the Sufic Order of America and connect thee with an indissoluble link with the Chain of all Murshids in Chain, all Prophets, Saints, and Leaders. Also Muhammad, the sum of all Prophets and Murshids, in order to elevate and enlighten thee toward the highest realization, that thou mayest know the mysteries of the material and spiritual world, and thereby accomplish the aim of life, and most sincerely serve humankind."

Love and blessings,
Moineddin

***

(Editor's note: An email to various senior leaders in the Sufi Order in the West.)

16 April 2000

Dear Atum, Devi, Taj, Himayat, and All,

I want to personally express my thanks to each one of you from the Sufi Order who attended the Federation Leaders' Retreat last week. The sense of gratitude I feel is profound. On a practical level I am grateful for the considerable time and expense you took to travel to Charlottesville [*Virginia*] for the retreat. Even more, I am grateful emotionally and spiritually for your clear and wholehearted participation and presentations.

We were so blessed to receive through each of you the spiritual wine that flowed from your souls into our hearts. The transmission, teachings and support of Pir Vilayat, despite his physical absence, were everywhere self-evident.

As Taj so beautifully expressed it, we were able to take off our organizational masks and share our feelings with naked and childlike hearts. Tears of joyous reunion were shed in the light and love of the Heart of Inayat.

I also want to pour out my thanks to Pir-o-Murshid Hidayat and our beloved brothers and sisters of the Sufi Movement. Without his inspiration and energy constantly working to make a reality of the Federation of the Sufi Message, the Leaders' Retreat would never have happened.

Our coming together represents as well the deep wish of Murshid Samuel Lewis whose whole life was dedicated to the spread of the Sufi Message beyond politics and personalities.

Pir-o-Murshid Hazrat Inayat Khan says, "There is no such thing as impossible. All is possible.... Man, blinded by the law of nature's working, by the law of consequences which he has known through his few years of life on earth, begins to say, 'This is possible and that is impossible.' If he were to rise beyond limitations, his soul would see nothing but possible" (Githa II, "The Spirit of Optimism").

Thank you all again from the depth of my heart. Special gratitude to Ananda Cronin who hosted our gathering with such a spirit of delight, and to Saul Barodofsky whose positive and energetic presence was a support throughout the retreat.

May our souls affirm the great possibility that beckons as we enter into new dimensions of cooperation and service to the Sufi Message of Love, Harmony and Beauty.

Love and blessings,
Moineddin

P.S. Thanks to you, Sarmad, for providing a pictorial record of this watershed event with your flashbulb and film! It was wonderful to see you.

At home in Maui, late 1990s.

Preparations for Dying (2000)

(Editor's note: From a letter sent to several mureeds.)

February 4, 2000

Dear All,

Many thanks for sharing your insights about the change of vibrational reality we call *death*. Your views are indeed of interest and value to all of us, coming as they do from intense and deep personal experience.

Yesterday our next door neighbor and land partner Karen died of liver cancer. She was surrounded by a circle of loving friends including her son. The last time I saw Karen was three weeks ago. I was doing my spiritual practice outdoors in the sunshine when she walked close by. I opened my eyes and said, "Just doing my yoga." She beamed a smile and said, "Yes, you are, keep doing it." Interestingly, her pet dog of many years died a month earlier.

Last night I dreamed of Karen. She appeared and said, "You didn't say goodbye." Then she opened her arms and we hugged a silent goodbye to each other.

I am reminded of something Murshid S.A.M. said about the approach of different schools to spiritual realization. He said, "Some schools of Zen rule out all phenomena short of absolute realization, whereas Sufism adopts a more gradual view. One approach is not necessarily better than the other, but the approach of Sufism may be more suited to greater numbers of people."

A similar comparison might be drawn between the way some Buddhist schools approach death and the Sufi approach. I've excerpted the following paragraphs from [Murshid S.A.M.'s commentaries on Hazrat Inayat Khan's] Series I Githas on "Spirit Phenomena," for general consideration.

"Initiation among the Sufis has, for one of its many objects, to find a caravan in the hereafter that journeys to the desired goal. Therefore, by initiation it is meant that a Sufi prepares himself here on earth to be capable of appreciating the spiritual souls, and unites with them in the brotherhood of initiation on the Path, which may keep him connected with the caravan which is continually journeying toward the goal....

"As spirits of every kind live mostly with their own kind, so the souls who have been in the path of illumination through life dwell in the hereafter among the illuminated spirits, where they are helped and guided by the advanced spirits towards a higher goal. It is this association of spirits which may be called the "White Brotherhood," Masters, Murshids, or Prophets. When the Prophet was asked to tell something about his journey to the heavens, he described how he met Abraham, Moses, Jesus, David, and Solomon. This explains both things: the one, that like attracts like; and the other, that the experience of the spirit world is an experience on the path towards the final goal....

"The further the soul journeys, the less it feels inclined to come back to the world. A traveler who has long left his country forgets it in time and has no inclination to return. Then how can a soul, whose country by no means was the world it was visiting for a time and then left for its own land, long for the place? The comfort of that land to which the soul belongs is much greater than that it has experienced in the world; the freedom of its own spheres was much greater than that it had on earth; the peace of its original dwelling has never been experienced by it when on earth.

"It is very wrong when people imagine the dead long to come to the earth. No doubt you cannot blame them, for they imagine from their experience in the world. For the world is interesting to them when they are in the world, but as soon as they leave it, their experience becomes different. Man on earth need not pity a spirit that has passed from the earth; it is he who should be pitied, even if he be in a palace, so great is the joy and comfort and peace of the higher spheres."

And yet, Sufis and Bodhisattvas do return from the joy and comfort and peace of the higher spheres. We return to balance karma and to fulfill dharma.

It is now almost midnight, February 5th, 2000—the 73rd *urs* of Hazrat Inayat Khan. This sharing seems well-suited to the occasion.

Love,
Moineddin

Last Urs (2001)

(Editor's note: This email to Ruhaniat mureeds was sent on January 15, 2001, less than six weeks before Moineddin passed, on 27 February.)

15 January 2001

Beloved Ones of God,

Tomorrow we shall commemorate the 30th *urs* of Murshid Samuel Lewis (Sufi Ahmed Murad Chishti). Enclosed is a paragraph from Murshid's Commentary on "The Spiritual Hierarchy" by Hazrat Inayat Khan, followed by a comment from me.

"*In the early years of his life the Prophet was ignored, then he was attacked, and finally he was followed by everybody until he had no rest. Then, because he had been properly recognized, he could and did withdraw. His mission was complete and perfect and there was no need for his further remaining upon earth. His followers would have been very happy and would have been intoxicated by the bliss of his companionship, yet that very intoxication would have hindered their further evolution. The pain of separation at his departure hastened the development of his followers as it has that of the disciples of all times.*"

So much of this paragraph could be applied to Murshid's own life—with one notable exception. As Wali Ali pointed out during his talk at the Eugene Jamiat Khas in October, Murshid's passing was *not* marked by the pain of separation. On the contrary, his *baraka* was so present and prevalent in the general atmosphere and in our hearts, despite his physical absence, that we didn't feel his loss. Perhaps it was because we were all so young and our hopes were alive and our inspiration was singing and ringing.

It was not until later that we would feel the impacts of the world, and the challenges of dealing with our shadow natures. Now we have the opportunity to balance heaven and earth, in depth, in our individual and collective lives.

And that opportunity enriches us as human beings and beckons us to grow spiritually, just as it has beckoned the prophets that have gone before, including Hazrat Inayat Khan and Murshid Samuel Lewis.

Ya Rahim,
Moineddin

Instructions for the Pir (1998)

(Editor's note: As mentioned in the correspondence above, in 1998 Moineddin wrote an additional paper in the series "Instructions for the Pir," originally begun by Murshid Samuel Lewis. The "Bowl of Saki" saying is by Hazrat Inayat Khan.)

Instructions for the Pir

Sangitha Series III   Number 33

TOWARD THE ONE, THE PERFECTION OF LOVE, HARMONY, AND BEAUTY, THE ONLY BEING,
UNITED WITH ALL THE ILLUMINATED SOULS WHO FORM THE EMBODIMENT OF THE MASTER, THE SPIRIT OF GUIDANCE.

BOWL OF SAKI: The great teachers of humanity become streams of love.

TASAWWUF: The Pir does not have to become a great teacher, but the Pir does have to become a stream of love. Without the capacity to become a stream of love, one is not properly a Pir.

Now, how does one become a stream of love? One becomes a stream of love by immersing oneself in the living waters of spiritual realization. And for a Pir this realization begins with *fana-fi-rassoul*, the effacement in the spirit of one or more of the great teachers of humanity, which can include the Christ Child and the Divine Mother.

The Pir, as a human being, will have frailties and fallibilities. Thus, the Pir will have a divine exemplar or series of divine exemplars toward whom to look as beacons of realization and behavior. The *tasawwuri* Walks shared by Murshid Samuel Lewis are particularly helpful in attuning one to the greater rhythm and being of the Messengers of God.

The specific portion of humanity assisted by the Pir is the body of mureeds entrusted to his or her care. *Care* is the operative word here. For without care, there is no love. The Pir is entrusted to love and care for the mureeds as if they were members of one's immediate family. A beautiful similitude of the caring attitude of the Pir can be found in the Biblical phrase, "And there were shepherds abiding in the field, keeping watch over their flocks by night."

V. AN EVOLVING SUFI PATH

All of the preceding lessons in this series emphasize the importance of the love-element in the work of the Pir. This love can come through a kind word, and it can come through a heartfelt silence. This love can come through the glance, through the breath, through the atmosphere. The heart of the Pir, having been proven through many tests of loss and pain, will be large enough to accommodate the sorrows of the mureeds, will be living enough to sympathize with their needs, will be strong enough to help them bear their burdens, will be peaceful enough to transform their losses into new beginnings.

For those on the Path of the Pir, it is well to remember the words of Pir-o-Murshid Inayat Khan:

"Our work is for eternity."

Lesson 33 is by Murshid Moineddin Jablonski
For the Inner School of the Pir

VI. Epilogue

Flying Clouds (poem 1977)

Looking up, the whole sky's
become an appaloosa's flank
rippling over ridge and rim
of these green hills.

The sun's an elusive rider;
his grinning face burns and burns
until he gives himself away.

Through the flying grey clouds
a glimpse of bright turquoise—
like a flash of bluejay
through the silver mist.

I ride home dreaming of new feathers!

Acid Trip, 1966 (poem 1991)

I swallowed hard and found myself
in the body of a horse.
A shaggy small horse,
huge in endurance,
rump to the blizzard's
bitter eye.

This horse is familiar, I think.

He insists there's a storm
raging on the steppes of Asia that never lets up.
And a white howling
too dense for sun.

Bull in a China Shop (poem 1994)

If Picasso
could command small fortunes
for his scribbled Minotaurs,
may I—all artless—trade
these naked lines of need
for the gold coins of
your lips, dear,
upon mine?

– VI. EPILOGUE –

Wings (poem 2000)

(Editor's note: This and the following poem were the last that Moineddin published. They appeared in the Ruhaniat's Heartbeat *journal in Fall 2000, Volume 14).*

> Raven swoops high, a dripping clam
> in her beak. She drops the clam
> on a fossil reef, breaking it open.
> Raven eats the clam's sweet
> sea-nurtured flesh, making
> its life her own.
>
> What do we really know
> of being taken,
> of letting go,
> of breaking?

The Wind (poem 2000)

You herd the clouds like sheep
in a blue pasture
crook in hand.

Or play the wolf scattering the flock,
ripping wool from the flanks
of a fat ewe. Or white tufts
from a lamb's throat,
intent on the kill.

Hours after the feast,
the flamingo sunset will array itself
like great wings in the sky—
wings the color of pigeons' feet.

And you will be there,
savage and calm,
breathing it out,
breathing it in.

VI. EPILOGUE

At the Voice of the Turtle, Southwest Sufi Center, New Mexico.

Acknowledgements

Many people helped create this testament to Moineddin's life and work.

Thanks go especially to Quan Yin Williams and Najat Roberts. Quan Yin served as my assistant editor. She believed in and supported the book, even before it began to take its final shape. In addition to contributing her invaluable editorial eye, she tracked down photos and documents, and engaged several of Moineddin's students in the process of reviewing the developing the manuscript. Najat, who also serves as the head of the nascent archive project for Moineddin's writings, unearthed many early letters and poems from the time that she served as Moineddin's esoteric secretary in the 1970s and 1980s. (She is referred to as "Fatima" Roberts, her earlier spiritual name, in two of the early letters included here.) Both Quan Yin and Najat were also enthusiastic proofreaders, surely a *tasawwuri*-emulation of Moineddin, who was well-known for his ability to find typos in any Ruhaniat publication.

Several of Moineddin's friends and fellow students of Murshid Samuel Lewis also contributed important letters that helped fill in gaps in the story. These include Allaudin William Mathieu and Mansur Johnson. Allaudin added several letters from the early Maui days. Mansur, one of Moineddin's earliest friends from Iowa, carried on a uniquely personal correspondence with him from the years 1975 to 1980. I highly recommend the entire online archive of these 82 letters, which can be found at www.mansurjohnson.com, along with Mansur's other books, including *Murshid*, about his time with Murshid Samuel Lewis. Mansur also contributed several early photos, both of Moineddin and Murshid Samuel Lewis.

Other longtime students of Moineddin who contributed invaluable time, proofreading help and support include Mariam Baker, Majida Nelson, Amrita Skye Blaine and Boudewijn Boom.

Jelaluddin Hauke Sturm in Berlin contributed the beautiful cover and interior design. I have collaborated with him on several book projects, and he is always a pleasure to work with! Longtime friend, publishing professional and fellow mureed Carol Sill in Canada, the archivist for Shamcher Beorse's writings, contributed the index. Final proofreading help came from Iman Michael Howden, Jivani Joyce Carlson and Jannat Janet Granger.

The story "Piktor's Metamorphosis" is reprinted with permission from *C.G. Jung and Hermann Hesse: A Record of Two Friendships* by

Miquel Serrano. All rights reserved. Copyright 1977 Daimon Verlag, Am Klosterplatz, Hauptstrasse 85, CH-8840 Einsiedelm, Switzerland. www.daimon.ch.)

The only royalty from this book goes to Moineddin's children, and virtually all of the work on this book was donated. We did have a few publishing costs, which were "crowd-funded" by the following Ruhaniat mureeds: Wajida Jamila Pape, Tarana Wesley, Vakil Forest Shomer, Salim Chisti Matt Gras, Rashid Andreas Beurskens, Fateah Saunders, Batina Ruth Vandam-Hinds, Jeanpierre David, Tawwaba Bloch, Basira Beardsworth, Zubin Westrick, Stella Cranwell, Khalisa Kitz, Kakuli Razina Judy Ballinger, Najat and Jaman Roberts, Mudita Sabato, Noor-un-Nisa Walsh, Mansur Kreps, Quan Yin Williams, Azima Lila Forest, Nicola Inana Prelle, Saraswati Rena Coon, Uwais Andre Bernard, Ahmed Alan Heeks, and the Soulwork Foundation.

Appendix I: Eulogy—Pir Moineddin Carl Jablonski, 1942–2001

(Editor's note: Published in Toward the One, *the journal of the Federation of the Sufi Message, shortly after Moineddin's passing.)*

"As long as I shall live, this is Murshid's house; therefore, O faithful companions, keep me living."
--Moineddin Jablonski, from "Job's Tears."

Pir Moineddin assumed leadership of the Ruhaniat in 1971 upon the death of Murshid Samuel Lewis after the latter designated him as his spiritual successor. Continuing his teacher's vision, Pir Moineddin oversaw the spread of the Sufi Message of Love, Harmony, and Beauty through spiritual practice, the Dances of Universal Peace, the Healing work, Soulwork counseling, and conscious community involvement. The Ruhaniat grew from some 150 people to a worldwide network of Sufi communities throughout forty-two states, the United Kingdom, Canada, Russia, Norway, Germany, The Netherlands, Belgium, Switzerland, Japan, Kuwait, The Philippines, Brazil, Australia, and New Zealand.

During his tenure as spiritual director of the Ruhaniat, Moineddin met a number of challenges faced not only by the Ruhaniat but also by other spiritual organizations that came out of the 1960s and 70s. Many of these challenges centered on issues of spiritual authority and accountability. With regard to the former, Moineddin shepherded the individuation of the Ruhaniat from the Sufi Order International in 1977, affirming the practice of Murshid Samuel Lewis that the living relationship between Sufi mureed and guide was more important than any attempt to impose organizational rules on the relationship. With regard to the latter, Moineddin instituted ethical guidelines and an ethics procedure in the Ruhaniat in the early 1980s and required all initiators to have an active supervisor or "check-in" person, as was the practice of Murshid Samuel Lewis in his own life. Both of the later developments were controversial at the time, although later adopted by many spiritual groups.

At the same time, Moineddin attempted to follow the vision of Murshid Samuel Lewis by increasing the importance of collaborative leadership, or as Murshid S.A.M. put it, "the group-unit becoming the nexus of spiritual authority." In this regard, Moineddin decentralized leadership from a small group in the San Francisco Bay area and encouraged various concentrations like Dances of Universal Peace and the Healing Ritual to flourish under their own vision and energy. With regard to this, Moineddin saw wisdom born of necessity as well as wisdom for its own sake. In a brief haiku, he expressed the former and in an aphorism from "Job's Tears" the latter:

SUFI POEM
Murshid lasted
three years
carrying everything.

"I am not Murshid; we are Murshid. I do not have all the answers; we may have the answers."

On the level of organizational structure, Moineddin reorganized Ruhaniat governance from a Board of Trustees and Jamiat Khas centered in the San Francisco Bay area to ones composed of representatives from throughout the USA and, more recently, the world. In addition, along with Pir Hidayat Inayat Khan of the Sufi Movement International, Moineddin cultivated the foundation and establishment of the Federation of the Sufi

Message, which now also includes the Sufi Order International, the Sufi Way, the Sufi Contact and the Fraternity of Light, all lineages of Sufi work that stem from the inspiration of Hazrat Inayat Khan.

Pir Moineddin was a great uniter, a man of tremendous heart and great humor who worked steadfastly on behalf of the greater good of all, even in the face of his own health concerns.

Frail after a kidney failure and subsequent transplant, Moineddin moved to Maui in 1981 to rejuvenate his body, mind, and spirit, and married Mei-Ling Chang of Ha'iku, Maui, an energetic woman of Hawai'ian/Chinese descent. Mei-Ling supplied Moineddin with the emotional fuel he needed to heal and to carry out his destiny and purpose. He survived with the help of two different kidney transplants ten years apart.

With his personal health concerns continually uncertain, he gave all he could to those of the community who asked for and sought out his counsel and guidance. For years he taught meditative practice and helped people uncomplicate their lives by offering fresh and noble angles from which to view life situations. His Midwest upbringing laid a foundation that made strangers feel like friends. His easygoing sense of humor and "don't tell me, show me" attitude challenged and inspired friends and students to uphold their integrity. His truthful feedback and simple common sense wisdom helped farmers, business people, doctors, lawyers, and politicians alike become better people, content within themselves and their community.

The breath is enough,
the heart is enough,
the eye is enough,
the atmosphere is enough.
—from "Job's Tears"

One of his great contributions was the emphasis on what he dubbed "Soulwork," a psychospiritual counseling approach that promotes clarity within an individual so that one may heal one's wounds and unite one's struggling internal personal identities. His Soulwork training was inspired by the late Frida Waterhouse as well as Harvey Grady, and is continued under the guidance of Murshida Mariam Baker.

During the last five years of his life, Moineddin founded the Southwest Sufi Community on 1900 acres outside Silver City, New Mexico. The SSC comprises Khankah Noor Inayat, a residential community; Voice of the Turtle Retreat Center; and Bear Creek Nature Preserve. He described this community with the following statement:

"As we prepare to come together for this experience in holistic living, remember that we are living in a time of rapid change and intensive growth—a process which brings out the worst and best in each one of us. Everywhere people are challenged to stick to their ideals in a world of fearful emotions which too often lead to abusive words and violent acts, even in our own homes. Our work is to root out these imbalances in ourselves, so that our hearts can become havens of safety, peace, and refuge for each other. Practicing thus, we develop individual spiritual capacities which, when transposed to the level of intentional community, create greater potential for harmlessness, compassion, and loving-kindness to arise planet-wide."

In one of his letters he writes, "To each of you I offer these words of counsel: Deepen your compassion. Love the wounded places in you that need healing. Open yourself to the grace of illumination. Give freely of your joy. Share your neighbor's burden. Through all these avenues, discover your soul."

(Editor's note: Contributions by Malik Cotter, Sharabi Hilal, Shabda Kahn and Saadi Klotz.)

Appendix II:
Piktor's Metamorphosis
by Hermann Hesse

(Editor's note: The following story is from the book C.G. Jung and Hermann Hesse: A Record of Two Friendships *by Miquel Serrano, which Moineddin mentions in the letter "Metamorphosis" in Section IV.)*

That night at Mr. Ceccarelli's inn I read the small book which Hesse had given me.

It was the story of a young man, Piktor, who had entered Paradise and found himself standing before a tree which represented both Man and Woman. He gazed at it with wonder and then asked, "Are you the Tree of Life?" The tree made no reply, but instead the Serpent appeared, and so Piktor continued on his way. He examined everything with care and was delighted with what he saw.

As he walked along, he saw another tree which represented the Sun and the Moon. "Perhaps you are the Tree of Life?" he asked. The Sun seemed to laugh in affirmation, and the Moon smiled. All about Piktor were clumps of wildflowers. They seemed to have faces like people, and some laughed richly and understandingly, while others swayed in a lighthearted manner. Still others neither moved nor laughed; they were somber and sunk into themselves, as though drunk with their own perfume. Some of the flowers sang to Piktor: one sang him the wistful song of the lilacs, another a dark blue lullaby. One flower had eyes like hard sapphire; another reminded him of his first love; still another made him recall his mother's voice when he had wandered with her as a child in the gardens at home. Most of the flowers were gaily laughing, and one stuck out her tongue at him. It was a little pink tongue, and Piktor leaned down to touch it. When he did, he met the wild bitter taste of wine and honey, and he knew that it was the kiss of a woman.

Alone amongst all these flowers, Piktor was overwhelmed by a mixed feeling of nostalgia and fear. His heart was beating rapidly as though anxious to respond to the rhythms of the place. Piktor then saw a bird lying on the grass a little distance away. The bird had feathers like a peacock reflecting all the colors of the spectrum. Piktor was overwhelmed by the beauty of the bird, and so he approached and asked, "Where can one find happiness?"

"Happiness?" replied the bird, "Happiness is everywhere—in the mountains and the valleys and in every flower."

The bird then stretched its neck and shook its feathers before settling back motionless. Suddenly Piktor realized that the bird had been transformed into a flower. The feathers had become leaves and the claws, roots. Piktor looked down in astonishment, and then almost immediately, the flower began to move its leaves. It had already grown tired of being a flower and began to float languidly up into the air. It had turned into a butterfly, and was a blaze of pure, floating color.

To Piktor's increasing amazement, this happy bird-flower-butterfly flew about him in circles. After a while, it glided to the earth like a snowflake and remained trembling by Piktor's feet. For a moment, its wings fluttered, and then suddenly it was transformed into a crystal, radiating a deep red light. It glistened on the grass with fantastic brilliance.

As Piktor gazed down upon it, it seemed to be gradually disappearing into the ground, as though it were being drawn into the very center of the earth. Just as it was about to vanish, Piktor reached down and grasped it. He held it tightly in his hand, because it seemed a talisman for every adventure in the world.

At that moment, the Serpent slid down from a nearby tree and whispered into Piktor's ear, "This jewel can turn you into anything you want to be. But tell it your wish quickly, before it disappears." Afraid of losing the opportunity, Piktor whispered the secret word to the stone, and suddenly he was transformed into a tree. Piktor had always wanted to be a tree, because he admired their strength and serenity. Soon he felt his roots sink into the earth and his branches reach towards the sky. New leaves and branches sprouted from his trunk, and he was content. His thirsty roots absorbed the water from the earth, and his branches were cooled by the languid air of the forest. Insects lived in his bark, and a porcupine took shelter at his feet.

In the forest of Paradise in which he stood, he observed the continuing metamorphosis that took place round about him. He watched flowers become precious stones, or turn themselves into birds. He saw a neighboring tree suddenly transform itself into a brook. Another became a crocodile, yet a third turned into a fish and swam off full of gaiety and happiness. All of creation took part in this game of change; elephants became rocks; giraffes, huge flowering trees.

In the midst of all this change, Piktor alone remained the same. When he began to realize his condition, he lost his happiness, and little by little, he began to grow old, taking on that tired, absent look that one can observe in many old trees. Nor is this phenomenon confined to trees; horses and dogs and even human beings begin to disintegrate with time and to lose their beauty because they have lost the gift of metamorphosis. They end their days in sadness and worry.

A long time afterwards, a little girl with blonde hair lost her way while dancing through Paradise. She wore a blue dress and sang gaily as she skipped along. Her presence was eagerly noticed by other creatures in the forest; the bushes reached out towards her with their branches, and many trees threw down fruit for her. But the young girl ignored their attentions. At length, she came into the little clearing where Piktor stood as a tree. When Piktor looked down at her, he was struck by a deep feeling of nostalgia and an immense desire to seize happiness before it was too late. He felt as though his whole being were commanding him to concentrate on the meaning of his existence and to force it to the surface of his consciousness. He recalled his past life, his years as a man before he entered Paradise. And he particularly remembered the time when he had held the magic jewel in his hands, because at that moment, with all changes possible, he had been most alive. He then recalled the bird and the gay tree which had represented the Sun and the Moon, and as he did so, he realized how fatal the Serpent's advice had been.

The girl sensed the restless movement of Piktor's leaves and branches, and when she looked up, she felt strangely disquieted. She sat in the shade, and intuitively began to understand that the tree was lonely and sad, while at the same time realizing that there was something noble in its total isolation. Leaning against the rough tree trunk, she sensed something of the turmoil that was going on in Piktor's being, and she too started to tremble in an inexplicable passion. Soon she was weeping, and as the tears fell on her dress, she wondered why it was that suffering existed. In her own solitude, she felt herself reaching out in compassion for the lonely tree.

Sensing her feelings, Piktor gathered all the forces of his life and directed them towards the young girl. He realized now how monstrous the Serpent's deception had been and how foolishly he had acted. Now as a single tree, he was overwhelmed with the vision of the tree that was Man and Woman together.

Just then, a green bird with red wings drew near and circled round the tree. The girl watched its flight and saw something bright and luminous fall from its beak into the nearby grass. She leaned over to pick it up and found that it was a precious carbuncle. She had hardly held the stone for a moment when the confused thoughts that had troubled her vanished, and she was overcome by a single desire. In a moment of ecstasy, she became one with the tree and was transformed into a new branch which grew out towards the heavens.

Now everything was perfect, and the world was in order. In that moment, Paradise had been found. Piktor was no longer a solitary old tree, but was fulfilled and complete and bore a new name which he called Piktoria. And thus he sang out, loud and clear, the word "Piktoria!" And this phrase also signified "Victoria" or Victory. At long last, he had been transformed, and he realized the truth of eternal metamorphosis, because he had been changed from a half to a whole.

From then on, he knew he would be able to transform himself as often as he liked. The force of continuing creation was now released within him, and he knew he could renew himself as a star or a fish or a cloud or a bird. But he also realized that whatever form he took would be a whole, and that in each image he would be a pair; he had both the Sun and the Moon within him, and he was at once Man and Woman.

That evening in Montagnola, when I finished reading the book and glanced once again at the drawings it contained, I thought of a phrase which Hesse himself had written only the year before: "In their old age, some men have the gift of once again experiencing the paradisiacal state of their childhood." That, I realized, was the key to the seemingly ingenious tale of Piktor. It was really a vision of Paradise regained. And then, too, there came back upon me with redoubled force Hermann Hesse's remark of the afternoon before when, with his hand on the stone bust, he had said, "We will return to form, to pure form...."

(Editor's note: Reprinted with permission. All rights reserved. Copyright 1977 Daimon Verlag, Am Klosterplatz, Hauptstrasse 85, CH-8840 Einsiedelm, Switzerland. Website: www.daimon.ch.)

Glossary

(Editor's note: This editor used a 'hybrid' approach to the use of italics and capitalization for esoteric terms. Where a term, like zikr, is used in the same sense as it generally is in classical Sufism, Vedanta or Buddhism, it is italicized in lower case. However, we treat the titles of papers or lessons, for instance Hazrat Inayat Khan's Githas on Sadhana differently, using a capitalized title without italics. In these cases, the term is not necessarily identical with its usage in classical Sufism or another tradition. A good example would be salat (italics), the form of Muslim prayer, and Salat (not italics, but capitalized), a particular English language prayer given by Hazrat Inayat Khan. Capitalization in Moineddin's poetry is at the poet's discretion. The general editing theory was that slavish consistency seldom increases readability and may inhibit understanding.)

Arabic (Ar) Hebrew (Heb) Sanskrit (Skr) Greek (Gr) Japanese (Jap) Persian (Per)

Abdal: "substitute." Ar. A rank of saints in the Sufi spiritual hierarchy, which involves being a "changeling"(*badal*)—transforming oneself by the will of Allah to be whatever the situation requires. Murshid Samuel Lewis said that he was an *Abdal*, and a number of references to this are made in the book.

agape: universal, unconditional or "selfless" love. Gr.

akhlak Allah: the "manner" of God, a practice or grace associated with experiences of *baqa*, subsisting in the divine. Ar.

Alhamdulillah: "all praise to the One," every praiseworthy essence returns to Allah. Ar.

Allaho Akbar: "Allah is greater," the essence of which Murshid Samuel Lewis translated as "peace is power." Ar.

Amal: literally, "hope," used here to mean a practice given by Hazrat Inayat Khan, involving dissolving gradually into Unity, drawn from the nexus of historical practice shared by Indian Sufism and yoga. Ar.

anahata: "unstruck," refers here to the heart chakra. Skr.

baqa: resurrection, salvation, "subsistence" occurring after *fana* (effacement). Ar.

baraka: blessing-magnetism, Ar.

bayat: pledge of loyalty to a Sufi teacher, used to mean the "first initiation" in the Inayati Sufi schools descended from Hazrat Inayat Khan. Ar.

bodhisattva: in Mahayana Buddhism, one who vows to attain enlightenment for the benefit of all sentient beings. Skr.

bhakti: spiritual path of love. Skr.

chakra: "wheel," an energy point or node in the subtle body. Skr.

chela: disciple in the Hindu path. Skr.

cherag(a): "lamp" or "light." Per. Here, a minister of the Universal Worship inspired by Hazrat Inayat Khan.

darood: literally, "health," "well-being," "thanksgiving." Per. Traditionally, any invocation made to invoke the presence of and blessing to and through the Prophet Muhammad. Also called in Arabic a *salawat*. Here the word Darood (capitalized) means a rhythmical breath meditaiton or *fikr* using the first words of the invocation originally used by Hazrat Inayat Khan to begin his talks and lectures: "Toward the One."

darquza: "Overlooking may be called in other words rising beyond things: one has to rise in order to overlook; the one who stands beneath life could not overlook, even if he wanted to."—Hazrat Inayat Khan. Per.

darshan: the giving of a blessing through the glance. Skr.

dhamma: also *dharma*, literally "that which supports or holds together," the "way" or "path," righteous duty. Skr.

dharmakaya: divine "form." Skr.

dhyana: meditation, or the process of entering into it. Skr.

Djabrut: sometimes spelled *jabrut*; from one of the Arabic words for "bridge," relating in Sufi cosmology to the realm of power or angelic realm that connects or bridges the various realms of unmanifested creation with those of manifestation. According to Murshid Samuel Lewis, "Divine breath is at the basis of personality. The soul has attuned itself to a certain keynote in *Djabrut* and gathered certain experiences and characteristics in *Malakut*. These remain as seeds until the body is big and strong enough to express them." Ar.

dervish: or *darvish*, a word with a number of variations in Persian and Urdu, with indistinct origins, meaning a wandering saint or medicant. Most often linked to the word "door," as "one who goes from door to door" or who "sits between the doorways" between this world and the next. Per.

dhikr: (also spelled *zikr*). remembrance of Allah, often using some form of the phrase *La ilaha ila 'llah*. Ar.

fana: effacement. Ar.

fana-fi-sheikh: effacement in the being of one's living teacher or sheikh. Ar.

fana-fi-pir: effacement in the being of a teacher who has passed. Ar.

fana-fi-rassoul: effacement in the being of one of the messengers or prophets. Ar.

fana-fi-lillah: effacement in the being of Unity itself. Ar. See also nirvakalpa samadhi.

fikr: from an Arabic word meaning to "think," here used to mean keeping a sacred phrase on the breath in the heart and so in consciousness. From Hazrat Inayat Khan: "The breath is like a swing which has a constant motion, and whatever is put in the swing, swings also with the movement of the breath. *Fikr*, therefore, is not a breathing practice. In *fikr* it is not necessary that one should breathe in a certain way, different from one's usual breathing. *Fikr* is to become conscious of the natural movement of the breath, and picturing breath as a swing, to put in that swing a certain thought, as a babe in the cradle, to rock it. Only the difference in rocking is an intentional activity on the part of the person who rocks the cradle." Ar.

Gatha: usually meaning one of the hymns of Zarathustra in Avestan, the ancient Persian language. In Sanskrit, the word means "song" or "verse." Here (capitalized) the word means one of the original written lessons for mureeds from the writings and talks of Hazrat Inayat Khan, which included the following series: Takua Taharat (Everyday Life), Etekad Rasm u Ravaj (Superstitions, Customs and Beliefs), Pasi Anfas (Breath), Saluk (Morals), Kashf (Insight), Nakshi Bandi (Symbology) and Tasawwuf (Metaphysics).

Al Haqq: the "truth" of being, "what is," one of the 99 "Beautiful Names" of Allah. Ar.

haqiqat: "fact," "truth," or "reality." Ar. The stage of mystical knowing or experience after *tariqat*. Hazrat Inayat Khan: "Haqiqat is to know the truth of our being and the inner law of Nature. This knowledge widens the heart of a person. When he has realized the truth of being, he has realized the One Being; he is different from nobody, distant from no one: he is one with all. That is the grade where religion ends and Sufism begins."

hal: a spiritual state of consciousness, something that passes with "time." Ar.

Al Hayy: life energy, one of the 99 "Beautiful Names" of Allah. Ar.

ilm: divine knowledge, as the understanding of levels, worlds, differences and distinctions. Ar.

iman: faith, confidence, trust; related to the Semitic root for ameyn, amin. Ar.

inshallah: by the will of the One. Ar.

ishk: divine love as passion, what brings or holds things or beings together. According to some Sufis, ishk in its most profound sense is what created the universes and is identical with the only Being. Ar.

Ishk Allah Mahebud Lillah: variation of a traditional sacred phrase frequently used by Murshid Samuel Lewis, and explained by him in the following manner, consistent with the literal meaning of Arabic: God is love (*ishk Allah*, love as passion); loving, being loved and love itself—the whole process (*mahebud*)—is *for* or *toward* (the meaning of the preposition *li-*) the One (*lillah*). Ar.

Jamiat: a gathering; in specific (as capitalized in the book), a Jamiat Khas was the gathering of leaders in the Sufi Islamia Ruhaniat Society. In most cases, this is what Moineddin refers to as a "Jamiat." A Jamiat Ahm was a more general gathering of initiated mureeds. Ar.

jelal: condition of expressiveness. Ar.

jemal: condition of responsiveness. Ar.

jhana: meditation; specifically, the meditative breathing practices of Buddha. Skr.

jihad: struggle, exertion. Ar.

jnana: spiritual path of knowledge, including self-knowledge. Skr.

Kabbalah: the various strands of Jewish mysticism. Heb.

Al Kafi: that which suffices, the "most necessary" remedy. Ar.

karamat: the power of miracle. Ar.

kasab: from a verb meaning "to earn," an alternative nostril breathing practice used by Hazrat Inayat Khan in his teaching. Ar.

kashf: direct mystical insight without an intermediary. Ar.

kemal: periods of the breath being in a state of stagnation or stasis, which is similar to the outer situation where two atmospheric pressures collide. Ar.

kensho: initial insight or awakening in Buddhism. Jap.

khalif: "steward" or "deputy." Ar. Here used, usually capitalized, to mean one of those permitted to give bayat and teach in various of the Hazrat Inayat Khan (Inayati) lineages.

khankah: sometimes also spelled *khanqah*, a building or group of buildings that house a Sufi community or provides a place for group gatherings or spiritual retreat. Per. The equivalent term in Arabic is *zawiyah*. Murshid Samuel Lewis had a khankah at the Mentorgarden in San Francisco and in Novato, California (Marin Country) at the Garden of Inayat.

ko-an: in Japanese Zen Buddhism, a story, question or statement meant to test a student's progress. Jap.

madzub: from the Persian *majzub*, "possessed," a God-intoxicated being. From Hazrat Inayat Khan: "The fifth form in which a person who lives the inner life appears is a strange form, a form which very few people can understand. He puts on the mask of innocence outwardly to such an extent that those who do not understand may easily consider him unbalanced, peculiar, or strange. He does not mind about it, for the reason that it is only his shield. If he were to admit before humanity the power that he has, thousands of people would go after him, and he would not have one moment to live his inner life. The enormous power that he possesses governs inwardly lands and countries, controlling them and keeping them safe from disasters such as floods and plagues, and also wars; keeping harmony in the country or in the place in which he lives; and all this is done by his silence, by his constant realization of the inner life. To a person who lacks deep insight he will seem a strange being. In the language of the East he is called *Madzub*." Per.

makam: (sometimes also spelled *maqam* in Sufi literature), the "stage" of consciousness that one maintains in everyday life. Ar.

maqbara: Arabic term referring generally to the gravesite of a revered religious figure in Islam or a Sufi saint. Capitalized here as Maqbara, it refers specifically in Moineddin's writing to the grave of Murshid Samuel Lewis at the Lama Foundation in New Mexico, USA. *Dargah* is the parallel term in Persian, also used in India. Ar.

Malakut: in Sufi cosmology, the realm of intelligence, the world of symbolic forms, the "mental plane," Ar. From Murshid Samuel Lewis: "Mental attitudes and opinions find their source in *Malakut*, the mental region or mind-world, which is compounded of various grades of light, shadow and darkness. *Djabrut*, the spiritual sphere, from which the spiritual attitudes arise is the heart plane and is compounded only of various grades of light—there is no darkness there." See also *Djabrut*.

marifat: from the Arabic verb *arafa*, to know. The stage of mystical knowing or experience after *haqiqat*. Hazrat Inayat Khan: "Marifat is the actual realization of God, the One Being, when there is no doubt anywhere. When these four classes [*shariat, tariqat, haqiqat, marifat*] are accomplished, then the full play of Sufism comes. Sufi means *safa*, pure—not only pure from differences and distinctions, but even pure from all that is learnt and known. That is the state of Allah, the pure and perfect One." Ar.

mashallah: what Allah has wished, or Allah has willed it. Ar.

mujahida: literally, "greater struggle." Used here to mean the process of clearing the heart from impressions that prevent one from accessing kashf or direct insight from Oneness. Ar.

muladhara: root chakra at the base of the spine. Skr.

murakkabah: concentration, focusing the mind on one theme. Ar.

mureed: (spelling used in the Inayati Sufi lineages, also spelled *murid* in some Sufi literature). An initiated student in a Sufi order or lineage, one who has made the pledge of bayat. Ar.

mushahida: Sufi practice of inner witnessing, seeing through the heart as through the eyes of Unity. See also listing under *shahud*. Ar.

nabi: a divine prophet, from the Hebrew *nebi*; also (capitalized) the name of a prayer of Hazrat Inayat Khan. Ar.

nafs: the "personal" breath or "self." Ar.

nafsaniat: the realm of personal name and form. Ar.

nafs alima: a state of "self" that knows or understands from the divine viewpoint. Ar.

nafs selima: the "peaceful" self, which gives blessing freely. Ar.

nirvakalpa samadhi: state of total absorption into Unity, excluding an awareness of individual "self." "The dew-drop slips into the Shining Sea." Skr.

nirvana: from the Sanskrit verb meaning to "blow out" a candle. A state in which all desires and aversions have been extinguished. From Murshid Samuel Lewis: "It is easy to imagine Nirvana far away from turmoil; it is marvelous to imagine and attain Nirvana in the midst of trouble. Therefore if the sage once finds the Universal Peace in the midst of strife, it will be natural for him to find it anywhere and everywhere. The descent of Jesus into Hell is nothing but the willingness of the awakened soul to face all and fear nothing for the sake of God." Skr.

prajna: insight, wisdom. Skr.

pralaya: "non-existence," a state in which the three gunas (sattva, rajas, tamas) are in perfect balance. Skr. From Murshid Samuel Lewis: "The stories of Creation (myths) all indicate numbers and symbols which presuppose rhythm. The statement is made 'By the Word of God were all things in heaven and earth made.' This also presumes the rhythms of God. The Indian people especially have a complex cosmology based on it, and the terms *pralaya* and *manvantara* all are associated with rhythmical breath as if of God Himself. It suggests that if God did not breathe rhythmically there would be chaos. And by analogy also if man, created in God's image did not breathe rhythmically there would be chaos within him."

Al Quddus: holiness, sacred spaciousness; one of the 99 "Beautiful Names" of Allah. Ar.

Ramnam: The mantra "Om Sri Ram Jai Ram Jai Jai Ram"—Homage to the One who is both personal and impersonal, both truth and power, victory! Skr.

rassoul: divine messenger; also (capitalized), the name of a particular prayer of Hazrat Inayat Khan. Ar.

ryazat: body of spiritual practices used in a particular Sufi school or *tariqat*. Ar.

rishi: seers who composed the Vedic hymns. Skr.

sadhana: "accomplishment." Skr. Hazrat Inayat Khan gave lessons for somewhat more advanced mureeds ("Githas"), which included a series he called "Sadhana," the path of attainment. From Hazrat Inayat Khan: "The secret of life is the desire to attain something; the absence of this makes life useless. Hope is the sustenance of life; hope comes from the desire of attaining something. Therefore this desire is in itself a very great power. The object which a person wishes to attain may be small compared with the power he develops in the process of attainment. The Hindus call attainment *sadhana*; the power gained through attainment is called in Sanskrit *siddhi*, and it is this which is the sign of spiritual mastership."

sahaja samadhi: "natural" or "open" vision, "*samadhi* with open eyes." "The Shining Sea slips into the dew-drop." Skr.

sahasrara: "thousand-petalled," refers here to the crown chakra. Skr.

sama: Sufi sessions of music and poetry. Ar.

samadhi: "together" or "integrated." Skr. A state of meditation in which subject and object become one. From Murshid Samuel Lewis: "It may be asked if there is perfection in meditation, and the answer to this depends largely by what one means. Yes, there is a state called '*samadhi*' wherein one continues to live, when one lives and moves and has his being in God, or at least one has a realization which is not limited by the ego outlook. The attunement to God which comes through meditation and heart-awakening is such that openly and consciously as well as conscientiously one finds himself beyond the distinctions and differences which divide men."

samsara: the cycle of life and death, of material existence. Skr.

samskara: impression upon the mind that remains for a period of time. Skr.

satori: Zen Buddhist term for an experience of initial awakening or enlightenment, often used interchangeably with *kensho*, "seeing into one's true nature." Jap.

sema: from the Arabic *sami*, to hear; see also *sama* above. Here *sema* refers to the turning ceremony of the Mevlevi Sufis, a form of zikr or remembrance begun by Mevlana Jelaluddin Rumi. Ar.

Ash Shafi: that which cures or quenches, source of divine healing. Ar.

shagal: "occupying," "filling up." Ar. A breathing practice used in the teaching of Hazrat Inayat Khan, from the ancient Hebrew word meaning "to be destroyed or ravished," but also present in Arabic and Persian as above. From Murshid Samuel Lewis: "Every breath taken with the thought of God or in praise of God preserves the light of the body. *Kasab* increases the capacity, *Shagal* increases the light and *Darood* and *fikr* prevent its loss. Therefore illumination can extend even to the physical vehicle."

shahud: direct sight, from the Arabic *shahid*, to witness or experience. Murshid Samuel Lewis: "Contemplation or Mushahida is an advanced practice among adepts. Lessons about *shahud* appear in 'The Sufi Message of Spiritual Liberty' and also in studies on *azan*, the call to prayer. No doubt these are proper introductions, but the real practice of *mushahida* comes when one delves deeply into one's whole heart, sees the universe as within one's own heart and identifies oneself with the Divine Mother, so to speak, feeling the whole creation as if within oneself." Ar.

shariat: traditional religious law. Ar. From Hazrat Inayat Khan: "Shariat means the law that it is necessary for the collectivity to observe, to harmonize with one's surroundings and with one's self within. Although the religious authorities of Islam have limited it to restrictions, yet a thousand places in the Qur'an and Hadith one can trace where the law of Shariat is meant to be subject to change to suit the time and place."

siddhi: "perfection" or "attainment." Skr. See also *sadhana above*.

sifat: a sacred quality or activity of the One. Ar.

sijda: position of placing the forehead in surrender upon the earth. Ar.

silsila: "chain," "link" or "connection." Ar. "The Hierarchical Chain, known as the *silsila sufian*, is a linkage of realized personalities whose teachings reflect the age in which they have lived and functioned. There are many such Chains, each associated with a particular Sufi order." –Murshid Samuel L. Lewis

Subhan Allah: "glory be to Allah," the purity of original Essence. Ar.

tanasukh: "transformation," or mantle of transmission. Ar. From Murshid Samuel Lewis: "We give names to various angels thereby making distinctions which may not exist in reality. For it is discovered by the sages that all the illuminated ones form the embodiment of a single Master. This has led to the promulgation of *tanasukh*, or return, a doctrine which has been confused with reincarnation. According to *tanasukh* there is One Divine Spirit which constantly ascends and descends, although Jacob saw it in symbolic form in dream." For more on this idea of Sufi cosmology, see Hazrat Inayat Khan's book "The Soul Whence and Whither."

tariqat: "way" or "path." Ar. A dervish order, but also the Sufi methods of discipline and meditation. From Hazrat Inayat Khan: "*Tariqat* is the understanding of law besides following it, that we must understand the cause of all things that we must do and must not do, instead of obeying the law without understanding."

tasbih: a form of zikr or remembrance. Ar. and Per. Often used, also here, as a term for the prayer beads used in the Sufi path.

tasawwuri: literally, "imagining," as in imagining oneself to be acting with or in the presence of one's teacher, a type of spiritual "gestalt" used in Sufism. Ar.

tawajjeh: also *tawajjuh*; attention, regard, turning toward. Ar. A practice used by Sufi teachers of giving blessing through the glance. From Murshid Samuel Lewis: "Sufis also have two practices which help increase *baraka* by the use of the eyes. When the power is concentrated upon a person, thing, place, affair, incident or thing— that which tends to a point, to contraction or *qabz*, it is called *sulp*.

When the same power is radiated over a larger area, covering many persons, things, affairs, incidents, it is called *tawajjeh*."

tawhid: unity with Reality, Oneness itself, and any philosophy or statement taking as its first assumption that Reality is all that exists. Ar.

At Tawwab: releasing and returning to ripeness; one of the 99 "Beautiful Names" of Allah. Ar.

urs: anniversary of the passing of a Sufi teacher. Ar.

urouj: "rising," "ascending." Ar. As evidenced in the breath, the desire or activity of acquiring or gathering towards a "self," an "initiating" energy. From Murshid Samuel Lewis: "One of the main reasons for the nufs was to bring about the existence of many forms. To create means to form discrete things out of a universal substance. This comes from the *urouj* activity of Allah by which the Supreme Spirit is converted into matter. This is the primordial matter called *hule* (*huyyal*) which means primal stuff, and was termed *aretz* by Moses and *arek* by the Chaldeans and which means nothing but 'hardened spirit.'"

Al Wakil: what solves problems, protects, one of the 99 "Beautiful Names" of Allah. Ar.

wazifa: "assignment," "lesson," work to do. Ar. Here used to mean the repetition of one or more sacred phrases, usually including the "Beautiful Names" of Allah.

zat (also spelled *dhat*): the sacred essence of the One. Ar. Both *sifat* (quality) and *zat* (essence) are grammatically feminine, to balance the grammatically masculine form of the word "allah."

Zen: Japanese school of Mahayana Buddhism, emphasizing direct insight into the nature of reality. Jap. From Murshid Samuel Lewis: "Kashf or Prajna is an operation of an immediate function of the insight of the entire personality. It is independent causally of time and space. It may or may not justify itself logically, but it certainly fulfills what Jesus has said: "By their fruits ye shall know them." One may also read of the benefits of meditation. Dr. Daisetz Suzuki has proclaimed that Zen in truth is not just meditative practice, it is operative Prajna function. Sufis would agree on this point."

Index

Symbols
40 Lessons on Breath 252
99 Names 60, 68, 361, 362, 369. See also Beautiful Names
112 Shiva practices 159

A

Abdal 24, 67, 155, 319-321
Abdul Aziz, Haji Baba 163
Abode of the Message 76
Adam 100, 151
Adam Kadmon 55
agape 131, 151, 153, 188
Ahmed, Shemseddin 42, 54
ahwal 108, 173
akhlak Allah 108, 128, 181
alchemy 19, 120, 217, 241
Al-Fattah 124
Al-Ghazzali 131, 280
Al-Hallaj, Mansur 170
alhamdulillah 31, 94, 103, 135, 193, 299
Ali, Pir Barkat 53, 54, 66, 100, 103, 106-107
Ali Qadr 298
Allah 14-15, 26-27, 29, 31-32, 42, 45-46, 60, 68-69, 71-72, 74-75, 77-80, 82, 84-86, 88, 91, 93, 98, 103, 106-111, 118, 128, 131, 133-135, 137, 149, 152, 157, 159, 164-165, 168, 171, 178, 181, 183-184, 186, 190, 198-199, 208, 217, 274, 304, 306, 311, 313, 317-318, 322
Alpert, Richard (Ram Dass) 205, 291
amal 108, 109, 117, 276
amaliat 108
anandashram 95, 159
aphorisms 68, 116, 307
Aramaic Lord's Prayer zikr 309
Arnold, Sir Edwin 62, 257, 304
art 102, 116, 138-140, 173, 174, 196, 202, 224-245
ashraf-ul-makluqat 125
Asrar ul Ansar 108
Auliya, Nizamuddin 76

Aurobindo, Sri 171
Avatar 47, 78, 80, 123, 194
Azrael 93

B

Baba, Neem Karoli 291
Bacchus 22
Baker, Murshida Mariam 349
Baker Roshi, Richard 281
balance 19, 54, 69-70, 98, 100, 114, 116, 129, 134, 136-137, 145-146, 150, 157, 171, 173-174, 178-180, 182, 183, 186-187, 236, 249, 254, 262, 274-277, 279, 299, 302, 315, 334-335
baqa 88, 108, 127, 143, 176-177, 181, 304.
baraka 27, 32, 42-43, 60, 71, 78, 96-97, 104, 120, 137, 147, 149, 150, 161, 163, 184, 240, 276, 310, 335. baraka, chain of 147, 161
Barodofsky, Murshid Saul 50, 331
Bartley, Abdul Aziz 95, 155
Baskin-Robbins 42-43
Baugh, Jaffar 275
bayat 70, 71, 74, 98, 101, 152, 287, 315, 330. See also initiation
Bear Creek 299, 302-303
Beautiful Names 110, 133, 170, 184, 186. See also 99 Names
Begg, W.D. 53-54, 76, 90-92
Bellach, David 59
Beloved, the 18, 46, 50, 68, 122, 129, 137, 153
Beorse, Evelyn 80
Beorse, Shamcher 42, 80, 87-88, 312
Bernal Heights 66
Bhagavad Gita 22, 150
Bhagawan, Sri 168
bhakta 22
Birth of the New Era, the 45
Bismillah Dance 59
Bismillah Magazine 26, 47, 59, 62, 69, 78, 80-82, 91, 95, 105-107, 114, 155, 304, 318
bodhisattvas 36, 50, 98, 100, 180, 238, 241, 257, 304, 314
body self 248, 252
Bolinas 32, 33, 39, 159
Book of Instructions for Murshid 330
Book of Job 62

Bowl of Saki 157, 163, 336
breath 36, 49, 50, 55, 58, 68, 71, 109, 117, 126, 133-134, 137, 146, 150, 159, 176, 185, 192, 196, 198, 209, 213, 252, 265, 278, 315, 316, 337
Brown, Byron 257
Buddha 31, 36, 47, 88, 96, 98, 127, 129, 161, 182, 185-186, 236, 238, 240, 257, 304
Burnham, Zeinob 62, 80, 290

C

caravan 333
categories of membership 287
chakra 31, 44, 214, 240, 246, 250, 278
Chang, Mei-Ling 209, 229, 244, 248, 275, 291, 298
cheragas and cherags 41, 285
Chinese Hospital 28, 50
Chishti Order 43, 108
Chisti, Sufi Ahmed Murad. See Lewis, Murshid Samuel L. (Murshid S.A.M.)
Chishti, Moineddin 91, 101, 102, 244
Chishti-Qadri-Sabri 327, 328
Chishti, Sheikh Selim 28
Chishti, Usman Haruni 244
Christian Holy Order of Mans 66
Christ, Jesus 57-58, 68, 71, 98, 101, 123, 125-126, 139, 143, 151, 158, 167, 170, 173, 176, 188, 189, 250, 253, 318, 320, 322, 336
Church of MANS 166. See also Christian Holy Order of Mans
circle 26, 241, 248, 273, 278, 290, 305, 333
Clementina Street 28, 33, 37, 66
Cohn, Amertat 44
commentaries 81, 108, 113-115, 167, 182, 333
concentration 34, 43, 55, 118-120, 126, 133-134, 136, 139, 140-145, 147-148, 172, 178, 181-182, 185, 186, 189, 193, 197, 240, 266, 285, 296, 310
Conference of the Birds, the 22
Confraternity prayers 102, 163
controlled schizophrenia 70
Coomeraswamy, Ananda 217
Corda, Murshida Vera 42, 75, 315
counseling 84, 215, 225
Coy, Salaman and Christine 199
Crescent and Heart 194, 290
Cronin, Ananda 199, 331

D

Dalai Lama 54, 197
Dances of Universal Peace 18, 26, 27, 30, 56, 108, 114, 143, 184, 294, 309, 310
dargah 91, 298
dark night of the soul 208, 209
darood 109, 126, 146, 150, 167, 216
darshan 31, 86, 93, 96, 99, 193, 220, 283
Davenport, Vasheest 41, 90, 91, 95, 204
death 38, 50, 67, 72, 77, 86-88, 93, 137, 155, 187, 188, 201, 207-209, 227, 248, 289-290, 296, 307, 309, 330, 333
Deborah, Reverend (Holy Order of MANS) 166
decentralization 323
Dede, Sheikh Suleiman 54, 59-60, 91, 96
de Jong-Keesing, Elizabeth 192
dervish 29, 30, 31, 47, 296
dharmakaya 125
Dharma Night meeting 34
dhikr 45
dhyana 108, 148
dialysis 54, 84, 93-94, 111, 162, 164, 166-167, 207, 208, 229, 231, 242, 248, 253
divorce 12, 81, 228, 242-243, 296, 309, 312
Diwan of Hazrat Inayat Khan 153
Djabrut 78
Douglas-Klotz, Murshid Saadi 264, 298, 309-310
dream 45, 102, 116-120, 164, 168, 171, 174, 282, 333
dunes, Oceano 62

E

Eat, Dance and Pray Together 310
ecstasy 22, 44, 60, 173, 181, 189
effacement 113, 141, 155, 176, 192, 274, 276, 336. See also fana
Effendi, Sheikh Muzaffer 54
eleventh degree (Murshids) circle 306, 307
Eliade, Mircea 217
Erickson, Amina 65
Er-Rahman, Er-Rahim Dance 31

esotericism 67, 73-74, 107, 115, 127, 142, 148, 169, 179, 279, 287
Etekad Rasm u Ravaj 108
ethical standards 280

F

Fairfax (California) 50
fana 70, 74, 108, 113, 141, 153, 155, 176, 177, 181, 192-194, 198, 274-276, 336. See also effacement
fana-fi-lillah 274, 276, 307
fana-fi-pir 274, 275-276
fana-fi-rassoul 274, 276, 306, 336
fana-fi-sheikh 70, 74, 153, 194, 267, 274, 276, 306
Federation of the Sufi Message 266, 317, 320, 324-331
Feild, Reshad 59
Fellowship of Universal Guidance 241
female self 244, 247 249, 253
feminine principle 243-244, 247, 266
fikr 50, 107-111, 133-135, 146, 148, 150, 159, 167
Fiske, Vocha 24, 42
Flower Service 285, 307
flute of Krishna 122, 150
funding 268

G

Gandhi 95, 171
Garden of Inayat 34-36, 40, 66, 69, 77, 155, 165, 222, 239, 275-276, 290
gas chambers 24
Gathas 108, 128, 139, 145, 266
Gathekas 115-131, 136-150, 169-190
Gebel, Suhrawardi 108
gender 12, 14, 205, 261, 264, 305
Ghalib 153
Gift of Life, the 307
Githas 108, 115, 139, 142, 193, 333
Githekas 160
glance (divine) 22, 31, 33, 58, 96-97, 110, 128, 337
glomerulo-nephritis 110
goddess 283, 285
Gospel of Thomas 150, 203

grades of initiation 266
Grady, Harvey 201, 241, 250, 254, 257
Grand Night 276
grassroots 319, 322
gravesite 60, 64, 65, 294. See also dargah, maqbara
great awakening 276
Great Mother 247, 265. See also goddess
Greer, Asha 61
grief 208-209, 226, 243
guidance 13-14, 42-43, 73-74, 81, 97, 125, 156, 178, 182, 206, 214, 229, 239, 240, 254, 273, 281, 287, 289, 329
Gulistan, the 121, 316
Guthrie, Dr. Wayne 241

H

Ha'iku 211, 213, 221, 225, 278
Hakuin Zen-shi 275
hal 283, 305
halo center 56, 250
Halveti-Jerrahi order 54
haqiqat 108
Hare Krishna, Hare Rama Dance 31
Hasiat 108
hatha yoga 182, 188
Hawaii 201, 209, 211-212, 215, 224
heart 26, 32, 41, 43-44, 58, 67, 78, 82, 84-85, 87, 99, 101-102, 107, 109-110, 113, 116, 119, 121-125, 127, 130-140, 142-145, 147, 148-149, 151, 153, 160, 170, 172-173, 176, 179, 182-186, 188, 193-194, 198, 202, 210, 214, 217, 227, 238, 246, 256, 260, 274, 276, 278, 279, 301, 305, 306, 311, 324, 326, 331, 337
Heartbeat Journal 322, 343
Helveti 91
Herz, Hassan 35, 39, 65, 69, 70-71, 95, 99, 101, 155
Herz, Jayanara 35, 39, 69, 95, 155-156, 290
Hesse, Hermann 202, 219
hierarchy (spiritual) 67, 157, 172, 174, 190, 319
high self 209, 214, 217, 224-225, 245-247, 251, 253-256, 293
hippie 19, 20, 205
Holy Biography of Hazrat Khwaja Muinuddin Chishti, the 90
Hoppe, Art 27

Hoppe, Merrice 298
Howden, Iman 213
hridaya 199
huna 202, 224, 267, 275
Hurkalya 59, 76, 82

I

I-A-U 314
imagination 113, 116-117, 119, 120, 122-124, 172-174, 181, 250
impression 33, 86, 96-97, 117-119, 122, 125, 133, 137, 141, 147-148, 179-180, 182, 196-197, 213, 237, 251, 307, 317. See also samskaras
Inayat Answers 192
India 20, 28, 54, 59, 76, 90, 95, 126, 171, 205, 260, 261, 301, 310, 330
initiation 41, 44, 74, 77, 98, 101, 103, 146, 151-152, 187, 239, 262, 266, 268, 274, 287-288, 307, 310, 315, 320-323, 327, 328, 330, 333. See also bayat
inner child 224, 242, 248-249
Instructions for the Pir 305, 319-320, 328, 336
In The Garden 315
intoxication (divine) 22
invocation 26, 41, 43, 73, 126, 176, 190, 313
Iradah, Anahata 310
ishk 107, 125, 162, 168

J

Jablonski, Murshida Fatima 31-33, 39, 40, 54, 65, 69, 75-76, 82, 84, 90-91, 94-96, 100-101, 152, 161-162, 165, 168, 198-199, 261, 290, 312, 346
Jamiat 220, 235, 262, 266-267, 269, 270-273, 277, 281, 283, 287, 289, 293, 298, 305, 306, 317, 325, 335
Japanese Noh 36
jelal 22, 100-101, 110, 116, 155, 179
jhanas 185-186
jihad 178
Jilani, Grand Sheikh Abdul Qadir 24, 71, 319, 320
Jinn 20
jnana 22, 162
Job's Tears 307, 347, 348, 349

Johnson, Mansur 21, 24, 33, 39, 93, 94, 155, 170, 192, 194, 199, 220, 237, 261, 275
Johnson, Robert A. 266
Journal of Somatics, the 264
judge self 250, 251, 252, 254, 255
Jung, C.G. 202, 219

K

kabbalah 136
kabbalistic invocation 245
Kashf ul Kabur 108
kadr and kaza 187
kahuna 225, 289
Kalama dance 31, 60, 91, 108
Kaleemi, Pir 42
Karish, Dr. Bella 241
Karunamayee 42
kasab 108-109, 146, 148, 163
kashf 108, 117, 162, 180, 182
kemal 101, 134
khalif 44, 72-73, 77, 86, 113, 273, 274, 276, 309, 327, 328
khankah 34, 59, 70, 76-77, 82, 109, 208, 242, 298-299, 309, 349
Khankah Darul Ehsan 109
Khankah Noor Inayat 320, 349
Khan, Noorunisa Inayat 320
Khan, Pir Hidayat Inayat 82, 87, 266, 317, 319-320, 322, 324-325, 328, 331
Khan, Pir-o-Murshid Hazrat Inayat 21, 23, 32, 41, 43, 45-47, 54, 57, 59, 65, 67, 69-70, 73-75, 77-78, 81-82, 85, 87, 91, 95, 98, 100-102, 108, 113-115, 127-128, 134, 136, 138-139, 145-148, 153, 156-157, 159-160, 163, 169, 172, 174, 176-179, 184, 186, 192, 194, 196, 208, 217, 227, 241, 244, 259, 260-262, 265-266, 274, 276, 277, 280, 285, 287, 293, 301, 320-324, 326-337
Khan, Pir Vilayat Inayat 19, 42-45, 54, 67, 69, 73, 75, 77-82, 194, 276, 278, 312, 317-318, 320-323, 326, 328, 331
Khan, Pir Zia Inayat 320, 321, 325-326, 328-329
Khan, Saadia Khawar 23
Khan, Seraphiel Inayat. See Khan, Pir Zia Inayat
Kahn, Pir Shabda 60, 324
Khan, Murshida Taj Inayat 75, 77, 331
Khawas 108

Khwaja Gharib Nawaz. See Chisti, Moineddin
kidney (renal) disease 34, 110, 242, 298
kidney transplant 54, 164, 198-199, 201, 207, 214, 229, 231, 242, 248, 309
Klein, Qayyum 299
koan, ko-an 44, 275, 279
Korzybski, Alfred 237
Krishna 21, 22, 30-31, 70, 96, 122, 126, 150, 168, 169, 217-218
Krishnabai, Mother 54, 95, 297
kun faya kun 169, 171
Kyung Bo Seo, Grand Master 64

L

Lama Foundation 32, 61-65, 275, 289, 291, 294-296, 309
Lamala 42
Lama Maqbara Camp 60, 61
Leila and Majnun 22
Lewis, Murshid Samuel L. (Murshid S.A.M.) 17-25, 31, 35-43, 46, 50, 53-55, 64-66, 71, 73-81, 93, 95, 101, 113-114, 134, 137, 143, 164, 201-203, 206, 208, 215-216, 220, 236, 252, 257, 261-262, 265, 267, 269, 270, 273-277, 287, 289, 291-296, 298, 303-304, 309, 315, 318-322, 327, 328-331, 333, 335-336
life counseling 215
Los Angeles 27, 62, 241, 313
love (divine) 20, 22, 27, 30, 41-43, 67-68, 70, 76, 79, 94, 99, 102, 109, 118, 125-126, 130-131, 137, 140-141, 149, 151-153, 155, 159, 161-162, 168-170, 173, 176, 184-185, 187-189, 193, 198, 205-206, 216, 222, 224, 239, 241, 245, 256, 273, 283, 305, 309, 331, 336-337. See also agape, ishk, karuna
love, harmony and beauty 26, 107, 133, 307, 324, 332
Love, Human and Divine 70
LSD 19, 204, 206, 238-239, 275

M

madzub 19, 20-23, 265
mahamudra 185
Maharshi, Ramana 96
makam 276, 283, 305
malakut 78

male self 243, 244, 247, 249, 253
mantra 98, 115, 126, 143, 160
maqamat 108
maqbara 60-61, 64, 104, 213, 289, 294-295, 309. See also gravesite
march on Washington 238
marifat 108
Marin (County, California) 26, 33-34, 59, 66, 75, 86, 299
marriage 22, 145, 152, 207, 222, 224, 241, 274
Martin, Murshida Rabia 330
Masnavi 93, 94, 174
masters, saints and Prophets 30
Mathieu, Allaudin William 59, 192, 220
Mathieu, Hafiza 95, 155, 159, 161, 167
Maui (Hawaii) 211-213, 215-216, 220-222, 224, 267, 278, 289, 293, 307, 309, 332
meditation 37, 55, 61, 71, 76, 122, 137, 142, 148, 150, 161, 182, 184, 207, 216, 217, 273, 294, 315
Mendocino Camp 93, 199, 212
Mental Purification 114, 115, 136, 157, 169, 260
Mentorgarten 27, 33, 34, 38, 66, 86, 168, 193, 262, 298
Message, the (Sufi Order magazine) 68, 75, 214
Mevelvi order 54
Meyer, Khadija 298
Meyer, Masheikh Wali Ali 32, 54, 65, 67, 69, 75-76, 79, 82, 84, 86, 97, 193, 207, 270, 275-276, 298-299, 307, 309, 321, 323-324, 327-328, 335
Miller, Guin 29, 42
Miller, Joe 29, 35, 38, 42, 44, 50, 62, 99, 102, 257, 304, 319
Miller, Murshida Kamae A 298, 310
Mishala al 'Ayan 80
mother (divine) 23, 128, 239, 262, 336
Muhammad see Prophet Muhammad
Muktananda, Swami 281
murakkabah 108, 119, 139, 143, 178
murshid, the 44, 105, 164, 322
Musafferedin, Sheikh 91
music 19, 81, 82-83, 102, 121-122, 124, 126, 140, 144, 173, 204, 210, 222, 238, 248
Mysticism of Sound, the 136

N

nabi 78, 156
Nabi (prayer) 32, 102, 148, 172
nafs alima 79, 117, 137, 151
Nakshi Bandi 108
Naqshibandi Order 101, 108
nasihat 108
Native American Church 20
nayaz 108, 145
Nembutsu Dance 31
Neumann, Erich 247, 265
Ninety-Nine Names. See 99 Names
Nirtan 23, 177
nirvakalpa and sahaja 265
nirvana 32, 50, 97-98, 137, 192, 274, 304
Noor Mahal 82, 86, 102, 161, 163, 199
Northwest Sufi Camp 93
Novato (California) 34, 69, 275

O

Occultism 108
Om Namo Shivaya Dance 31
O'Neill, Eugene 102
original mureeds meeting 272-273
overlooking 196

P

Paderewski 140
pagyambar 78
Pakistan 23, 29, 54, 66, 79, 106, 276, 310, 327
Palo Alto 208, 242-243
parables 153, 236
Pasi Anfas 108
Pasnak, Murshid Nawab 329
Passover 129
PeaceWorks 283, 309-310
Perez, Murshida Ana 275
Petaluma (California) 82, 242
Pettersen, Shems 104, 105
Piktor's Metamorphosis 219

Pinckley, Jemila 33, 39, 289
Pir-o-Murshid 66, 67, 105
Pir, Pir(a) 44, 47, 203, 274, 282, 301, 305, 319-321, 323-326, 328-329, 336-337
Pluto practice 55
poetry 102, 108, 121, 122, 124, 140, 150-151, 173, 190, 238, 248
Prajna Paramita Hridaya Sutra 190
pralaya 88
Pran Nath, Pandit 42
pratyekabuddhas 146
prayer 32, 59-60, 62, 67, 71, 73, 80, 82, 102, 109, 110-111, 119, 121-122, 127, 138, 143, 145, 147-148, 152, 155, 159, 163, 172-173, 182-184, 186, 217, 223, 241, 291, 300, 310
Precita Park (San Francisco, California) 27
presence 21, 24, 30, 43, 85, 97, 108, 110, 134, 144, 167, 170, 176, 181, 183-184, 186, 190, 217, 240, 243, 244-246, 250, 260, 261, 276, 279, 305, 322, 327, 331
Prophet Muhammad 24, 31, 43, 45-46, 72, 73, 79, 91, 98, 101, 119, 121, 124-125, 131, 138, 140-141, 143, 149, 156, 161, 170-171, 174, 177-178, 181, 183, 184-185, 189-190, 220, 235, 240, 275, 295, 322, 330
psychedelics 19, 20, 80, 205, 206, 207, 239
psychology (spiritual) 209, 241
Puck 24, 25

Q

Qadri Order 108, 327, 328
Qur'an 20, 45, 98, 131, 161, 280

R

Radha 21
Ramakrishna, Sri 23, 128, 162
Ramdas, Papa 47, 62, 96, 162, 163
Ramdas Speaks 163
ramnam 31, 125, 159
rassoul 78, 91, 102, 147, 156, 161, 194, 309
Reich, Ted 42
remembrance 45, 109, 144, 224, 236. See also dhikr, zikr, zikar
Reps, Paul 42, 235
retreat 43, 73, 177, 259, 264, 275, 295, 296, 299, 303, 325, 331

rind 103, 283
risalyat 193
Roberts, Fatima (Najat) 161, 162, 313
Robinson, Nizamuddin 298
ruhaniat 80
Rumi, Jelaluddin (Mevlana) 19, 60, 122, 174, 190, 321
Ryazat 108, 115

S

sabbath 136
Sabri, Allauddin 323, 327-328
sacred phrase 26, 27, 30, 45, 91, 133, 144, 150, 163, 184
sadhana 98, 108, 176
sahaja samadhi 97
Saladin 169, 216, 252
Salarwala, West Pakistan 66
Salat (prayer of Hazrat Inayat Khan) 60, 73, 102, 108, 127
Saluk 108
sama 173
samadhi 23, 50, 97, 117, 119, 239, 240, 276
samsara 32, 97, 117, 137, 181
samskaras 115, 125, 137. See also impression
San Anselmo 26, 76
San Francisco 27, 32-34, 37, 38, 41, 59, 64, 66, 193, 207-209, 225, 243, 245, 262, 277, 298
San Francisco Chronicle 27
sangathas 108, 159
sangithas 193, 274, 277, 336
Sasaki Roshi, Joshu 64
satori 206, 239, 275
Saum (prayer of Hazrat Inayat Khan) 59, 102, 110
Schachter-Shalomi, Rabbi Zalman 42
schism: Sufi Order and SIRS 78, 81
Schuon, Fritjof 217
Scott Hall (San Anselmo, California) 26
seekers 47, 142
self-sacrifice 170
sema 59
Senzaki, Nyogen 45, 47, 88, 235, 236
Serrano, Miguel 202, 219, 347

shadow 57, 114, 118, 141, 158, 161, 201, 205, 235-238, 240, 250, 254, 256-257, 261, 267, 274, 335
shafayat 108
shaghal 108, 109, 303
Shams-i-Tabriz 19, 321
shariat 102, 108
sheikh 28, 44, 54, 59, 90, 91, 103, 268-269, 273, 274, 313, 327-328
Sherif, Pir Dewwal 79, 327-328
Shiva 30, 96, 159, 217, 218, 232, 297
Shomer, Vakil 75, 347
Siddiq, Abu Bakr 72, 322
sifat 124, 149, 169, 202
sign of a teacher 131
sijda 213, 278
Sikander 75-76
silsila 43, 73, 121
Silver City 31, 298-299
Simmons, Akbar 275-276, 327
SIRS 41, 42, 44-45, 75, 222, 269, 270, 273-274, 279, 287, 299, 310, 312, 322, 325. See also Sufi Islamia Ruhaniat Society
Siva, Siva 30
Six Interviews 81, 163, 193
Snake Dance 31
sobriety 173, 181, 220, 315
Socialist Discussion Club 238
soul 14, 22-23, 32, 45, 58, 62, 73-74, 83, 88, 94-95, 97-98, 100, 114, 116, 122, 127-128, 133, 135, 141, 143-145, 148-150, 153, 156-158, 160, 168, 170-173, 176, 181, 184, 186, 188, 192, 201, 208-209, 217, 226, 227, 236, 238, 241-242, 248, 255-256, 260, 272, 287, 293, 304, 312, 331, 334
Soulwork 201-203, 241-242, 244, 248, 251-253, 255, 256, 347, 349, 357
Sound, the (newsletter) 41, 42, 43, 44, 45, 204, 266
Southwest Sufi Community 298-299, 301-303
Spirit of Guidance 26, 63, 66, 71, 73, 107, 115, 133, 167, 172, 251, 262, 274, 275, 277, 283, 285, 305, 317, 336
Spirit Phenomena 333
Spiritual Architecture 102, 137
spiritual practices 19, 37, 55-56, 71, 100, 109, 115, 125-127, 133, 139, 146, 150, 159, 163, 167, 173, 178, 181, 183, 185, 187, 206-207, 211, 213, 239, 264, 274, 278, 301, 303, 330

spiritual teacher 26, 29, 44, 66, 99, 101-102, 129, 149, 155, 172, 174, 260, 289, 301, 315
spring cleaning meeting 271
Stadlinger, Hayat 42
states 20-21, 117, 160, 173, 256, 265, 274
stations of the cross 57
St. Denis, Ruth 28, 310
Student Non-violent Coordinating Committee 238
subhan allah 31, 133, 196
succession 77, 86. See also successor
successor 17, 44, 54, 73, 77, 81, 96, 270, 307, 317, 328. See also succession
Sufi Choir 60, 220
Sufi community 54, 87, 208, 214, 241, 299
Sufi invocation 26, 43, 126, 176, 190, 313
Sufi Islamia Ruhaniat Society 32, 40-41, 44, 57, 59, 64, 66-69, 71-75, 78-81, 87, 90, 92, 101, 106, 111, 148, 157, 163, 164, 193, 202-203, 212, 222, 235, 261, 262, 266, 268, 269, 271, 273-274, 279-282, 287-288, 294-296, 298, 305-307, 309-313, 315, 318, 321-324, 327-329, 335, 343, 346-348, 357. See also SIRS
Sufi Message 59, 68, 74, 77, 83, 91, 95, 100, 102, 108-109, 114, 123, 169, 196, 214, 222, 271, 301, 307, 309, 312-313, 317-320, 323-327, 329-332
Sufi Message of Spiritual Liberty, a 108
Sufi Message, the (volume series) 100, 114, 169, 196
Sufi Movement 261, 262, 277, 291, 312, 317-319, 321, 323-325, 327-331
Sufi Order International 54, 64, 67-69, 73, 75-76, 78, 81, 285, 307, 312, 317-318, 321, 323-325, 327, 328, 331
Sufi rock (Pir Dahan, Fairfax, California) 50
Sufi Vision and Initiation 81, 261
Suhrawardi Order 108
Sunseed (film) 44, 101, 102, 168
Suras of the New Age 30
Suresnes 277

T

Tackett, Victoria 264
Taj Mahal 120, 169
Takua Taharat 108, 145
Tales 278
talim 108
tariqa 66, 75, 90, 259-261, 274, 280

tariqat 108
tasawwuf 108, -131, 136-151, 169-190, 336
tasawwuri Murshid 70-71, 95, 164-165, 193
tawajjeh 110. See also glance
tawhid 280
ten ox-herding pictures 150
the proof of Hazrat Inayat Khan 192
Thomas, Dylan 170
three self 293
Three Wazifas dance 31
Thursday night meetings 158, 196, 198, 222
Tidjani, Ahmed 66
Tidjaniyya, the 66
Toward Spiritual Brotherhood 168
Toward the One 26, 73, 100, 107, 115, 126, 133, 146, 190, 255, 295, 316, 336, 347
transcendental meditation 148
transmission (spiritual) 18, 41, 43, 53, 67, 69, 73, 75, 81, 99, 101, 104, 110, 121, 147, 163, 183, 261, 270, 274, 296, 304, 309, 310, 321-323, 325, 330-331
Trikkanad, Premanand 62
Trungpa, Chogyam 281
Turkey 54, 91
twenty purification breaths 134, 145-146, 163, 213

U

united with all 56, 190, 313
Unity of Religious Ideals, the 73
Universal Worship 41, 102, 283, 285, 318
University of Iowa Writer's Workshop 238
Upanishads 62
urouj 122, 193
urs 18, 50, 75, 114, 208, 220, 278, 334-335
Use of Centers, the 214
US Forest Service 65

V

visions 26, 61, 64, 119, 275
Vivekananda, Swami 162

voice (divine) 66, 97, 148, 150, 169, 180, 303
Voice of the Turtle Retreat Center 349

W

Wagner, Eugene 42
Wailuku 213
Walker, Darwesh 238
walk (training) 28, 31, 55-57, 66, 143, 144, 155, 181-182, 184, 186, 213-214, 296, 336
Warwick, Dr. Anjari 29, 33, 42
wasiat 108
Waterhouse, Frida 19, 42, 165, 168, 201, 209, 216, 225, 241-243, 257, 264-265, 293, 315
wazifa 91, 108, 115, 143, 148, 150, 196
Welch, Halim 65
Whitman, Walt 55
wisdom 70, 73, 79, 109, 125, 128-129, 138, 140-141, 146, 148, 155, 162, 177, 179, 180-183, 205, 218, 260-261, 301, 326
Wisdom Comes Dancing 310
Witteveen, Karimbaksh 328
women 21-22, 29, 31, 44, 60, 75, 100, 110, 155-156, 199, 205-206, 248, 264-266, 285-286, 320
world peace 23
World War II 24, 261

Y

Ya Fattah 60, 124, 306
Ya Haqq 134
Ya Hayy 134, 167
Yahuvah 314
Ya Quddus 133
Ya Shafi Ya Kafi 134
Ya Tawwab 133
Ya Wakil 135, 163
Yogi Bhajan 38
yogis 117, 119, 128-129, 186

Z

zat 124, 169, 202
zazen 182, 186
Zen Flesh, Zen Bones 159, 207, 235, 239
Zen Ko-An, the 275
zikr, zikar 19, 45-46, 50, 60, 108-109, 133, 144, 146, 148, 150, 184, 190, 278, 283, 309. See also dhikr, remembrance
Ziraat 179

The Sufi Ruhaniat International

The Sufi Ruhaniat International is dedicated to helping individuals unfold their highest spiritual purpose, manifest their essential inner being, and live harmoniously with others, with the hope of relieving human suffering and contributing to the awakening of all of humankind. The organization was founded by Murshid Samuel L. Lewis shortly before he died in 1971. We are in the stream of the ages-old wisdom lineage of Sufism brought to the West in 1910 by Hazrat Inayat Khan under the title "The Sufi Message of Spiritual Liberty" and his disciple Murshid Samuel L. Lewis (Sufi Ahmed Murad Chisti). This work was continued by Pir Moineddin Jablonski, the spiritual successor of Murshid Samuel Lewis, who guided the Ruhaniat from 1971 until his death in 2001. It continues today under the guidance of Pir Shabda Kahn, the successor of Pir Moineddin.

The Ruhaniat family is composed of sincere mureeds (initiated students) who tread the path of initiation and discipleship, seeking the truth of the inner life through personal practice and direct experience. Because Sufism is based on experiences and not on premises, we affirm the preciousness of an initiatic relationship of spiritual transmission between initiator and mureed. It is a fundamental principle of the Sufi Ruhaniat International that each mureed have an initiator to serve as friend, guide and reality check. This primary initiatic relationship provides a living matrix within which students as well as teachers may develop in character and spiritual experience. Retreats and classes are open to all, both initiates and non-initiates alike.

Further activities of the Ruhaniat include an Esoteric Studies program, the International Network for the Dances of Universal Peace, the Dervish Healing Order, the Service of Universal Peace and ministerial training, Spiritual Psychology and SoulWork, Ziraat (Sacred Agriculture), Retreat and many other inspired teachings of the leaders and lineage holders of the Ruhaniat.

We have recently crossed the threshold between the old millennium and the new. Many contemporary tools are available to help us in our personal and spiritual growth. At the same time, we represent a tradition that has its roots in prehistory. The sacred practices and teachings that have come down to us from diverse climes and cultures in an unbroken line have been carefully cultivated and prepared for us by innumerable spiritual forebears.

Contact: website: **www.ruhaniat.org** or **info@ruhaniat.org**

The Sufi Soulwork Foundation

Established as a non-profit organizational body in 2013, the SoulWork Foundation is dedicated to the development and presentation of SoulWork as developed by Moineddin Jablonski, an educational and practical tool for psychological healing and transformation. This will help individuals and groups learn to resolve conflicts and live harmoniously. SoulWork is open to all faiths, races, ages and genders. The Foundation is directed by Mariam Baker, the current lineage holder of SoulWork.

Moineddin Jablonski writes:

"We are living in a time of rapid change and intensive growth -- a process which brings out the worst and best in each one of us. Everywhere people are challenged to stick to their ideals in a world of fearful emotions which too often lead to abusive words and violent acts, even in our own homes. Our work is to root out these imbalances in ourselves, so that our hearts can become havens of safety, peace and refuge for each other."

The SoulWork Foundation is the healthy womb in this time for planting the seeds for personal and planetary healing and integration. Using the tools of science, psychology, shamanism, quantum physics and mysticism, the SoulWork Foundation supports the organic movement of humanity crossing the threshold into greater balance and vitality, ever evolving and unfolding.

The Foundation supports the healing art of developing relationship to the many parts of the self with inner guidance as the central focus. Acceptance and integration of the self happens through relationship, which naturally leads to a fuller, passionate, grounded interaction with life. Active imagination, body awareness, journaling, meditation and inquiry provide a container for the process.

The aim of the Foundation is to increase the availability of Soulwork: through individual sessions, groups, retreats, presentations; through providing training for Soulwork practitioners, through curriculum development, and by locating facilities for ongoing trainings. The Foundation will use a variety of media, and academic formats to accomplish this aim. Contributions are welcome and fully tax deductible for U.S. citizens.

Please contact us through our website (**www.soulworkfoundation.org**), Facebook page ("The SoulWork Foundation") or at our business address: The SoulWork Foundation, PO Box 5773, Eugene, OR 97405 USA.

Printed in Great Britain
by Amazon